*Praise for the Previous Edition*

# The Luxury Guide to
# Walt Disney World® Resort

"Luxury means different things to different travelers: an elegant guest suite, a hotel atrium full of exotic blooms, a romantic dinner with fireworks as a backdrop. However you define it, Cara Goldsbury's book tells you where to find it."

—Faye Wolfe, *Disney* magazine

"Expertly written . . . an impressively informative vacation planning guide for any individual or family seeking to maximize their experience of the 'Disney magic' to the fullest."

—James A. Cox, *Midwest Book Review*

## Help Us Keep This Guide Up to Date

We would love to hear from you concerning your experiences with this guide and how you feel it could be improved and kept up to date. Please send your comments and suggestions to:

editorial@GlobePequot.com

Thanks for your input, and happy travels!

# The Luxury Guide to Walt Disney World® Resort

*How to Get the Most Out of the*
*Best Disney Has to Offer*

Cara Goldsbury

THIRD EDITION

travel

Guilford, Connecticut

All the information in this guidebook is subject to change. We recommend that you call ahead to obtain current information before traveling.

To buy books in quantity for corporate use
or incentives, call **(800) 962–0973**
or e-mail **premiums@GlobePequot.com.**

ISSN 1555-6050
ISBN 978-0-7627-6040-4

Printed in the United States of America
10 9 8 7 6 5 4 3 2 1

# CONTENTS

# ABOUT THE AUTHOR

Cara Goldsbury is a travel agent specializing in Walt Disney World with over twenty-five years of experience. She has appeared as a leading Disney expert on two Travel Channel specials and has been cited as such in numerous national news articles. She lives in Port Aransas, Texas, and spends many weeks throughout the year in Orlando researching the book. Visit her at www.wdwluxuryguide.com or www.caragoldsbury.com.

# ACKNOWLEDGMENTS

Many thanks to the creative and caring people of Globe Pequot Press and to my editor Amy Lyons.

My great appreciation to the Walt Disney World Company for their guidance and assistance, in particular Geoffrey Pointon in Public Relations and Bill Downs with Disney Destinations.

Thanks go to David Brady, media/communications manager at Disney's Grand Floridian Resort, Jennifer Hodges, director of public relations at Loews Hotels at Universal Orlando, Kristi Pericht at Grande Lakes Orlando, Keith Salwoski and Michelle Smith at Gaylord Palms Resort, Mary Deatrick of Deatrick Public Relations in association with Rosen Shingle Creek, and Laura Richeson (Bennett & Co.) at the Hyatt Regency Grand Cypress. Also Sara Moore and Steve Trover of All Star Vacation Homes, Laura Skowyra at SeaWorld, and Treva Marshall and Joel Kaiman with TJM Communications in association with the Walt Disney World Swan and Dolphin. My thanks to Allison Tom with Edelman Productions and the Travel Channel. And last but certainly not least to Tom Parke, Kim Westhoff, Ragini Stearns, and Eva Cooper at the Waldorf Astoria.

To all my readers whose enthusiasm for Disney inspires me, and to the many Disney webmasters, authors, and travel agents who have been such a support.

And always to my family who give me such encouragement and love.

# INTRODUCTION

Walt Disney World.

These three words instantly fill the mind with images of Mickey Mouse, Peter Pan, Cinderella, and Snow White. For children they send the imagination soaring to places only dreamed of in their wildest fantasies. For adults they offer a trip back to the idyllic innocence of childhood when nothing was unattainable and the world was filled with unlimited possibilities. What other place could be all this to so many people?

Walt Disney World is a destination that renews hopes and dreams, an adventure of the heart, true magic. Disney's four theme parks are so totally distinct that it's almost like taking a different vacation each day of your visit. Enhancing the experience are Disney's themed resorts, transporting you to a unique time and place: early twentieth-century New England, nineteenth-century Florida, even a lodge in deepest Africa. With only a small percentage of its 30,000 acres fully developed, you'll find lush grounds dotted with lakes, wetlands, and stunningly landscaped resorts and parks. With so many delightful diversions, it's difficult to know where to begin. Allow this guidebook to step in and show you the way.

Is it possible for sophisticated travelers to really enjoy themselves in the land of Mickey Mouse? Absolutely! This unique travel guide overflowing with tips and techniques for a splendid vacation is designed for those who wish to tour Walt Disney World but also want to reside in luxurious resorts and dine at many of the best restaurants. I'm prepared to direct you in planning a visit in which each day comes with the best Disney has to offer. Together we will arrange a relatively stress-free vacation by utilizing each component of this travel guide to best suit your needs. Together we will decide the most convenient time of year for your vacation, which resort best fits your personality, what rooms are perfect for you, where to dine, and much, much more. Helpful tips throughout can make the difference between a mediocre trip and a fantastic one. Now let's get going!

# HOW TO USE THIS GUIDE

To help you choose which accommodations and restaurants best suit your needs, we've developed the following codes:

## Accommodations

The following symbols represent the average cost (without any discounts) of standard through suites for one night in regular season, excluding tax; and studio through three-bedroom villas at Disney Deluxe Villa Resorts:

| | |
|---|---|
| $ | $200 or less |
| $$ | $201 to $350 |
| $$$ | $351 to $500 |
| $$$$ | $501 to $1,000 |
| $$$$$ | $1,001 to $2,500 |

## Restaurants

The following symbols represent the average cost of an adult dinner entree or buffet, excluding tax and tip:

| | |
|---|---|
| $ | $12 or less |
| $$ | $13 to $20 |
| $$$ | $21 to $30 |
| $$$$ | $31 and over |

This symbol indicates the most luxurious accommodations, restaurants, and entertainment.

# PLANNING YOUR TRIP

The most successful vacations are those that are carefully planned and researched months ahead of time. In fact, the planning is, for some, half the fun. Disney is so extensive and offers so many choices to fit the personalities of so many types of vacationers that it demands at least some forethought. You'll discover a wealth of options, some suitable for just about everyone, others frivolous for some but perfect for others. Neglecting to do your homework oftentimes results in disappointment and frustration. The outcome can mean the difference between a smooth trip and an exasperating one.

Begin by reading this book cover to cover and visiting its companion Web site at www.wdwluxuryguide.com. Send for a free Disney vacation planning DVD at http://disneyworld.disney.go.com, call the Orlando/Orange County Convention and Visitors Bureau (800-551-0181 or 407-363-5871), or visit www.orlandoinfo.com for maps of the area as well as a visitor's guide on the many area attractions. For those interested in visiting Universal Orlando (and you should be), call (800) 837-2273 or visit www.universalorlando .com. Check out the sites listed in the following section, and remember, the help of a travel agent who specializes in Disney may be the key to your best vacation ever.

## Disney and Orlando Web Sites

Log on to these excellent Disney-related sites for hundreds of tips along with pictures, menus, and much, much more.

**The Luxury Guide to Walt Disney World** (www.wdwluxuryguide .com or www.caragoldsbury.com). Companion site to this guidebook with continual book updates, menus, recipes, photos, and loads of information and photos on Walt Disney World.

**Walt Disney World Online** (http://disneyworld.disney.go.com). Walt Disney World's official Web site, with a wealth of information useful in planning your vacation.

**AllEarsNet** (www.allears.net). Fabulous for up-to-date detailed news including complete Disney restaurant menus. Sign up for the great free weekly newsletter.

**Carlson's Disney Resort and Parks Picture Site** (www.wdwfun.com). Featuring more than 1,800 photos of the Walt Disney World Resort.

**The DIBB** (www.thedibb.co.uk). A UK–based Disney and Orlando interactive site with information, tips, and planning advice along with an active forum and photo gallery.

**The DIS** (www.wdwinfo.com). Great information site with the best Disney discussion group around.

**Discovery Cove** (www.discoverycove.com). Discovery Cove's official Web site.

**Disney Echo** (www.disneyecho.emuck.com). A fun and friendly online connection to like-minded Disney fans from all over the world.

**Disney World and Orlando Unofficial Guide** (www.wdisneyw.co.uk). Includes Walt Disney World theme park info and tips, resort descriptions and reviews, money-saving advice, photos, maps, and more.

**Disney World Trivia** (www.wdwradio.com). From the author of the *Walt Disney World Trivia Books,* and host of the "The WDW Radio Show— Your Walt Disney World Information Station" podcast, Lou Mongello's site contains trivia, secrets, and fun facts about WDW, as well as news, rumors, games, downloads, forums, photos, articles, and more.

**Explore The Magic** (www.explorethemagic.com). Discounts, tickets, resorts, news, forums, and information for the Disney World tourist.

**INTERCOT** (www.intercot.com). A great, comprehensive guide to Walt Disney World featuring information covering the major theme parks, travel information, pictures, audio clips, video clips, tips, trivia, and interactive discussion about the world's most popular vacation destination.

**Magical Definition Disney Podcast** (www.magicaldefinition.com). Join award-winning Disney podcaster Nathan Rose (of Magical Mountain and Flick Direct) along with Tim Devine (the Magic in Pixels) on a magical journey into the world of Disney. Featuring the latest Disney news and rumors, interviews with Disney Imagineers, Disney photography tips, debates on a variety of Disney topics, and much more Disney magic.

**Magical Mountain** (www.magicalmountain.net). Information about Walt Disney World, Disney company news, exclusive software, Disney merchandise for sale, theme park photos, columns, and more.

**MagicTrips** (www.magictrips.com). Practical information, reader restaurant reviews, and a discussion site.

**Mickey News** (www.mickeynews.com). The latest Disney news as well as park photos, dining, and movie reviews. Check out the column sections for great tips and information.

**MousePlanet** (www.mouseplanet.com). Practical advice, news, and reader reviews.

**MouseSavers** (www.mousesavers.com). A running list of current discounts available at Walt Disney World and Universal resorts.

**SeaWorld** (www.seaworld.com). Official Web site of SeaWorld.

**Tikiman's Polynesian Resort Pages** (www.tikimanpages.com/tiki/). Loads of pictures and information on Disney's Polynesian Resort.

**Universal Orlando** (www.universalorlando.com). Official Web site includes park hours, ticket options, theme park attractions, and hotel information.

**Walt Disney World Live Entertainment** (http://pages.prodigy.net/steve soares). Current Walt Disney World entertainment schedules, descriptions, photos, and links.

**The WDW Radio Show—Your Walt Disney World Information Station** (www.wdwradio.com). Join Lou Mongello each week as he covers Walt Disney World News, visits the WDW Rumor Mill, and interviews

Disney Imagineers, authors, and special guests. He also shares trivia and explores the history of the Walt Disney World theme parks and resorts. With the help of other authors, cast members, and other experts, get vacation planning tips and advice as well as attraction, dining, and resort reviews.

**WDW Magic** (www.wdwmagic.com). Information on upcoming Disney attractions and plenty of park photos.

# TRAVEL TIPS
# FOR THE BUSIEST TIMES

If at all possible, avoid like the plague the hot summer months and most importantly any major holiday at Walt Disney World. The busiest holiday periods are President's Day, the two weeks surrounding Easter, July Fourth, Thanksgiving weekend, and Christmas through New Year's—the busiest time of year. Memorial Day is a toss-up, with the only exception to the rule being Martin Luther King, Jr. Day, Labor Day, Columbus Day, and Veterans Day, when parks are crowded but not unbearable.

If you must travel in busy seasons, remember to make advance dining reservations and utilize FASTPASS (described in chapter 4 on the parks) whenever possible, and pick a resort on Disney property for easy access and midday breaks. When parks reach full capacity, and they do during the busiest of times, only Disney resort guests are allowed admission to at least one park, making it even more important to stay on-property if visiting in high season. Those staying off-property should arrive at the parks well before opening time, when a large percentage of Disney resort guests are still sleeping, to assure access. Although such information is never released in advance, Disney sometimes opens earlier than official opening time during holiday periods in anticipation of record crowds.

**WDW Today** (www.wdwtoday.com). Podcast covering various topics from around Walt Disney World, airing new episodes three times a week on Monday, Wednesday, and Friday with a live call-in show every month.

## Important Walt Disney World Phone Numbers

Advance Dining Reservations (407) WDW-DINE or (407) 939-3463

Behind-the-Scenes tours (407) WDW-TOUR or (407) 939-8687

Boating and tennis (407) WDW-PLAY or (407) 939-7529

Child's Activity Centers reservations (407) WDW-DINE or (407) 939-3463

Fishing information and reservations (407) WDW-BASS or (407) 939-2277

General information (407) 824-4321

Golf tee times (407) 938-4653

Park tickets (407) 566-4985

Switchboard (407) 824-2222

Transportation information (407) 939-7433

Updated park hours (407) 824-4321

## When Should I Go?

Always a tough decision. Should you plan a summer trip when the children are out of school, knowing full well the parks will be sweltering and jam-packed? What about a slower time of year when parks are half-empty but with shortened operating hours in which to tour them? How about over a long holiday weekend, or would it be preferable simply to take the children out of school? These are all questions you must weigh, questions that will help you reach a decision best for you and your family.

Each season has its pros and its cons. The busy season brings congested parks, long lines, and higher resort rates but also greatly extended park hours. The slower seasons bring half-filled parks, little waiting in line, and lower resort rates along with later opening times, earlier closing times, and attractions that are closed for rehab. For me, slow season can't be beat. If you are able to do so, avoid the busiest times of the year. If not, the summer months or holidays are certainly better than nothing and, with a bit of planning and a lot of energy, can be more than enjoyable.

The following guidelines may not be exact since each year comes with different Florida resident offers, special celebrations, conventions, and so forth that affect crowd size. Use them as a general guide to avoiding the parks at their worst.

## How Busy Will It Be?

**Busiest:** President's Day week; mid-March to the week after Easter (staggered spring break around the country); the second week of June to the third week of August; Thanksgiving Day through the weekend; the week of Christmas to New Year's Day.

**Busy:** The last two weeks of February (avoid President's Day week) to the first part of March before the onset of spring break; the week after Easter until the second week of June; the month of October (a big convention month, the PGA Golf Classic, and Halloween celebrations at the Magic Kingdom and Universal Orlando); the first two weeks of December.

**Least busy:** Just after New Year's Day to the first week of February (avoiding the Martin Luther King holiday weekend in January); the third week of August to the beginning of October; the month of November excluding Thanksgiving weekend; just after Thanksgiving and again the week preceding Christmas week, a special time when the parks and resorts are festively decorated for the holidays.

# What Will the Weather Be Like?

Because Orlando is a year-round vacation destination, you probably won't encounter bitter cold weather. Winter has many days of sunshine along with the occasional cold snap, while summer brings uncomfortably muggy and warm days with almost daily afternoon showers. Peak hurricane season begins in August and runs through October, so be prepared for a washout (just about every store in the parks sells inexpensive Mickey-motif rain ponchos for that afternoon shower). The best months of the year—with delightfully mild and low-humidity weather, relatively small amounts of rainfall, and little if no danger of hurricanes—are November, March, April, and early May. Before leaving, call (407) 824-4104 for daily weather information or check one of the many excellent weather sites on the Internet.

| Month | Average High Temp (°F) | Average Low Temp (°F) | Average Rainfall (inches) |
|---|---|---|---|
| January | 72 | 50 | 2.43 |
| February | 74 | 51 | 3.25 |
| March | 79 | 56 | 3.54 |
| April | 83 | 60 | 2.4 |
| May | 88 | 66 | 3.74 |
| June | 91 | 71 | 7.35 |
| July | 92 | 73 | 7.15 |
| August | 92 | 73 | 6.25 |
| September | 90 | 72 | 5.76 |
| October | 85 | 65 | 2.73 |
| November | 79 | 59 | 2.32 |
| December | 73 | 53 | 2.11 |

# What Should I Pack?

Think casual! Park attire is appropriate throughout Disney with the exception of the more stylish resort restaurants (for dress codes, see individual restaurant descriptions). In the warmer months of April through October, bring shorts, light-colored short-sleeved or sleeveless shirts (darker colors really attract the heat), comfortable walking shoes (bring two pairs to switch off), cushy socks, sunglasses, hat, bathing suit and cover-up, water-resistant footwear, and a rain jacket. Women should bring a light purse or backpack; nothing's worse than lugging a heavy bag around the parks. For evenings away from the park at one of the more sophisticated dining venues, dress is business casual: Women should plan on wearing a simple dress, dress shorts, or casual pants or jeans with a stylish blouse and sandals; men will be comfortable in khakis or nice jeans or dress shorts, and a short or long-sleeved collared shirt with loafers or sandals. Only at Victoria and Albert's is a jacket required for men.

The remaining months are anyone's guess. The weather is usually mild, but bring an assortment of casual clothing in the form of shorts and comfortable long pants along with short- and long-sleeved shirts, a sweater, hat, sunglasses, bathing suit and cover-up (pools are heated), rain jacket, light coat, and of course comfortable walking shoes and socks. For evenings away from the parks, women should wear smartly casual transitional clothing, and men casual pants and long-sleeved shirts. Florida is known (particularly November through February) for unexpected cold fronts that will find you in shorts one day and a winter jacket the next, although it never gets uncomfortably hot. Don't get caught off guard or you'll find yourself with an unwanted Mickey Mouse wardrobe. Check the Internet for a weather forecast before packing for your trip.

Water-resistant footwear and fast-drying clothes are desirable at the Animal Kingdom (you'll get quite wet on the Kali River Rapids attraction) and most importantly at Universal's Islands of Adventure, where several rides will give you a thorough soaking. And don't forget plenty of sunscreen, film, memory cards, and batteries, all of which can be purchased almost anywhere in Disney but at a premium price.

## How Long Should I Plan on Staying?

With four major theme parks at Disney, two at Universal Orlando, plus SeaWorld, specialty parks like Discovery Cove, and several water parks, a long weekend will barely give you a taste of the many attractions in the area. Staying seven days or more allows enough time to truly enjoy much of what Orlando has to offer. In one week you'll have time to visit all four of Disney's theme parks, spend a day at Universal, hit one of the water parks, and still have a day left over to relax by the pool and rest your feet. Ten days would really be a treat, allowing a trip to both SeaWorld and Discovery Cove plus a bit of time to stop and smell the roses.

Of course, if you can spare only a long weekend, go for it. You will certainly have some tough decisions to make. With only a few days for touring, go when the parks are not as crowded and plan on visiting the Magic Kingdom, Epcot, and either the Animal Kingdom or Disney's Hollywood Studios with a trip in mind for another year to pick up all you've missed.

# Should I Rent a Car?

Does driving in an unknown place make you uneasy? Do you plan on visiting just Disney, or are SeaWorld and Universal also of interest to you? Will you be staying at a resort serviced by the monorail or at a more isolated one? Would you like to dine at other resorts, or do you see yourself eating at the parks or simply staying put at your hotel? All these factors play a large part in your decision.

The drive from the airport on the Central Florida GreeneWay is a no-brainer, and finding your way around Disney is easy. Traffic is fairly light and there's excellent signage. However, if driving a car in new situations tends to be a nerve-wracking experience, use Disney's more-than-adequate transportation system.

If your plans include a stay at the Animal Kingdom Lodge or Villas, Wilderness Lodge, the Villas at Disney's Wilderness Lodge, or an off-site property, renting a car provides you with many more options. If you plan to visit Universal Studios or SeaWorld, a car is by far the best choice.

No matter what your plans, a car is usually the best option for traveling to the Animal Kingdom or Disney's Hollywood Studios (parks not serviced by the monorail), the water parks, or evening restaurant-hopping at the many excellent resort dining spots. Think about trying Disney transportation for a day or two and, if it doesn't work for you, then rent a car. Alamo has free shuttle service to its Car Care Center location near the Magic Kingdom, and most non-Disney deluxe hotels have car rental desks in their lobbies.

Those who would like to sample some of Disney's excellent resort restaurants will find it time-consuming, not to mention complex, to resort-hop using Disney transportation. It requires a trip to an open park or Downtown Disney and then another bus to the resort and the same thing back again (of course you can always simplify things and take a cab). A stay at one of the Magic Kingdom resorts offers easy monorail access to the Magic Kingdom, other Magic Kingdom resorts, and Epcot. The Epcot Resorts are just a walk or boat launch away from Epcot, the Board-Walk, and Disney's Hollywood Studios, greatly expanding your restaurant choices.

I consider a car a must at any of the non-Disney properties, where transportation options are quite sparse—and don't let them tell you differently

# TIPS FOR WALT DISNEY WORLD FIRST-TIMERS

- Slow down and enjoy the magic. Resist the urge to see everything at breakneck speed, and take time to enjoy the many amenities offered at your resort (you certainly paid enough for them). You can't possibly see it all, so think of this as your first trip to Disney, not your last. There will be time to pick up the things you missed on the next go-round.

- Think ahead. Decide your priorities before your vacation begins.

- Get to the parks early! It's amazing, particularly in busy season, how many of the popular rides you can knock off before half the "World" gets out of bed.

- Plan for a rest in the middle of the day if you have children in tow or the parks are open late. Stay at one of the Magic Kingdom or Epcot resorts, allowing an easy return to your room in the middle of the day for a nap or a plunge in the pool.

- If a meal at Cinderella's Royal Table in the Magic Kingdom is tops on your child's list, you must—I repeat must—call exactly 180 days prior at 7 a.m. Orlando time (Eastern standard time) for Advance Dining Reservations or risk missing this highly coveted restaurant. The only time you might get away with sleeping in and booking a bit later in the day is during extremely slow seasons.

- Always come prepared for an afternoon shower during the rainy summer months even if the sky looks perfectly clear in the morning. Rent a locker to store your rain gear, circling back if skies start to look threatening. If you're caught unprepared, just about every store in the parks sells inexpensive rain ponchos.

- If a lounge chair is a priority at the water parks, you'll need to arrive at opening time to secure one (or reserve one of the private cabanas). And remember that in the busy summer months, water parks are sometimes filled to capacity by midmorning, with new guests kept from entering until late afternoon.

- Use FASTPASS, Disney's nifty time-saving device offered at all four theme parks, saving hours in line (see the FASTPASS section for each park in chapter 4).

- Make Advance Dining Reservations, especially in the busier times of year (see chapter 8, Dining, for a more detailed explanation), to save hours of waiting and frustration.

- Allow plenty of time to reach the theme parks each morning. It's easy to miss your breakfast reservations when enough time has not been allocated.

- Be selectively spontaneous. If something catches your eye, even if it's not on your daily list of things to do, be ready to stop and explore or you may miss something wonderful.

- Be attuned to the limitations of your children. If they're tired, take a break; if their feet hurt, get them a stroller (forget that they outgrew one years ago); if a ride scares them, don't force the issue. It will make your day and the day of other park visitors a lot less stressful.

- Wear broken-in, comfortable footwear. Better yet, bring two pairs and rotate them. Nothing is worse than getting blisters on your first day and then having to nurse them for the remainder of your vacation.

(although the Waldorf Astoria seems to have a better system with almost hourly shuttles to the Disney theme parks). Transportation from off-site properties is inconvenient at best, offering only the bare necessities. The only exceptions are Universal resorts, extremely convenient to the Universal theme parks and CityWalk; if Universal is all you plan on, a car is really not necessary.

In short, you will probably be using a combination of Disney transportation and a car for added convenience. And if you're like me and hate waiting for public transportation, rent a car to save hours of frustration.

Do remember that if your plans include a rental car, parking will be a factor. Although parking is complimentary to guests of a Walt Disney World resort, those staying off-property will pay $14 per day to park at the Disney theme parks. And instead of being dropped off in front of the theme park entrance, those with a car will need to catch a shuttle from the parking lot. Self-parking is complimentary at the Disney resorts, but valet parking will set you back $12 per day. That doesn't include the Walt Disney World Swan and Dolphin, where it's $10 for self-parking and $16 for valet. And factor in an even bigger charge off-property where prices vary according to resort.

# ARRIVAL AT
# WALT DISNEY WORLD

## Getting to Walt Disney World

### Orlando Airports

Most travelers arrive at the Orlando International Airport (MCO), approximately a twenty-five-minute drive from Walt Disney World and fifteen minutes from Universal Orlando. Private jets will want to land at Kissimmee (ISM), the closest airport to Walt Disney World. Other choices for private aircraft include Orlando International (MCO), closest to Universal Orlando, and Orlando Executive (ORL), closest to downtown.

### By Car

Walt Disney World is located off I-4, about 25 miles southwest of Orlando and west of the Florida Turnpike. From Interstate 95 or U.S. Highway 1 from the Florida Turnpike, take I-4 west and follow the signs to the correct Walt Disney World exit for your resort or theme park destination. Those traveling south on the Florida Turnpike will want to shorten their travel time by taking the new Walt Disney World's Western Way—look for 429 West Toll Road (Tampa) to exit the turnpike and in 14 miles take the Walt Disney World exit. Those traveling northbound on the turnpike should take the Osceola Parkway that will lead directly to Walt Disney World.

Once inside Walt Disney World, excellent signage will direct you to all destinations; however, you'll need to know what area your resort belongs to

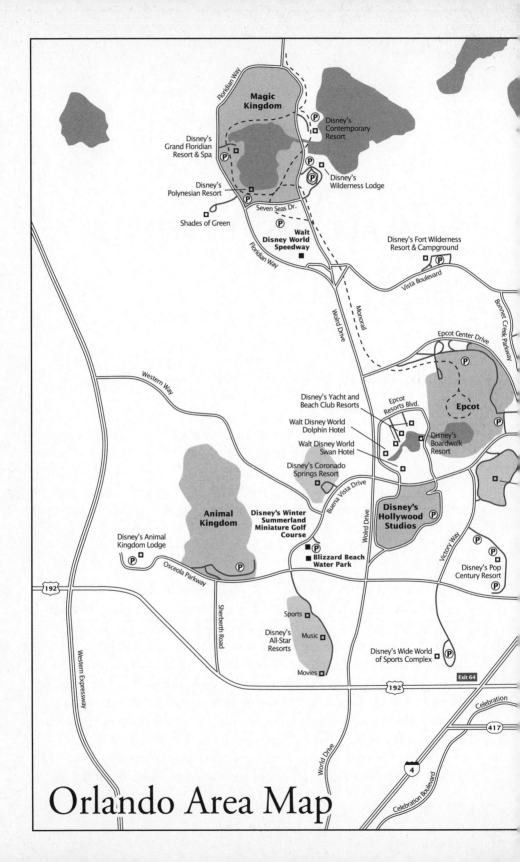

# Orlando Area Map

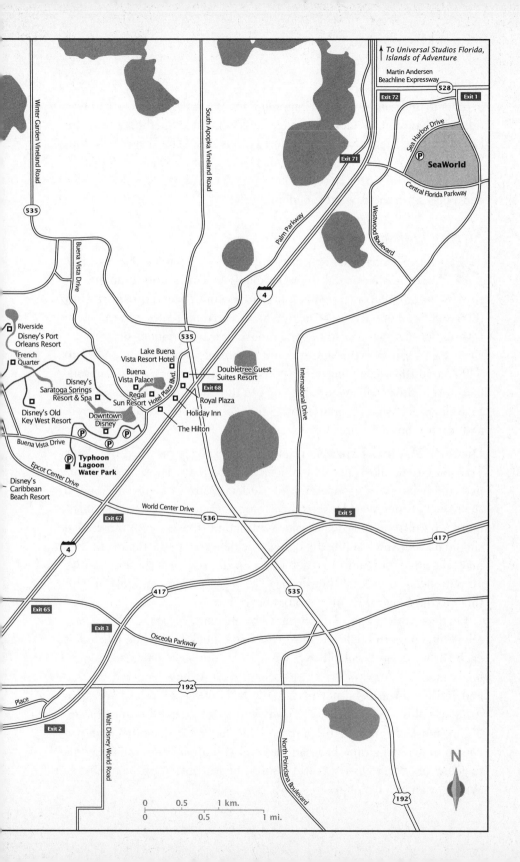

To Universal Studios Florida,
Islands of Adventure

Martin Andersen
Beachline Expressway

528

Exit 72          Exit 1

Sea Harbor Drive

P

**SeaWorld**

Central Florida Parkway

Exit 71

Westwood Boulevard

Palm Parkway

Winter Garden Vineland Road

South Apopka Vineland Road

535

4

Buena Vista Drive

535

International Drive

Riverside
Disney's Port
Orleans Resort

French
Quarter

Lake Buena
Vista Resort Hotel

Buena
Vista Palace

Doubletree Guest
Suites Resort

Disney's
Saratoga Springs
Resort & Spa

Regal
Sun Resort

Hotel Plaza Blvd.

Exit 68

Royal Plaza

Disney's Old
Key West Resort

Holiday Inn

Downtown
Disney

The Hilton

P          P

Buena Vista Drive

P

P  **Typhoon
Lagoon
Water Park**

Epcot Center Drive

Disney's
Caribbean
Beach Resort

World Center Drive

536

Exit 5

Exit 67

4

417

417                535

Exit 65

Exit 3

Osceola Parkway

192

Place

Walt Disney World Road

North Poinciana Boulevard

Exit 2

N

192

0        0.5        1 km.
0        0.5        1 mi.

in order to find your way. The Contemporary, Bay Lake Tower, Grand Floridian, Polynesian, Wilderness Lodge, and Villas at Wilderness Lodge are located in the Magic Kingdom Resort Hotels area. The BoardWalk Inn, Yacht and Beach Club, and the Walt Disney World Swan and Dolphin Hotels are in the Epcot Resort Hotels area. The Animal Kingdom Lodge and Villas sit in the Animal Kingdom area.

## Airport Transportation

For personalized service book private car or limousine transfers prior to your arrival from **Quicksilver Tours and Transportation** (888-468-6939 or www.quicksilver-tours.com), **Star Transportation** (866-888-5530 or www.gostarmgt.com), or **Garden Tours & Transportation** (866-698-5466 or www.gardentoursandtransportation.com). Towncars cost $115 to $170 round-trip and limousines approximately $240 to $290 round-trip (depending on the transportation company and size of your party). Your driver will meet you as you exit the escalator downstairs at baggage claim. A customary gratuity of 15 to 20 percent should be considered, and reservations are mandatory.

**Disney's Magical Express,** a motor coach service provided by Mears Transportation, allows guests to check their bags at their hometown airport and bypass baggage claim at the Orlando airport before heading to their Walt Disney World resort. Buses stop at up to four resorts so it takes quite a bit of time to arrive at your destination (those short on patience should book private car transfers). Bags are delivered to the room, but they may take up to four hours to reach you. Guests arriving at the airport after 10 p.m. need to pick up their luggage at baggage claim and take it with them to the Magical Express motor coach.

On departure day avoid airport lines by checking luggage and receiving a boarding pass through the Resort Airline Check-In Service located at each Disney resort (available to passengers of American, Delta, Continental, United, US Airways, Northwest, Southwest Airlines, AirTran, Alaska, and JetBlue). You need not necessarily be utilizing Magical Express to make use of this handy service. Those with a flight departure time before 8 a.m. must check in at the airport. This service is complimentary (of course individual airline baggage fees will still apply) and available only to guests of a Walt Disney World resort (not available at the Walt Disney World Swan and Dolphin).

## Car Rental

**Alamo Rent A Car,** the official car rental company of Walt Disney World, is located both at the airport and at the Car Care Center near the Magic Kingdom, with free shuttle service provided to and from your Disney resort. For convenience stick with the companies located on airport property—**Alamo, Avis, Budget, Dollar, Enterprise, L&M, National,** and **Thrifty**—whose cars are parked a quick walk away from the baggage claim area. Off-property car companies include **Hertz** and **Payless**. All companies have another location somewhere in the vicinity of Walt Disney World.

Both National and Alamo offer XM radios in many of their luxury and premium rentals, a real bonus when cruising. For something more luxurious try the **Hertz Prestige Collection,** offering Volvo C70 convertibles, Cadillac Escalades, Hummer H2s, Mercedes C and E class, and Audi Q-7 AWDs. Specific models may be reserved, and a complimentary NeverLost navigational system is included. Avis has a Cool Cars Collection including Super Sport Camaros, Toyota Camry and Prius Hybrids, CTS Cadillacs, Titan and Tundra trucks, VW Beetle Convertibles, and Corvettes.

Excellent signage and a great toll road from the airport make for an easy twenty-five-minute drive. Take the South exit out of the airport to toll road State Route 417 South, also known as the Central Florida GreeneWay, and follow the signage to Walt Disney World and your resort or theme park destination. The drive is approximately 22 miles. Another option is the north route out of the airport to toll Highway 528, also known as the Bee Line Expressway, then to I-4. This is the quickest way to Universal Orlando, but it's best to avoid it as a route to Disney during rush-hour traffic; it's the old route before the GreeneWay and only slightly shorter.

# Disney Transportation

Disney's complimentary transportation system, designed for the exclusive use of Disney resort guests (although only on the busiest days do they require an ID to ride), is in most cases efficient, particularly the monorail. In addition, taxis can be found at every resort, all four theme parks, and Downtown Disney. For more information call (407) WDW-RIDE or (407) 939-7433.

## Bus Transportation

Disney has an extensive and reliable system of more than 700 clean, air-conditioned buses traversing the extent of the property. Designed for the exclusive use of Disney's registered guests, buses depart approximately every twenty minutes, carrying guests to all four theme parks, both water parks, Downtown Disney, and all resort hotels. However, it takes more time than a car, what with multiple stops at several resorts and what sometimes seems like a roundabout direction. Some buses are direct (to the theme parks and Downtown Disney) while others require a change at Downtown Disney. Buses operate as early as 6:30 a.m. for those with before-park-hours breakfast reservations until one and a half hours after park closing time. One advantage of bus transportation is the convenient drop-off directly in front of the park entrance, translating into no parking hassles and no waiting for a tram. The downside occurs after park closing when quite a line can form; consider leaving just a few minutes before the fireworks are over or hanging out to shop at one of the stores near the exit.

Getting easily from one resort to another is a different story altogether. Those staying at a Magic Kingdom or Epcot resort have many choices within walking distance or a monorail ride away, but those utilizing bus transportation find the only way to accomplish this feat is to take the quickest form of transportation to the nearest open theme park and then a bus to the resort of choice. After park hours it's necessary to bus to Downtown Disney and then to the resort. For example, it takes a good hour or more to travel between say the Yacht Club Resort and Wilderness Lodge. If you want to resort-hop, I strongly encourage renting a car or utilizing a taxi for optimum convenience.

## Monorail

Twelve monorails, each holding 300 passengers, travel over 13 miles of track at up to 40 mph on three lines: the monorail between Epcot and the Transportation and Ticket Center (TTC), the express monorail to the Magic Kingdom, and the Magic Kingdom Resorts monorail. All use the TTC as their central hub. Monorails traveling counterclockwise around the Seven Seas Lagoon offer a nonstop ride between the TTC and the Magic Kingdom. Monorails running clockwise stop at the Grand Floridian,

# TIPS FOR ROMANCE

- If you're traveling with children, plan an evening or two on your own at a romantic restaurant (Victoria and Albert's takes the cake) or a night at Downtown Disney or one of the theme parks. Leave the kids at one of Disney's excellent resort childcare centers. If your child is under four or not potty trained, call **Kid's Nite Out** at (407) 828-0920 for in-room childcare.

- Consider springing for two rooms. Disney guarantees connecting rooms for families with children.

- Bring along a bottle of wine to enjoy in your room or on your balcony. The bottled wine selections at the Disney resort shops tend to be a bit sparse; of course In-Room Dining usually has a nice selection.

- Arrange for a couples massage at the Grand Floridian Spa in a candlelit room.

- Pick up a glass of wine at the kiosk in France or Italy, then stroll Epcot's World Showcase in the evening when all the countries are beautifully lit by twinkling lights.

- Watch the evening fireworks spectacular from one of the resort beaches. Perfect spots can be found at the beaches of the Polynesian and Grand Floridian.

- Take a Fireworks Cruise from one of the Magic Kingdom or Epcot resorts; order a bottle of champagne delivered to the boat from In-Room Dining and enjoy! For super romantic luxury rent the 52-foot Grand I yacht for a moonlight spin around the Seven Seas Lagoon.

- For the ultimate in romance get married or renew your vows at Walt Disney World. To make arrangements call a Disney wedding specialist at (321) 939-4610.

the Polynesian, the Contemporary, and the TTC. Between Epcot and the Magic Kingdom is a lovely ride with easy access between the parks.

## Boat Service

Ferryboats found at the TTC are a fun form of transportation for Magic Kingdom visitors. The Magic Kingdom is also accessible by water taxi from the Polynesian, Grand Floridian, Contemporary, and Wilderness Lodge and Villas. Both Epcot and Disney's Hollywood Studios are accessible by water taxi from the BoardWalk Inn, Yacht and Beach Club, and the Walt Disney World Swan and Dolphin.

# Basic Disney Reference Guide

**Alcoholic beverages.** You'll find alcohol served at every park and hotel on Disney property, except at the Magic Kingdom. The legal drinking age in Florida is twenty-one; however, most of Disney's lounges allow minors as long as they do not drink alcohol or sit at the bar. Bottles of liquor, wine, and beer can be purchased in at least one shop in every Walt Disney World resort and/or from In-Room Dining.

**ATMs.** Chase automated teller machines (ATMs) are located at each park, in Downtown Disney, at the TTC, and in or near the lobby of each resort.

**Business centers.** Disney resorts with convention center facilities (Yacht and Beach Club, BoardWalk Inn, Contemporary, Grand Floridian, and Walt Disney World Swan and Dolphin) offer a complete office environment including personal computers, high-speed Internet, fax machines, copiers, and secretarial services.

**Car care and gasoline.** Hess Express has three stations in Disney World open twenty-four hours: on Floridian Way near the Magic Kingdom, across from Downtown Disney, and at the entrance to the Board-Walk. For car repair go to the AAA Car Care Center (407-824-0976) adjoining the Hess station near the Magic Kingdom. Open Monday through Friday from 7 a.m. to 6 p.m. and Saturday 7 a.m. to 4 p.m. If your car becomes disabled while on Disney property, AAA has complimentary towing to the Car Care Center; after hours call Disney security at (407) 824-4777.

**Child care.** Disney's Children's Activity Centers include the Cub's Den at Wilderness Lodge, the Sandcastle Club at the Yacht and Beach Club Resort, the Mouseketeer Club at the Grand Floridian, Simba's Cubhouse at the Animal Kingdom Lodge and Villas, Camp Dolphin at the Swan and Dolphin Resort, and the Never Land Club at the Polynesian (my favorite), all offering child care services for potty-trained children ages four through twelve. See individual resort descriptions for detailed information. Cost is $11.50 per hour per child, including a meal, with a minimum of two hours. Reservations should be made at least twenty-four hours in advance by calling (407) WDW-DINE or (407) 939-3463. For Camp Dolphin call (407) 934-4241.

Many off-property resorts have excellent child care facilities. At the Hyatt Regency Grand Cypress is Camp Hyatt, Camp Omni at the Omni ChampionsGate, at the Ritz-Carlton and JW Marriott there's Ritz Kids, and at the Waldorf Astoria the WA Kids Club.

For in-room child care, nanny, or mother's helper services, Disney recommends Kid's Nite Out. All employees of this service receive a thorough background check. Call (800) 696-8105, extension 0, or (407) 828-0920 at least seventy-two hours in advance; four-hour minimum charge.

**Dietary requests.** Dietary requests such as kosher, no sugar added, low-carb, or low-fat as well as special dietary requests regarding allergies to gluten or wheat, shellfish, soy, lactose, peanuts, or other foods can be accommodated at full-service restaurants; a 14-day advance notice is requested by calling (407) WDW-DINE or (407) 939-3463 or e-mailing specialdiets@disneyworld.com. Kosher meals can be found at Cosmic Ray's Starlight Café at the Magic Kingdom, ABC Commissary at Disney's Hollywood Studios, Liberty Inn and Electric Umbrella at Epcot, and Pizzafari at the Animal Kingdom. Most full-service and many quick-service restaurants offer at least one vegetarian choice, which I have tried to reflect in my entree examples in the restaurant section.

**Environmental awareness.** Disney's environmental commitment is more than commendable. Efforts include the recycling of more than 30 percent of waste; distribution of prepared, unserved food to local missions; collection of food waste for compost production; purchase of recycled products and products with reduced packaging; and use of reclaimed water for irrigation. Recycling containers can be found in every guest room and throughout the parks. Walt Disney World Resort has earned the

Florida Department of Environmental Protection's (DEP) Green Lodging Program designation for 100 percent of its lodging with green features such as a towel and linen reuse program, low-flow faucets and showerheads, an advanced computerized energy management system, and a recycling program for visitors and staff.

**Flowers and such.** Flowers and gourmet food baskets can be delivered, and magical in-room experiences created anywhere on Disney property. Call (407) 827-3505; www.disneyflorist.com.

**Groceries.** The closest full-service grocery store to Walt Disney World is twenty-four-hour Goodings, located in the Crossroads Shopping Center of Lake Buena Vista near Downtown Disney, or order online at www .goodings.com for resort delivery (minimum $50 per order plus a $20 service charge). Just north of Goodings is a new Winn Dixie near the Hyatt Grand Cypress at 11957 South Apopka-Vineland Rd. A Publix services the Omni and Reunion Resort on ChampionsGate Blvd. Near Universal is a Whole Foods on the corner of Turkey Lake and Sand Lake Road in the Restaurant Row area. Shop online ahead of time at www.gardengrocer .com from a large selection of grocery items that can be delivered to your resort for a fee of only $12 (free with an order of $200 or more). A small selection of groceries is also available at each Disney Deluxe Villa Resort.

**Guests with disabilities.** Vehicles equipped with lifts to accommodate wheelchairs and most ECVs service all bus routes. Watercraft access varies according to the type of craft and water levels. All monorails, many park attractions, and most restrooms are wheelchair accessible. Special parking areas are available at all four theme parks. Wheelchairs and electric controlled vehicles (ECVs) may be rented in limited quantities at each theme park.

Each resort offers special equipment and facilities for guests with disabilities. Features vary by resort but may include wider bathroom doors, roll-in showers, shower benches, handheld shower heads, accessible vanities, portable commodes, bathroom and bed rails, bed shaker alarm, text typewriter, strobe-light fire alarm, and phone amplifier. Other features include double peepholes in doors, closed-captioned television, and braille on signage and elevators.

Most theme park attractions provide access through the main queue while others have auxiliary entrances for wheelchairs and service animals along with up to five members of your party. Certain attractions require guests to transfer from their wheelchair to a ride system. For detailed information the helpful *Guidebook for Guests with Disabilities* is available at Guest Relations at each park or at the front desk of each Walt Disney World Resort. Handheld receivers are available to read captions at more than twenty park attractions. Each park offers assistive listening devices, video captioning, braille guidebooks, and audiotaped tours, all available for a refundable $25 deposit, and handheld captioning is available with a $100 deposit. Reflective captioning can be found at many theater-type attractions. A sign language interpreter for live shows can be made available with one week's notice on certain days of the week (see each individual park for details). Additional information can be found at http://disneyworld.disney.go.com or by calling (407) 824-4321 (voice) or (407) 827-5141 (TTY).

For further detailed information consider purchasing *Walt Disney World with Disabilities* by Stephen Ashley or *Passporter's Open Mouse for Walt Disney World and the Disney Cruise Line,* by Deb Wills and Debra Martin Koma. Both are comprehensive resources for people with mobility, sensory, and other impairments, but also cover such diverse topics as food allergies, special dietary needs, motion sickness, and more.

**Hair salons.** Full-service salons are located at the Grand Floridian, Contemporary, Yacht and Beach Club, and Dolphin as well as at the Waldorf Astoria, Hyatt Regency Grand Cypress, Gaylord Palms, Omni, Rosen Shingle Creek, Reunion Resort, Portofino Bay Hotel at Universal, and the JW Marriott/Ritz-Carlton. An old-fashioned barber haircut can be had on Main Street in the Magic Kingdom.

**International travelers.** Visitors who speak languages other than English may ask at Guest Services in each theme park for a park guide versed in that language. Guides are available in more than a dozen languages. Also available at Guest Relations, with a $100 refundable deposit, are complimentary language translation headsets with wireless technology that provide synchronized narration in Spanish, French, German, Japanese, or Portuguese for more than thirty attractions. Interpreters are available by calling the Foreign Language Center at (407) 827-7900. Many restaurants offer menus in several languages. Foreign currency may be exchanged at any Walt Disney World resort.

**Internet services.** In-room high-speed Internet access is available for a fee at all resorts. Additional access can be found at the business centers of all resorts offering convention services. High-speed wireless Internet access (WiFi) is available at the BoardWalk, Contemporary, Grand Floridian, Yacht and Beach Club, and the Walt Disney World Swan and Dolphin.

**Laundry and dry cleaning**. Self-service, coin-operated washers and dryers are located at every Disney resort in addition to same-day dry cleaning and laundry service.

**Lockers.** Lockers can be found in all four Disney parks as well as both water parks, Downtown Disney, and the Transportation and Ticket Center (TTC).

**Lost and found.** Lost item claims may be made at each individual park's Lost and Found. The central Lost and Found is located at the TTC, where items not claimed the previous day are sent; call (407) 824-4245.

**Mail.** The closest post office is at the Shoppes of Buena Vista, 12541 Highway 535; open Monday through Friday from 9 a.m. to 4 p.m. and Saturday from 9 a.m. to noon. Stamps may be purchased and letters mailed at all four theme parks, Downtown Disney, and all Walt Disney World resorts. All shops at Walt Disney World offer worldwide shipping for a fee.

**Medical care.** All theme parks offer first aid during park hours. Twenty-four-hour, in-room medical care for nonemergencies is handled by Physician Room Service (407-238-2000). Florida Hospital Centra Care Walk-In Medical Center (407-934-2273) has a Lake Buena Vista location near Downtown Disney, with complimentary transportation available and most insurance plans accepted. Emergency medical needs are met by the Dr. P. Phillips Hospital at I-4 exit 74A or at Florida Hospital Celebration Health located on Walt Disney World property in the town of Celebration.

**Money matters.** Walt Disney World accepts cash, traveler's checks, Disney Dollars (available at Disney Stores, Guest Relations, and Resort Services), and six types of credit cards: American Express, MasterCard, Visa, Discover, Japanese Credit Bureau, and Diners Club.

Guests of a Disney-owned resort may charge throughout Disney by using their room key as long as a credit card imprint is given at check-in. ATMs are readily available throughout Walt Disney World, with locations at each resort, each theme park, Downtown Disney, and the TTC.

**Parking.** Parking at Disney theme parks is free to all registered guests of Walt Disney World resorts and Annual Passport holders. All others pay $14 per day. Make sure you make a note of what section and aisle you have parked in; lots are enormous. Save your receipt if you plan on park-hopping; it allows you to park for that day only at any of the other Disney theme parks for no additional fee.

All Disney resorts charge $12 per day for valet parking; no charge for self-parking. Be forewarned that after 11 p.m. most resorts have only one valet parking attendant on duty, not a grand welcome after returning from dinner or a late night at the parks.

**Pets.** Only service dogs for guests with disabilities are allowed inside Disney's theme parks and resorts. Disney's newest pet centers, run by Best Friend Pet Care, are located at the TTC near the Magic Kingdom, Epcot, Disney's Hollywood Studios, the Animal Kingdom, and Fort Wilderness Resort and Campground. Goodies such as deluxe bedding, private doggy suites, kitty condos with piped-in bird sounds, playgroups for puppies, ice cream breaks, cuddle time, and grooming are available. Proof of vaccination is required. For more information go to www.bestfriendspetcare .com/centers.cfm#fl.

**Rider Swap.** Parents traveling with young children who don't meet height restrictions should consider utilizing the rider swap program. One parent waits with the child while the other rides, then the second parent hands off the child and goes to the head of the line. Just speak to the cast member on duty.

**Safety.** Walt Disney World is a relatively safe environment, but caution must still be taken. Be alert at all times, particularly at night. Always lock your guest room door, and make sure you verify who is knocking before allowing anyone entry. Use the safe provided in your room to store money and valuables. Park in well-lit areas, lock your car, and be aware of your surroundings when leaving the car. Take extra care when traveling to Orlando and places outside Walt Disney World where security is less stringent.

**Security.** All bags are checked prior to entering the theme parks by uniformed security cast members; allow yourself extra time if you've booked Advance Dining Reservations. High-security, antiterrorist barricades that can stop speeding trucks have been installed at Walt Disney World, an added level of protection for the theme parks' service entrances.

**Smoking.** All Walt Disney World resort guest rooms (including room balconies), restaurants, and public areas are smoke-free environments. Tobacco products are not sold in the theme parks and water parks, where smoking is limited to designated areas; look for the cigarette symbol on the guide maps. Because of the implementation of the Florida Indoor Clean Air Act, smoking is not allowed at any of Disney's resort lounges.

**Strollers and wheelchairs.** Strollers, wheelchairs, and electric controlled vehicles (ECVs) may be rented at all major theme parks and Downtown Disney. Retain your receipt for a replacement at any other Disney theme park for that day only. A limited number of wheelchairs are also available at all Disney resorts.

Another great option that will save you money is Orlando Stroller Rentals at www.orlandostrollerrentals.com, which uses only high-end strollers including a PushChair designed for older children. Strollers are delivered to your hotel's bell service/luggage room and picked up upon checkout.

**Telephone calls.** Orlando has a ten-digit calling system, meaning you must dial the area code of 407 followed by the number when making a local call.

**VIP tour services.** Those wishing to make their visit to the theme parks as seamless and easy as possible should consider Disney's personalized theme park tours. For $175 to $195 per hour ($215 for non–Disney resort guests) with a six-hour minimum, a Disney VIP guide will maximize your time by assisting you and up to nine others with a customized day at the parks and plenty of Disney trivia along the way. Don't expect to move to the front of the line, but do expect plenty of help with the FASTPASS system and special seating for parades, stage shows, and dining. Private transportation with back entrance into the parks can be added for $120 more per day. A Premium VIP Tour option for $275 to $315 includes private transportation to the parks with back-door entrance, allows more flexibility of start time, and quite a bit more flexibility in obtaining FASTPASS. Reservations must be made at least forty-eight hours in advance by calling (407) 560-4033.

# ANNUAL WALT DISNEY WORLD EVENTS

**January:** Walt Disney World Marathon the second week of January.

**February:** ESPN The Weekend late in the month.

**March:** Ten-week Epcot International Flower and Garden Festival begins.

**April:** Epcot International Flower and Garden Festival continues.

**May:** Epcot International Flower and Garden Festival continues; Star Wars Weekends at Disney's Hollywood Studios begins.

**June:** Star Wars Weekends at Disney's Hollywood Studios continues.

**September:** Night of Joy at Disney's Hollywood Studios; Mickey's Not So Scary Halloween Party at the Magic Kingdom begins.

**October:** Six-week Epcot Food and Wine Festival begins; Mickey's Not So Scary Halloween Party at the Magic Kingdom continues until the end of the month; PGA golf tournament at Disney's Magnolia and Palm Golf Courses.

**November:** Epcot Food and Wine Festival; Festival of the Masters at Downtown Disney; Mickey's Very Merry Christmas Party at the Magic Kingdom begins; Osborne Family Spectacle of Dancing Lights at Disney's Hollywood Studios begins.

**December:** Mickey's Very Merry Christmas Party at the Magic Kingdom continues; Osborne Family Spectacle of Dancing Lights at Disney's Hollywood Studios continues; Epcot's Holidays Around the World.

Do not discount using a non-Disney tour guide, a less expensive and excellent option. Good choices include: Michael's VIPs, www.michaels vips.com; VIP Theme Park Tours, www.vipthemeparktours.com; Suntastic Tours, www.suntastictours.com; and Elite Orlando VIP Tours, http:// eliteorlandoviptours.com.

## Disney Weddings

*Bride's* magazine lists Disney among the top ten U.S. wedding destinations. In fact, Walt Disney World hosts about 2,000 weddings a year. More than 23,000 couples have taken their wedding vows in Disney's storybook atmosphere, and countless more have picked Disney as their choice for a dream honeymoon. Imagine being escorted to your wedding in Cinderella's glass coach with horses and footmen in attendance or perhaps a Hollywood Extravaganza at Disney's Hollywood Studios. Everything can be arranged, from the flowers to the photographer, the waiters to the music. To speak to a wedding planner, call (407) 566-6540.

### Wedding Locations

Although weddings are allowed just about anywhere on Disney property, there are several very popular sites; if you want a theme park wedding, expect the price to skyrocket. On an island surrounded by the Seven Seas Lagoon is the **Wedding Pavilion** at the Grand Floridian Resort, offering a magical view of Cinderella's Castle. The **Swan Boat Landing** fronting Cinderella's Castle at the Magic Kingdom is another top pick. At Epcot choose any of the romantic **World Showcase pavilions**—perhaps a sunrise wedding in Japan or a ceremony among the koi ponds in China. **Sea Breeze Point** at Disney's Board-Walk Inn offers a white gazebo overlooking Crescent Lake. Or you may want to consider the wedding gazebo in the Yacht Club Resort's serene rose garden. **Sunset Pointe** at the Polynesian Resort is on a grassy hill overlooking the Seven Seas Lagoon with Cinderella's Castle in the background while **Sunrise Terrace** at the Wilderness Lodge has a fourth-floor balcony overlooking the pine trees and Bay Lake. You can also have your marriage ceremony on Disney Cruise Line's private island, **Castaway Cay**.

## Wedding Themes

Choose from a traditional wedding to a variety of Disney-themed weddings. Some theme ideas include a Beauty and the Beast Ball Wedding or a Winter Wonderland Wedding. How about an Animal Kingdom Safari reception? What about inviting Mickey to your cake cutting? Just about anything is possible at Walt Disney World.

## Wedding Packages

Disney's Escape Weddings are small and intimate, with eighteen or fewer guests at one of six locations at Walt Disney World. Prices start at $4,750 depending on the location. Included are bouquet and boutonniere, wedding cake and bottle of champagne, violinist, limousine, photographer and photo album, wedding coordinator, and a personalized wedding Web site. Many alternative arrangements can be planned for an additional price such as flowers, transportation in Cinderella's Coach or a vintage car, or Disney characters to join in your celebration. Since a reception is not included in the basic cost, consider a post-wedding dinner at a romantic restaurant, an Illuminations dessert party, or perhaps tea at the Grand Floridian.

More elaborate weddings with ten or more guests can be completely customized and are considered Wishes Weddings with prices beginning at $12,000. Ceremonies can take place just about anywhere on property, but think about a dream-come-true option at the Magic Kingdom's Swan Boat Landing with Cinderella's Castle as a backdrop, a fanfare trumpeter, a horse-drawn coach, and transportation down Main Street for your guests in motorized cars.

Disney has teamed up with celebrity wedding planner David Tutera and created glamorous Couture Weddings starting at $65,000. These grand affairs begin with save-the-date cards as well as wedding invitations created by David. For your ceremony the stage is dressed in sophistication. Your reception is chosen from four heavenly styles that include shimmering fabrics, floral arrangements, props, furniture, elegant flatware, stemware, and table settings. What about a cocktail soiree in contemporary colors like ice blue and chocolate brown, and a custom lounge area with an illuminated bar and floor-to-ceiling draped walls? Or perhaps a classic elegance look with crystal chandeliers, gold drapery and candelabras, and gilded mirrors and pedestals? Specialty drinks can even be created that match your color scheme, your bridesmaid's dresses, or flowers. For more information go to http://disneycoutureweddings.com.

Disney Cruise Line's Weddings at Sea begin at $2,500 and can be performed either onboard or on Castaway Cay, Disney's private island. Included is the marriage license, on-site wedding coordinator, officiant, solo musician, flowers for the bride and groom, cake and champagne reception, dinner for two at Palo (the adults-only dining room) on the wedding night, a special wedding gift, and a $100 onboard credit.

# LUXURY ACCOMMODATIONS

alt Disney World is rich in choices for the deluxe traveler, but which resort is best for *you?* Let's try to narrow down the field of possibilities by pinpointing your party's personality and preferences.

Those traveling with small children will find themselves spending quite a bit of time at the Magic Kingdom. Strongly consider choosing one of the Magic Kingdom Resorts, where the park is just a short monorail hop away, easily accessible for a quick afternoon nap or a dip in the pool.

Adults traveling without children will probably enjoy being closer to Epcot and Disney's Hollywood Studios. It's just a short walk or boat ride away to both parks from any of the excellent Epcot resorts. You'll also find a world of possibilities in nearby dining and entertainment.

Those who enjoy nature and like a quiet, more isolated resort should opt for the Animal Kingdom Lodge, where hundreds of animals roam just 30 feet from your room balcony, or perhaps Wilderness Lodge, surrounded by pine forest fronting Bay Lake. If the convenience and comfort of a living area and kitchen are appealing, think about one of the Disney Deluxe Villa Resorts located throughout Walt Disney World. If you plan on spending several days at Universal with a visit to SeaWorld or Discovery Cove, book two or three nights at one of the hotels near Universal and then afterward move to a Disney resort.

Also consider room type preferences. Is a view of the water or pool important? Or would you rather pay less and have a view of the resort's gardens?

Will a standard room be all that you need, or should you consider one on the concierge level or maybe a roomy suite? Of course budget together with how much time will be spent in your room are major considerations and will play a large part in your decision. If hanging out at your resort sounds appealing, the concierge rooms are a smart idea. These accommodations, located on a keyed-access floor, come with the use of a private lounge with complimentary continental breakfast, snacks throughout the afternoon, before-dinner hors d'oeuvres and cocktails, and late evening cordials and desserts. These amenities are in addition to private check-in and checkout and the assistance of a concierge staff ready to help you with Advance Dining Reservations, recreation, show tickets, or anything else within their power. Definitely a nice plus to your vacation. Suites in each of the deluxe resorts come in virtually all shapes and sizes, some as large as 2,000 or more square feet, certainly the most luxurious option if your pocketbook allows.

Would you rather stay within Walt Disney World, or do you prefer an off-property location? Staying on property certainly has its pluses. In addition to the many benefits (see the sidebar in the next section for more details), consider the ease of transportation and quick access to the parks. Parents of teens can allow them time on their own without worrying about their every move. And teens will love the freedom of hopping aboard the monorail or a Disney bus to tour the parks without parents. Those with small children will be close enough to head back from the parks for an afternoon nap. That said, several off-property resorts are deluxe, all of them within ten to twenty minutes from Walt Disney World with the new Waldorf Astoria practically in the middle of Disney property. Of course always consider Universal's hotels if your plans include a few days at the Universal parks. One of the chief reasons to consider a stay off-property is if someone (particularly someone who is paying) is Mickey Mouse phobic. For them, Disney theming, though terrific, is a bit of overkill and the thought of spending the entire day in the park and then returning to more of the same is just too much.

## Walt Disney World Resorts

Although many resorts are owned and operated by Disney, only those meeting the standard of superior first class or deluxe have been considered

# DISNEY RESORT GUEST BENEFITS

- Complimentary and convenient Disney transportation by monorail, bus, and water taxi.
- Complimentary parking at Disney's theme parks.
- Easy access to the parks, making midday breaks and naps possible, plus allowing parties to effortlessly split up to go their independent ways.
- Charge privileges to your resort account for purchases throughout Disney.
- Guaranteed entry to a Disney theme park, particularly important during busy holiday periods when filled-to-capacity parks often close to non-Disney resort guests.
- Extra Magic Hours whereby one of Disney's theme parks opens an hour early or up to three hours later than regular park hours exclusively for Disney resort guests.
- Disney's Dining Plan, which can save up to 30 percent per adult if purchased as part of your Magic Your Way Package, allowing a choice from over 100 select restaurants.
- Complimentary Titleist and Cobra club rentals with a full round of golf at any Disney golf course.
- Package delivery from anywhere on-property directly to your resort.
- Access to Disney's child care facilities available only to resort guests.
- Complimentary airport transportation via Disney's Magical Express buses.
- The magic of Disney twenty-four hours a day.

for review in this guidebook. All have attractive guest rooms, landscaped grounds of sheer artistry, top-notch recreational facilities and services, and at least one excellent restaurant if not two or three. And all, with the exception of the off-site properties, offer Disney's special touch.

## Disney Resorts

Although Disney offers a nice range of resorts in every price category, we will consider only the deluxe resorts and the newer Disney Deluxe Villa Resorts. The moderate properties, though interesting and well themed, do not fit this book's designation of luxury, and of course the value properties do not even come close.

### DISNEY'S DELUXE RESORTS

Disney's deluxe properties are graced with impressive lobbies, painstakingly landscaped grounds, first-rate restaurants, elaborately themed pools, and lovely, if not five-star, accommodations. These properties include the Grand Floridian, the Polynesian, the Contemporary, the Wilderness Lodge, the Animal Kingdom Lodge, the BoardWalk Inn, the Yacht and Beach Club, and the Walt Disney World Swan and Dolphin.

The Wilderness Lodge as well as the Animal Kingdom Lodge are a slightly different level of deluxe. Standard rooms here are smaller than other deluxe resorts; however, what they lack in room space they more than make up for in atmosphere. Those who frequent five-star properties such as the Ritz-Carlton or Four Seasons should not expect the same amenities at Disney (although a Four Seasons resort is slated to open in 2012 on Disney property). While I love Disney resort's theming, and I absolutely adore the wonderful atmosphere, they do tend to rest on their laurels a bit and there is definitely room for improvement. You'll find somewhat smallish guest rooms, and the pool areas have lounge chairs so tightly packed that you can forget about peace and quiet. Thankfully mattresses and pillows have been upgraded, and the paper-thin towels have been replaced. Even the old embarrassing Mickey Mouse soaps have given way to H2O bath products. Please don't expect butlers, marble baths (except in Disney's suites), pay movies, HBO, and your choice of one hundred channels. The point is just to enjoy the unparalleled theming and friendly service in the four-star-rated rooms at "the Most Magical Place on Earth."

For those choosing to stay off-property, deluxe resorts include the Waldorf Astoria Orlando, Hyatt Regency Grand Cypress, the Gaylord Palms Resort, the Omni Orlando Resort, and the Reunion Resort. At Universal are the Hard Rock Hotel, the Portofino Bay Hotel, and the Royal Pacific Resort. The Ritz-Carlton, JW Marriott, and Rosen Shingle Creek are located between Universal and Disney. All are excellent alternatives to the Disney resorts, but be prepared to deal with conventioneers who tend to take over most of these hotels with private dinners and outdoor evening events. While Disney also hosts conventions, the events usually take place out of sight in their convention facilities.

**DISNEY'S DELUXE VILLA RESORTS**

The Villas at Disney's Wilderness Lodge, Bay Lake Tower at the Contemporary Resort, and the new Animal Kingdom Villas are Disney's most luxurious Vacation Club Resort choices (called Disney's Deluxe Villa Resorts), properties leased out to non-owners when rooms are available. It's a great way to enjoy Disney with all the conveniences of home, including a full kitchen, a living room, and a bathroom for each bedroom.

I do feel, however, that the Disney Deluxe Villa Resort studio accommodations' only advantage is their mini-kitchen consisting of a microwave, small refrigerator, and sink. A better choice for just about the same price is a guest room at one of the deluxe hotels. The new Bay Lake Tower has the distinct advantage of being on the monorail with super access to the Magic Kingdom and Epcot as well as the other monorail resorts and their exceptional restaurants. The Villas at Disney's Wilderness Lodge property is just a hop, skip, and jump away from the facilities of the adjoining Wilderness Lodge and a boat ride away from the Magic Kingdom. The Animal Kingdom Villas, while remote, do have access to three very good restaurants and the advantage of some of Disney's best theming.

**CHECK-IN AND CHECKOUT**

Check-in time is 3 p.m. at all Disney resorts and 4 p.m. at all Disney Deluxe Villa Resorts. If arriving early in the day, go straight to your resort to register and have your luggage stored until check-in time (or if arriving on Magical Express, luggage will be delivered directly to your room), then head off to a park or spend time exploring the property. In slower seasons it's sometimes possible to check in early.

At check-in you'll receive a bulletin with up-to-date information on resort services, recreation, and special events as well as a *Walt Disney World Update* with park hours, rehabs (attractions closed for renovation), and special events. If you'd like a head start, ask for a copy of the park guide maps. Re-request any preferences at registration. Be sure to have your room pointed out on a resort map; if the location is undesirable, say so before leaving the desk. And if you've booked the concierge level or a suite, remember to identify yourself as a concierge guest to the bellhop or valet on arrival to be escorted directly to your private check-in.

If you're taking a late plane home on checkout day, store your luggage with either the bell desk or valet parking and head out to the parks. Those traveling on participating airlines can simply check their bags and pick up boarding passes at the Resort Airline Check-in Service desk, making it a cinch at the airport. If you're staying at more than one Disney property, valet services will transfer your luggage free of charge with luggage arriving by 3 p.m.

## Disney Discounts

Yes, this book is about a Disney deluxe vacation, but even the biggest spenders like a bargain. And bargains are as easily available at the deluxe resorts as they are at the value ones. Better yet, opportunities to save on everything from dining to entertainment to behind-the-scenes tours abound. With the many discounts available, only in the busiest seasons or when reserving a suite should anyone pay full price for a **Disney resort.** Following are some of the many ways to save.

**Seasonal discounts.** Rooms at Walt Disney World are priced using a four-season system that varies according to resort type. Remember, the busier the season, the more expensive the room. Approximate seasons for deluxe resorts and Disney Deluxe Villa Resorts are as follows:

- Value season: Just after New Years to mid-February, mid-July to early October, and late November to right before Christmas
- Regular season: mid- to late April (depending on the Easter holiday) to mid-July and again early October until Thanksgiving
- Peak season: mid-February until mid- to late April (depending on the Easter holiday)
- Holiday season: just before Christmas through New Years

**Annual Pass rates.** This is one of Disney's better bargains. With the purchase of an Annual Pass, you'll not only receive unlimited park admission for one year but also excellent resort rates. Only one person in the room need be a pass holder to obtain sometimes up to a 45 percent discount available throughout most of the year. Also included is a quarterly *Mickey Monitor* newsletter; discounted admission to Blizzard Beach, Typhoon Lagoon, DisneyQuest, and Cirque du Soleil; free parking at the theme parks; as well as discounts on special ticketed events, selected dining, merchandise, car rentals, behind-the-scenes tours, spa treatments, water sports, boat rentals, Richard Petty Driving Experience, and golf. Room discounts aren't typically available until two to three months in advance and are, of course, limited. A good strategy is to hold a room at the regular price just to be safe and continue calling periodically until the pass holder discount becomes available, at which point the reservation agent will lower your rate (or have your Disney specialist travel agent, who is always in the know about Disney's discounted room rates, do this for you). With the amount saved, the additional cost of an Annual Pass could more than pay for itself in a couple of nights.

**Disney discount codes.** Throughout the year Disney offers great promotions associated with special discount codes. Have your Disney specialist travel agent keep an eye out for you or keep up online at www .mousesavers.com, a great Web site that stays on top of the discount game.

**AAA/CAA discounts.** Receive a discounted room price of 10 to 20 percent with a AAA or CAA membership for all but the busiest times of year.

**Florida residents.** Residents of Florida receive great Disney benefits, particularly during the slower times of the year. Call your travel agent or go to http://disneyworld.disney.go.com/florida-residents for special prices on resort rooms and theme park passes.

## Reservations

Before calling for reservations, narrow the field down to two or three resorts that best suit your needs. Reserve as soon as possible, particularly for travel during major holidays, to ensure that your preferred resort and room type are available. Again, decisions need to be made. Is it best to go with a package deal or book a "room only" reservation and treat your air, resort, and car as separate elements? Is it wiser to make reservations yourself or call a travel agent? How about booking your trip on the Internet? All good questions. With such a wide array of booking choices on the market, there is no substitute for a good travel agent, particularly one that specializes in Disney. This professional can certainly save you a lot of time, headaches, and usually money.

## DISNEY AND UNIVERSAL BOOKING NUMBERS

Call a travel agent or Central Reservations at the Walt Disney World Travel Company at (407) 939-7675 or go online at http://disneyworld.disney.go.com for all on-site Disney resorts. Universal's on-site hotels may be booked through your travel agent, online at www.universalorlando.com, or by calling (888) U ESCAPE, (888) 273-1311, (866) LOEWS-WB, or (866) 563-9792.

## MAJOR AIRLINES SERVICING ORLANDO

Airlines servicing Orlando include AirTran, Alaska Airlines, American, Continental, Delta, Frontier, JetBlue, Midwest, Northwest, Southwest, Spirit, Sun Country, United, US Airways, and WestJet. International carriers include Air Lingus, Aeromexico, Air Canada, British Airways, Copa, Lufthansa, Mexicana, Taca, Tam, and Virgin Atlantic. Find the lowest airfare by calling your travel agent or each individual airline servicing your city (a lot of work) or by shopping the Internet, particularly sites such as Expedia, Orbitz, and Travelocity. No one should ever pay full fare for a coach-class seat unless booking at the last minute. Most important, shop, shop, shop! Fares to Orlando tend to be quite a bargain.

## TRAVEL AGENCIES SPECIALIZING IN DISNEY

There's nothing quite like a Disney expert when it comes to choosing a travel agent. These are Authorized Disney Vacation Planners who can make the difference between a mediocre vacation and an excellent one.

- **Cara Goldsbury and Luxury Orlando Vacations:** (800) 930-9954 or www.wdwluxuryguide.com. As a service to her readers and others interested in experiencing a luxury Disney vacation, Cara Goldsbury, this book's author, offers personalized travel consultation and planning to the Walt Disney World Resort and Disney Cruise Lines.

- **WDWTravels:** (800) 709-4573 or www.wdwtravels.com

- **The Magic for Less Travel:** (888) 330-6201 or www.themagicfor less.com

- **MEI-Travel:** www.mei-travel.com

**DISNEY'S VACATION PACKAGE PLANS**

The Walt Disney World Travel Company as well as many of the afore-mentioned travel agencies offer Disney's special package plans. The more elaborate ones are a good buy only if you think you'll use all of the additional features. Beware of purchasing a plan with elements you do not want or need.

Disney also has air/sea vacations. Those who love cruising should consider three or four nights on the Disney Cruise Line combined with several days at a Disney resort, the best of both worlds (see the last chapter of this book for more information on cruising with Disney).

Disney's package plans, including Magic Your Way tickets, are as follows:

**Disney's Magic Your Way Package:** Resort accommodations and Magic Your Way Base Tickets.

**Disney's Magic Your Way Package Plus Quick-Service Dining:** Resort accommodations, Magic Your Way Base Tickets, and a Disney dining plan that includes two quick service meals and two snacks per person per night plus a resort refillable mug per person.

**Disney's Magic Your Way Package Plus Dining:** Resort accommodations, Magic Your Way Base Tickets, and a Disney dining plan at more than one hundred on-property restaurants including per-person, per-night the following: one table-service meal (entree, dessert, and non-alcoholic beverage, or one full buffet), one quick-service meal (entree, dessert, and nonalcoholic beverage), and one snack. A table-service meal can be exchanged for a character meal, or two table-service meals can be exchanged for a signature dining experience (appetizer, entrée, dessert, and a nonalcoholic beverage) at places such as California Grill, Citricos, Flying Fish, and Cinderella's Royal Table, for private dining, or a Disney dinner show like Hoop-Dee-Doo Revue or Spirit of Aloha.

**Disney's Magic Your Way Package Plus Deluxe Dining:** Resort accommodations, Magic Your Way Base Tickets, and a Disney dining plan at more than one hundred on-property restaurants including the following: three meals per person per night at either a quick-service spot (entrée, dessert, and non-alcoholic beverage) or a full-service restaurant (appetizer, entrée, dessert, and one non-alcoholic beverage or one full buffet or character meal) as well as two snacks. Two dining credits will be needed for signature dining experiences, Disney dinner shows, and private dining.

**Disney's Magic Your Way Premium Package:** Resort accommodations, Magic Your Way Premium Tickets, breakfast, lunch, dinner, and two snacks per person per night including In-Room Dining, unlimited selected recreation including golf, fishing, water sports, boating, and tennis, admission to Cirque du Soleil, admission to Disney Children's Activity Centers at selected resorts, and unlimited admission to theme park tours.

**Disney's Magic Your Way Platinum Package:** Resort accommodations, Magic Your Way Premium Tickets, breakfast, lunch, dinner (including Victoria and Albert's), and In-Room Dining, unlimited recreation including golf, fishing, water sports, boating, and tennis, unlimited select tours, preferred fireworks viewing, reserved seating for Fantasmic!, private golf lessons, one selected spa treatment, tickets for Cirque du Soleil, unlimited child care in the resort Child Activity Centers, in-room child care, a Fireworks Cruise, unlimited theme park tours, Disney PhotoCD and Professional Portrait Service, and a Richard Petty Ride Along Experience.

**Wine and Dine add on:** If you enjoy a bottle of wine with dinner this is a great addition to any of the packages above that include dining. For around $40 more per room per night you'll receive one bottle of wine from a designated list at full-service restaurants where alcohol is served. It really is a nice discount—for instance, at the California Grill the $54 bottle of Wild Horse Pinot Noir was included as a choice. In fact, there were six bottles priced over $50 and twenty-five $45 dollars and above.

## CONSIDERATIONS

When considering a concierge-level room, take into account the schedule you will more than likely keep during your vacation. If you plan on spending most of the day and into the evening at the parks, the additional price for concierge service will not be worth the expense. You'll probably only have the time to take advantage of the continental breakfast and perhaps the late-night cordials and dessert, with the remaining offerings wasted. If returning to your resort to dress and relax before dinner or an afternoon swim at the pool sounds more to your liking, the concierge level can't be beat. The almost continuous food and beverages, the extra-attentive service, and that special feeling of staying in a small hotel within a larger complex certainly go a long way.

It's a good idea to inquire when a resort has last been renovated. If it's been over five years, pick another. Disney does seem to stretch room reno-vations about two years too long resulting in overpriced and underwhelm-ing accommodations that are not up to par. This is where a good Disney travel specialist will come in handy, someone who has that information at their fingertips.

Inquire whether any major construction will be in progress at your resort of choice during your visit. If so, book another property. No matter how nicely they try to cover up a pool reconstruction or an all-encompass-ing face-lift, it most certainly will affect your overall resort experience. Take my word for it.

At the time of booking, request anything special or important to you, such as a particular view, the desire to be far from the elevator or pool, or a certain bed type. Remember that these requests are never guaranteed unless you are reserving a suite with an assigned room number (usually only the Presidential or Vice Presidential Suites). The only guarantee Disney will make is connecting rooms for families with children.

Remember to take advantage of any discounts such as Annual Pass-holder or AAA rates described earlier in this chapter. Consider reserving tee times, child care, special dinner shows, or Advance Dining Reserva-tions when making your resort reservations.

## Magic Kingdom Area Resorts

This is the most enchanting area in all of Walt Disney World. Six resorts hug the shoreline of two bodies of water, the Seven Seas Lagoon and Bay Lake, all accessible by either monorail or boat to the Magic Kingdom. Disney's Contemporary, Bay Lake Tower, Grand Floridian, and Polynesian

# THE BEST OF EVERYTHING

### BEST RESORT POOLS

- The Yacht and Beach Club's Storm-along Bay, a three-acre miniature water park
- The Swan and Dolphin's grotto-style lagoon pool
- The Volcano Pool at the Polynesian Resort with its luxuriant waterfall, smoking peak, and perfect views of Cinderella's Castle
- The boulder-strewn wonderland at the Wilderness Lodge with its own erupting geyser
- The lush pool at the Hyatt Regency Grand Cypress cooled by twelve waterfalls
- The JW Marriott's Lazy River, 24,000 square feet of winding delight
- The sophisticated pools at the Waldorf Astoria Orlando with luxury cabana options.

### BEST DELUXE RESORT

On Disney property it's the Grand Floridian with its upscale Victorian ambience and lagoonside setting facing the Magic Kingdom. Off-property, it's the new Waldorf Astoria where you may never even feel the need to go to the parks. At Universal go for the Portofino Bay Hotel, with its unsurpassed atmosphere of an Italian seaside resort.

### BEST DISNEY DELUXE VILLA RESORT

The Bay Lake Tower at the Contemporary Resort with its hip, modern look, monorail access, and spectacular views of the Magic Kingdom. Or the Animal Kingdom Villas where exotic animals are roaming just outside your guest room.

### BEST ATMOSPHERE

The Animal Kingdom Lodge, where hundreds of animals roam the savanna and the air is pulsating to the beat of African drums. Running a close second is Universal's Portofino Bay Hotel, where guests are transported to a seaside Italian village.

### BEST LOBBY

How to choose? Three make the cut: the Wilderness Lodge, the Grand Floridian, and the Animal Kingdom Lodge, all eye-popping in their grandeur.

### BEST ACCESS TO THE PARKS

The Contemporary, Polynesian, Bay Lake Tower, and Grand Floridian with monorail access to the Magic Kingdom, Epcot, and the Transportation and Ticket Center. At Universal, the Hard Rock Hotel is just a five-minute walk or boat ride to Universal Studios, Islands of Adventure, and CityWalk.

### BEST FOR ROMANCE

The Polynesian Resort, whose lush tiki-torch-lit grounds and white-sand beaches with views of Cinderella's Castle are simply dreamy, or Universal's Portofino Bay Hotel, where an evening stroll along the bay with Italian arias playing in the distance can't be beat.

### BEST FOR NATURE LOVERS

Wilderness Lodge, a nature lover's dream of rushing waterfalls, spouting geysers, and bubbly creeks, all surrounded by stately pine trees and sparkling Bay Lake.

### BEST FOR TENNIS

The great tennis centers at the Hyatt Regency Grand Cypress and Reunion Resort.

## BEST FOR GOLF

At the Ritz-Carlton Grande Lakes you'll find a Greg Norman–designed course set on the headwaters of the Everglades and an innovative Caddy-Concierge Program; the Reunion Resort has three outstanding courses designed by Arnold Palmer, Jack Nicklaus, and Tom Watson; and the new Waldorf Astoria whose Rees Jones–designed course winds through a wetland preserve.

## BEST RESORT LOUNGES

- **California Grill Lounge.** The Contemporary Resort's fifteenth-floor lounge offers unrivaled views of the Magic Kingdom and the Seven Seas Lagoon. Sip on cocktails, nosh on fantastically fresh sushi, and catch one of the best views of the Wishes fireworks display. *CARA'S TIP:* If you're only coming for drinks, it can be difficult to get in around fireworks time. You'll need to check first at the second-floor podium.

- **The Waldorf Astoria's Peacock Alley** where chic guests gather for cocktails and snacks. And there's more at Sir Harry's Lounge with its masculine, private club atmosphere and live piano music.

- **Bluezoo.** This restaurant bar at the Dolphin is the coolest place around.

- **Velvet.** The Hard Rock Hotel is where you'll find this ultrahip cocktail lounge.

- **Bar America.** Portofino Bay's upscale lounge overlooks the romantic piazza.

- **Il Mulino.** The Walt Disney World Swan's hip restaurant bar, a study in refinement and style.

- **Sora.** One happening sushi/cocktail bar at Gaylord Palms Resort. Along with it's contemporary Asian flair are cool cocktails with ingredients such as green tea liquor, ginger lemon grass infused vodka, and muddled shisho leaves.

- **The Wave.** Futuristic glowing blue lounge at the Contemporary Resort where wines from the Southern hemisphere, organic beers, and antioxidant cocktails are the norm.

### BEST CONCIERGE LOUNGE

The Grand Floridian's Royal Palm Club where there's Disney's best spread of appetizers and pleasant music wafting up from the Grand Lobby below. And the Ritz Carlton's exceptional lounge with great views and the best food and drinks around.

### BEST SPA

- **Spa by Guerlain at the Waldorf Astoria,** a respite you'll never want to leave.
- **The Mandara Spa at the Walt Disney World Dolphin** where you'll find exotic Balinese-inspired atmosphere and treatments.
- **The Ritz Carlton Spa,** a tranquil oasis in the center of theme park craziness.

### BEST SUITES

- **The Royal Assante Presidential Suite at the Animal Kingdom Lodge** with its thatch roof ceiling, hand-carved furnishings, African textiles, and sweeping views of the resort's savanna.
- **The Emperor's Suite at the Walt Disney World Dolphin,** a two-story delight in a divine contemporary style with views for miles and miles.
- **The Hemingway Presidential Suite at Gaylord Palms,** a masculine beauty in the style Ernest would have loved.
- **The Waldorf Astoria's Presidential Suite** whose lush furnishings, lofty views, and sheer elegance are a dream come true.

Resorts surround the Seven Seas Lagoon and feature magical views of Cinderella's Castle; all four connect to one another as well as to the Magic Kingdom and Epcot (via the Transportation and Ticket Center, or TTC) by monorail. Disney's Wilderness Lodge and the Villas at Disney's Wilderness Lodge are not connected by monorail to the Magic Kingdom; however, they are accessible to the park by boat, with the plus of a pristine setting smack-dab in the middle of a pine forest fronting beautiful Bay Lake.

Those driving for the first time to the Magic Kingdom Resorts may feel confused when the signage seems to be leading straight into the Magic Kingdom parking lot. Drive up to the second turnstile on the right, advise the parking lot attendant that you're checking in, and he or she will wave you past. Stay to your right and follow the signs to your resort.

## Bay Lake Tower at Disney's Contemporary Resort

**428 units. 4600 North World Drive, Lake Buena Vista 32830; phone (407) 824-1000, fax (407) 824-3539. Check-in 4 p.m., checkout 11 a.m. For reservations call (407) WDW-DISNEY or (407) 939-3476, or contact your travel agent. $$$–$$$$$**

**Why Stay Here?** Disney's only Deluxe Villa Resort located on the monorail.

**Rooms to Book.** Theme park view rooms with stellar views of the Magic Kingdom and the Seven Seas Lagoon. The Grand Villas here are Disney's most spectacular three-bedroom option.

**Don't Miss.** The Wishes fireworks show from the balcony of your Magic Kingdom view room.

This new, 16-story Disney Deluxe Villa Resort adjoining the Contemporary Resort offers dramatic views of the Magic Kingdom, the Seven Seas Lagoon, and Bay Lake. The crescent-shaped tower is linked by pedestrian sky bridge to the Contemporary Resort with access to the monorail and all the Magic Kingdom area has to offer. The resort's small, circular lobby is bright and sunny due to huge glass windows with ultra-contemporary seating, tropical palm trees, and a fun glass bubble chandelier hanging overhead. Just outside the lobby is an area faintly Asian in design with dramatically lofty bamboo and a sparkling fountain that leads to the pool area and Bay Lake.

I do feel that a resort that could have been darn near perfect misses the mark for two reasons: check-in is far away next-door at the Contemporary Resort; and, worse yet, the resort's amazing Top of the World Lounge on the sixteenth floor is available only to Disney Vacation Club owners (it's an absolutely ridiculous concept that resort guests of the Bay Lake Tower are not allowed access!).

## REST

Villas are quite impressive with modern furnishings that are soothing to the eye. Contemporary artwork adorns the walls, and stylish charcoal gray carpeting adds a soft look to the rooms. All enjoy an iPod docking station, electronic safe, DVD player, iron and ironing board, Pack 'n' Play, coffee maker, vacuum, and hairdryer. One irritation is that ice machines are found on only three of the fifteen floors—an unbelievable inconvenience.

**Studios.** While studios units are pleasant, they are unusually small at just over 300 square feet. Adorning the room is a queen bed topped with a soft white duvet and a gold and pumpkin hued bed runner, a linen-look beige sofa sleeper with celery-colored throw pillows, sky blue leather ottoman coffee table, a two-person dining table, full-size bureau over which is a wall-mounted, flat-panel TV, and adjoining balcony (first-floor units have a patio). Off the entry hall is an open, somewhat cramped room where one side is the mini-kitchen with wet bar, pull-out pantry, undercounter refrigerator, and microwave, and, strangely enough, the other side a bathroom vanity with a single sink (you're never sure whether to wash the dishes or wash your face). Separated from the hallway by a sliding frosted glass door is the marble bath with a commode area and tub accented with glass tiles.

**One-Bedroom Villas.** Striking one-bedroom villas are 807 square feet. The kitchen has contemporary, dark wood cabinets, sea blue backsplash, and white and gray granite countertops with stainless steel refrigerator, dishwasher, stove, and microwave. A granite island features two yellow leather bar stools. Just opposite is booth dining seating four. The adjoining living area is furnished with a white sleeper sofa adorned with bright yellow pillows, blue leather oversized ottoman/coffee table, a sand-colored leather sleeper chair, chocolate brown occasional chair, and a bureau over which is mounted a flat-panel TV (turn on channel 20 to hear the accompanying Wishes fireworks music). A sliding door leads to the balcony. Off the living area is a full-size bonus bath with a small, corner single sink. You'll also find a stacked washer/dryer in the hallway. In the bedroom is a king-sized bed with an interesting black and white woven leather headboard intermixed with dark wood. A moss green throw tops a white duvet with a punch of nautical blue in the bolster. Two glass-topped black side tables flank the bed. A dark wood bureau with a white cabinet front holds another flat-panel TV and a built-in luggage rack. There's also a vanity-style marble desk, an easy chair with chrome arms, and a door leading to the balcony. One area of the master bath has a whirlpool tub and single sink set in a taupe granite vanity backed by a wall of shimmering glass tile; in the other area is the shower with chic hardware and splashes of glass tile, the commode, and a small corner single sink.

**Two-Bedroom Suites.** A two-bedroom suite is simply a combination of the one-bedroom and a studio at 1,152 square feet. Some are dedicated with the second bedroom offering two queen beds and no mini-kitchen.

**Grand Villas.** With 2,044 square feet, the spectacular Grand Villas offer magical views (fourteen in all with six Magic Kingdom and eight Bay Lake views). Although these are the exact same layout as the Animal Kingdom Villas Kidani, the Bay Lake villas seem larger because of the lighter decor. The first thing you notice is the amazing view, so heavenly that you'll simply refuse to lower the shades. Offering three bedrooms and four baths on two levels, you'll find the kitchen, dining area, living room, master bedroom, laundry room, and extra bath on the first floor and two bedrooms, two baths, and a TV room on the second floor (entry doors are found on both floors). The kitchen is open to the living area with a small island, and there's an adjoining eight-person dining table. A balcony is found off the kitchen. The soaring, two-story living area has hardwood flooring topped with a colorful, contemporary rug, a sleeper sofa, two occasional chairs, ottoman-style coffee table, and entertainment center with TV and stereo system. A master, similar to the one found in the one-bedroom villa, is just off the living area with its own balcony. Climb the hardwood floor and stainless steel cable railing staircase to the second floor where two identical bedrooms, each with two queen beds and balcony, flank the loft TV room with sleeper sofa. Sleeps twelve.

Villas' view choices range from a standard view with a look at either the parking area or the pool, to a Bay Lake view or a Magic Kingdom view.

But like the next-door Contemporary Resort, Magic Kingdom views here also offer a not-so-nice look of the giant parking lot below.

*CARA'S TIP:* If you are in a Magic Kingdom view villa, request one on the north side of the building closest to the park, which affords a superb vista of Space Mountain and the Castle. On the Bay Lake side request floors nine and above for an Epcot view. A few bonus type villas on the far north side considered Bay Lake View units actually have a view of the Magic Kingdom from their balconies only.

### DINE

**Cove Bar.** Pool bar; Caesar salad with chicken, club sandwich, five-spice chicken lettuce wraps, vegetable summer rolls with sesame green beans; bento box meals available poolside from private dining including an Italian deli sandwich, club sandwich, cheeseburger, and vegetarian sandwich; specialty cocktails, frozen drinks, wine.

**In-Room Dining.** Available 24/7 from the next-door Contemporary Resort.

### PLAY

**Children's Activities.** Disney trivia challenges, campfire/marshmallow roast, pool games, ceramics, arts and crafts, bingo.

**Bocce Ball and Shuffleboard.** Courts just outside the lobby; pick up equipment at Community Hall.

**Community Hall.** Located just off the lobby area offering recreation for the entire family; DVD rentals, foosball, game stations.

**Swimming.** Zero entry Bay Cove Pool fronting Bay Lake with a fun tower water slide and interactive water feature; kid's splash pool; whirlpool; BBQ/picnic area; small, but pleasant sand beach accented with Spanish moss-dripping trees.

**Tennis.** Two lighted courts with nice views of Bay Lake on the north side of the property; complimentary equipment at Community Hall.

### WORK, MOVE, SOOTHE

The Bay Lake Tower shares all services with the adjacent Contemporary Resort. See the subsequent entry for the Contemporary Resort.

**GO**

Take the Skyway Bridge to the Contemporary's fourth-floor monorail or walk the pathway to the Magic Kingdom. The monorail stops at the Transportation and Ticket Center, where you can transfer to the Epcot monorail. Buses run to Disney's Hollywood Studios, Animal Kingdom, Blizzard Beach, Downtown Disney, and Typhoon Lagoon. Take the monorail to the Polynesian and Grand Floridian Resorts. To reach other Disney resorts during park operating hours, take the monorail to the Magic Kingdom and from there pick up a bus to your resort destination. After park hours, take the bus to Downtown Disney and transfer to your resort destination. Wilderness Lodge and Fort Wilderness are reachable via the Blue Flag Launch found at the Contemporary's Bay Lake marina.

## Disney's Contemporary Resort

**654 rooms. 4600 North World Drive, Lake Buena Vista 32830; phone (407) 824-1000, fax (407) 824-3539. Check-in 3 p.m., checkout 11 a.m. For reservations call (407) WDW-DISNEY or (407) 939-3476, or contact your travel agent. $$–$$$$$**

**Why Stay Here?** What other resort do you know of that has a monorail running through it?

**Rooms to Book.** Theme park view rooms overlooking the Magic Kingdom with perfect vistas of the Wishes fireworks spectacular.

**Don't Miss.** Cocktails followed by a superb meal at the California Grill with the best views in all of Walt Disney World.

The fifteen-story, A-frame Contemporary Resort has long been a familiar landmark. What used to be considered a modern façade is now pretty darn austere, with its soaring, open interior and its sharp edges and angles. Love it or hate it, its accessibility to the Magic Kingdom can't be beat, and a resort makeover has given the term "contemporary" more meaning. Of course, the sight of the monorail silently gliding through its core is simply magical. The property consists of a high-rise tower, a three-story wing, and a next-door convention center, making this resort a favorite choice for groups.

Wacky trees cut in futuristic forms line the entrance leading to a marble lobby with sleek, chocolate colored, chenille sofas and woven grass chairs. To feel the grandeur of the resort, you'll want to head to its centerpiece, the fourth-floor Grand Canyon Concourse, whose soaring space boasts floors of guest rooms surrounding the vast atrium. At its heart stands a charming 90-foot mosaic mural of Native American children, which is surrounded by shops, restaurants, and the monorail station, all constantly buzzing with traffic. High above it all sits the fifteenth-floor California Grill, one of Disney's best restaurants, with a bird's-eye view of the Magic Kingdom.

**REST**

**Guest rooms.** Upscale, elegant decor with dark, rich wood furnishings, beds covered in cream-colored down duvets topped with celery green bolsters, soft triple sheets, comfy mattresses, and loads of pillows make these some of the nicest rooms in Disney's repertoire. If it weren't for the dated low ceilings you would think you were in a brand new resort. Other nice touches include a gold-and-taupe-toned, suede-covered headboard stretching to the ceiling with soft built-in lighting, a flip-over sofa bed in a soft celery green, a sleek, frosted-glass-topped desk with ergonomic chair, contemporary pendant lighting, and a copper-lined mirror. Carpeting and wall color are a lovely shade of taupe, and the 32-inch LCD flat-panel TV, set in a shallow wall unit, is a real bonus. Baths are elegant with chocolate brown and cream marble floors, and elongated sinks in a stainless steel and frosted glass vanity. A bath/shower adjoins the two sinks with the commode in a separate area. The foyer's two closets are designed with frosted glass panels trimmed in rich wood with a granite vanity that hides a refrigerator and coffeemaker. Amenities include a laptop-size electronic safe, fluffy towels, non-lighted makeup mirror, hairdryer, iron and ironing board, iPod clock radio, and morning newspaper.

Tower rooms, all with balconies, are the ticket here and worth the additional cost with knockout views of either the Magic Kingdom and glorious sunsets (for a higher price) on one side, or Bay Lake on the other. The higher the floor, the quieter the room and the better the view. Rooms can be noisy due to their suspended position over the Grand Canyon Concourse where the clamor of Chef Mickey's character breakfast begins in the wee hours of the morning—request a room on the opposite side of the tower.

The three-story Garden Wing guest rooms offer the same decor and basic configuration as Tower rooms, but they come with a bit of a walk to the main building and the monorail. Bottom-floor rooms have a patio, but the top two floors are minus balconies. Spend a bit more for a Garden View with vistas of either the gardens, the marina, the pools, or Bay Lake instead of a parking lot.

Garden Wing Deluxe Rooms sit in the corner of the building, making them angular in shape with both the king bed and the living area all in one large space. The living area holds modern furnishings including a sleeper sofa, cool-looking but not-too-comfortable chair with ottoman, coffee table, entertainment center, and desk. The bath is slightly oversize with two areas: two sinks and tub in one area with a shower and toilet in a separate space. A wet bar is in the foyer.

*CARA'S TIP:* Although Tower rooms on the Magic Kingdom side have a marvelous view of the park, they also come with a not-so-marvelous view of the parking lot; however, it's worth it for front-row seats of the night-time fireworks display.

**Concierge rooms.** The Contemporary Resort has two concierge levels: one on the twelfth floor and another on the fourteenth floor. Guest rooms here have the addition of desktop computers.

The Contemporary's relaxing Atrium Club on the resort's twelfth floor is one of Disney's standout concierge lounges where you'll find continental breakfast, afternoon snacks, evening appetizers and wine, and after-dinner desserts and cordials as well as private check-in/checkout, robes, turndown service, DVD players, and the services of a concierge staff. The best part is its lengthy balcony and unbeatable views of the Magic Kingdom and Seven Seas Lagoon. At breakfast are the usual suspects of fruit, juice, pastries, cereal, toast, donuts, croissants, cinnamon rolls, mini-muffins, and bagels, and afternoon snacks are cookies, brownies, mini-cupcakes, Hello Dollys, pecan bars, goldfish, pretzels, fruit, coffee, sodas, etc. What used to be pretty lackluster offerings in the evening are now quite savory with two hot items like kefta skewers, rock shrimp with hummus and lavash, macadamia nut chicken, tamarind spiced short ribs, beef tenderloin skewers with balsamic drizzle, prosciutto flatbread, conch fritters with spicy remoulade, mini blue crab cheesecakes with chipotle mayo, crunchy chicken lollipops, prosciutto wrapped scallops, beef flatbreads with caramelized onions and goat cheese, duck confit with apple slaw, spring rolls, and pot stickers with soy glaze along with cold items such as smoked tomato jam bruschetta with fresh mozzarella cheese, crudités with dip, hummus, and PB&J sandwiches. Excelsior Cabernet, Rock Rabbit Syrah, Fess Parker Chardonnay, and Beringer White Zinfandel are the wines of choice along with a nice variety of beer. Desserts are mini-tarts, cannoli, chocolate-covered strawberries, and petit fours with cordials—children enjoy gummy worms, pudding, and cookies.

Fourteenth-floor rooms and suites have been renovated in a nice modern-day style with new furnishings and contemporary lighting and accessories. Regular guest rooms on this floor are larger than the rest of the tower's, with leather headboards, deep balconies, larger baths, and spectacular views, but most of the accommodations are suites. All have the exclusive use of the Tower Club concierge lounge offering the same amenities as the Atrium Club above, but in a more intimate setting. And because it is the only guest room floor not suspended over the Grand Concourse it is quieter—that is, until the California Grill just above it on the fifteenth floor closes and the clean-up begins and continues until the wee hours of the morning; totally unacceptable for any room, much less suites at this price tag.

**Suites.** All of the following suites are located on the fourteenth floor.

One-bedroom suites have 1,428 square feet and come with either a Bay Lake or a Magic Kingdom view. The living area has a modern decor with soothing charcoal-toned carpeting, four easy chairs, sofa, six-person dining table, oversized flat-panel TV, desk with computer, wet bar, and a deep balcony. A full bath with single sink and shower sits off the marble entry hall. The suite's bedroom is similar to a standard-type guest room with two queen beds, but with a bath slightly larger than a standard with tub and sink in one room and a toilet and sink in another area. A king-bedded guest room can be added to make this a two-bedroom suite with 1,892 square feet.

The two-bedroom, three-bath Presidential Suite sports 2,061 square feet. Deep balconies span the length of the suite and afford spectacular Magic Kingdom views. A spacious living room decorated in a neutral color scheme comes with a wet bar and microwave, sofa bed, two easy chairs with ottomans, large flat-panel TV, desk with computer, and six-person dining table. Off the dining area is a two-person bar that opens into the suite's kitchen with full-size refrigerator, wet bar sink, and microwave.

Guests love the huge king-bedded master bedroom with its large sitting area, TV, oversized bureau, two easy chairs with ottomans, and full-size working desk, as well as a mammoth whirlpool bathtub, separate marble shower with wall jets, double sinks, two closets, and vanity desk inside the walk-in closet. The second bedroom comes with two queen-size beds and single-sink bath. An additional full bath is off the marble entry hall.

The two-bedroom, three-bath Vice Presidential Suite at 1,985 square feet has fun contemporary furnishings, fantasy lighting fixtures, and divine dove gray carpeting. Off the foyer is a single-sink full bath with shower and in the living area (believe it or not it's smaller than the living area in a one-bedroom suite) is a six-person dining table, wet bar and microwave, two easy chairs, sleeper sofa, desk with computer, oversized flat-panel TV, and deep balconies spanning the length of the suite with views of Bay Lake and Epcot's Spaceship Earth. There are two queen-size beds and working desk in the sizable master bedroom and a king in the second bedroom. The master bathroom's tub is sans a whirlpool, but there is a shower with wall jets, bidet, vanity desk, and walk-in closet.

## DINE

**California Grill.** Popular fifteenth-floor restaurant; dinner only. Innovative cuisine accompanied by sweeping views of the Magic Kingdom and the Seven Seas Lagoon. (See full description in Dining chapter.)

**Chef Mickey's.** Breakfast and dinner home-style buffet with Chef Mickey and friends Goofy, Minnie, and Donald Duck.

**The Contempo Café.** 24/7 quick-service dining; *breakfast:* oatmeal, grits, waffles, grilled breakfast sandwich, French toast, breakfast burrito, egg platter; *lunch:* marinated beef, cheese, or pepperoni flatbreads, chicken Caesar or chopped salad, roasted curried vegetable bulgur salad, steakhouse salad with goat cheese and tomatoes, multigrain turkey BLT sandwich, stacked sandwich with ham and havarti on ciabatta, hot sandwiches of turkey with brie and arugula, spiced crusted mahi with slaw, honey lime chicken with pepper jack, Angus cheeseburger; *dinner* has the additions of pasta with marinara, chicken basil cream pasta, hot open-faced roast beef sandwich, and a vegetable bake; *children's menu:*

pizza, mini turkey sandwich on multigrain bread, chicken nuggets, burger; self-service bakery.

**Sand Bar and Grill.** Pool bar; specialty drinks, beer, wine, frozen coolers; double bacon cheeseburger, hot dog, turkey sandwich, Caesar salad with chicken, nachos; ice-cream bars, fruit cup, chocolate chip cookie.

**The Wave.** Healthy American cuisine serving breakfast, lunch, and dinner (See full description in Dining chapter).

**In-Room Dining.** Available 24/7.

### SIP

**California Grill Lounge.** Fifteenth-floor lounge in the California Grill restaurant with spectacular views of the Magic Kingdom and Seven Seas Lagoon; sophisticated wine and cocktail list, pristine sushi and sashimi, inventive appetizers; check-in at the second floor podium.

**Contemporary Grounds.** Lobby gourmet coffee bar with specialty coffees, smoothies, and assorted pastries.

**Outer Rim.** Downsized and glaringly bright (due to the next-door Contempo Café) fourth-floor lounge with sweeping views of Bay Lake; specialty drinks, martinis, wine, beer.

**The Wave Lounge.** Glowing blue bar, the largest at any Disney Deluxe Resort; wine and beer flights including organic choices; cocktails featuring organic spirits; *appetizers:* beef, chicken, or tofu skewers served with green papaya salad, lump crab nachos with black bean salsa, miso marinated fresh fish and edamame salad, crispy vegetable summer rolls, five spice chicken lettuce wraps, pepper seared ahi tuna; *desserts:* coconut panna cotta with passion fruit drizzle, sorbet, almond pineapple raisin baklava, zucchini carrot cake, fresh fruit compote with yogurt gelato; organic coffees.

### PLAY

**Arcade.** Super-sized arcade located on the fourth-floor concourse.

**Beach.** Small white-sand beach dotted with hammocks located near the marina.

**Boating.** Boat on miles of Bay Lake and the adjoining Seven Seas Lagoon; Sea Raycers, Suntracker Pontoons, Boston Whaler Montauks; specialty cruises; call (407) WDW-PLAY or (407) 939-7529 for reservations.

**Children's activities.** Disney trivia, temporary tattoos, sidewalk chalk, pool games, sand art, pool parties, arts and crafts; campfire sing-along and Movie Under the Stars on the shores of Bay Lake most evenings.

**Electrical Water Pageant.** On the Seven Seas Lagoon nightly at 10:05 p.m.; best viewed from bay-view tower room balconies, pool, or the beach. Delightful 1,000-foot string of illuminated barges featuring King Neptune and his court of whales, sea serpents, and other deep-sea creatures. May be canceled due to inclement weather.

**Fishing.** Guided two-hour fishing excursion for as many as five people include boat, guide, and gear; catch-and-release only (call 407-WDW-BASS or 407-939-2277 for reservations).

**Swimming.** The pool area has been renovated with the addition of a kids' splash zone as well as fountain jets in the main pool; two heated pools and two hot tubs with little theming; largest pool (6,500 square feet) has 149-foot waterslide; smaller pool surrounded by marvelous lake vistas; cabanas available for rent at the smaller pool with 32-inch flat-panel TVs, chic lounge furnishings, fruit, and sodas.

**Tennis.** Two lighted courts to the north of the adjoining Bay Lake Tower.

**Volleyball.** Sand volleyball court located on the beach.

**Waterskiing and parasailing.** Only Disney resort offering waterskiing, wakeboarding, Jet Skiing, and parasailing. (See chapter 6, Sporting Diversions, for full details.)

## WORK, MOVE, SOOTHE

**Business center.** Located at the Contemporary Resort Convention Center, with personal computers, Internet service, shipping, fax machine, and copier.

**Hair salon.** American Beauty Salon & Barber located on third floor; open 9 a.m. to 6 p.m.; hairstyling, color, facials, manicures, pedicures.

**Fitness Center.** Olympiad Health Club located on third floor; open 6 a.m. to 9 p.m.; Life Fitness treadmills, bicycles, and ellipticals; Cybex strength training machines; free weights; coed dry sauna; personal training, Swedish massage (including in-room) and reflexology by appointment; fitness center is complimentary to resort guests.

**GO**

Board the monorail or walk for about ten minutes along the short path to the Magic Kingdom. The monorail stops at the Transportation and Ticket Center, where you can transfer to the Epcot monorail. Buses run to Disney's Hollywood Studios, Animal Kingdom, Blizzard Beach, Downtown Disney, and Typhoon Lagoon. The monorail takes you to the Polynesian and Grand Floridian Resorts.

To reach other Disney resorts during park operating hours, take the monorail to the Magic Kingdom and from there pick up a bus to your resort destination. After park hours, take the bus to Downtown Disney and transfer to your resort destination. Wilderness Lodge and Fort Wilderness are reachable via the Blue Flag Launch.

## Disney's Grand Floridian Resort & Spa

**867 rooms. 4401 Floridian Way, Lake Buena Vista 32830; phone (407) 824-3000, fax (407) 824-3186. Check-in 3 p.m., checkout 11 a.m. For reservations call (407) WDW-DISNEY or (407) 939-3476, or contact your travel agent. $$$–$$$$$**

**Why Stay Here?** A stunning setting on the Seven Seas Lagoon, some of Disney's best restaurants, and a spot on the monorail as an added bonus.

**Rooms to Book.** Those in the main building with a Theme Park View and access to the Royal Palm Club concierge lounge.

**Don't Miss.** Dining at Victoria and Albert's, the only AAA Five-Diamond awarded restaurant in Central Florida.

Spreading along the shore of the Seven Seas Lagoon with views of the Magic Kingdom, this world-class resort is Disney's flagship. Its red-gabled roofs and Victorian elegance transport you to the time of Florida's nineteenth-century grand seaside "palace hotels." Impeccably maintained and manicured grounds are strung with fragrant, blossom-filled lanes that meander among the gracious four- and five-story buildings fabricated with gleaming white clapboard siding, red shingled roofs, fairytale turrets, and intricate latticework; a favorite sight is the housekeepers in Victorian period costumes strolling the grounds twirling lacy parasols.

Guests' preferred gathering spot is the soaring, five-story Grand Lobby topped with stained-glass cupolas and massive filigreed chandeliers. Strewn with potted palms, cushy seating, and extravagant flower arrangements, it's at its liveliest in the late afternoon and evening hours when entertainment rotates between a relaxing piano player and a dynamic ragtime/jazz band. Because the resort possesses a popular wedding chapel, don't be surprised to see white-gowned brides frequently roaming the lobby; if you're in luck, a Cinderella coach with footmen and white ponies will be on hand to whisk away the newly wedded couple.

Aquatic enticements include a sugar-soft sand beach dotted with brightly striped, canopied lounge chairs, a large swimming pool in the central courtyard, a beachside Florida springs–style pool, and a marina sporting a wide assortment of watercraft including a 52-foot yacht. A full-service spa and health club, tennis courts, three lounges, and upscale shopping round out the list of exceptional offerings. The restaurants here are also quite a draw, notably Victoria and Albert's, central Florida's rightly famous, award-winning gem.

**REST**

**Guest rooms.** Guest rooms, at just over 440 square feet, are decorated in a cheery, Victorian floral motif, each with either one king or two queen beds (only a few have kings), full-size sofa (some come with an additional easy chair), two chairs and a table, and minibar. The addition of 32-inch plasma flat-panel TVs, under-counter refrigerators, and iHome clock radio with iPod docks are a nice bonus along with a writing desk and bureau. DVD players can be added on request. Cream-colored marble baths have twin sinks, an extra phone, Spa H2O bath products, full-length and make-up mirrors, and hair dryer. The closet contains an electronic safe, iron and ironing board, and robes, and all rooms have daily newspaper delivery, coffeemaker, and nightly turndown service. Most accommodations come with generous balconies and vary only in the view of either the gardens, the lagoon, or the Magic Kingdom.

If you're smart, you'll book a Theme Park view room with vistas of the Magic Kingdom, but remember that it doesn't always mean a view of the castle (request the Sago Key or Conch Key building for a castle view;

Boca Chica looks mostly at Space Mountain). Lagoon-view rooms are also a nice choice facing the Seven Seas lagoon and the Polynesian Resort. Garden views overlook the flowering grounds, the sparkling courtyard pool, or the marina. Top-floor guest rooms have vaulted ceilings along with very private balconies that require standing for a view; although their high ceilings give them a more open feel, they are actually a bit smaller than a normal guest room.

Lodge Tower rooms are located in turreted corners of many of the buildings. Similar to a standard room with balcony, they offer the bonus of an additional sitting area with an extra phone and TV.

*CARA'S TIP:* Theme Park views are found in the Boca Chica, Sago Cay, Conch Key, and the Main Building (concierge), but the Boca Chica and Conch Key buildings do have trees that sometimes block part of your view. Rooms in Sago Cay have maximum peacefulness in a setting far from the pool; however, they also require a longer walk to the main building. Sugar Loaf and Big Pine are closest to the main building and the monorail, but because they are near the courtyard pool, they tend to be a bit noisier.

**Concierge rooms.** Accommodations on the concierge level vary from standard guest rooms to larger Deluxe Rooms to suites. Deluxe Rooms at 634 square feet are in the main building offering a spacious sitting area within the guest room with a sofa, coffee table, entertainment center, wet bar, writing desk, two chairs and a table, and two queen-size beds, but never a Magic Kingdom view—there are three on the fourth floor and three more on the third floor (if you want a quieter location request the third floor since fourth-floor rooms are found just off the lounge).

Deluxe King Rooms sleeping two are in the main building and are privy to the Royal Palm Club, but there are two variations: six turreted rooms with 648 square feet offering a 4-poster bed, bay window-type sitting area with sofa and easy chair, and wet bar, but no balcony with only one offering a view of the Magic Kingdom; and 440 square feet, standard-size guest rooms located on the second floor above Gasparilla Grill, all with a marina/Magic Kingdom view, balcony, and whirlpool tub.

The Royal Palm Club, located on the fourth floor of the main building in a prime position overlooking the Grand Lobby, is the more upscale of the two concierge lounges with views of the Seven Seas Lagoon and the resort's lovely courtyard. Serving all rooms of the main building and all suites throughout the property regardless of location, you'll find a concierge staff on duty near the main elevator of the third floor. The Lodge Concierge lounge in the Sugar Loaf building offers the services of a concierge desk and the same food and drink as the Royal Palm Club, but in a less grand setting. Don't look for a lagoon view room in this building— you'll find only garden, marina, or pool views. Of course, the prices are lower than those in the Royal Palm Club.

At both lounges you'll find a continental breakfast of juice, fruit, yogurt, cereal, toast, bagels, muffins, sticky buns, danish, brioche, cheese coffeecake, strawberry turnovers, croissants, cheese, and ham. Midday offerings of pretzels, chips, vegetable crudités with dip, hummus, brownies, cookies, two types of lemonade as well as iced tea, and late afternoon tea of scones with clotted cream and jam, trifle, fruit, banana bread, cookies, jam tarts, coffee, and tea are served. Early evening brings appetizing hors d'oeuvres such as chayote slaw, Virginia ham and biscuits, sweet and sour chicken skewers, crab cakes, chicken Caesar salad, stuffed chicken with fig relish, green mussels, spanakopita, beef empanadas, quiche, dates with proscuitto and Parmesan, salmon with potato salad, mozzarella salad, crudités with dip and hummus, cheese and crackers, guacamole and chips, and Southwestern chicken salad. Wines include Penfolds Cabernet, Coppola Merlot and Riesling, Beringer Zinfandel, Chateau St. Jean Chardonnay, and Iron Horse sparkling wine with a nice assortment of beer. Kids look forward to their own spread of tuna and PB&J sandwiches, fish nuggets, cookies, brownies, and cupcakes with the occasional adult sneaking an irresistible taste of their own. After-dinner desserts like éclairs, cream puffs, tarts, petit fours, cookies, cupcakes, brownies, and Rice Krispies treats are served with a selection of liqueurs. And everyone enjoys the self-service cappuccino machine and the refrigerator filled with beer and sodas.

**Suites.** The Grand Floridian's twenty-five suites can be had in all shapes and sizes. All have upgraded robes and H2O bath products, DVD players, and fresh flowers. In the main building are four Signature Suites: the Grand Suite, Walt Disney Suite, Roy O. Disney Suite, and Victorian Suite.

From its fifth-floor perch, the Grand Suite at 2,220 square feet features five dormer-style balconies with sweeping views of the Seven Seas Lagoon, Cinderella's Castle, Space Mountain, the Contemporary, the

Polynesian, even Spaceship Earth in the distance. A long entry hall with marble half bath leads to the sunny, turreted living room with hardwood flooring, and massive chandelier lighting. Thankfully an unattractive wall of mirrors has been removed and furnishings now include two fern green and buttercream sofas atop an area rug, a strange faux stacked book side table, two coffee tables, two peach-colored easy chairs, a dining table for four, desk, Bose stereo system, an oversized LCD TV with DVD player, an upright shiny white piano, and a corner marble wet bar with under-counter refrigerator, coffee maker, and microwave. Off one side of the large foyer is the master bedroom with a four-poster, king bed decorated in a soft green spread. It has a desk and entertainment center with flat-panel TV with balcony views of the Polynesian, the wedding chapel, and the Floridian-style pool. The solid marble master bathroom has double sinks, mini LCD TV, two closets, large whirlpool tub, huge shower, and a separate toilet and bidet. On the other side of the entry foyer is a second bedroom with a twin bed and sleeper chair, entertainment center, a single-sink bath with mini-LCD TV, and a balcony with the suite's best view of Cinderella's Castle.

The 1,690-square-foot Walt Disney Suite is a favorite filled with Walt memorabilia including railroad models and family pictures; you almost feel you're in Walt's apartment, expecting him to return any minute. Enter into a marble foyer with half bath to a cozy living room in shades of rose, green, and cream with wet bar, desk, entertainment center with flat-panel TV, chaise lounge, sofa, easy chairs, coffee table, and four-person dining table. The master bedroom has a king-size bed, desk, sofa, entertainment center, a huge walk-in closet with a bureau, and a marble bathroom with two sinks, whirlpool tub, and separate shower. The second bedroom has twin beds, two easy chairs, an entertainment center, and another bathroom. Balconies face the courtyard pool, the beach, and the lagoon with views of the Polynesian resort.

Just below the Walt Disney Suite is the Roy O. Disney Suite, comparable in shape and size, with a moss green and salmon color scheme and memorabilia representing Walt's brother Roy, including a wall of family photographs.

The intimate Victorian Suite at 1,083 square feet, on the top floor of the main building, is bedecked in soft green, peach, and rose hues. The living area holds a small sofa, coffee table, entertainment center, wet bar with refrigerator, four-person dining table, and even an old Victrola. Overlooking the courtyard pool are three balconies with views of the top of Cinderella's Castle and Space Mountain, the Polynesian, and the Seven Seas Lagoon. Through French doors is the bedroom with a four-poster king-size bed covered in a standard spread, desk, oversize easy chair and ottoman, and bureau with flat-panel TV. The master bath has a large walk-in closet with dressing area, double-sinks, mini TV, and oversize tub. Off the small foyer is a half bath.

You'll also find one- and two-bedroom suites, all with a variety of views including marina, lagoon, theme park, and garden. Located in both the main building and the other outlying lodge buildings, they all come with concierge services regardless of location. *CARA'S TIP:* If you're staying in a suite outside the main building you may choose to use either concierge lounge for convenience.

Two-bedroom Outer Lodge Suites found throughout the resort are basically two standard-size guest rooms (one with a king and the other two queens), a living room with sleeper sofa, two occasional chairs, coffee table, desk, and four-person dining table. All have an additional full bath off the living area.

Two-Bedroom Theme Park Suites with 1,792 square feet offer the distinction of a straight on view of the lagoon and Cinderella's Castle; only two of these suites exist: the Everglades Suite in Conch Key and the Cape Coral Suite in Sago Cay, both located on the ground floor with a waterfront, oversized patio. For more privacy and quiet request the Cape Coral Suite (the Everglades Suite is near the boat launch). The double-size living area features a full-size dining table and wrap-around wet bar. A standard-size bedroom is found (one with a king and the other two queens) on either side of the living area.

**DINE**

**Citricos.** Innovative New American cuisine and a world-class wine list; dinner only. (See full description in Dining chapter.)

**Garden View Tea Room.** Lobby tearoom open 2 to 4:30 p.m.; advance reservations available; English-style tea served in high style; wide assortment of teas, scones, tarts, trifle, pound cake; pâté, fruit and cheese, tea sandwiches, champagne; come after 3 p.m. when tea is accompanied by live entertainment from the Grand Lobby.

**Gasparilla Grill.** Snack bar open 24/7; grill items served 6:30 a.m. to 11:30 p.m.; dine inside adjacent to the arcade or outside overlooking the marina; *breakfast:* bagel with cream cheese, biscuits, croissant or bagel breakfast sandwiches, scrambled eggs, hash brown casserole, grits, oatmeal, sausage, bacon, pancakes, waffles, cereal, muffins, donuts, Danish pastries, croissants, cinnamon buns; *lunch and dinner:* chicken nuggets, pizza, burgers, Reuben hot dog, Southwestern chicken sandwich, roast beef sandwich, Italian meat sandwich, jerk chicken sandwich, tabbouleh wrap, grilled chicken Caesar salad; *children's menu:* hot dog, burger, chicken nuggets; anytime items: slushies, salads, cold sandwiches, fruit, fat-free frozen yogurt, soft-serve ice cream, cookies, pastries; wine, beer, margaritas.

**Grand Floridian Café.** Casual cafe serving breakfast, lunch, and dinner in a garden-view setting; *breakfast:* frittata, three-egg omelet, lobster eggs benedict, steak and eggs, breakfast skillet; *lunch:* great Niçoise salad prepared with fresh, seared rare tuna and a tart vinaigrette, cobb salad, orange glazed salmon salad, Reuben sandwich, the Grand Sandwich (open-faced hot ham, turkey, bacon, and tomato with Boursin cheese sauce and fried onion straws); *dinner:* shrimp and chicken feta sausage penne pasta with asiago cream, spice-dusted tuna with warm roasted pepper-garbanzo purée, grilled rib eye with red wine sauce, salmon with shiitake and leeks on a potato-chive beurre blanc.

**Narcoossee's.** Fresh seafood with a perfect waterside setting; dinner only; views of the Magic Kingdom fireworks. (See full description in Dining chapter.)

**1900 Park Fare.** Breakfast and dinner character buffet; Supercalifragilistic breakfast with a bevy of characters; evenings bring the Cinderella's Happily-Ever-After Dinner.

**Victoria and Albert's.** Disney's grandest dining establishment; dinner only; the only AAA Five-Diamond awarded restaurant in Central Florida. (See full description in Dining chapter.)

**Private dining.** Twenty-four-hour In-Room Dining; dining aboard the *Grand I* yacht or in one of the many secluded and romantic venues located throughout the property.

## SIP

**Beachside Pool Bar.** Cocktails, beer, frozen drinks, nonalcoholic beverages; deli sandwiches of ham and cheese or turkey and cheese, PB&J sandwich.

**Citricos Lounge.** Small bar found within Citricos restaurant; international wines, martinis, cocktails, espresso; appetizers; desserts.

**Courtyard Pool Bar.** Specialty drinks, beer, wine, nonalcoholic beverages; cold sandwiches.

**Mizner's Lounge.** Second-story lobby lounge with picturesque views of the resort courtyard and pool; cocktails, fine wine, beer, cordials; appetizers from Citricos including gateau of crab, artisan cheeses, or sautéed shrimp with lemon, white wine, tomatoes, and feta; open 5 p.m. to midnight.

**Narcoossee's Lounge.** Small bar inside Narcoossee's restaurant; specialty drinks, wine, espresso; *appetizers:* crab cakes with Cajun remoulade sauce, Prince Edward Island mussels, shrimp and crab chowder, duck confit with balsamic lentils and tangerine marmalade, Rhode Island fried calamari; *entrees:* Tanglewood Farms chicken breast with bacon vinaigrette, grilled filet mignon and choron sauce, pan seared scallops and apple gastrique; *desserts:* almond crusted cheesecake and blackberry sauce, gelato sampler, key lime crème brûlée; step outside to the boat dock for views of the Magic Kingdom fireworks and the Electrical Water Pageant.

## PLAY

**Arcade.** Very small arcade located inside Gasparilla Grill.

**Beach.** Found near the Florida Natural Springs Pool; lovely crescent of white-sand beach with canopy-covered lounge chairs; no swimming allowed in lagoon.

**Boating.** Rentals at the Captain's Shipyard Marina; Sea Raycers, pontoon boats, Boston Whaler Montauks, 13-foot catamaran; specialty cruises.

The 52-foot Sea Ray yacht found at the Grand Floridian's marina is a true indulgence, a perfect venue for viewing the Wishes fireworks for up to eighteen people; call (407) WDW-PLAY.

**Children's activities.** Some of the very best children's activities are here at the Grand Floridian for those between the ages of four and twelve; Disney's Pirate Adventure, a two-hour supervised sail to a deserted island in search of buried treasure including lunch, offered every day except Sunday, 9:30 to 11:30 a.m. ($34); Wonderland Tea Party, Monday through Friday, 2 to 3 p.m., hosted by characters from *Alice in Wonderland* ($40).

For children ages three through eleven, the My Disney Girl's Perfectly Princess Tea Party offered Sunday, Monday, Wednesday, Thursday, and Friday, 10:30 a.m. to noon, at which children accompanied by an adult receive the royal treatment in the Garden View Lounge, including a meet and greet with Princess Aurora, a My Disney Girl Princess Aurora doll, a tiara and bracelet, and tea for two along with storytelling, sing-alongs, and a Grand Princess Parade through the resort's lobby ($250 for one adult and one child, $165 per additional child, and $85 per additional adult); dressing in royal finery encouraged; royal princes may attend and receive a princely crown and a Disney plush bear. Reservations for all activities can be made up to 180 days prior by calling (407) WDW-DINE or (407) 939-3463.

Adventure Time is offered Monday through Friday at 1 and 3 p.m. with activities at the Beach Pool; campfire and a movie on the beach most evenings with a Mickey-shaped firepit and s'mores.

**Electrical Water Pageant.** On the Seven Seas Lagoon nightly at 9:15; best viewed from the beach or the boat dock near Narcoossee's; may be canceled due to inclement weather. Delightful 1,000-foot string of illuminated barges features King Neptune and his court of whales, sea serpents, and other deep-sea creatures.

**Fishing.** Two-hour guided bass fishing excursion includes guide, boat, and gear for as many as five guests; catch-and-release only (call 407-WDW-BASS or 407-939-2277 for reservations).

**Jogging.** A 1-mile trail along the beach to the Polynesian Resort and back.

**Swimming.** Florida natural springs–style beach pool with a cooling waterfall, sunbathing deck, changing rooms, kiddie pool, waterslide, and pool bar; twenty-four-hour free-form pool cools the central courtyard along with a children's wading pool and whirlpool; both pools are heated. Beach pool cabanas with LCD cable TV, DVD/CD/MP3 player, satellite radio, wireless Internet, beverage-stocked refrigerator, ceiling fan, lounge furniture, and fruit basket can be rented for $110 half day and $185 full day (private massage available for an additional fee).

**Tennis.** Disney's Racquet Club located at the Grand Floridian Tennis Center boasts two professionally maintained clay courts; gazebo-style pro shop offers private lessons, a play-the-professional option, and restringing services; court fees are $12.50 per person per hour; for information or to book lessons, clinics, and private instruction, call Michael Dublin, director of tennis operations, at (407) 621-1991.

**Volleyball.** Sand volleyball court located on the beach.

### WORK, MOVE, SOOTHE

**Business center.** Fax, Internet, copying, shipping, and receiving; open 7 a.m. to 5 p.m. daily.

**Child care.** Mouseketeer Club; Disney movies, art activities, video games; open 4:30 p.m. to midnight daily for potty-trained children ages four to twelve; dinner included; only for guests of the Grand Floridian or those dining at the resort. Call (407) WDW-DINE or (407) 939-3463 for reservations.

**Hair salon.** Ivy Trellis Salon open daily 9 a.m. to 6 p.m.; full range of salon services including haircut, color, styling, and manicures.

**Spa and fitness center.** Grand Floridian Spa and Health Club; 9,000-square-foot facility; spa: massage, shiatsu, reflexology, facials, water therapies and soaks, hand and foot treatments, body treatments and wraps; fitness center (complimentary to guests): Life Fitness treadmills, Precor elliptical cross trainers, upright and recumbent cycles, Smith machine, LifeFitness and Precor strength training equipment, free weights; personal training available by appointment; locker rooms equipped with whirlpools, Turkish bath, and Finnish saunas. Treatment hours 8 a.m. to 8 p.m.; fitness center open 6 a.m. to 9 p.m.; call (407) 824-2332.

### GO

Transportation choices to the Magic Kingdom include both monorail and water taxi. Take the monorail to the Transportation and Ticket Center (TTC) and transfer to the Epcot monorail. There is a direct bus to Disney's Hollywood Studios, Animal Kingdom, Downtown Disney, Typhoon

Lagoon, and Blizzard Beach. Use monorail service to reach the Contemporary Resort. Walk (ten minutes) or take the water taxi or monorail to the Polynesian Resort.

To reach other Disney resorts during park operating hours, take the monorail to the Magic Kingdom and from there pick up a bus to your resort destination. After park hours take a bus to Downtown Disney and then transfer to your resort destination.

## Disney's Polynesian Resort

**853 rooms. 1600 Seven Seas Drive, Lake Buena Vista 32830; phone (407) 824-2000, fax (407) 824-3174. Check-in 3 p.m., checkout 11 a.m. For reservations call (407) WDW-DISNEY or (407) 939-3476, or contact your travel agent. $$$–$$$$$**

**Why Stay Here?** A prime location on the monorail with lush gardens and idyllic views of Cinderella's Castle.

**Rooms to Book.** Theme Park View concierge rooms facing the Seven Seas Lagoon and the Magic Kingdom with access to the Royal Polynesian Lounge.

**Don't Miss.** A late night stroll on the tiki torch-lit beach with the sight of Cinderella's Castle in the distance. Stick around to enjoy the Wishes fireworks show.

Along with a warm aloha and a lei greeting, guests are invited to enter the soothing South Seas environment of the Great Ceremonial House, a green oasis sheltering the front desk, shops, and restaurants. Vines encase the rugged lava rock cataracts that cool the two-story lobby resting below towering palm trees. The centerpiece garden has a profusion of flowering orchids, bromeliads, ginger, and anthurium scattered throughout banana trees, elephant's ears, and rubber plants. High-backed rattan and cane chairs, and sofas with striking tangerine and moss green cushions and textiles sit on floors of polished flagstone while overhead brilliantly colored macaws perch in the branches of the surrounding foliage. Two-story picture windows draw the eye outdoors to the lush landscape surrounding the Volcano Pool and the Seven Seas Lagoon beyond. Located on the monorail system and within walking distance of the Transportation and Ticket Center, the Polynesian is the most convenient of Disney's resorts with direct access to both the Magic Kingdom and Epcot. Lodging is in eleven tangerine- and mahogany-tinted longhouses scattered throughout the luxuriant grounds composed of more than seventy-five species of dense vegetation. Ducks and ibis roam the thick grassy lawns and rabbits hop along meandering pathways lined with volcanic rock. In the evenings the resort is torch-lit, and soft Hawaiian melodies set a romantic mood. Three white-sand beaches dotted with hammocks and lounge chairs are a spectacular place to sun or relax while viewing the Magic Kingdom fireworks. *CARA'S TIP:* Some find this resort a bit hokey and old-fashioned, but it has a loyal following. There are, however, many complaints of lackluster service and poor management. I have had a few unpleasant experiences myself so don't expect a flawless stay here each and every time.

## REST

**Guest rooms.** Some of the largest standard rooms in Disney with around 440 square feet are here at the Polynesian. Rooms are quite nice with chocolate and cream-colored batik print carpeting, and furnishings that are a mixture of dark and blond wood. Bamboo bed frames go well with the batik-style bedspreads rich with rust, blue, and brown tones, and the drapery is fun with a tropical leaf motif. A rattan chair with ottoman sits in the corner.

Running the length of the wall opposite the bed is a bamboo bureau attached to a vanity/desk atop which sits a built-in 32-inch LCD flat-panel TV. Many rooms also offer a daybed. In the entry are built-in closets with reed motif etched glass paneling that feature a marble-topped bar with an under-the-counter refrigerator, coffeemaker, and an electronic safe. Smallish baths come without Disney's typical split-bath configuration and many without double sinks, but all are handsomely festooned with rich green marble vanities, rust-colored marble flooring, seagrass wallpaper, tiki god fixtures offering very poor lighting, and rounded shower rods with sea green batik print curtains. Baths in the Tokelau, Tahiti, and Rapa Nui longhouses are a bit larger. Amenities include an iPod docking station clock radio, iron and ironing board, full-length mirror, dual-line phones, and daily newspaper. *CARA'S TIP:* Walls are particularly thin, resulting in a bit too much noise heard from surrounding guest rooms. Your best chance of receiving the perfect room (of which there are many) is to educate yourself before check-in and request exactly what you would like, both at reservation time and again at the front desk before being handed your key. The following information may sound excessive, but it could make the difference between a perfect vacation and a disappointing one. The longhouses of Tokelau, Tahiti, and Rapa Nui feature the largest rooms, all of which come with patios or balconies and a convenient location near the Transportation and Ticket Center. Older longhouses, closer to the Great Ceremonial House, lack second-floor balconies.

The two-story Niue and Tonga longhouses, with the Tonga being an all-suite building, are small and intimate; the Tonga has second-floor balconies, the Niue does not. Water-view rooms in the Tahiti building front a lovely beach with great views across the lagoon but are also located very close to the Transportation and Ticket Center with noise from the ferryboat during park hours. One side of the Samoa and the Niue buildings faces the rambunctious Volcano Pool, a plus or minus depending on your personality. One side of the Fiji longhouse looks at the marina but is considered a garden view. One side of the Aotearoa, Tonga, and Rarotonga longhouses faces the monorail, and one side of the Rapa Nui can see the parking lot, although these are actually considered "garden" views. A few garden-view rooms closest to the concierge lounge in the Hawaii building look at another building.

If staying in the Fiji, Tuvalu, Tonga, and Aotearoa, you had better enjoy the beat of drums, because the Polynesian Luau is held nearby. The worst view is from the so-called garden-view side of the Tuvalu longhouse that stares at one end of the Fiji building only a few feet away. And now there's a Magic Kingdom lagoon view category that guarantees you a spectacular view of the park but at a higher price tag.

**Concierge rooms.** Nestled up against the beach is the Hawaii concierge building, offering the services of a concierge staff as well as private check-in and checkout. The bi-level Royal Polynesian Lounge is among the best in Disney's repertoire, affording a fantastic view of Cinderella's Castle and the Magic Kingdom fireworks with quite delicious food to boot. Accommodations come with either a lagoon view, theme park view (a guaranteed view of the castle without obstructions), or a garden view, but second-floor rooms do not have balconies. Additional amenities include robes, DVD players, and nightly turndown service. Open from 7 a.m. to 10 p.m., the concierge lounge has complimentary food and beverages, beginning with a continental breakfast of juice, coffee, tea, fresh fruit, hot oatmeal, pastries, bagels, English muffins, and cereal. From noon to 4 p.m., fresh fruit, cookies, orange guava juice, lemonade, coffee, and iced tea are served along with snacks such as cookies, gummy worms, and goldfish crackers. Evening choices include fresh pineapple with caramel dipping sauce, hummus, cheese and crackers, crudités and dip, PB&J sandwiches, and two hot appetizers such as sushi rolls, vegetable spring rolls, BBQ pulled pork, duck pot stickers, chilled banana and coconut soup, Maui onion potato au gratin, scallop bacon wraps, chicken satay, Asian slaw, and Kona sticky wings, as well as wine and beer. After dinner are cordials and mini desserts of brownies, éclairs, cream puffs, fruit tarts, and petit fours. There's also a self-service espresso and cappuccino machine.

**Suites.** All suites are located in the small and intimate two-story Tonga longhouse. Their only drawback is the inconvenient walk to the Hawaii longhouse concierge lounge for food offerings since the only meals served in the Tonga building are continental breakfast and afternoon snacks and beverages. All suites are decorated in an ethnic island style with impressive rattan and bamboo furnishings, seagrass wallpaper, bedspreads in tropical prints, and granite countertops throughout.

For the ultimate vacation, try the King Kamehameha, a two-story wonder with two bedrooms, two and a half baths, a parlor, and a kitchen. At 1,863 square feet, the upstairs master offers a balcony, bamboo king bed, entertainment center, easy chair with ottoman, an enormous two-part bath with a sink, bidet, commode, whirlpool tub, TV, and walk-in closet on one side—and a tub, shower, sink, and commode on the other. The second bedroom has two queen beds, easy chair with ottoman, entertainment center, bath with double sinks and separate shower and tub, as well as a balcony. Downstairs is a great parlor with flagstone-style tile flooring, entertainment center, six-person dining table, a seagrass sleeper sofa, easy chairs, bamboo coffee table, overhead paddle fans, half bath, and granite kitchen with microwave, dishwasher, sink, toaster, and coffeemaker. A balcony spanning the length of the suite overlooks the marina and Cinderella's Castle in the distance. *CARA'S TIP:* The Honeymoon Room can connect to the King Kamehameha Suite to make a three-bedroom, three-and-a-half bath suite.

The two-bedroom, three-bath Ambassador Suites at 1,513 square feet have a master with a king bed, entertainment armoire, chaise lounge, desk, table and two chairs, large bath, and balcony. The living room features two small sofas, a large TV, chaise lounge, dining table for four, sleeper sofa, large garden-view balcony or patio, wet bar, full bath, and separate full kitchen (minus a stove). The second bedroom is the same size as a standard guest room with a balcony. A few caveats here: there are two Ambassador Suites: one on the first floor and one on the second with preference on request only. The downstairs suite faces a small fenced garden; the upstairs suite has a view of the parking lot. Both are close to and have a view of the monorail.

The marina/Cinderella Castle–view two-bedroom/two-bath Princess Suite has dark rattan furnishings in the seagrass wallpapered living area with daybed, settee, two easy chairs, coffee table, glass-topped bamboo side tables, flat-panel television and DVD/VCR player, granite wet bar with microwave, and patio. Off to each side of the living area are two master-type bedrooms each with two queen beds, TV, easy chair, and ottoman. Each bedroom has a bath with granite-topped, double-sinked vanities, and a separate room with a bathtub, stand-alone granite shower, and toilet (one bath is wheelchair accessible). A One-Bedroom Princess Suite simply eliminates the second bedroom.

The Honeymoon Room is a slightly oversized standard guest room offering a marina/Space Mountain view, king bed with orchid-motif duvet, an easy chair and ottoman, bamboo table and chairs for two, and patio. The bath is found off the foyer with a whirlpool tub, double sinks, and separate shower.

## DINE

**Captain Cook's Snack Company.** Snack bar located in the Great Ceremonial House with indoor and outdoor seating and touch-screen ordering; open 24/7 with grill closing at 11 p.m.; *breakfast:* Tonga Toast (battered and deep fried banana-stuffed sourdough bread), Mickey waffle, breakfast croissant sandwich, breakfast platter, cereal, fruit, pastries, specialty coffees; *lunch and dinner:* bacon double cheeseburger, multigrain turkey club, grilled cheese sandwich, pulled pork sandwich, chicken Caesar salad, chicken and vegetable stir-fried noodles, Hawaiian flatbread, prepackaged cold sandwiches and sushi; *dessert:* Dole whip (soft-serve pineapple ice cream), brownies, cupcakes, apple pie, muffins, croissants, cookies; *children's menu:* cheeseburger, grilled cheese, chicken nuggets, turkey and cheese sandwich.

**Kona Café.** Casual dining for breakfast, lunch, and dinner; American cuisine with delicate hints of Asia; *breakfast:* famous Tonga Toast (batter-fried, banana-stuffed sourdough bread rolled in cinnamon sugar), macadamia pineapple pancakes, steak and eggs, poached eggs with hollandaise over smoked pulled pork hash; *lunch:* Asian noodle bowl, barbecued pork taco, Asian chicken chop salad, Polynesian plate lunch; *dinner:* teriyaki New York strip, Pan-Asian noodles, miso-glazed mahi mahi, coconut-almond chicken, tuna Oscar.

**Kona Island.** Quick-service stand near the monorail platform; coffee and pastry morning hours with Kona coffee, latte, cappuccino, café au lait, espresso; sushi in the evening hours along with a small collection of cocktails and sake.

**Ohana.** Breakfast and dinner only; all-you-care-to-eat Polynesian feast prepared on an 18-foot semicircular fire pit; Mickey Mouse hosts a family-style *breakfast* with scrambled eggs, fried potatoes with caramelized onions, sausage, bacon, breakfast breads, fruit; *dinner:* mixed greens with honey-lime dressing, pork dumplings with sweet and sour sauce, honey-coriander wings, marinated sirloin steak, Asian barbecue pork loin, mesquite grilled turkey, spicy grilled peel 'n' eat shrimp, lo mein noodles, stir-fried vegetables, bread pudding with bananas foster sauce.

**Spirit of Aloha Polynesian Luau.** Luau dinner show with modern song and dance from Lilo and Stitch, as well as traditional Polynesian entertainment; salad, pineapple coconut bread, roasted chicken, barbecued pork ribs, Polynesian rice, seasonal vegetables; unlimited drinks, including beer and wine; children's meal available; three-category pricing according to seating. Held at the Luau Cove Tuesday through Saturday, 5:15 and 8 p.m.; subject to cancellation in inclement weather; call (407) WDW-DINE or (407) 939-3463 for reservations.

**In-Room Dining.** Available 7 a.m. to 10 p.m.

## SIP

**Barefoot Pool Bar.** Volcano Pool thatch-roofed bar; tropical alcoholic and nonalcoholic drinks, beer, wine, sangria.

**Tambu Lounge.** Located upstairs in the Great Ceremonial House overlooking the pool with the picturesque Seven Seas Lagoon in the distance; tropical drinks served in hollowed-out pineapples and coconuts, wine, beer; appetizers including honey-ginger chicken wings, grilled tuna flat-bread, lump crab cakes with Asian tartar sauce, sushi roll, crisp breads and dips; open 1 p.m. to midnight, with appetizers served 5 to 10 p.m.

## PLAY

**Arcade.** Moana Mickey's Fun Hut; open 24/7; located next to Captain Cook's Snack Company with the latest in video equipment.

**Beaches.** Three idyllic beaches with perfect vistas of Seven Seas Lagoon and the Magic Kingdom; swimming prohibited in the lagoon; lounge chairs, beach hammocks, swings; prime viewing for the Magic Kingdom fireworks; best views: beach in front of Tahiti longhouse; closest to Volcano Pool: beach in front of Hawaii longhouse; most secluded: beach on the Grand Floridian side of the property.

**Bicycles.** Bicycles and two- and four-seater surrey bicycles for rent at the marina.

**Boating.** Boat rentals available at the Mikala Canoe Club; Sea Raycers, 17-foot Boston Whaler Montauks, Suntracker pontoons, 14-foot dual- or mono-hull Hobie sailboats; fireworks boating excursion with driver (call 407-WDW-PLAY or 407-939-7529 for reservations).

**Children's activities and playground.** Arts and crafts daily in the Great Ceremonial House, noon to 2 p.m.; beach and pool games, treasure hunt, chalk art, tiki masks, hula lessons, duck races.

**Electrical Water Pageant.** On the Seven Seas Lagoon nightly at 9 best viewed from the beach, Ohana restaurant, or a lagoon-view room; may be canceled due to inclement weather. Delightful 1,000-foot string of illuminated barges features King Neptune and his court of whales, sea serpents, and other deep-sea creatures.

**Fishing.** Guided two-hour fishing excursions for as many as five people include boat, guide, and gear; catch-and-release only (call 407-WDW-BASS or 407-939-2277 for reservations).

**Jogging.** A 1.5-mile scenic jogging path circles the resort.

**Swimming.** Nanea Volcano Pool features a smoking volcano slide, under-water music, sparkling waterfall, and kiddie pool, all with a superb view of the Seven Seas Lagoon; no whirlpool; quieter East Pool is often filled with ducks in the morning; both pools are heated.

**Volleyball.** Sand court located on beach in front of Volcano Pool.

### WORK, MOVE, SOOTHE

**Child care.** At the Never Land Club, Peter Pan–themed facility with a replica of Wendy's bedroom; arcade games, arts and crafts, Disney classic movies on a giant screen. Open 4 p.m. to midnight, for potty-trained children ages four to twelve of registered guests of any Disney-owned property. Cost includes buffet dinner; call (407) 939-3463 for reservations.

**Spa and fitness center.** Grand Floridian Spa located between the Grand Floridian and the Polynesian; see previous entry on Grand Floridian Resort.

### GO

Transportation choices to the Magic Kingdom include both monorail and water taxi. To reach Epcot, walk to the Transportation and Ticket Center (TTC)—you'll find excellent signage throughout the resort—and take a direct monorail. There is a direct bus to Disney's Hollywood Studios, Animal Kingdom, Downtown Disney, Typhoon Lagoon, and Blizzard Beach. Take the monorail or water taxi or follow the walking path to the Grand Floridian Resort (about a ten-minute walk). Monorail service will get you to the Contemporary Resort.

To reach other Disney resorts during park operating hours, take the monorail to the Magic Kingdom and from there pick up a bus to your resort destination. After park hours, take a bus to Downtown Disney and then transfer to your resort destination.

## Disney's Wilderness Lodge

**727 rooms. 901 Timberline Drive, Lake Buena Vista 32830; phone (407) 824-3200, fax (407) 824-3232. Check-in 3 p.m., checkout 11 a.m. For reservations call (407) WDW-DISNEY or (407) 939-3476, or contact your travel agent. $$–$$$$$**

**Why Stay Here?** Surrounded by nature, you'll feel as if you're ensconced in a cabin out West.

**Rooms to Book.** The Yosemite and the Yellowstone Suites, some of Disney's most reasonably priced top accommodations.

**Don't Miss.** The resort's geyser show occurring every hour along the shores of Bay Lake.

Teddy Roosevelt would exclaim "bully" to Disney's dramatic depiction of an early 1900s national park lodge, an atmosphere that simply can't be beat. I challenge you to keep your jaw from dropping open on your first encounter with its awesome eight-story lobby. A marvel of timber, sheer walls of lodgepole pine logs, and rugged rock surround the huge, open expanse filled with oversize leather chairs and Native American crafts of beaded moccasins, feathered headdresses, textiles, and drums. Relax in old-fashioned rockers fronting the massive, 82-foot-tall fireplace composed of rockwork replicating the diverse strata of the Grand Canyon. Two authentic 55-foot Pacific Northwest totem poles overlook rustic stone and hardwood floors topped with Native American rugs, tepee chandeliers, and a bevy of "park ranger" staff who roam the lodge attending to guests. Quiet and seductive nooks and crannies on the floors above the lobby offer hours of privacy, and rows of back porch rockers facing the resort grounds look out to a serene scene of natural beauty.

Seven floors of guest rooms are found above the lobby and in two six-story wings composed of quarry stone, chunky logs, and green tin rooftops surrounded by a breathtaking scene of roaring waterfalls, rushing creeks, and towering pines. What begins in the lobby as a bubbling hot spring turns into Silver Creek that widens to become a sparkling waterfall emptying into the boulder-lined, hot springs–style swimming pool, one of Disney's best. The chirping of crickets is heard beneath the bridges and along the meandering pathways lined with natural grasses, junipers, sotols, and wildflowers. On the shore of Bay Lake, the resort's very own re-created geyser, surrounded by a steaming expanse of geothermal activity, erupts hourly from early morning to late night. After dark when the waterfall is lit, it's even more spectacular.

**REST**

**Guest rooms.** Those who have experienced other deluxe Disney resorts may be surprised at the smallish guest rooms here, measuring only 340 square feet. Though pleasant, they don't leave room for a sitting area. Bedding is either two queen-size beds, a king-size bed (wheelchair-accessible rooms), or a queen-size bed and a set of bunk beds (an extremely popular choice with the kids). You'll find bedspreads in a Native American quilted print with rich blue dust ruffles, gold/green carpeting in a pine cone motif, and a built-in, 32-inch flat-panel TV. Two-poster beds have padded leather headboards accented with a carved woodland scene, triple-sheeted linens with nice downy pillows, and a not-so-comfortable mattress. All rooms come with a table and two chairs, under-counter refrigerator, keyed safe, iPod clock radio, and coffeemaker. Bathrooms, a few feet smaller than other deluxe resorts, have attractive black/gold granite countertops in the separate vanity area holding two sinks and a hair dryer—an adjoining bathtub/commode area is embellished with white-and-gold tiles and wallpaper in an etched leaf print. There's no makeup mirror, but the full-length mirror, curved shower curtain, and rain shower–style shower head are a plus. Other room amenities include a small keyed safe, iron and ironing board, and daily newspaper.

Room view choices include a standard view with a look at either the parking lot or rooftops; a lodge view of either the forested area facing the Magic Kingdom (views of the park and the fireworks are mostly obscured by the trees except from some rooms on the top floors) or the next-door Villas at Wilderness Lodge; or a picturesque courtyard view of the pool and Bay Lake. Sixth-floor rooms in the outer wings closer to the lake come with dormer balconies that require standing for a view.

**Concierge rooms.** Concierge rooms on the seventh floor include standard rooms with a variety of views, four Honeymoon Suites, and the Vice Presidential and Presidential Suites. Guests receive the services of a private concierge staff and access to the Old Faithful Club. Plenty of tables set up around the balcony overlooking the lobby, a sizeable serving room, and an accommodating staff add to the appeal. Breakfast consists of fresh fruit, juice, yogurt, pastries, cereal, oatmeal, mini muffins, croissants, and bagels, and afternoon snacks are goldfish crackers, fruit, pretzels, gummy bears, sugar and chocolate chip cookies. Evenings bring hearty food catered from either Whispering Canyon Café or Artist Point where the spread includes tomato basil dip, tapenade, fruit, crudités, cheese, and PB&J sandwiches, accompanied by one soup such as corn chowder, vegetable, tomato basil, and potato cheese, along with one hot dish such as chicken and pesto pasta, pork loin with Artist Point macaroni and cheese, sausage and peppers, beef stroganoff, beef stir-fry, pulled pork, or grilled chicken with mashed potatoes. Wine offerings are King Estate Oregon Pinot Gris, Washington State 14 Hands Merlot, Columbia Crest

Cabernet, and Kenwood Zinfandel. There's also a self-service cappuccino machine. After dinner wine and cordials are served with scrumptious hot cobbler along with an assortment of yummy homemade cookies, brownies, and rightly famous Magic Bars. Extra concierge amenities include DVD players, robes, and nightly turndown service. All concierge rooms have dormer balconies that require standing for a view.

Although they're the same size as a standard room, the Honeymoon Suites surrounding the lobby feel larger because they come with only one king-size bed, leaving more room to walk around. Their claim to fame is a large chocolate-brown marble whirlpool tub perfect for romance. Rooms also hold a table with two chairs and clothes bureau with built-in flat-panel TV. Remember, they come with dormer balconies, so you must stand for a view—two of the suites offer a not-so-great look at the rooftops and the Villas at Wilderness Lodge in the distance, while the other two enjoy a view of the Seven Seas Lagoon, the Grand Floridian, the Contemporary, and the top of the Magic Kingdom fireworks.

**Suites.** If a larger room is more to your liking, consider a Deluxe Suite sleeping six. At 500 square feet, these offer a comfortable but not huge balconied parlor area holding a charcoal gray, queen-size leather sofa bed, two easy chairs, coffee table, two-person table and chairs, a flat-panel TV, wet bar, coffeemaker, and small refrigerator. The crowded bedroom, separated by curtained French doors from the parlor, has two queen-size beds, TV, and a stand-up balcony. The double-sinked bathroom with separate commode and shower area can be accessed from either the bedroom or the foyer. Deluxe Suites come with some sort of a view of the water (some rooms are nicely obstructed with trees). Although they are not located on the club level seventh floor, they do come with concierge privileges.

The 885-square-foot Vice Presidential Suite (also known as the Yosemite) is outfitted in upscale cowboy style featuring rawhide curtains, branding-iron towel bars, wood-paneled walls, Native American artwork, and lodgepole trim. The living area offers a distressed leather sleeper sofa, two leather easy chairs, oversized desk, Remington-style lamp, Southwestern rug, and an armoire with a flat-panel TV, DVD player, and stereo. A wooden walk-in bar is complete with swinging doors, microwave, under counter refrigerator, sink, toaster, blender, coffeemaker, and two leather barstools. The small dining room has hardwood flooring with a circular, six-person table with rustic twig chairs. An amazing balcony, actually better than the resort's Presidential Suite because of its deepness, wraps the suite with marvelous views of the resort's pool and geyser as well as sparkling Bay Lake. In the bedroom is a king bed with western-style bedding and leather throw pillows, drum lamps, an armoire with flat-panel TV, and leather easy chair and ottoman. Off the entry hall is a half bath with single sink. The only disappointing aspect of the suite is the master bath's ultra-sensitive, automatic motion-detector vent fan that turns on whenever entering the bath for irritating 30-second intervals causing quite a problem during the night for someone trying to sleep. There's also the earth-toned mosaic tile that needs a good grout job, and lack of good lighting and a makeup mirror. Its pluses are the oversized, oval whirlpool tub, double sinks, and giant separate shower. But the Yosemite Suite is one of the better priced V.P. suites at the Disney Deluxe properties and certainly one to consider for a nice upgrade.

On the opposite side of the courtyard is the 1,000-square-foot Presidential Suite (also known as the Yellowstone), a Teddy Roosevelt delight with shiny hardwood flooring, an elk-horn chandelier, and balconies running the length of the corner suite overlooking Bay Lake and the pool. The living area comes with a leather/chenille sleeper sofa, coffee table, three easy chairs (one leather), and wet bar with sink, under-counter refrigerator, microwave, coffeemaker, and dishes. A rustic dining table, separated from the living room by a granite buffet/bar, seats eight. Off the foyer is a half bath as well as a cozy office with a balcony overlooking the courtyard. The bedroom is outfitted with twig-style furnishings and a leather easy chair and ottoman. An attractive chocolate and black marble bathroom has two sink areas, a commode and bidet in a separate room, vanity, large stand-alone shower, and a fantastic whirlpool tub.

**DINE**

**Artist Point.** Outstanding Pacific Northwest cuisine and wine with views of Bay Lake and the courtyard waterfall; dinner only. (See full description in Dining chapter.)

**Roaring Forks Snacks.** Cozy atmosphere indoors and picturesque outdoor area near the pool; *breakfast:* croissant breakfast sandwich, scrambled egg plate, bacon, hash browns, pancakes, oatmeal, grits, create-your-own yogurt parfait, fruit, assorted pastries, muffins, croissants, donuts; *lunch and dinner:* ham and Tillamook cheddar sandwich, smoked turkey and brie sandwich, grilled vegetable sandwich on seven-grain bread, roast beef and blue cheese on focaccia, grilled chicken salad with apple vinaigrette, vegetarian salad with orange sesame vinaigrette, burger, chicken nuggets, pizza; *desserts:* frozen yogurt, soft-serve ice cream, chocolate bundt cake, Magic Bars, brownies, cupcakes; open 6 a.m. to midnight; grill items available 7 a.m. to 11 p.m.

**Whispering Canyon Café.** Open breakfast, lunch, and dinner for Western-style fun and hearty food; kids love this place where smoked meats are served in an all-you-care-to-eat skillet along with plenty of hoo-tin' and hollerin'; *breakfast:* beef brisket and eggs skillet with barbecue hollandaise sauce, western omelet, raisin bread French toast, Belgian waf-fle; *lunch:* smoked beef brisket salad, whiskey maple-glazed trout, pulled pork sandwich, Brunswick stew; *dinner:* meat loaf, smoked pork loin with mango chutney, chorizo-Tillamook grits, chicken vegetable penne pasta, grilled rib eye steak.

**In-Room Dining.** Available 7 to 11 a.m. and 4 p.m. to midnight.

**SIP**

**Territory Lounge.** Rustic atmosphere of lodgepole pine posts, old ter-ritorial maps, prints of the American West, vintage surveyor equipment, and carved wooden bears; Pacific Northwest wine, beer, martinis, spe-cialty drinks and coffees; appetizers of nachos with beef chili, cheese plate, Asian-inspired salmon cakes, honey-ginger wings, BLT or pulled pork flatbread.

**Trout Pass Pool Bar.** Log cabin pool bar; specialty drinks, beer, wine, bag snacks, nonalcoholic smoothies.

**PLAY**

Services and recreational activities here are shared with the adjacent Vil-las at Wilderness Lodge.

**Arcade.** Buttons and Bells Game Arcade with state-of-the-art video games for all levels.

**Beach.** The smallish Bay Lake Beach is nestled against tall pine trees.

**Bicycles.** Rentable at the marina for exploration of wilderness trails connecting to Fort Wilderness; bicycles, two- and four-seat surrey bikes.

**Boating.** Rentals available for the enjoyment of Bay Lake and the Seven Seas Lagoon at Teton Boat Rentals; Sea Raycers, Boston Whaler Montauks, 21-foot Sun Tracker pontoon boats; Magic Kingdom fireworks cruise (call 407-WDW-PLAY or 407-939-7529 for reservations).

**Children's activities and playground.** Children's playground located on the beach; family arts and crafts in the Cub's Den, 2:30 to 4 p.m. (children must be accompanied by a parent); magic cookie hour, dance parties, bingo, Disney trivia, pool activities, beach games; next-door Fort Wilderness, just a boat ride away, offers pony rides and nightly carriage and wagon rides (extra fee), and a complimentary sing-along campfire, marshmallow roast, and Disney movie program hosted by Chip 'n Dale.

**Electrical Water Pageant.** On the Seven Seas Lagoon nightly at 9:35; best viewed from the beach, boat dock, or a Bay Lake–facing room; may be canceled due to inclement weather. Delightful 1,000-foot string of illuminated barges features King Neptune and his court of whales, sea serpents, and other deep-sea creatures.

**Fishing.** Two-hour fishing excursion for as many as five guests includes boat, fishing equipment, and guide; catch-and-release only (call 407-WDW-BASS or 407-939-2277 for reservations).

**Jogging.** Jogging paths connect to Disney's Fort Wilderness, where several trails through a forest of pines and along Bay Lake make for pleasant exercise routes.

**Swimming.** A top attraction at Wilderness Lodge is its boulder-lined, free-form pool featuring waterfalls, rocky overlooks, waterslide, and nearby geyser; kiddie pool, two whirlpools.

**Tours.** Meet in the lobby for a "Wonders of the Lodge" ranger-led tour of the resort; check your resort guide for day and time with no reservations necessary.

**Volleyball.** Sand volleyball court located on Bay Lake Beach; equipment at Teton Boat Rentals.

## WORK, MOVE, SOOTHE

**Child care.** The Cub's Den features video and arcade games, Northwestern arts and crafts, and Disney movies. Open 4:30 p.m. to midnight for potty-trained cubs ages four to twelve; also open to registered guests of any Disney-owned property; cost includes dinner; call (407) WDW-DINE or (407) 939-3463 for reservations.

**Fitness center.** Sturdy Branches Health Club located at the adjoining Villas at Wilderness Lodge. (See description in Villas of Wilderness Lodge section).

## GO

Since the monorail doesn't reach this neck of the woods, Wilderness Lodge is definitely less accessible than other Magic Kingdom resorts. Take the bus to the Magic Kingdom or better yet a boat departing from the Northwest Dock and Ferry (a separate area from the marina) to the Magic Kingdom, Contemporary Resort, and Fort Wilderness. There is a direct bus to Epcot, Disney's Hollywood Studios, Animal Kingdom, Downtown Disney, Typhoon Lagoon, and Blizzard Beach.

To reach other Disney resorts during park operating hours, take the boat to the Magic Kingdom and pick up a bus or monorail from there to your resort destination. After park hours take a bus to Downtown Disney and then transfer to the resort.

## The Villas at Disney's Wilderness Lodge

**136 units. 801 Timberline Drive, Lake Buena Vista 32830; phone (407) 938-4300, fax (407) 824-3232. Check-in 4 p.m., checkout 11 a.m. For reservations call (407) WDW-DISNEY or (407) 939-3476, or contact your travel agent. $$–$$$$**

**Why Stay Here?** A sense of Florida's natural environment with the convenience of larger living quarters.

**Rooms to Book.** Request a villa on the back side of the resort with a view of the surrounding pine forest.

**Don't Miss.** Dinner at the next-door Artist Point at the Wilderness Lodge.

Sharing the same lobby, check-in desk, and amenities with the adjoining Wilderness Lodge (a short, covered walkway connects the two), this Deluxe Villa Resort property is a tribute to the Western railroad hotels built in the early 1900s. Rooms not occupied by owners are available to the many visitors who wish to stay on Disney property but who would also like the convenience of a kitchen and the extra breathing space of a living area.

The overall effect here is one of coziness and intimacy. Its four-story buildings, tucked away in the pine trees, are tinted with soothing earth tones of soft brown and green. Inside the lobby, guests step into a rustic four-story atrium of log construction adorned with detailed wood carvings and paintings of the Pacific Northwest. A rock and timber living room made snug with fireplace, leather easy chairs, and window seats features railroad memorabilia, some belonging to Walt Disney. Outdoors a small springs-style pool is surrounded by towering pine trees and natural vegetation. For additional information on the Villas' sister property, Disney's Wilderness Lodge, see the appropriate sections in the previous entry.

**REST**

Villa choices come in studios as well as one- and two-bedroom units (three-bedroom units are not offered at this property), each with a balcony or patio. The villas are looking nice and fresh and flat-panel TVs have been installed in all villas. Autumn colors in splashes of rich red and forest green intermingle with rustic pine furnishings. Sofas in Native American print fabrics mix well with curtains and chairs sporting a whimsical gingham design, woodland scene prints decorate the cream, gold, and crimson walls, and the carpet is imprinted with a pinecone motif. The small but efficient full kitchens are done in a cream-colored granite with forest green cabinetry. Beds feature headboards carved with woodland scenes and down-home quilt bedspreads in a pinecone print. Views from all units are of either the pool or the woods, with some of the units on the higher floors enjoying a glimpse of Bay Lake.

The 356-square-foot studios sleep a maximum of four people plus one child age two or younger. They include either two queen-size beds or one queen-size bed and a double sofa bed, armoire with TV, small dining table with two chairs, patio or balcony, microwave, small refrigerator, coffeemaker, and wet bar. Studio bedspreads are done in a country quilt with blue and white ticking dust ruffle. Bathrooms have a single sink with a separate, but small bath-commode area decorated with color-splashed tile. A closet holds an iron and ironing board. Just slightly larger than the next-door Wilderness Lodge guest rooms, their advantage is the addition of a sofa bed and mini-kitchen but at a higher nightly rate.

The one-bedroom villas, at 727 square feet, sleep a maximum of four plus one child age two or younger. Each unit has a small living area with a queen-size sofa bed, easy chair, entertainment center containing a TV with DVD player, two-person dining table, two-chair eating bar, and balcony or patio. The kitchen, open to the living area, contains a small refrigerator plus stove, dishwasher, coffeemaker, toaster, microwave, and all utensils, dishes, and pots, and pans to make a complete meal. The spacious bedroom holds a king-size bed, armoire with TV, small table, and rattan chair. The bedroom adjoins a two-room bath, one area holding a whirlpool tub, vanity sink, and hair dryer and the other containing a commode (in a separate enclosure), shower, and additional pedestal sink. There's also a large closet with portable crib, iron and ironing board, and keyed safe. A nice feature is the stacked washer-dryer. I like unit number 2523 with views of the pine trees and the Hidden Springs Pool in the distance and no adjoining balconies to disturb the peace and quiet.

Two-bedroom villas sleep a maximum of eight people plus one child age two or younger and offer 1,080 square feet of room. This unit is exactly the same as the one-bedroom unit, with the addition of a studio bedroom, which adds up to two bedrooms, two baths, living area, kitchen, three TVs, and two balconies or porches. Dedicated two-bedroom villas, of which there are very few, have two queens minus the sofa and mini-kitchen in the second bedroom.

*CARA'S TIP:* Avoid units at the extreme far end of the property, which come with a not-so-great side view of the service area.

## PLAY

**Swimming.** The scent of pine perfumes the air at peaceful Hidden Springs, a free-form pool with geyser bubbles; no lifeguard on duty.

## WORK, MOVE, SOOTHE

**Fitness center.** Sturdy Branches Health Club; Cybex strength training equipment, Smith machine, Life Fitness treadmills and ellipticals, Life

Cycles, free weights; coed dry sauna; personal training, Swedish massage, reflexology, facials, aromatherapy, and in-room massage available by appointment; fitness center is complimentary to resort guests; open 6 a.m. to 9 p.m.

## Epcot Area Resorts

Those who plan to spend a lot of time at Epcot and Disney's Hollywood Studios should strongly consider selecting one of the resorts in this terrific area. Options include Disney's Beach Club Resort, Disney's BoardWalk Inn, Disney's Yacht Club Resort, the Walt Disney World Swan, and the Walt Disney World Dolphin. All front Crescent Lake, and all are within walking distance or a boat ride to Epcot, Disney's Hollywood Studios, and the Boardwalk. With such easy access to so many resorts and Epcot just a few minutes away, you'll find more restaurant and entertainment choices than you can count.

### Disney's Beach Club Resort

**583 rooms. 1800 Epcot Resorts Boulevard, Lake Buena Vista 32830; phone (407) 934-8000, fax (407) 934-3850. Check-in 3 p.m., checkout 11 a.m. For reservations call (407) WDW-DISNEY or (407) 939-3476, or contact your travel agent. $$$–$$$$$**

**Why Stay Here?** Super easy access to Epcot, just a five-minute walk away.

**Rooms to Book.** A Lagoon View concierge room with access to the Stone Harbor Club and a panorama of Crescent Lake.

**Don't Miss.** An afternoon enjoying Stormalong Bay, the resort's great swimming pool complex.

Five-story, blue and white, Cape Cod–style buildings fronting a white-sand beach bordered with soft sea grass bring to mind late-nineteenth-century Martha's Vineyard. Relax in inviting white rockers on the front porch, or while away time in the lobby where airy, high ceilings centered by a seahorse chandelier, curtained alcove sitting areas, gold-and-cream-striped seating, high-back canopy-style chairs, and potted banana plants create a cabana ambience. A sunny solarium overlooks the resort's lovely gardens.

The casually elegant grounds surrounding the resort are planted with a variety of crape myrtles, gardenias, and roses, but the highlight is the fantastic Stormalong Bay, a winding wonderland of a small-scale water park shared with the Yacht Club. Since this is the closest resort to Epcot, it offers super easy access to the International Gateway entrance, a convenience that can't be beat. I must say that if balconies are important to you choose a room at the Yacht Club instead where full-size balconies are found in every guest room; the majority of the Beach Club's room balconies are 1 foot by 3 feet, standing-room-only.

**REST**

**Guest rooms.** New room renovations are a great improvement featuring a more adult look. With 380 square feet, guest rooms are bedecked in a sea-blue and chocolate color scheme with striped curtains, cream duvets, and shutter-style distressed cherry wood headboards. Above a large cottage-white bureau is a wall-mounted flat-panel TV. There's delicate seahorse imprinted wallpaper, an additional bureau in the foyer, and in the corner sits a work desk with a lifeguard Mickey lamp. Some rooms also come with a daybed. The lively decor continues in the bath where sailing ship motif wallpaper and shower curtain adorn a separate tub and commode area of pale gold ceramic tile. Outside is a gray and white marble vanity with pickled green mirrors, two sinks, non-lighted makeup mirror, and hair dryer. Amenities include a small keyed safe, iron and ironing board, coffeemaker, refrigerator, iPod docking station clock radio, and daily newspaper.

CARA'S TIP: Request a room facing Epcot for a view of Illuminations, and remember that standard-view rooms could have a view of the parking lot. Water-view rooms aren't always of Crescent Lake; many times they face Stormalong Bay, a somewhat noisy location.

**Concierge rooms.** Fifth-floor concierge-level rooms include the amenities of the Stone Harbor Club, a small but cozy lounge (one that tends to be a bit crowded and frenzied when the occupancy level is high) with complimentary food and beverages throughout the day. Expect a continental breakfast of three types of juice, donuts, bagels, pastries, muffins, croissants, fruit, and cereal along with afternoon snacks of beverages, goldfish crackers, cookies, popcorn, pudding, nuts, pretzels and, in late afternoon, cake. Early evening brings wine (Kenwood White Zinfandel, Ravenswood Zinfandel, Castle Rock Pinot Noir, Two Princess Riesling, Sartori Pinot Grigio) with a small spread of hot and cold hors d'oeuvres such as cheese and crackers, hummus, olives, crudités with dip, pinwheel and PB&J sandwiches, fresh mozzarella and cherry tomato salad, asparagus salad, bourbon beef kabobs, and roasted salmon as well as a daily soup like clam chowder and roasted tomato cream. After dinner you'll find desserts such as mini tarts and cheesecake, cookies, and Rice Krispies squares along with liqueurs. There's also a self-service espresso and cappuccino machine. Additional amenities include the services of a friendly concierge staff, private check-in and checkout, DVD players, nightly turndown service, and robes.

**Suites.** The 2,200-square-foot Presidential Newport Suite has a large marble foyer leading to a living room with a somewhat small seating area and seahorse motif fireplace. You'll also find a wet bar, dining room with seating for eight, butler's pantry-style kitchen, and half bath. In the colossal master bedroom is a king bed, desk, easy chair and ottoman, armoire, and loads of windows. The marble master bath holds a whirlpool tub, separate toilet area with bidet, separate walk-in shower, mini TV, double sinks, and large walk-in closet. The second bedroom is actually the size of a one-bedroom suite with king bed, walk-in closet, balcony, and separate sitting area. Three extended balconies almost encircle the entire suite, affording views of the gardens, quiet pool, and lagoon. A half bath is found off the foyer.

The fifth-floor Vice Presidential Nantucket Suite at 996 square feet is a one-bedroom, one-and-a-half-bath suite with a parlor holding a sofa, coffee table, easy chairs, wet bar with microwave and small refrigerator, four-person dining table, desk, armoire, and balcony overlooking a quiet garden courtyard. The bedroom has a small standing-room-only balcony facing Stormalong Bay and a marble bathroom with whirlpool tub, separate shower, double sinks, and mini TV.

Enter two-bedroom suites through a small marble foyer to a living area with a table and two chairs, sofa, easy chair, coffee table, bureau, wall-mounted flat-panel TV, and wet bar with coffeemaker and under-counter refrigerator. Off the living area is a long, narrow bathroom with a double-sinked vanity and closet outside of the separate shower/tub and toilet area. The smallish master bedroom is accessed through French doors. A standard guest room is off the living area. These accommodate a maximum of seven people.

One-bedroom suites at 726 square feet offer a small parlor with a daybed, coffee table, and flat-panel TV. Through French doors is the bedroom with a king bed, desk, daybed, second TV, and love seat. A standard-size bath and walk-in closet are located off the parlor with a balcony running the length of the suite. Sleeps four.

Water-view Deluxe Rooms are corner rooms found on every floor except the fifth. At 533 square feet they afford extra room for a more comfortable stay. Just past the small marble foyer is a standard-size bath then a long, narrow room with two queen beds and a daybed set in a small alcove. The small balcony is a stand-up only. All come with concierge lounge access, as do all suites regardless of floor location.

## DINE

**Beach Club Marketplace.** Located within the Atlantic Wear and Wardrobe Emporium; counter service available all day; *breakfast:* omelet sandwich on a croissant, made-to-order yogurt parfait, fresh-baked pastries, muffins, bagels, croissants; *lunch and dinner:* roast beef and brie on ciabatta roll, turkey and mozzarella on sourdough baguette, smoked ham and Black Diamond cheddar on a multigrain bun, grilled vegetable wrap, grilled chicken made-to-order salad, New England clam chowder; variety of fresh desserts and gelato; espresso, cappuccino, wine; *children's menu:* turkey sandwich, PB&J.

**Beaches and Cream.** Disney's best milk shake and ice-cream stop; burgers and sandwiches; open for lunch and dinner.

**Cape May Café.** Open for breakfast and dinner; breakfast buffet with Goofy and friends; evening New England–style clambake buffet; *breakfast:* scrambled eggs, omelets, biscuits and gravy, French toast, pancakes, breakfast pizza, smoked salmon, bread pudding with vanilla sauce, and more; *dinner:* clam chowder, assorted salads, steamed clams, snow crab legs, mussels, shrimp, fish of the day, prime rib, dessert table.

**In-Room Dining.** Available 24/7.

## SIP

**Hurricane Hanna's Grill.** Poolside bar and grill; full bar, cocktails, beer, alcoholic and nonalcoholic frozen drinks; grilled chicken flatbread, turkey sandwich, cheeseburger, hot dog, vegetable wrap, grilled chicken salad; *children's menu:* grilled cheese, hot dog, turkey sandwich, cheeseburger.

**Martha's Vineyard.** Cocktail lounge adjoining Cape May Café.

## PLAY

**Arcade.** Lafferty Place Arcade located next to Beaches and Cream soda shop.

**Beach.** An enticing white-sand beach dotted with lounge chairs fronting Crescent Lake with views of the BoardWalk and the Epcot fireworks; swimming not allowed in Crescent Lake.

**Children's playground and activities.** Playground located near Stormalong Bay; pool parties and games, scavenger hunts, bingo, Wii bowling and tennis, Guitar Hero jam sessions, dance parties; Albatross Treasure Cruise sets sail in search of treasure each Monday, Wednesday and Friday at 9:30 a.m. for a two-hour cruise ($34); a Campfire Singalong and Movie Under the Stars is offered each evening on the shore of Crescent Lake with marshmallows and s'mores available for purchase.

**Croquet.** Croquet court located at Beach Club Resort; complimentary equipment available at Ship Shape Health club.

**Fishing.** See "Play" section for Disney's Yacht Club Resort.

**Jogging.** Joggers utilize the 0.75-mile circular BoardWalk as their track.

**Swimming.** Stormalong Bay is an eye-popping, free-form, miniature water park complex that meanders between the Beach Club and the Yacht Club. The most divine pool at Disney, its three acres of winding, watery delight offer sandy-bottom pools, a 230-foot-long "shipwreck" waterslide, a snorkeling lagoon, tidal whirlpool, bubbling hot tubs, a kiddie pool with its own slide next to the beach, and enough length to float lazily in inner tubes to your heart's content. Inner tubes are available for rent. A quiet pool and whirlpool are located at the Epcot end of the resort at the Beach Club, with another at the Dolphin end of the Yacht Club. All pools are heated.

**Tennis.** See "Play" section in subsequent entry for Disney's Yacht Club Resort.

**Volleyball.** Sand court located at Beach Club Resort; ball available at Ship Shape Health Club.

### WORK, MOVE, SOOTHE

**Child care.** Sandcastle Club features video and board games, arts and crafts, Disney movies, play kitchen; open 4:30 p.m. to midnight, for potty-trained children ages four to twelve; cost includes dinner and late night cookies and milk; open only to registered guests of the Yacht Club, Beach Club, Beach Club Villas, and BoardWalk Inn and Villas; call (407) WDW-DINE or (407) 939-3463 for reservations.

**Hair salon.** Periwig Beauty and Barber Salon; haircuts, perms, color, manicures, pedicures; open daily 9 a.m. to 6 p.m.

**Fitness center.** Ship Shape Health Club; Cybex strength training machines, Life Fitness treadmills, bicycles, elliptical machines, Stairmaster stair-climbers, free weights; whirlpool, steam room, and sauna; massage available by appointment, including in-room; fitness center is complimentary to resort guests; 24-hour access with attendant on duty 6 a.m. to 9 p.m.

### GO

Take the watercraft taxi to Disney's Hollywood Studios from the Bayside Marina at the Yacht Club. Although boat transportation is available to Epcot, it's quicker to walk to the park than to walk to the marina to catch the boat. The BoardWalk is a stroll around the lagoon. Bus service is available to the Magic Kingdom, Animal Kingdom, Typhoon Lagoon, Blizzard Beach, and Downtown Disney.

To reach other Disney resorts outside of the Epcot area, you must first bus to Downtown Disney or an open theme park and then transfer to your resort destination.

## Disney's BoardWalk Inn

**371 rooms. 2101 Epcot Resorts Boulevard, Lake Buena Vista 32830; phone (407) 939-5100, fax (407) 939-5150. Check-in 3**

**p.m., checkout 11 a.m. For reservations call (407) WDW-DIS-NEY or (407) 939-3476, or contact your travel agent. $$$–$$$$$**

**Why Stay Here?** A charming ambience, easy access to Epcot, and some of the friendliest concierge cast members to be found.

**Rooms to Book.** Deluxe Club concierge rooms are one of Disney's best bargains with over 600 square feet of space and prime views of Crescent Lake and the bustling Boardwalk.

**Don't Miss.** Dinner at the Flying Fish whose creative seafood is something to write home about.

The BoardWalk Inn's intimate charm captures the feeling of a 1930s mid-Atlantic seacoast retreat. In the lobby is a nostalgic living room scene of chintz-covered, oversize chairs, invitingly plump sofas, floral rugs, and potted palms set atop gleaming hardwood floors and plush area rugs. Looming overhead is the barrel-shaped, chandeliered ceiling embellished with delicate latticework. Views from the lofty windows are of a lush courtyard green fronting a festive, old-fashioned boardwalk. Step outside to the wide veranda lined with wicker rocking chairs, a perfect early evening spot from which to bathe in the pink glow of sunset as the BoardWalk slowly comes alive.

The resort's gleaming white four-story buildings, dotted with latticework and crowned with sea green roofs and striped awnings, surround interior courtyards fragrant with blooming roses. The inn is just a short walk away from Epcot's International Gateway entrance.

**REST**

**Guest rooms.** Well-appointed accommodations average 434 whimsical square feet, all with French doors leading to full-size balconies or patios. Renovated guest rooms have a crisp new look with white duvets and a brocade bed runner topped with a cherry red accent pillow. Most offer two queen-size, two-poster beds, a blond wood bureau topped with a built-in flat-panel TV, and a desk/vanity with Mickey lamp. Apple green, twin-size sofa sleeper and gold-and-white-striped wallpaper combined with soft yellow paint and fresh blue and cream carpeting complete the soothing look. A second clothes bureau is near the bathroom. In one area of the bath is a white vanity topped with cream-colored marble, pewter-hued mirrors, double sinks, hair dryer, and makeup mirror. In a separate room is the commode and a tub/shower surrounded by white tile and curved shower curtain in sea blue and green. Amenities include H2O bath products, keyed wall safe, iron and ironing board, iPod docking station alarm clock, coffeemaker, small refrigerator, and daily newspaper. Standard-view rooms could mean either a view of the front of the resort and perhaps a bit of the parking lot or a delightful one of the peaceful, interior courtyard and, with any luck, the Illuminations fireworks. Water-view rooms are pleasing, but those closest to the BoardWalk or overlooking the pool could be a bit noisy. Keep in mind that ground-floor rooms have open patios that afford little privacy, with vistas sometimes blocked by too-tall hedging.

**Concierge rooms.** Consider upgrading to one of the sixty-five concierge-level rooms. The Innkeeper's Club lounge on the fourth floor enjoys a view of Illuminations from its balcony and a great concierge staff. Breakfast is fruit, bagels, toast, croissants, pastries, yogurt, cereal, juice, coffee, and tea. Midday refreshments are cookies, chips and salsa, popcorn, pretzels, goldfish, and beverages. Early evening comes with hot and cold hors d'oeuvres of hummus, crudités, PB&J sandwiches, cheese and crackers, and two hot dishes such as chicken nuggets, chicken skewers with pineapple, pot stickers, vegetable spring rolls, pork wontons, empanadas, and crab phyllo purses along with wine (Chateau Ste. Michelle Chardonnay, Columbia Crest Merlot, Beringer White Zinfandel) and beer. After dinner are cordials and desserts like chocolate-covered strawberries, fruit tarts, parfaits, chocolate mousse, and cookies. There's also a self-service cappuccino machine. All this along with nightly turndown, private check-in and checkout, and robes makes for one delightful vacation.

As well as standard-size rooms (six of which offer king beds), the concierge level has ten very spacious, 644-square-foot Deluxe Rooms, all with a spectacular view of the BoardWalk and Crescent Lake, even a view of the Magic Kingdom's fireworks in the distance. They come with two queen beds, bureau with flat-panel TV, desk, and an open seating area outfitted with a sleeper sofa, coffee table, easy chair, and extra bureau with another flat-panel TV and DVD player. Five Deluxe Rooms are on the third floor and the other five are on the fourth floor. Two actually adjoin, room numbers 3227 and 3229, perfect for families (on request only).

**Suites.** A gated, white picket fence encircles the serene, two-storied Garden Suites (915 to 1,100 square feet), most with a private front yard complete with rose garden, arbor, mailbox, birdhouse, and porch. Downstairs is a homey living area with a flat-panel TV, malachite green, L-shaped sectional sleeper sofa, coffee table, desk, closet, half bath, and wet bar with microwave, coffeemaker, and small refrigerator. Upstairs is a loft bedroom with a king bed, bureau with built-in flat-panel TV, and a bathroom with double sink, whirlpool tub, separate shower, and mini-TV. Instead of a loft, three of the fourteen Garden Suites (rooms 1205, 1206, and 1207) have a large, upstairs bedroom with French doors leading out to a balcony that overlooks the quiet pool. Be sure to request your preference; honeymooners should request the unit with the heart-shaped shrubbery. All require walking outside and over to the main building to access the concierge lounge.

Two-bedroom suites with 1,288 square feet offer a small parlor decorated in soft green and gold and furnished with a sleeper sofa, coffee table, easy chair, desk, bureau with built-in flat-panel TV, and small dining table for four. There's also a wet bar with microwave and small refrigerator with a half bath off the foyer. French doors lead from the living room to the standard-size master with king bed and walk-in closet, and a cream-toned marble bath featuring a whirlpool tub, separate commode area, double sinks, shower, and mini-TV. Off the other side of the living area is a standard guest room with two queen beds. There are three balconies, and all have a view of the gardens. Suite number 4205 has a bonus of an Illuminations view but also a view of two satellite dishes and a slice of the road; good nighttime view, but not so great during the day.

The Vice Presidential Sonora Suite's lovely living room is perfect for entertaining, with plush Victorian-style, floral furnishings in a mellow mint and butterscotch palette combined with two easy chairs, sofa, coffee table, eight-person dining table, wet bar, buffet, flat-panel TV with stereo, service kitchen, marble half bath, and balcony the length of the suite. On one side of the living area is a standard guest room with two queens and upgraded bedspreads; on the other side a somewhat feminine master bedroom featuring a four-poster king-size bed, armoire with TV, and easy chair. The marble master bathroom comes with double sink, separate shower, whirlpool tub, mini-TV, and separate commode area. The outstanding view from the balcony is an all-encompassing panorama of Crescent Lake. I do like the story behind the suite's name: Sonora Carver was a woman who had a diving-horse act in the 1920s at the Atlantic City Boardwalk, plunging 40 feet on the back of a horse to land in a tank of water.

From deep balconies that run the length of the two-bedroom, two-and-a-half-bath Presidential Steeplechase Suite are sweeping views of the BoardWalk and Crescent Lake. This 2,170-square-foot beauty comes with a muraled domed ceiling above the massive living room. Done in shades of soft blue, gold, and yellow, it features hardwood flooring topped with large area rugs, two seating areas, and an eight-person dining table. Off the dining room is a service kitchen with wet bar, undercounter refrigerator, and microwave, with a pass-through counter to the dining room. The lavish master bedroom boasts a curtained king four-poster bed, and in the marble bath is a giant-size walk-in closet, vanity area, gargantuan whirlpool tub, shower, separate bidet and commode area, and double, hand-painted sinks. The second bedroom is standard in size but with two queens and upgraded bedding and wallpaper. A marble half bath is off the hardwood floor entry.

**DINE**

See Dining section for Disney's BoardWalk in chapter 5, Beyond the Theme Parks.

**In-Room Dining.** Available 24/7.

**SIP**

**Belle Vue Lounge.** Sentimental music the likes of Benny Goodman plays from vintage radios in this comfy bar; additional balcony seating overlooks the BoardWalk; cocktails, specialty drinks, single-malt scotch, wine, beer; continental breakfast served mornings from 6:30 a.m. until 11 a.m.

**Leaping Horse Libations.** Luna Park pool bar; cold sandwiches, beer, specialty drinks.

**PLAY**

**Arcade.** Sideshow Arcade is just off the Village Green with the newest in video and computer games as well as the old reliable pinball machines.

**Bicycle and surrey rentals.** In front of the Village Green; two-, four-, and six-seater surreys available for rent 10 a.m. to 10 p.m., weather permitting; single and tandem bicycles for rent at Community Hall.

**Children's activities and playground.** Playground next to Luna Park Pool; arts and crafts in Community Hall such as ceramics, create-your-own souvenir, and customize a banner. Other activities include family game night, ping pong tournaments, poolside bingo and parties, and Wii bowling and tennis tournaments. Join in at the Yacht & Beach Club's Campfire Sing-along and Movie Under the Stars each evening on the shores of Crescent Lake.

**Ferris W. Eahlers Community Hall.** Video games, air hockey, table tennis, arts and crafts; bikes, books, DVDs, and videos for rent.

**Jogging.** Either the circular 0.75-mile BoardWalk or the path encircling the canal leading to Disney's Hollywood Studios can serve as a jogging track.

**Swimming.** 180,000-gallon Luna Park Pool with 200-foot-long Keister Coaster waterslide; kiddie pool and whirlpool; smaller Inn Pool and whirlpool in Rose Courtyard on Epcot side of inn; quiet Villa Pool and whirlpool next to Community Hall; all pools heated and open 24/7; no lifeguard on duty.

**Tennis.** Two hard-surface, lighted courts; complimentary to registered guests; make reservations at Community Hall where you'll find complimentary rackets.

### WORK, MOVE, SOOTHE

**Business center.** Located at the BoardWalk Conference Center; personal computers, Internet, fax machine, copier, package mailing, secretarial service.

**Muscles and Bustles Health Club.** Cybex strength training equipment, Life Fitness treadmills, elliptical trainers, bicycles; free weights; coed sauna and steam room; massage and reflexology available, including in-room; fitness center complimentary to resort guests; attendant available from 6 a.m. to 7 p.m.; twenty-four-hour access.

**GO**

A water taxi to Epcot and Disney's Hollywood Studios departs from the BoardWalk dock. It's a five- to ten-minute walk to Epcot's International Gateway and about a fifteen-minute walk to Disney's Hollywood Studios along the walkway found behind the resort. Bus service is available to the Magic Kingdom, Animal Kingdom, Typhoon Lagoon, Blizzard Beach, and Downtown Disney.

To reach other Disney resorts outside of the Epcot area, you must first take a bus to Downtown Disney or an open theme park and then transfer to your resort destination.

## Disney's Yacht Club Resort

**621 rooms. 1700 Epcot Resorts Boulevard, Lake Buena Vista 32830; phone (407) 934-7000, fax (407) 934-3450. Check-in 3 p.m., checkout 11 a.m. For reservations call (407) WDW-DISNEY or (407) 939-3476, or contact your travel agent. $$$–$$$$$**

**Why Stay Here?** Easy Epcot access and fun in the sun at Stormalong Bay, the resort's great pool complex.

**Rooms to Book.** A Lagoon View concierge room with vistas of Crescent Lake and access to the Regatta Club's lounge.

**Don't Miss.** An Illuminations cruise on the *Breathless,* a replica of a 1930s Chris Craft Runabout.

The theme here is one of a sophisticated, exclusive yacht club where a navy blue blazer should be in order for a stay. Four- and five-story oyster gray clapboard buildings with balconies shaded by red and white striped awnings front Crescent Lake and a sliver of groomed beach that stretches over to the adjoining Beach Club Resort. The resort's prime location, within walking distance of Epcot's International Gateway entrance as well as the BoardWalk and just a short boat ride away from Disney's Hollywood Studios, is near perfect. The polished, sleek lobby of ship-shiny hardwoods, potted palms, roped nautical railings, leather sofas, and overstuffed, striped easy chairs creates an environment reminiscent of a classy eastern seaboard hotel of the 1880s. The antique globe in the center of the room along with detailed ship models and oceans of gleaming brass complete the picture. The resort shares Stormalong Bay, a fantasyland pool complex, and all recreational areas and facilities with its sister property, the Beach Club.

## REST

**Guest rooms.** Enter your casually elegant room through a yellow yacht-style door where inside you'll find updated guest rooms. Two queen-size beds with a gleaming white headboard in a ship's wheel motif are covered in white duvets with blue piping and topped with a nautical bed runner and red velvet throw pillow. Brass sconce lighting, gold and blue striped drapery, and lots of maritime accents add to the charm. Rooms are fairly spacious at 380 square feet, with cheery white furnishings including a writing desk, a bureau above which sits a wall-mounted flat-panel TV, and an additional bureau near the bathroom. French doors lead to a private balcony or patio with a variety of views. Guest rooms come with comfortable mattresses, triple sheeting, and downy pillows. Some rooms have a blue chenille daybed, others a deep red anchor motif easy chair and ottoman. The marble bath vanity holds double sinks, hair dryer, non-lighted makeup mirror, and porthole-style mirrors. There is a separate tub and commode area. Amenities include an iron and ironing board, coffeemaker, refrigerator, keyed safe, iPod docking station clock radio, and daily newspaper.

*CARA'S TIP:* Standard rooms come with a view of either the gardens or the less desirable front of the resort with perhaps a slice of the parking lot. Try for the standard rooms on the back side near the quiet pool that look out to a grassy area with a fountain and duck pond. Water views face Crescent Lake, Stormalong Bay, or sometimes both; ask for one facing Epcot for a view of the fireworks. If a lot of walking is not your idea of a vacation, request a room close to the lobby; the resort is quite spread out, and long treks to your room are not uncommon.

**Concierge rooms.** Concierge rooms and suites located on the fifth floor are privy to the Regatta Club, one of only a few Disney concierge lounges with a balcony, but alas with a view of the front of the resort instead of Crescent Lake. Rooms here can be booked in either a standard or lagoon view—standard rooms overlook the gardens or the parking lot. Sunrise Starters in the mornings include coffee with a self-service cappuccino machine, three types of juice, donuts, muffins, croissants, bagels, pastries, fruit, and cereal. Midday Seaside Snacks consist of popcorn, pudding, pretzels, goldfish crackers, nuts, cookies, and beverages. Early evening brings wine (Kenwood White Zinfandel, Ravenswood Zinfandel, Castle Rock Pinot Noir, Two Princess Riesling, and Sartori Pinot Grigio choices), beer, and hors d'oeuvres such as hummus, crudités, cheese and crackers, pinwheel sandwiches, and fresh mozzarella with balsamic along with a hot item like duck quesadillas and chicken skewers, beef kabobs, salmon, or barbeque pork ribs, as well as a nightly soup such as chicken vegetable, minestrone, tomato bisque, or clam chowder (kids feast on PB&J sandwiches). After dinner Regatta Delights is a selection of cordials and desserts the likes of mini tarts and cheesecake, cookies, and Rice Krispies treats. Extra amenities include robes, turndown service, private check-in and checkout, DVD players, and the services of a pleasant concierge staff.

**Suites.** A variety of suites are available, all having been upgraded to include new wallpaper and carpeting, upgraded flat-panel TVs, and fresh new bedspreads or duvets. All suites regardless of location have concierge lounge access.

The smallest suites are the 654-square-foot Deluxe Rooms, all located on the third and fourth floors, and all with a balcony and view of Crescent Lake. There are two queen-size beds and a small parlor separated by a partial privacy wall.

Turret Two-Bedroom Suites offer 1,160 square feet. Long and narrow, you'll first encounter a standard guest room off the entry hall with two queen-size beds and bath. A narrow hallway leads to the second bedroom also with two queens and a slightly larger-than-standard bath; off it is a six-sided turreted living area with sofa, two easy chairs with ottoman, TV, and four-person dining room. The suite's only balcony is in the standard guest room.

Almost identical at 2,017 square feet but with different decor are the two-bedroom, two-and-a-half-bath Presidential (fourth floor) and Admiral Suites (fifth floor). The Presidential Suite overlooks the BoardWalk and Crescent Lake and is decorated in shades of rose and blue. There's a hardwood foyer with half bath as well as two living areas: one turreted with hardwood flooring and porthole-style windows; the other a carpeted area with a sofa, two easy chairs, coffee table, game table, desk, and gas fireplace. A separate eight-person dining room adjoins a service kitchen. The master bedroom offers a four-poster king bed and in its marble bathroom is an oversized whirlpool tub, shower, separate toilet area with bidet, vanity area, and two sinks. A second bedroom with two queens is standard size with upgraded bedding. Balconies are found in each bedroom and off the living area.

The largest suite at 2,374 square feet is the first-floor, two-bedroom, two-and-a-half-bath Captain's Deck Suite. A marble octagonal foyer leads to a nautically decorated suite decked out in a rich sea blue and rose palette. The parlor features an open sitting area, living area, large business desk in its own alcove, dining room with seating for ten, full kitchen (minus a stove), and oversized brick garden patio (shrubbery blocks the view of the adjoining parking area). Each of the bedrooms has its own private patio, and the plush master bedroom offers a king-size bed, bureau, entertainment center, easy chair and ottoman, walk-in closet, and luxuriously large marble bathroom with vanity area, TV, immense shower, whirlpool tub, separate commode area, and double sinks. The second bedroom is similar to a regular guest room with slightly upgraded decor.

## DINE

**Yacht Club Galley.** Casual all-day eatery open for breakfast, lunch, and dinner; *breakfast:* crab cake Benedict, ham and eggs, buttermilk pancakes with blueberries or chocolate chips, brioche French toast; *lunch:* lobster roll, fish and chips, steak salad, tomato and mozzarella on ciabatta roll; *dinner:* wild mushroom and onion tart, snow crab legs, lump crab cakes, oven-roasted chicken breast, grilled NY strip with red onion jam.

**Yachtsman Steakhouse.** Oak grilled steaks and seafood; dinner only. (See full description in Dining chapter.)

**In-Room Dining.** Served 24/7; limited menu after 10 p.m.

## SIP

**Ale and Compass Lounge.** Lobby bar serving specialty drinks, wine, beer, cordials; continental breakfast served 6 to 10:30 a.m.

**Crew's Cup Lounge.** Cozy seaport-style lounge adjoining Yachtsman Steakhouse; what used to be a very individual lounge now has Disney's cookie-cutter cocktail menu instead of beers from around the world (what a shame); appetizers such as buffalo chicken breast nuggets, honey-ginger chicken wings, and spinach dip as well as a limited menu from the adjoining Yachtsman Steakhouse including chilled seafood salad, seared Maine diver scallops, lobster bisque, heirloom salad, twin tournedos, grilled beef sirloin with peppercorn-brandy sauce, and sides of creamed spinach or mushroom caps.

**Hurricane Hanna's Grill.** Poolside bar and grill; full bar, cocktails, beer, alcoholic and nonalcoholic frozen drinks; grilled chicken flatbread, turkey sandwich, cheeseburger, hot dog, vegetable wrap, grilled chicken salad; *children's menu:* grilled cheese, hot dog, turkey sandwich, cheeseburger.

## PLAY

The Yacht Club shares all recreational activities with the adjacent Disney's Beach Club Resort. See also the Play section in the earlier entry for the Beach Club.

**Bicycles.** Brunswick bicycles available for rent at Bayside Marina.

**Boating.** Rentals at Bayside Marina for touring Crescent Lake and the adjacent waterways; Sea Raycers, Boston Whaler Montauks, pontoon boats.

Illumination cruises on a pontoon boat or on the *Breathless,* a 24-foot Chris Craft reproduction of a 1930 runabout—the viewing point under Epcot's International Bridge is unrivaled; call (407) WDW-PLAY or (407) 939-7529 for reservations.

**Children's activities.** Albatross Treasure Cruise sets sail in search of treasure each Monday, Wednesday and Friday at 9:30 a.m. for a two-hour cruise including lunch; children ages four to twelve ($34).

**Fishing.** Two-hour guided fishing excursions on Crescent Lake depart both morning and afternoon from the Yacht Club marina for a maximum of five guests, including gear and beverages; strictly catch-and-release (call 407-WDW-BASS or 407-939-2277 for reservations; twenty-four-hour notice required).

**Tennis.** One lighted hard-surface court available for complimentary use; complimentary equipment available at Ship Shape Health Club.

## WORK, MOVE, SOOTHE

The Yacht Club shares all services with the adjacent Disney's Beach Club Resort. See also the Work, Move, Soothe section in the earlier entry for the Beach Club.

# ORLANDO HOT SPOTS

Not everyone comes to Orlando to spend all their time in the theme parks. There are some who crave a freshly-shaken martini and a hip crowd. Here are options that will satisfy that need:

- **Il Mulino Bar at the Walt Disney World Swan.** This ever-so-happening spot adorned in shades of tangerine and chocolate and a cool illuminated bar is the place to be. Along with cigars and Italian wines are savory antipasti selections and a spiffy crowd.

- **Bluezoo Lounge at the Walt Disney World Dolphin.** Chic lounge with chocolate brown leather booths, mango orange accents, and copper lighting. Sip on a martini while savoring the action and a selection from the restaurant's raw bar.

- **Starlight Lounge at Timpano Chophouse & Martini Bar on West Sand Lake Road.** I love this place! Frank Sinatra–style live music along with martinis in a retro-swank 1950s bar. What more could you possibly want?

- **Seasons 52 bar on West Sand Lake Road.** A super buzzing bar scene adjoins the restaurant of the same name where live piano music, seventy wines by the glass, and a full menu with nothing over 500 calories is served in the midst of in-the-know locals.

- **Velvet at the Hard Rock Hotel.** Monthly Velvet Sessions (the last Thursday of the month) with live music from hot rock bands bring the crowds in to party. Take your drink outside on the verandah for super views of the resort and Universal's theme parks in the distance.

- **Eleven at the Reunion Grande Resort.** Wow! A see-and-be-seen rooftop bar surrounding a South Beach–style pool with tapas and panoramic views of Disney's fireworks display in the far distance.

- **Sir Harry's Lounge at the Waldorf Astoria Orlando.** Old money atmosphere where leather club chairs, single malt scotch, and live piano music are the order of the evening.

**Business center.** Located at the Yacht Club Convention Center; personal computers, Internet, fax machine, copier, secretarial services; open 7 a.m. to 6 p.m. Monday through Friday and 8 a.m. to 4 p.m. Saturday and Sunday.

**GO**

Take a water taxi to Epcot and Disney's Hollywood Studios from the Bayside Marina. It's a ten-minute walk to Epcot's International Gateway entrance and five minutes to the Boardwalk. Take a bus to the Magic Kingdom, Animal Kingdom, Typhoon Lagoon, Blizzard Beach, and Downtown Disney.

To reach other Disney resorts outside the Epcot area, you must first take a bus to Downtown Disney or an open theme park and then transfer to your resort destination.

## Walt Disney World Dolphin

**1,509 rooms. 1500 Epcot Resorts Boulevard, Lake Buena Vista 32830; phone (407) 934-4000, fax (407) 934-4099. Check-in 3 p.m., checkout 11 a.m. For reservations call (407) WDW-DISNEY, (407) 939-3476, or (888) 828-8850, or contact your travel agent. Reservations and information also available online at www.swan dolphin.com. $$–$$$$$**

**Why Stay Here?** Great access to Epcot and Disney's Hollywood Studios at a good price.

**Rooms to Book.** The top suites here are some of Disney's best with sweeping views and lovely furnishings. Consider the Emperor's Suite for a taste of sheer luxury.

**Don't Miss.** Dinner at Todd English's Bluezoo, Disney's chicest restaurant.

What can I say about the Swan and Dolphin? It's a tough call. The reason I include both in the book is for their fabulous, newly renovated suites, attractive public areas, great pools, super dining options, the best spa on Disney property, super comfortable beds, and a location in the midst of Epcot, the BoardWalk, and Disney's Hollywood Studios area. But you must be willing to contend with claustrophobic, low-ceiling hallways with gaudy wallpaper and loud carpeting, and the smallish and outdated standard baths. Either be content with a bargain priced guest room, or pony up for one of the stunning Presidential or Governor's Suites and be done with it.

Operated by Sheraton Hotels but situated within the grounds of Walt Disney World, the Dolphin's pyramid-shaped, Michael Graves–designed look can certainly be described as whimsical. All eyes are immediately drawn to the pair of five-story dolphins high atop the twenty-seven stories of the structure and then are immediately lured to the exterior fountain composed of giant clamshells cascading down nine stories. Shades of rich sea blues and bronze are featured throughout the resort and into the lobby draped with a billowing fabric, underneath which sits a fanciful fountain of dolphins. Outside you'll find a super Grotto Pool fronting the white-sand beach of Crescent Lake.

Extensive meeting facilities, ballrooms, and exhibit halls make this property a popular choice for conventioneers, so come prepared for large groups roaming the public areas both here and at the next-door Swan, which shares all recreational and service facilities with the Dolphin.

Although this is not a Disney-owned resort, guests receive the same amenities as at other Disney properties, including Extra Magic Hours, Disney transportation to all attractions, complimentary parking at Disney's theme parks, package delivery, and guaranteed park admission. However, charging privileges to your resort account do not extend outside of the Dolphin or Swan, and Disney's Magical Express is not offered.

**REST**

**Guest rooms.** Guest rooms have a soft, contemporary style with sleek, maple wood furnishings and frosted blue accents. Heavenly Beds feature pillow-top mattresses, triple-sheeted linens, down blankets and pillows, and snow-white duvets. Some upgrades have occurred recently with new earth tone accents including chocolate and taupe tinted carpeting, pumpkin-colored bolsters, and taupe and sea blue drapery as well as 32-inch flat-panel TVs. While comfortable, guest rooms at 360 square feet are a bit cozy. They come with either two double beds with an easy chair and ottoman or a king-size bed with a sofa. A single sink in a cramped corner marble vanity sits just outside the small, separate tub/shower and toilet area with its outdated tub and old-fashioned tile and sink. In the slate-floored foyer is a vanity with hair dryer and coffeemaker. Amenities include thick, fluffy towels, Bath & Body Works toiletry products, an iron and ironing board, two dual-line telephones, undercounter refrigerator, electronic safe, high-speed Internet connection, and cable TV with on-demand movies. A nice option is a room with a balcony (for which an extra charge is assessed). The best views are on the higher floors facing Epcot with a panoramic vista of Spaceship Earth, World Showcase, Crescent Lake, Illuminations, and the entire BoardWalk area. A mandatory $10 resort fee includes two bottles of water daily, twenty minutes of domestic long-distance phone calls per day, unlimited local calls up to an hour, fitness center, and in-room Internet access.

**Suites.** Premium Suites offer quite a bit more room than a regular guest room along with upgraded furnishings. In one large room is a king bed, sleeper sofa, desk, bureau with 42-inch flat-panel TV, four-person dining table, wet bar, and two easy chairs totaling 650 square feet.

Executive Suites are even larger. The parlor includes a sofa, easy chairs, coffee table, bureau with TV, full bath with two sinks, and wet bar. One or two guest rooms (one with a king-size bed and the other with two doubles) can be added on either side of the living area.

The Dolphin has several presidential suites, each with a different theme. The Caesar and Pharaoh Suites, on the nineteenth floor, are 2,451 square feet and similar in layout; both have been lovingly renovated in a sumptuous new decor. In the Caesar Suite the massive living area has two separate seating areas; one side with a white sectional sofa and wall-mounted flat-panel TV, the other with a pumpkin tinted curved sofa and two oversized brown leather easy chairs, all adorned with contemporary artwork and accessories. Other luxuries include a hardwood floor entry, six-person circular dining table, wet bar, extra full bath, and kitchen with a microwave, full-size refrigerator, wine cooler, dishwasher, and sink. The suite's master bedroom has a king with a leather headboard, chaise lounge, and leather-topped desk. In the bath is chocolate marble flooring with a whirlpool tub and a single sink outside of which sits a somewhat cramped single sink vanity. The guest bedroom is a standard size with two queen beds sporting dressy spreads in a soft blue and gray coral motif; its standard size bath is stylish in a sleek and modern black and cream color scheme with marble flooring and contemporary sink and fixtures. Alas, there is no balcony, but there is a distant Magic Kingdom view from the master.

On the twentieth floor sit the loftiest suites on property: two presidential suites, both two-story, three-bedroom units, both 2,589 square feet, and both beautifully redesigned. Their only glaring drawback is the dated outside hallway leading to these incredible abodes; however, once inside, all thoughts of the outside world are forgotten. The Emperor's Suite offers a breathtaking panorama of Disney's Hollywood Studios, Epcot, and the BoardWalk, seen not only through massive windows but also from the splendid downstairs balcony running the length of the living area. The look and feel of opulence begins when you walk across the hardwood floor of the entry hall onto soothing charcoal gray carpet. Enter a capacious vaulted living room with two luxe, tastefully contemporary sitting areas: one with a cherry red, chenille sectional sofa, the other with a charcoal and white seating arrangement, both centered with a shiny black baby grand piano. Proceed through rooms filled with live palms and orchids, multiple flat-panel TVs, leather-topped desks, and other spiffy furnishings. An eight-seat dining room allows guests to enjoy meals prepared in the full kitchen. Work, if you must, on a trendy desk in the spacious office. All baths, including the living room's half bath, have been refitted with stunning contemporary fixtures, cream marble countertops, cutting-edge square sinks, and chocolate marble flooring. Both the downstairs and upstairs guest rooms are fit for a king (or an emperor for that matter) with two queen beds upstairs and a king downstairs adorned in white silk spreads and chocolate and white marble baths. Upstairs the enormous master is striking with its red and chocolate decor; the bath is outfitted with a walk-in closet, square double sinks, whirlpool tub, stand-alone shower, and a separate commode and bidet room. In short, this suite is modern renovation at its best.

## DINE

**The Fountain.** Retro 1950s soda fountain; open for lunch and dinner; albacore tuna and cheddar melt, Cuban sandwich, buffalo chicken salad, build your favorite hot dog or hamburger, ahi tuna burger; *fountain treats:* hand-scooped and soft-serve ice cream, banana split, floats, sundaes, malts.

**Fresh Mediterranean Market.** Open for breakfast and lunch; *breakfast buffet or a la carte:* pastries, fruit, breakfast and rotisserie meats, hot and cold cereals, omelets, pancakes, waffles; *lunch:* chicken marsala, Italian charcuterie panini sandwich, beef sliders, pappardalle pasta with porcini mushrooms, seared black bass with bacon and lentils.

**Picabu Buffeteria.** Twenty-four-hour cafeteria (grill usually open until 11 p.m. but hours are seasonal); *breakfast:* fresh fruit, omelets, cinnamon buns, funnel cake, oatmeal, grits, cereal, hot cinnamon rolls, biscuits and gravy, corned beef hash, eggs-your-way, ciabatta breakfast sandwich, fruit turnovers; *lunch and dinner:* chicken sandwich, loaded nachos, burgers and hot dogs your way, Oriental glazed salmon, chicken pot pie, potato bar, strip steak and caramelized onions, pizza, beef lasagna, cold sandwiches, salads; self-service wine station; *children's menu:* hamburgers, hot dogs, mac 'n' cheese, chicken fingers.

**Shula's Steakhouse.** Best steak on Disney property; dinner only; clubby, luxurious atmosphere. (See full description in the Dining chapter.)

**Todd English's Bluezoo.** Fresh seafood in a stunning setting; dinner only. (See full description in Dining chapter.)

**In-Room Dining.** Available 24/7.

**SIP**

**Bluezoo Lounge.** Chic lounge adjoining Todd English's Bluezoo restaurant; open 3:30 to 11 p.m. daily; full bar, specialty cocktails, and martinis; raw bar; *appetizers:* flatbreads, crab nachos, lamb mezze; full restaurant menu also available; classic Happy Hour Monday through Friday 5 to 7 p.m.

**Cabana Bar and Beach Club.** Updated pool grill; full bar, alcoholic and nonalcoholic frozen tropical drinks; tuna tostada, seared grouper salad, chopped salad, bacon asparagus flatbread, crab cake sliders, soft shell crab sandwich, Cuban cheese steak.

**Lobby Lounge.** *Morning:* coffee and pastries; *late afternoon and evening:* seasonal cocktail service.

**Shula's Lounge.** Sports bar adjoining Shula's Steakhouse; cocktails, wine, champagne, port, single-malt scotches; full restaurant menu available.

**PLAY**

**Arcade.** A small arcade is downstairs near the fitness center.

**Basketball.** Courts on each side of Grotto Pool.

**Boating.** Electric Fun Boats with water cannons for Crescent Lake cruising.

**Children's playground.** Located in the pool area.

**Jogging.** Four miles of jogging trails surround the resort; jogging strollers and pedometers available; ask at fitness center or concierge desk for a map.

**Swimming.** Rambling, three-acre Grotto Pool with waterfall and waterslide located between the Dolphin and the Swan; children's pool, four whirlpools, Spring Pool, two lap pools, sand beach; Grotto and Spring pools are heated; irritating towel check-in and-out.

**Tennis.** Four lighted tennis courts located just across Epcot Resorts Boulevard; round robin classes from 2 to 4 p.m. on Saturday; private lessons available; racquet rentals available at the fitness center.

**Volleyball.** Sand courts on beach.

### WORK, MOVE, SOOTHE

**Business center.** Packaging and shipping, printing, computer and laptop workstations, copying, fax, office supplies; open 24/7 and staffed 7 a.m. to 6:30 p.m. Monday through Friday and 7:30 a.m. to 5 p.m. on Saturday.

**Car rental.** Alamo/National Car Rental desk located just off lobby.

**Child care.** Camp Dolphin with arts and crafts, trip to the game room, movie time; open 5:30 p.m. to midnight, for potty-trained children ages four to twelve; cost includes dinner at Picabu; open to all Walt Disney World guests; complimentary two hours for children of Il Mulino, Bluezoo, and Shula's diners (one child admitted for each adult entrée purchased) as well as spa-goers at Mandara Spa who purchase a treatment of 75 minutes or more; call (407) 934-4241 for required reservations.

**Hair salon.** Located within Mandara Spa; cut and color, shampoo and blow dry, hair and scalp conditioning, manicures, pedicures, acrylics, waxing, makeup.

**Health studio.** Free weights, Life Fitness strength training machines, cycles, treadmills, elliptical trainers; dry sauna in each locker room, coed whirlpool; open 6 a.m. to 9 p.m.; personalized training available by appointment.

**Spa.** Mandara Spa featuring Balinese treatments; retail store and hair salon; open from 8 a.m. until 9 p.m. (See full description in Spas section of chapter 5, Beyond the Theme Parks.)

### GO

The resort has a boat launch to Epcot's International Gateway and Disney's Hollywood Studios and bus service to the Magic Kingdom, Animal Kingdom, Downtown Disney, Typhoon Lagoon, and Blizzard Beach. If you prefer to walk, it's a pleasant ten- to fifteen-minute walk to Epcot's International Gateway entrance (one that is sometimes quicker than the boat service) or a fifteen- to twenty-minute walk to Disney's Hollywood Studios.

## Walt Disney World Swan

**758 rooms. 1200 Epcot Resorts Boulevard, Lake Buena Vista 32830; phone (407) 934-3000, fax (407) 934-4099. Check-in 3 p.m., checkout 11 a.m. For reservations call (407) WDW-DISNEY or (407) 939-3476, or (888) 828-8850, or contact your travel agent. Reservations and information also available online at www.swandolphin.com. $$–$$$$$**

**Why Stay Here?** Great Epcot and Disney Studios access by boat and a great price point for guest rooms.

**Rooms to Book.** The Governors Suite with plenty of room to spread out in gracious surroundings.

**Don't Miss.** Dinner at Il Mulino where great Italian food and a sophisticated ambience make for a perfect meal.

Designed by Michael Graves and operated by the Westin, the Swan, composed of a twelve-story main building and two seven-story wings, is a bit more subdued than the Dolphin. Linked by an awning-covered walkway (the place to catch the boat launch to Epcot and Disney's Hollywood Studios), it shares the same glorious three-acre grotto pool. The lobby is small but impressive with dazzling, cylindrical glass lighting, potted palms, contemporary seating, and a sparkling swan fountain. If the colossal style of the Dolphin is simply not your scene, the smaller-scale Swan is the place for you.

Although not a Disney-owned resort, guests receive the same amenities as at other Disney properties including Extra Magic Hours, Disney transportation to all attractions, complimentary parking at Disney's theme parks, package delivery, and guaranteed park admission. However, charging privileges to your resort account do not extend outside of the Swan or Dolphin, and Disney's Magical Express is not offered.

## REST

**Guest rooms.** Guest rooms embody a contemporary style with room size, furnishings, and decor the same as at the Dolphin (see "Rest" section of previous entry for the Walt Disney World Dolphin). At the Swan there are two queens instead of two double beds, carpeting in the entries instead of slate, and a different bathroom configuration. As at the Dolphin, baths have not been upgraded. Here there are two sinks: one outside the bath area with a hair dryer, non-lighted makeup mirror, and coffeemaker; one inside with the tub-shower and toilet. Amenities include an iron and ironing board, minibar, a pair of two-line telephones, high-speed Internet connection, and cable TV with on-demand movies. Views from the upper floors can be impressive, with panoramas of either Disney Studios or Epcot and the Grotto Pool. A nice option is a room with a balcony, albeit a rusty one, for which an extra charge is assessed. Corner balcony rooms come with an extra wall of windows that make for a bright, airy space; from Room 626 you also get a view of both the Magic Kingdom and Epcot fireworks. A mandatory $10 resort fee includes two bottles of water, twenty minutes of domestic long-distance phone calls per day, unlimited local calls up to an hour, and in-room internet access.

*CARA'S TIP:* A small percentage of guest rooms offer a view of the Epcot fireworks. Request one at the time of booking and again at check-in.

**Suites.** At 500 square feet, Swan Studio Suites offer quite a bit more square footage than a regular guest room, but with the same basic decor. The bedroom contains a king-size bed, queen-size sofa bed, easy chair, and bureau with TV, opening up to a bonus room with four-person dining table and wet bar; baths are also larger. Some suites have balconies (on request only).

Grand Suites feature charcoal-colored carpeting and upgraded, contemporary living room furnishings. Two standard rooms with standard decor, one with a king bed and the other with two queens, flank a 680-square-foot parlor with sleeper sofa, two easy chairs, TV, eight-person dining table, desk, service kitchen, and a single sink full bath. There's a total of four balconies. This suite can also be booked as a one-bedroom.

The one-bedroom Governors Suite is exceptional with all new decor even in the guest rooms. Ice blue and chocolate tones accent the luxuriously modern furniture surrounded by sleek accessories and lighting, but it's the bedroom that adds the extra flair. In the king-bedded bedroom is a sectioned-off sitting area with sofa and three easy chairs. The double-sinked bath features marble flooring and a separate shower and tub. You'll find two balconies in the living area and two more in the bedroom. A dining table seats six and there is an additional full-size bath in the entry hall as well as a service kitchen.

Newly renovated in attractive pumpkin and gold hues, the Executive Suites feature a standard guest room (with no balcony) connected to a parlor in which you'll find a wet bar, desk, four-person dining table, buffet, sofa, two easy chairs, sofa table, oversized flat-panel TV, an extra full bath, and a balcony. This type of suite also can be reserved as a two-bedroom with another standard guest room opening from the other side of the parlor.

There are four presidential suites, each with a different decor and theme. On the twelfth floor is the large Japanese Presidential Suite. It comes with two bedrooms (the master with a king bed and the second bedroom with two queen beds), three full baths, large parlor with a grand piano, dining room with seating for eight, and full kitchen. The same layout but a different decor is in the Italian Presidential Suite. On the eleventh floor is the Oasis Suite, offering a somewhat Egyptian decor and a view of Crescent Lake. Here you'll find a master bedroom with a king-size bed, an additional guest room, three full baths, immense living area with a grand piano, dining table for eight, and kitchen. The Southwest Presidential Suite is similar and is located on the twelfth floor.

**DINE**

**Garden Grove.** Serving breakfast, lunch, and dinner; *breakfast:* buffet and a la carte items such as a healthy frittata, banana pancakes, veggie Benedict, almond crusted French toast, steak and eggs with chipotle hollandaise sauce, Belgian waffles; Saturday and Sunday character breakfast with Goofy and Pluto; *lunch:* panzanella salad, chicken caprese panini, beef sliders, "stuffed" burger, French dip sandwich; *dinner:* buffet themed nights (Mediterranean Night on Saturday, Tuesday, and Thursday; Southern Barbeque on Monday and Sunday; Fisherman's Wharf seafood buffet on Monday and Friday).

**Il Mulino New York Trattoria.** Disney's best Italian restaurant; open for dinner only. (See full description in Dining chapter.)

**Splash Grill.** Lap pool grill with full-service bar; open seasonally for lunch only; cobb salad, tuna wrap, chicken club, Cuban "cheese steak," grass-fed organic burger, roasted vegetable wrap.

**In-Room Dining.** Available 24/7.

### SIP

**Il Mulino Lounge.** Superslick bar with specialty drinks, Italian wines, and antipasti of zucchini and calamari fritti, Italian rice balls, carpaccio, flight of three mini pizzas; illuminated wine bar; outside cigar terrace.

**Kimonos Lounge.** Sushi and sake bar; wine, single-malt scotch, port, small batch bourbons; hot appetizers, sushi, and sashimi; superfun karaoke nightly beginning at 9 p.m.

### PLAY

The Swan shares all recreational activities with the Dolphin. See the "Play" section in the previous entry for additional information.

**Arcade.** A small arcade with pool table and foosball is located near Splash Grill.

### WORK, MOVE, SOOTHE

**Business center.** Packaging and shipping, printing, computer and laptop workstations, copying, fax, office supplies; open 24/7 and staffed 7 a.m. to 6:30 p.m. Monday through Saturday.

**Child care.** Available at adjacent Dolphin Resort (see "Work, Move, Soothe" section of previous Dolphin entry).

**Fitness center.** Swan Health Studio; very small workout room with Life Fitness strength training machines, elliptical trainers, treadmills, free weights; locker rooms outfitted with dry saunas; guided runs; open daily 6 a.m. to 9 p.m.

**GO**

See "Go" section of previous entry for Walt Disney World Dolphin.

# Animal Kingdom Area Resorts

Disney's only deluxe resort in the Animal Kingdom area is the extraordinary Animal Kingdom Lodge. Here you'll also find Jambo House villas with studio, one-, and two-bedroom units found on the fifth and sixth floor of the resort. And next-door is the wonderful Animal Kingdom Villas Kidani Village. Although its solitude adds to the allure, that isolation also makes for a less convenient choice than resorts in the Magic Kingdom or Epcot area. If choosing these properties, consider renting a car to take full advantage of all that Walt Disney World has to offer in the way of resort restaurants and entertainment. Nearby is, of course, the Animal Kingdom as well as Blizzard Beach, Winter Summerland miniature golf, and Disney's ESPN Wide World of Sports.

## *Disney's Animal Kingdom Lodge*

**1,188 rooms including Jambo House villas. 2901 Osceola Parkway, Lake Buena Vista, FL 32830; phone (407) 938-3000, fax (407) 938-7102. Check-in 3 p.m., checkout 11 a.m. For reservations call (407) WDW-DISNEY or (407) 939-3476, or contact your travel agent. $$–$$$$$**

**Why Stay Here?** Magical views of the resort's savanna teaming with exotic wildlife.

**Rooms to Book.** The Royal Assante Presidential Suite, Disney's best accommodation.

**Don't Miss.** The Wanyama Sunset Safari, an evening game drive on the savanna followed by a multicourse dinner at the resort's premier restaurant, Jiko.

Disney's version of a safari lodge is truly a stunner, a faithful celebration of African wildlife, culture, and cuisine. Its authentic architecture combined with grasslands filled with hundreds of roaming exotic animals is simply a stroke of genius. The six-story, horseshoe-shaped structure topped with extravagant thatch rooftops is rustically surrounded by eucalyptus fencing and a glorious savanna. Though often compared to the Wilderness Lodge in design and pricing, the Animal Kingdom Lodge is a step above in terms of sophistication.

The imposing, five-story thatch-roofed lobby is a wonder. Just as at Disney's Wilderness Lodge (both designed by architect Peter Dominick) the first impression is nothing but *wow!* Resplendent overhead chandeliers formed by Masai shields and spears tower over the boulder-lined lobby. Safari-chic seating areas are extraordinary, with hand-carved coffee tables, handsome handwoven rugs, richly tinted rattan and cane chairs, and relaxing leather sofas adorned with African textile throw pillows (whose fabrics are in need of a bit of freshening). A rope suspension bridge spans the lobby and draws the eye to balconies carved with graceful antelopes and a 46-foot picture window framed with the branches of an intricate iron-work tree. The centerpiece of the lobby is the one-of-a-kind sacred Ijele, a 16-foot, dazzling mask created by the Igbo people of Nigeria.

Out back sits a massive yellow flame tree poised atop Arusha Rock, an outcropping with panoramic views of the savanna. Nearby, a fire pit surrounded by rocking chairs is the site of nightly storytelling by the African staff. Lobby and restaurant greeters together with the savanna guides are all cultural representatives from Africa, more than delighted to answer questions or share information and tales of their homeland.

Located within a five-minute drive to the Animal Kingdom theme park (but with no walking path to the park), the animals you'll see here are exclusively the lodge's and not part of the theme park's menagerie. The design is one that encourages observation of the animals from both common lookouts as well as from 75 percent of the rooms. Several viewing platforms are staffed by guides helpful in identifying wildlife as well as communicating interesting information about the animals. Each savanna holds different species, and patience is sometimes required to spot them. But more times than not, you'll find the savanna brimming with an abundance of prime viewing opportunities including zebras, giraffes, gazelles, ankole (African cattle), wildebeests, exotic birds, and more.

If you can somehow find the time, take a tour of the resort's outstanding collection of more than 500 pieces of museum-quality African art, including intricate masks, amazing beadwork, artifacts dating as far back as 8,500 B.C., and much, much more.

## REST

**Guest rooms.** Don't even consider booking a room without a savanna view, well worth every penny for a front-row seat from which to view the animals. And remember to bring your binoculars from home! Through a shield-covered door is an attractively designed, honey-colored room outfitted with handcrafted and carved furnishings, torch-shaped lamps, tribal baskets, and ethnic prints. Intricately engraved headboards are draped in a gauzy fabric reminiscent of mosquito netting and beds are covered in vibrant African print spreads. Flat-panel TVs are built into a bureau (one that takes up too much room space), beside which sits a table and two chairs. Baths have a separate granite-topped vanity area with double sinks, hair dryer, full-length mirror, and too-dim lighting. The bathroom walls are papered with maps of Africa, and the vanity is topped with a wonderful hand-carved mirror.

Amenities include an iron and ironing board, keyed safe, refrigerator, coffeemaker, and daily newspaper. All rooms have balconies, with 75 percent of them offering savanna views, but guest rooms at 344 square feet are a bit cramped. Room bedding includes one king, two queens, or a queen-size and bunk beds. Views are standard, overlooking the front of the resort and the parking lot; savanna, overlooking one of three savannas; and pool, overlooking the pool area.

*CARA'S TIP:* At the Animal Kingdom Lodge are three savannas, each with its own charm. The Kudu Trail savanna now faces the new Animal Kingdom Villas. Beware the standard view rooms that look at the parking area and could possibly be in the valet parking drop-off area with a constant stream of buses and cars passing by your room balcony at all hours of the day and night.

**Concierge rooms.** Concierge-level guest rooms come with a view of the savanna and are located on the fourth and fifth floor. The thatch-roofed, sixth-floor Kilimanjaro Club overlooking the lobby offers unusual food and a pleasant ambience, and would be perfect if not for the indifferent wait staff. Extra amenities include the services of a concierge staff, curbside check-in, DVD players, and turndown service. In the morning there's a continental breakfast of mango, pineapple, and orange juice,

Danish pastry, muffins, bagels, croissants, fresh fruit, oatmeal, quinoa, and cereal. Later you'll find afternoon beverages and snacks of African smoothies, Kettle Chips, cookies, trail mix, spiced nuts, fruit, banana chips, granola bars, goldfish crackers, and gummy bears, with the addition of scones and biscuits at tea time. In the evening enjoy South African wine and beer as well as cold hors d'oeuvres and hot items from the on-site restaurants, Boma and Jiko, including such goodies as a nightly soup like carrot ginger and butternut squash, samosas, meatballs with Tunisian tomato sauce, palaver stew, mini vegetable bobitie, chicken wings, barbecue pork ribs, assorted cheeses, hummus, yogurt dip, and crudités. Kids enjoy PB&J sandwiches. After-dinner treats include cookies, pineapple cheesecake, minitarts, Rice Krispies treats, mango-filled phyllo dough, cordials, and sometimes zebra domes (ganache-covered chocolate-coffee mousse) from Boma. Lemonade, iced tea, and sodas are available throughout the day. You'll even find a self-service espresso and cappuccino machine.

A special early morning excursion, the Sunrise Safari Breakfast Adventure, is available to Animal Kingdom Lodge concierge guests only on Thursday and Sunday at 6:30 a.m. It includes a forty-five-minute, before-park-hours ride through the Animal Kingdom's Kilimanjaro Safaris followed by a buffet breakfast at Pizzafari. Advance reservations can be made 180 days prior through the concierge itinerary planning office by calling (407) 938-4755.

**Suites.** One-bedroom suites at 777 square feet feature a separate parlor with a queen-size sofa bed, easy chair, coffee table, entertainment center, four-person dining table, wet bar with small refrigerator and microwave, writing desk, half bath, and balcony with savanna view. In the bedroom are two queen-size beds, entertainment center, vanity desk, and balcony. The bath has a double sink, both a tub and a large shower, and a separate room for the commode. Sleeps six.

Two-bedroom suites have the same living room layout, but the master bedroom has a king-size bed, easy chair and ottoman, and a separate vanity area. A standard-size second bedroom with two queen-size beds sits off the foyer with a standard bath. Sleeps eight.

For something grand, book the newly renovated, two-bedroom, two-and-a-half-bath Royal Assante Suite with more than 2,115 square feet of exotic luxury. Located on the fifth floor and reminiscent of famous African lodges, it offers panoramic views of the main savanna teeming with exotic wildlife.

In my opinion this is Disney's best suite. Just off the entry is the dining room boasting a massive table made from a single tree trunk and eight faux zebra-upholstered chairs. The suite's highlight is its circular living room with a fascinating thatch ceiling completely surrounded by a stand-up balcony, hardwood and stone flooring, rich African textiles and artwork, a rock fireplace, and hand-carved furnishings including an assortment of easy chairs and a curved sofa. The master bedroom comes with a mosquito net–draped king bed composed of tree trunks, a wall of reed built-ins filled with drawers and a flat-panel TV, and a sitting area with sleeper sofa and drum-style table. The adjoining bath is one of Disney's best with its free-standing soaking tub, double sinks, vanity, shower, mini TV, and separate commode and bidet area. The second bedroom is standard size with two queen beds. A deep balcony with lounge chairs and outdoor dining table runs the length of both bedrooms, perfect for dinner overlooking the savanna. You'll also find a half bath with a river rock vanity and raised basin, an office featuring a grass cloth and copper clad desk, and a service kitchen with a full-size refrigerator, wet bar, microwave, and separate entry.

The two-bedroom, two-and-a-half-bath Royal Kuba Vice Presidential Suite at 1,619 square feet, also located on the fifth floor, is another gem. Similar to the Royal Assante Suite, it simply comes with rooms that are a bit smaller in size and without an office, but with the same amazing decor, thatch ceiling, master bedroom, bath, and balcony.

**Animal Kingdom Villas Jambo House.** In the existing Animal Kingdom Lodge and located on the fifth or sixth floors are the Jambo House Villas, available in studio, one-, and two-bedroom units. Similar to the lodge's guest rooms with rich, warm fabrics, lovely carved wood furnishings, earthy colors, and a warm atmosphere, they are winners in my book.

Studios offer 316 to 365 square feet and come with a queen bed adorned with mosquito netting above the headboard, sleeper sofa, table and two chairs, flat-panel TV in a bureau, freestanding armoire closet, and a balcony. There's also the typical wet bar mini-kitchen with microwave, sink, and refrigerator. In the bath is a tub and single sink with the commode separate.

The one-bedroom villa has 629 to 710 square feet. You'll find a small kitchen with a full-size stove and refrigerator, sink, and dishwasher and a very small, free-standing island. The parlor has a chocolate brown sleeper sofa, an oversized, pumpkin-colored sleeper easy chair, a table with a two-person bench and two chairs, coffee table, flat-panel TV, and balcony. Most sleep five. The master comes with a king bed, leopard motif carpeting, bureau with TV, desk, and a second balcony. In the bath are double sinks in a granite vanity, whirlpool bathtub decorated with a setting sun Lion King mural, and separate commode area. There's also a washer, dryer, and two balconies.

A two-bedroom villa is a one-bedroom plus a connecting studio with 945 to 1075 square feet.

There are six Grand Villas with three bedrooms, four baths, and 2,349 glorious square feet. All are on one level and are located at the end of each wing.

CARA'S TIP: What the Animal Kingdom Villas Jambo House call Value Villas are smaller villas minus the sleeper chair in a living area.

## DINE

An interesting array of dining choices, many with an African flair, will please even the most timid eaters. Wine connoisseurs will love the fact that the Animal Kingdom Lodge has one of the largest offerings of South African wines in the United States.

**Boma.** Lively African and American buffet open for breakfast and dinner. (See full description in Dining chapter.)

**Jiko.** One of Disney's loveliest restaurants; dinner only; international food with an African flair and an extensive South African wine list. (See full description in Dining chapter.)

**The Mara.** Self-service snack bar; open 6 a.m. to 11:30 p.m. (grill opens at 7 a.m.); *breakfast:* scrambled eggs, waffles, brioche French toast, egg and bacon croissant sandwich, breakfast pizza or wrap, fruit smoothies, oatmeal, pastries, croissants, cinnamon rolls, muffins, specialty coffees; *lunch and dinner:* flatbreads, African stew, falafel pita, chicken pita, chicken Caesar salad, chicken nuggets, turkey ciabatta, fried shrimp, burger, rotisserie chicken, fresh fruit, cold sandwiches, salads; South African bottled wine and beer; *children's menu:* hot dogs, rotisserie chicken, mac 'n' cheese, pizza; *dessert:* zebra domes (ganache-covered chocolate-coffee mousse), cheesecake, paw print brownies, carrot cake, freshly baked cookies.

**In-Room Dining.** Available 6 a.m. to midnight.

## SIP

**Capetown Lounge and Wine Bar.** Jiko's very small but eye-catching bar; one of the largest South African wine lists in the United States.

**Uzima Springs.** Thatch-roofed pool bar; specialty drinks, beer, wine, nonalcoholic smoothies.

**Victoria Falls.** Lounge overlooking Boma (Sigh! Too bad it doesn't overlook the savanna); open 4 p.m. to midnight; African bush lodge atmosphere; cocktails, South African wine, port, and beer; *appetizers:* fruit and cheese platter, nut mix with African spices, shrimp cocktail, crisp breads and dip.

## PLAY

**Arcade.** Pumba's Fun and Games arcade located near the pool.

**Children's playground and activities.** Hakuna Matata playground near pool with a nice view of the flamingo area and the savanna; flamingo feedings, medallion rubbing, cookie decorating, wildlife games, African games and crafts at the pool, primal parades.

**Jiko Wine Dinners.** Begin with a reception on the terrace followed by dinner and wine pairings in Jiko's private dining room; offered at various dates throughout the year; call (407) 939-3463 for reservations or (407) 938-7149 for specific information.

**Storytelling.** African folktales shared each evening around the outdoor Arusha Firepit.

**Swimming.** Uzima Pool, the lodge's 11,000-square-foot version of a watering hole, highlighted by a 67-foot waterslide; cement is darkened to create the effect of swimming out in the bush, minus the crocodiles; two secluded whirlpools; kiddie pool.

**Tennis.** Two courts located next-door at Animal Kingdom Villas Kidani Village.

**Tours and activities.** Culinary tour of the resort's restaurants; animal tracking; animal viewing with night vision; cultural safaris.

**Wanyama Safari.** Open only to Animal Kingdom Lodge guests, this is one of Disney's best resort tours, which includes a game drive around the resort's savannas in an open-air safari van followed by a preset, multicourse meal with wine pairings at Jiko; just before sunset on Monday, Wednesday, Friday, and Saturday but can also be reserved on the other days of the week with a minimum of four guests; minimum age is eight; reservations taken at (407) 938-4755 as early as 180 days in advance; only eight guests per evening allowed so book early.

### WORK, MOVE, SOOTHE

**Child care.** Simba's Cubhouse with classic Disney movies, play kitchen, viewing window to the savanna, arts and crafts, arcade and computer games. Open 4:30 p.m. to midnight, for potty-trained children ages four to twelve; cost includes dinner and snacks; open to all registered guests of Walt Disney World resorts; call (407) WDW-DINE or (407) 939-3463 for reservations.

**Fitness center.** Zahanati Massage and Fitness Center; free weights, Cybex strength training equipment, Life Fitness treadmills, exercise bicycles, ellipticals; steam room and sauna in each locker room (fitness center is complimentary to resort guests); personal training; facials, massage, and body treatments with in-room service available for an additional fee; open 6 a.m. to 9 p.m.

### GO

Bus transportation is available to all four Disney theme parks, Downtown Disney, Typhoon Lagoon, and Blizzard Beach. To reach other Disney resorts, you must first take a bus to Downtown Disney or an open theme park and then transfer to your resort destination.

## The Animal Kingdom Villas Kidani Village

**492 units. 3701 Osceola Parkway, Lake Buena Vista 32830; phone (407) 938-3000, fax (407) 938-4799. Check-in 4 p.m., checkout 11 a.m. For reservations call (407) WDW-DISNEY or (407) 939-3476, or contact your travel agent. $$–$$$$$**

**Why Stay Here?** Great savanna views in roomy villas and a remote resort far from the madness of the theme parks.

**Rooms to Book.** Definitely one with savanna views, but the three-bedroom, two-story Grand Villas, if the pocketbook allows, are quite the treat.

**Don't Miss.** Time spent at the fire pit, the perfect place to enjoy the wildlife on a starry night.

As at the next-door Animal Kingdom Lodge, this new Deluxe Villa Resort property has the advantage of a savanna teeming with wildlife along with roomy and distinctive villas. You'll also find a full-service restaurant, feature pool, fitness center, and water play area. An attractive two-story lobby area with African rustic chic seating, hardwood flooring, and tribal rugs sports a delightful thatched ceiling. Scattered here and there throughout the resort are superb viewing areas with rockers, perfect for those guests without a savanna view, and off the lobby is the Library offering a restful sitting room with a fireplace as well as a balcony with savanna views. Guests are entitled to all privileges of the next-door Animal Kingdom Lodge including the pool, playground, and childcare, but plan on a 10-minute walk to reach it.

## REST

Villas here are atmospheric and very similar to the next-door Jambo House with hand-carved furnishings, tile entries, ostrich egg lamps, muraled tub surrounds, chocolate brown granite countertops, animal print carpeting, khaki curtains with leather strapping, a Lion King theme, and a chocolate and persimmon-colored decor with African textile touches. Headboards are made of carved, dark wood, bedspreads are the same as at the next-door Jambo House, and each bed is topped with a mosquito netting decoration. Every bedroom has its own TV, DVD player, and iPod docking station clock radio. And each unit has a laptop-size electronic safe, vacuum, iron and ironing board, and Pack 'n' Play.

**Studios.** Studios sleep up to four with 366 square feet. A queen-size bed (not terribly comfortable, made up with a thin blanket and no duvet) is accompanied by a sleeper sofa, table and two chairs, bureau with built-in flat-panel TV, and DVD player. Two closets are to be found, one a carved wood armoire. Strangely missing is a table on one side of the bed (I used an upside-down trash can to make do). You'll also find a mini-kitchen with sink, under-counter refrigerator, microwave, toaster, and coffee maker. Baths have a single-sink granite vanity (no makeup mirror), a tub/shower combination, and separate commode area. All have a balcony with varying views.

**Villas.** One-bedroom villas sleep five with 807 square feet. The living room has a chocolate brown sleeper sofa as well as a persimmon-colored sleeper chair, a flat-panel TV, and DVD player. The villa's small granite kitchen comes with a two-seat dining bar, coffee maker, dinnerware, glassware, flatware, pots and pans, microwave, toaster, stove, refrigerator, and dishwasher. A laundry area closet contains a stacked washer and dryer, and in the entry is an extra full bath. The master bedroom suite is comfortable with its king-size bed, desk, and bureau with flat-panel TV. The adjoining terra cotta bath is all one space (as opposed to the two-room baths in the other Deluxe Villa properties) with a whirlpool tub, large shower, single sink, and separate commode area. The villa's balcony is accessed from both the living area and master bedroom.

The two-bedroom villa is a studio plus a one-bedroom villa and sleeps up to nine people with 1,173 square feet. A dedicated two-bedroom's second bedroom has two queen-size beds and lacks a mini-kitchen and its own entry.

Sixteen Grand Villas sleep up to twelve people and offer spectacular views (avoid those located at the very end of the property whose views are not up to par). With three bedrooms and four baths on two levels, you'll find the kitchen, dining area, living room, master bedroom, and extra bath on the first floor, and two bedrooms, two baths, and a TV room on the second floor (entry doors are found on both floors). The kitchen is open to the adjoining six-person dining table and buffet. In the soaring, open, two-story living area is tile flooring topped with a colorful rug, a sleeper sofa, sleeper chair, easy chair, and entertainment center with TV and stereo system. A balcony covers the length of the bottom floor. A king-bedded master, similar to the one found in the standard villas, is just off the living area with a whirlpool tub and extra TV in the bath. Climb the kraal fence stairwell to the second floor where two identical bedrooms, each with two queen beds and its own balcony, flank the loft TV room with sleeper sofa. A full-size laundry room is found downstairs. 2,201 square feet.

*CARA'S TIP:* Standard villas offer a view of the front of the resort or the pool, but worse yet could possibly face the valet parking drop-off area with a constant stream of buses and cars passing by your room balcony at all hours of the day and night. From all of the savanna view rooms you will also have a view of the next-door Animal Kingdom Lodge. A lobby level villa (floor two) comes with up-close-and-personal savanna view so think about requesting one.

## DINE

**Sanaa.** The villas' only full-service restaurant offering African cooking with Indian flavors for lunch and dinner; huge picture windows overlook the resort's savanna. (See full description in Dining chapter.)

## SIP

**Maji Pool Bar.** Great pool bar with interesting views of a bird sanctuary; club sandwich, Caesar salad with tandoori chicken, or order from private dining with food served in a bento box with choices of turkey club sandwich, tandoori Angus chuck burger, naan wrap sandwiches (grilled shrimp and vegetable, vegetarian chickpea salad, tandoori chicken and vegetable, or grilled lamb); frozen novelties, smoothies; specialty drinks, beer, wine, sangria.

**Sanaa Lounge.** Small but unique, thatch roof bar located within Sanaa restaurant with specialty drinks such as African mojitos, Malawi mango margaritas, and Kande coconut coolers; beer and an international wine list including South African choices; *appetizers:* Indian-style bread service with your choice of three breads and three accompaniments, potato and pea samosas, lamb kefta with dried papaya sauce.

## PLAY

**Arcade.** Safari So Good Arcade located near the lobby area.

**Barbeque Pavilion.** Fire up the grills and picnic alfresco in this atmospheric natural setting with views of a wildlife pond; located near the sports court.

**Basketball and shuffleboard.** Courts are located across the street in a nature setting; complimentary equipment available at Community Hall.

**Children's playground and activities.** Arts and crafts, pool parties, trivia, bingo, Wii tournaments; Camp Kidani is a fee-based activity time from 6 to 8 p.m. at Community Hall learning about animals and African cultures with rotating activities throughout the week: reptiles and amphibians, birds, sports and games, African art, or mammals.

# CHRISTMAS AT WALT DISNEY WORLD

Christmas is a special time at Walt Disney World, when it's adorned with more than 1,200 Christmas trees, 10 miles of garland, eight million lights, and 300,000 yards of ribbon. If you'd like to bring your Christmas spirit up a few notches, just head to one of the following locations:

- The Magic Kingdom features a huge Christmas tree in Town Square, garland and lights draped down Main Street, and a special Christmas parade. Mickey's Very Merry Christmas Party, an after-park-hours ticketed event, is one of the most popular holiday events, so book early.

- Epcot's Liberty Inn has Santa's Bakeshop, a life-size gingerbread house selling Christmas cookies and beverages. World Showcase features Christmas storytelling from around the world, and each night Mickey and his friends hold a Christmas tree lighting ceremony. There's even a special Illuminations finale. Best of all is the Candlelight Processional, staged three times each evening from late November through December 30, with a massed choir, fifty-piece orchestra, and celebrity narrators who tell the story of Christmas.

- Disney's Hollywood Studios is one of the most popular places around, with its fantastic Osborne Family Spectacle of Lights, millions of colorful, twinkling Christmas lights on the Streets of America. And don't forget to catch the Hollywood Holly-Day Parade each afternoon.

- The Animal Kingdom hosts Mickey's Jingle Jungle Parade complete with Santa, Goofy, and falling snow. Carolers greet guests around the 65-foot-tall Christmas tree at the park's entrance, and children have the opportunity to meet Disney characters dressed in holiday finery at Camp Minnie-Mickey.

- At Disney's Contemporary Resort is Walt Disney World's largest wreath, as well as Gepetto's workshop featuring Pinocchio, all made of chocolate and sugar.

- The Grand Floridian lobby's life-size, 300-square-foot gingerbread house is a wonder. It doubles as a real bakeshop from which you can purchase all sorts of Christmas goodies.

- Animal Kingdom Lodge features an entirely edible miniature African village of sugar, chocolate, and gingerbread.

- The Beach Club display is a life-size gingerbread and chocolate carousel.

- The Yacht Club presents a miniature train running through a sugary village and a mountain made of sweets.

**Community Hall.** Head here for arts and crafts, board games, table tennis, foosball, game stations, and TV viewing; located on the second floor just off the lobby area.

**Firepit.** An atmospheric fire is found nightly, perfect for stargazing.

**Swimming.** Samawati Springs Pool is located in a tranquil area off to the side of the resort; 128-foot water slide; two whirlpools; Uwanja Camp, a super-fun interactive water play area for children with water cannons, overflowing water tower, spitting snakes, rope bridges, geyser jets, and a waterfall lagoon with three zones for different age groups (watch out for the spitting African masks!).

**Tennis.** Two lighted hard courts are located across the street in a nature setting; complimentary equipment available at Community Hall.

**Tours and activities.** Cultural tour of Sanaa, African artifacts tour, African Inspired Disney Designs Tour, and a nightly African celebration in the lobby.

**WORK, MOVE, SOOTHE**

The Animal Kingdom Villas Kidani Village shares all services with the adjacent Animal Kingdom Lodge. (See the earlier entry for the Animal Kingdom Lodge.)

**Fitness Center.** Survival of the Fittest Fitness Center located in the pool area; free weights, Life Fitness treadmills, exercise bicycles, elliptical cross trainers; twenty-four-hour access.

**GO**

Bus transportation is available to all four Disney theme parks, Downtown Disney, Typhoon Lagoon, and Blizzard Beach. To reach other Disney resorts, you must first take a bus to Downtown Disney or an open theme park and then transfer to your resort destination.

# Other Notable Resorts Near Disney

Those who want a resort with easy access to the theme parks (but without Mickey Mouse at every turn) should consider one of the luxury resorts within a five- to twenty-minute drive from Disney. These include the Gaylord Palms Resort, the Hyatt Regency Grand Cypress, the Omni Orlando Resort at ChampionsGate, the Waldorf Astoria Orlando, and the Reunion Resort. Another great choice is All Star Vacation Homes with four, five, or more bedrooms.

## All Star Vacation Homes

**7822 West Irlo Bronson Highway, Kissimmee, Florida 34747; phone (407) 997-0733, fax (407) 997-1370. Check-in 4 p.m., checkout 11 a.m. For reservations call (800) 572-5013 or book online at http://allstarvacationhomes.com. $$–$$$**

**Why Stay Here?** Up to seven bedrooms at a less expensive nightly price than a standard Disney Deluxe Resort room.

**Home to Book.** Acadia #8016 is a seven-bedroom/six-and-a-half-bath delight with a media room and swimming pool.

**Don't Miss.** Asking for the complimentary rental car or $100 gas or grocery gift card that comes with a 7-night stay.

Those looking for the comforts of an estate-style house close to Disney property should consider All Star Vacation Homes. With three to seven bedrooms, they accommodate from eight to sixteen people for about the price of a hotel room at a deluxe Disney resort. I think you'll be surprised how very close they are to Disney, actually closer to the Animal Kingdom than the Magic Kingdom is to the Animal Kingdom, with each property within 4 miles of Walt Disney World.

At the All Star office, check-in is quick and well-organized with an efficient and friendly staff happy to help you with dining reservations, car rentals, golf tee times, and more (concierge service is available prior to arrival and even includes arrangement for grocery delivery for a small fee). Here you'll also find complimentary Internet terminals as well as DVDs and PlayStation games available for checkout.

Although All Star has a wide range of accommodations to choose from, I've only reviewed the 5-Star Homes for maximum luxury. Each has a screened-in heated pool, fully equipped gourmet kitchen, barbecue grill, entertainment systems, and washer/dryer, and all have multiple master bedrooms, just the thing for a family reunion or couples traveling together. Beds come with pillow-top mattresses, and each bedroom has a TV and DVD or VCR. In the baths are plenty of thick towels, hair dryers, and high-quality bath products. A mid-size car rental is complimentary with a seven-night stay (or $100 worth of gas or groceries) except during holiday periods. A cleaning fee is assessed unless your stay is six nights or longer and varies according to the size of the rental; daily or mid-stay cleans can be requested for an additional charge. The nice thing is that each home, along with photos of every room in the house, is viewable online at http://allstarvacationhomes.com, making it simple to pick the perfect decor to fit your personality. Do expect granite countertops in the kitchen, but you'll find that many of the homes have non-stone counters in the baths. And many of the homes have heavy leather furnishings, which may or may not be to your taste.

The cons: There is a four-night minimum except during Easter, Christmas, and New Year's, when a seven-night minimum is imposed. And the homes are located off U.S. Highway 192 in Kissimmee, certainly not my favorite stretch of highway, loaded with fast-food chains and franchise restaurants. The good thing is that you'll only have to travel about 2 blocks of it before turning down a quiet avenue to your roomy, comfortable vacation home.

**REST**

5-Star Home accommodations are found in three communities within a few blocks of the All Star office:

**Formosa Gardens.** A gated community with the largest homes in All Star's repertoire. Ranging from about 3,400 to 3,600 square feet, homes are freshly painted and clean as a whistle. All have screened-in private pools with hot tubs. The caveat is that they have less stringent decor regulations, making them a bit hit or miss. But the online photos will help you choose the decor that appeals. Pluses such as big-screen TVs, game rooms, super-comfortable mattresses, and plenty of room to spread out overrides any interior decoration concerns. My home even had a computer with high-speed Internet.

**Acadia Estates.** The five-, six-, and seven-bedroom homes in the gated community of Acadia Estate are newer and more standardized than Formosa Gardens, but each has its own personal touch. Most are around 3,000 square feet, all with screened-in private pools with hot tubs, and each has a garage that has been converted into a home theater. The only caveat are the smaller lots compared to the larger ones in Formosa Gardens. I love home #8006 and its tropical wall colors, Tommy Bahama–style decor, and the fact that it has both a game room and home theater.

**Windsor Hills.** The difference here is that there are game rooms instead of media rooms in four-, five-, and six-bedroom homes, all with private pools. There's also a water park pool with clubhouse stocked with billiards tables, video game area, sundry shop, and fitness room with top of the line fitness equipment.

Whatever home you choose, I believe you will feel as if you've received a super vacation value.

## Gaylord Palms Resort

**1,406 rooms. 6000 West Osceola Parkway, Kissimmee 34746; phone (407) 586-0000, fax (407) 586-1999. Check-in 3 p.m., checkout 11 a.m. For reservations call (407) 586-2000 or your travel agent, or go online at www.gaylordpalms.com. $–$$$$$**

**Why Stay Here?** A delightful atmosphere, a super spa, and one of the best restaurants around, Old Hickory Steakhouse.

**Rooms to Book.** The Hemingway Suite, a masculine charmer that you won't soon forget.

**Don't Miss.** A half-day enjoying the resort's Relâche Spa.

The Gaylord Palms' claim to fame is its fascinating, four-acre glass-domed atrium. Conveniently located at I–4 and Osceola Parkway, it's only a five-minute drive to Walt Disney World and just fifteen minutes to Universal Studios. Beneath the stunning Grand Atrium sit the Emerald Bay and St. Augustine areas, where visitors will find a replica of a Spanish fort, lush vegetation, towering palms, rushing waterfalls, shopping opportunities, and Gator Springs with its juvenile alligators and native turtles. Escape to the tropics in the festive, five-story Key West wing where a 60-foot schooner is moored in a blue lagoon surrounded by piers, palm trees, sand sculptures, and daily sunset celebrations. Everyone's favorite locale is the intimate Everglades, where elevated boardwalks cross over a foggy swamp filled with metal-roofed shanties (one of which is the upscale Old Hickory Steakhouse), lofty cypress trees, croaking frogs, and flashing lightning bugs. All of this under one giant dome.

Because this is a major convention hotel with more than 400,000 square feet of meeting facilities and ballrooms, I suggest steering clear of here when any large conferences are occurring. The best times for leisure travelers are the summer months or around Christmas and New Year's, when more than two million pounds of ice are carved into a wintry wonderland at the resort's ICE! extravaganza.

Girlfriend Getaways can be organized and are customized with your own Experience Coordinator. Great ideas include a private wine tasting, a manicure party, game night with cocktails and snacks, private shopping spree, a pedicure party, even a bachelorette getaway or boot camp. Designated group planners get upgraded to a suite, a perfect place for the group to gather.

**REST**

**Guest rooms.** Very comfortable guest rooms offer 410 square feet with one king-size or two queen-size beds, a desk with two chairs, and armoire with old-style TV and mini-fridge stocked with water. Amenities in each room include an iron, ironing board, coffeemaker, CD player/alarm clock, a pair of two-line telephones (one of them cordless), on-demand movies, guest room doorbells with electronic "do not disturb" indicators, and laptop-size safes wired for recharging. One super feature is the in-room computing system with high-speed Internet, message center, and online guest services including housekeeping, valet, and bell services. Bathrooms have granite countertops, double sinks, lighted makeup and full-length mirrors, and hair dryers. What I'm hoping for is a change from bedspreads to more contemporary duvets, and with room renovations scheduled for 2010 this may be in the works. Most rooms have oversize showers in place of bathtubs. Inner rooms facing the atrium offer French doors leading to a pleasant balcony or patio, but be prepared to hear the noise from below; ask for a higher floor, avoid a room over one of the restaurants, or simply consider one of the Florida-view rooms that face the exterior but come without balconies and may have a view of the highway. A $15 per-night per-room resort fee covers Internet service, daily newspaper, two bottles of water daily, use of the fitness facility, shuttle service to Disney theme parks, and local phone calls up to twenty minutes.

The casual beach decor in the Key West area is a combination of white-washed cottage furnishings, energetic cabana-striped bedspreads awash in a myriad of bright tones, turtle motif sheers, and sea blue carpeting (probably my least favorite of the resort's room decors). Everglade rooms have light wood furnishings, moss green bedspreads, forest green carpeting, green granite baths (with a very strange striped mirror), and cheery dragonfly and fern motif curtains and wallpaper. Florida's Spanish influence is seen in the St. Augustine guest rooms located in the Grand Atrium. They feature a neutral color scheme of black and taupe, walnut furnishings, explorer map pillows and bed skirt fabric, carpeting reminiscent of Spanish tile, and tapestry and mosaic touches. Rooms in Emerald Bay are the most expensive. They have marble foyers, butternut-colored walls, dark walnut and mahogany furnishings, and whimsical gold-and-blue monkey motif bedspreads. Guests love the palm-imprinted wallpaper and elegant touches such as elevated beds, marble baths, and crown molding. Extra amenities for Emerald Bay include turndown service and robes.

**Suites.** There are plenty of choices in upscale accommodations with 115 suites on-property. All are one bedroom, one bath, but many come with the option of adding standard rooms on either side to make a two- or three-bedroom suite.

There are three types to choose from in the nine Presidential Suites, all found in either the Emerald Bay or St. Augustine areas. All come with Celebrity Services, a truly amazing personal concierge service. On my last visit they helped arrange spa treatments, dining reservations, airport limo, and more, all with that super personal touch, so rare in this day and age; one evening when I stayed in for dinner they even sent up a basket of DVDs along with milk and cookies.

The standard Presidential suite is beautifully decorated in updated decor and lavish fabrics. In the foyer you'll find a half bath and a sizeable office, then proceed to the living area with marble flooring, wet bar, baby grand piano, sofa, easy chairs, coffee table, and entertainment center. There's also a formal dining room seating ten adjoined by a kitchen and breakfast room. The master bedroom features a comfortable sitting room with large flat-panel TV and DVD player, four-poster king bed with a second TV, and large marble bath with whirlpool tub, separate shower, double sinks, mini TV, and toilet area. Several balconies run the length of the suite overlooking the atrium.

One of my favorite suites in Orlando is the oh-so-masculine Heming-way Suite, certainly a departure in style from the resort's other Presidential Suites. A bit smaller, it offers Ernest Hemingway memorabilia and is surrounded by balconies (five in all). In the living room you'll find a leather sofa, three easy chairs, animal-print rug, settee, chaise, desk, entertainment center with DVD player and TV, silk drapery, and a stereo system. Separated by a half-wall is an eight-person circular dining table with rattan chairs and animal print cushions, an oriental rug, and buffet. Off the dining area is a kitchen with sink, dishwasher, refrigerator, microwave, and two-person breakfast table. A half-bath is found near the foyer. The angular bedroom has a rattan bed, sofa, and entertainment center. In the bath is an extra large whirlpool tub, separate steam shower, and double sinks. This can become a two-bedroom suite with the addition of a standard room that connects off the entry hall.

A third type of Presidential Suite faces the front of the resort, is octagonal in shape, and lacks an atrium view.

Other suite types, located throughout the resort with furnishings according to area, include Executive Suites and Deluxe Suites, both great choices.

Executive Suites, available in each resort themed area, have a separate living area from the bedroom with a sleeper sofa, coffee table, entertainment center with TV and DVD player, desk, easy chair, and balcony. In the king bedroom is another TV, and the bath is similar to a standard guest room's. Deluxe Suites, also available in each resort themed area, come with a parlor where you'll find a dining table, two easy chairs, ottoman coffee table, sleeper sofa, entertainment center, and wet bar. Off the hallway between the living room and the bedroom is a balcony (only in those suites located in a corner) as well as a slightly larger-than-standard-size bath. In the oversized bedroom you'll find a desk, king bed, entertainment center, chair, and ottoman, as well as a second balcony. Those in Emerald Bay have an eight-person dining table and two balconies off the living/dining area.

## DINE

**Ben and Jerry's.** Hand-scooped Ben and Jerry's ice cream, sundaes, banana splits, milk shakes, fruit smoothies.

**H20 Sports Bar & Grill.** Pool bar with indoor and outdoor seating and ten TV screens for sporting events; Mediterranean salad, Florida cobb salad, flatbreads, shaved prime rib sandwich, crab cake sandwich, caprese sandwich, blackened mahi sandwich with remoulade sauce, buffalo chicken sandwich; specialty drinks, beer, wine; open 11 a.m. to 11 p.m.

**Java Coast.** Twenty-four-hour coffee shop; specialty coffees, wine, beer, sodas, juice; pastries, cereal, yogurt, bagels, turnovers, muffins, oatmeal cookies; soup, salads, fruit, sandwiches, quiche; cakes, pies.

**Old Hickory Steakhouse.** Dine above the swamps of the romantic Everglades on steaks and seafood; dinner only. (See full description in Dining chapter.)

**Sora.** Ultra hip sushi bar open early evening and for dinner; feast on sushi and sashimi, spicy tuna nachos, coconut curry crab bisque, bento box of the day, bao bun sandwiches, oven roasted five spice duck, miso glazed Chilean sea bass, and lobster fritters; Asian cocktail concoctions come with ingredients like green tea liquor and plum sake; favorites include the Zen cocktail with green tea liqueur, peach schnapps, and sauvignon blanc, or the Fragrant with gin, simple syrup, pomegranate juice, lemon juice, and club soda.

**Sunset Sam's Fish Camp.** Delightfully fun Key West–style seafood restaurant open for lunch and dinner; 60-foot sailboat bar overlooking the lagoon with island-style entertainment nightly, colossal drinks, and raw bar; conch and clam chowder, fresh fish and shrimp tacos, crab cakes, crispy whole yellowtail snapper, seared George's Bank sea scallops, fisherman's stew.

**Villa de Flora.** Mediterranean buffet with chef stations in an Old World–style mansion atmosphere; open for breakfast, lunch, and dinner. Italian-themed meals on Monday and Friday, Spain on Tuesday and Saturday, France Wednesday and Sunday, and Greece on Thursday; build your own Ben & Jerry's sundae and strawberry shortcake bar; nightly live entertainment; popular Sunday brunch.

**In-Room Dining.** Available 24/7.

### SIP

**Auggie's Jammin' Piano Bar.** Sing along with comedic dueling pianos playing old favorites; open 7 p.m. to 1:30 a.m.; piano music begins at 9 p.m.

**Old Hickory Steakhouse Bar.** Attractive candlelit bar adjoining the Old Hickory Steakhouse overlooking the misty swamps of the Everglades; martinis, port, sherry, wine, beer, single-malt scotch, specialty drinks, cognac; *appetizers:* shrimp or crab cocktail, smoked salmon, steak tartare, artisanal cheese plates, tenderloin of alligator lasagna, oysters Rockefeller, jumbo lump crab cakes, warm pear Gorgonzola tart, foie gras. If you're in luck, Apalachicola oysters will be on the menu.

**Sunset Sam's Fish Camp Bar.** Sixty-foot sailboat bar anchored in the lagoon in front of Sunset Sam's Fish Camp Restaurant; oversize island-style drinks on the SS *Gaylord;* raw bar; evening sunset celebration Jimmy Buffett–style with steel band, stilt walkers, and balloon animals for the kids.

### PLAY

**Arcade.** Located in the shopping area.

**Children's playground.** Sand beach playground next to Clearwater Cove Pool.

**Golf.** At nearby Falcon's Fire Golf Club, an eighteen-hole Rees Jones signature designed course, just 2 miles away; complimentary transportation and reserved tee times for registered guests. Coquina Dunes, a 9-hole executive putting course complete with sand traps, roughs, and dogleg bends, is located near the South Beach Pool.

**Recreation park.** Located between the hotel and convention center is an executive putting course (see Golf above), bocce court (complimentary), and croquet lawn (complimentary).

**Swimming.** Clearwater Cove with zero-depth entry, delightful octopus slide, whirlpool, water-jet play area, and kiddie pool; adjoining sandy beach and children's playground; adults-only South Beach Pool with two whirlpools.

**Tours and fun activities.** Tuesday Horticulture Tour; Tuesday, Thursday, and Saturday Alligator Feedings at Gator Springs in the Grand Atrium at 6:30 p.m.; fish feedings at Key West Lagoon Monday through Friday at 3 p.m.

**Volleyball.** A sand volleyball court is near the South Beach Pool.

### WORK, MOVE, SOOTHE

**Business center.** Located within the convention center with copying, faxing, printing, mailing, packing, shipping, computer stations, laptop connections, office supplies, and equipment rentals; open daily 7 a.m. to 8 p.m.

**Car rental.** Hertz Car Rental counter in the lobby.

**Child care.** In-room childcare can be arranged through Kid's Nite Out.

**Hair salon.** Relâche Spa Salon; hair and nail treatments, makeup consultation, makeovers; open 8 a.m. to 8 p.m. Monday through Thursday and 8 a.m. to 9 p.m. Friday through Sunday.

**Fitness center.** A 4,000-square-foot fitness facility is complimentary to guests; Life Fitness exercise machines, treadmills, elliptical cross trainers, upright and recumbent bicycles, free weights, Smith press system; fee-based classes including yoga, Pilates, kickboxing, meditation, body sculpt, tai chi; open 5:30 a.m. to 9:30 p.m.

**Spa.** Relâche Spa, a 20,000-square-foot facility with twenty-five treatment rooms; spa boutique; open 8 a.m. to 8 p.m.; call (407) 586-4772 for reservations. (See full description in Spas section of chapter 5, Beyond the Theme Parks.)

**GO**

Complimentary shuttle service is available to all four Walt Disney World parks, departing almost hourly during park operating hours. Ten daily shuttles go to SeaWorld, Universal Orlando, and Wet 'n' Wild. A car is suggested for added convenience.

## Hyatt Regency Grand Cypress

**750 rooms. 1 Grand Cypress Boulevard, Orlando 32836; phone (407) 239-1234, fax (407) 239-3800. Check-in 4 p.m., checkout noon. For reservations call (800) 233-1234 or your travel agent, or go online at www.hyattgrandcypress.com. $$–$$$$$**

**Why Stay Here?** Newly upgraded, contemporary rooms, lovely gardens, and close proximity to Downtown Disney.

**Rooms to Book.** Regency Club rooms with a view of Walt Disney World.

**Don't Miss.** Hopping on one of the resort's bicycles to explore the fascinating cypress swamp nature preserve.

Located less than a mile from Walt Disney World and around the corner from Downtown Disney is the Hyatt Regency Grand Cypress Resort. Don't be put off by the slightly dated pyramid exterior—all doubts evaporate as you enter the luxuriant, eighteen-story atrium lobby, a soothing tropical atmosphere of verdant palm trees, flowering foliage, and trickling streams that complement a notable art collection. The warm welcome continues with a glass of champagne and a congenial staff ready and waiting to assist.

Opulent grounds quickly lure guests outside to a 1,500-acre wonderland of lush landscaping featuring more than 20,000 shrubs, 50,000 annuals, a private lake, and a fantasyland pool. Stroll along meandering pathways through exotic tropical foliage intermingling with moss-covered boulders, trickling waterfalls, sculpture gardens, and soothing ponds. Or relax lakeside in swaying hammocks while swans glide gracefully across the waters of Lake Windsong. There's plenty of room to spread out with miles of golf courses and the most extensive nature trails around. Hop on a complimentary bicycle and pedal to your heart's content.

With 65,000 square feet of meeting space, be prepared for plenty of conventioneers. Here, however, ballrooms are in a separate downstairs

area out of the way of public spaces, giving the resort a much more inviting feel than most convention hotels.

**REST**

**Guest rooms.** Glass elevators rise to understated but elegant and chic
guest rooms with 360 square feet of space. Sophisticated and newly
restyled, they feature a contemporary look with crisp white bedding offset
with soothing soft blue accents in bolsters, throw pillows, and duvets, all
with a slightly tropical feel. Hyatt Grand beds feature a 13-inch-thick,
pillow-top Sealy Posturepedic mattress, Egyptian cotton sheets, sleek
leather headboards and a white down duvet topped with a sea blue runner. Natural colored walls are mixed with grass cloth, and artwork is
tropical pop. New additions include a 36-inch flat-panel TV mounted on
resin artwork, iHome clock radio with iPod dock, touch-sensitive lighting,
and a marble-topped walnut swivel desk with a designer leather and stainless chair. A full-length mirror and closet are found in the hallway behind
a frosted glass sliding door and include a laptop-size electronic safe. The
entry hall marble tile continues in the adjoining bath with contemporary
Toto fixtures, a single sink in a white Corian vanity over which sits a
frosted glass framed mirror, a frameless glass shower with a ceiling rain
shower in king rooms, and a glass enclosed bath/shower in rooms with two
double beds. The commode area is in a separate space. Extra amenities
include a lighted makeup mirror, scale, and dark rattan bath accessories.
Also included are an undercounter refrigerator, coffeemaker, daily newspaper, robes, two dual-line telephones, a standing-room-only balcony,
iron and ironing board, coffeemaker, and on-demand movies. King rooms
have the addition of a beige sleeper sofa. The only difference between a
standard and a deluxe room is simply in the view. An $18 per-room per-
day resort fee covers access to high-speed Internet in guest rooms, local
and toll-free telephone service charges, fitness center, shuttle to theme
parks, Pitch 'n' Putt Golf, rock climbing wall, golf driving range, bicycles,
tennis court time, and non-motorized boats.

*CARA'S TIP:* Light sleepers will want a room away from the atrium in
order to avoid the music wafting up from the lobby bar. Views include a
Buena Vista view (a view of the front of the resort and the surrounding
area), pool view, and lake view.

**Concierge rooms.** For about $100 more per night, consider upgrading to the Regency Club, located on the privately accessed eleventh and seventeenth floors. What you get for the extra cash outlay is an eleventh-floor lounge with a sweeping view, a professional and friendly concierge staff, complimentary fax service, robes, turndown service (with a fresh rose on the pillow), and of course plenty of food and snacks. An excellent continental breakfast includes specialty coffees, smoked salmon, cold cuts, cheese, bagels, toast, breakfast breads, croissants, donuts, muffins, fruit, yogurt, and cereal, and in the afternoon are beverages, cookies, nuts, and dried fruit. From 5 to 8:30 p.m. are appetizers like crudités, fruit, chips and salsa, spring rolls, cheese and lunchmeats, chicken flautas, quesadillas, cream cheese and artichoke pastries, spinach salad, chicken empanadas, wrap sandwiches, shrimp pasta, chicken and shrimp Caesar salad, wine, beer, and mixed drinks, and from 8:30 to 10 p.m. mini desserts and liqueurs in an adults-only atmosphere. Most guests seeking a quieter spot head to the tables set up outside the lounge, offering great vistas of the pool, the surrounding area, and the Epcot and Magic Kingdom fireworks.

**Suites.** After the guest room renovations are completed, work will begin on the suites. Executive Parlors have one or two standard guest rooms connecting to a living area with full-size sofa bed, easy chair, four-person table, and an extra full bath. In the VIP Suites is parquet flooring in the living area, which holds a sofa, three easy chairs, glass coffee table, wet bar with refrigerator, six-person dining table, full-size bath, and two stand-up balconies. A half bath is found off the marble foyer. To one side of the parlor is a standard guest room with two doubles and a balcony. From the other side is another king guest room with balcony, but with two baths and a vanity area in between. It can be reserved as either a one- or two-bedroom suite.

The one-bedroom, two-bath Hospitality Suites offer a standard guest room with king-size bed connected to a living area with a six-person marble dining and meeting table, large wet bar, and additional full bath. Ask for a twelfth-floor Hospitality Suite, which comes with one of the largest terraces I've ever seen, perfect for a reception. None of these suites has Regency Club access.

Five Penthouse Suites, each with a different color scheme and decor, are found on the seventeenth floor. Two of them are considered Owners Suites with a bilevel configuration—upstairs is a loft bedroom with king-size bed, desk, and armoire with TV as well as a bathroom with lovely whirlpool tub, separate shower, double sink, vanity, and upgraded toiletries. The downstairs living area boasts a six-person dining table, sizable sitting area, one with a baby grand piano, large wet bar with refrigerator, half bath, and giant-size patio with spectacular views. These two suites not only have access to the Regency Club but private butler service as well. An option is the addition of a downstairs connecting standard bedroom with two double beds.

Now for something really different, consider the intimate President's House, a gated home located on the shores of Lake Windsong. Enter through a marble foyer with a half bath to a living area with shiny hardwoods topped with an area rug, fireplace, sofa, love seat, two easy chairs, game table, baby grand piano, stereo system, plasma TV, and a six-person dining table, all with several sets of French doors leading to a wraparound screened deck overlooking the beach and lake. The full kitchen has granite countertops with a stove, refrigerator, dishwasher, and cappuccino machine. The king-bedded master comes with a lake view as well as a bureau, settee, entertainment center, deck, granite double-sinked bath with whirlpool tub, plasma TV, and separate shower. Off to the other side of the living area is a bedroom with a double bed, walk-in closet, and double-sink bath, and down the hall is a nice-size office with fax machine as well as an exercise room with treadmill, exercise bicycle, Stairmaster, and free weights with a double-sinked bath attached. There is also a full-size washer and dryer.

## DINE

**Cascade.** Casual dining spot centered around a 35-foot cascading mermaid fountain and views of the lush Hyatt grounds through its almost solid wall of windows; open for breakfast and lunch; Saturday and Sunday breakfast buffet.

**Hemingway's.** Steak and seafood in a Key West atmosphere; dinner only. (See full description in Dining chapter.)

**La Coquina.** Orlando's best Sunday champagne brunch overlooking Lake Windsong; Chef's Table dining in the kitchen Saturday nights; open only seasonally, late September through June; call (407) 239-3853 for reservations; complimentary valet or self-parking for restaurant guests.

**Palm Café & General Store.** Grab and go snack bar near pool; *breakfast:* Krispy Kreme doughnuts, French toast, omelets, pancakes, waffles, oatmeal, fruit; *lunch:* soup, pizza, Caesar salad, Mediterranean chicken salad, Italian wrap sandwich, ham and cheese, tuna, and roast beef sandwiches, fruit bowl; full-service dining with food from the next-door Cascade.

**Sushi Bar.** Located in the lobby bar area with traditional sushi and sake along with beer, martinis, and plum wine.

**White Horse Bar & Grill.** Upscale sports lounge open daily for dinner; sushi, sashimi, grilled beef tenderloin sandwich, Angus burger, crab cake sandwich, NY strip steak, grilled salmon; signature cocktails, martinis, sake, beer, wine.

**In-Room Dining.** Available 24/7.

### SIP

**Hurricane Lounge.** Atmospheric cocktail lounge adjoining Hemingway's restaurant; full bar with food from next-door Hemingway's; open nightly from 5:30 to 11 p.m.

**On the Rocks.** Pool bar located behind the waterfall in the grotto; cocktails, beer, smoothies; light meals of buffalo chicken wings, crisp calamari, chips and dip, Caesar salad, mixed fruit, tuna pita, grilled chicken club with avocado and jack cheese, crab cake sandwich, burgers.

**Trellises.** Hopping atrium lobby bar with cocktails, sushi, and live entertainment nightly; outside seating available; open 5 p.m. to midnight.

### PLAY

**Arcade.** Located behind the grotto pool's waterfall; video entertainment and pinball machines.

**Basketball.** Court located near Racquet Club; balls available from Racquet Club attendant.

**Beach.** A 1,000-foot beach on the shores of twenty-one-acre Lake Windsong with hammocks and lounge chairs.

**Boating.** Paddleboats, aqua cycles, hydro bikes, kayaks, sunfish sailboats, and canoes available at the Towel Hut next to pool for recreation on Lake Windsong; nonmotorized equipment complimentary for guests.

**Bicycles.** Available at the Towel Hut next to the pool; two bike paths, one 3.2 miles and the other 4.7 miles; complimentary for guests.

**Climbing rock wall.** Climbing rock wall found behind the Towel Hut; minimum height 42 inches; must weigh between 40 and 250 pounds; complimentary for guests.

**Fire pit.** Lit on the shore of Lake Windsong Thursday through Sunday evenings.

**Fishing.** Fishing permitted on Lake Windsong for guests only; catch-and-release.

**Golf.** The Grand Cypress Golf Club boasts four Jack Nicklaus–designed golf courses: the nine-hole North, the nine-hole South, the nine-hole East, and the eighteen-hole, St. Andrews–style New Course. At the Golf Club, located on the grounds of the resort's sister property, the Villas of Grand Cypress, are lessons and state-of-the-art computer instruction as well as a restaurant and sports bar; call (877) 330-7377 for information and reservations; golf desk in lobby available 8 a.m. to 4 p.m.

**Jogging.** Three jogging courses ranging from 1.3 miles to 4.7 miles meander through the property; map available at the fitness center or concierge.

**Nature area.** Fascinating forty-five-acre cypress swamp maintained in conjunction with the Florida Audubon Society; 1 mile of raised boardwalks with three side trails.

**Pitch 'n' Putt Golf.** On Lake Windsong; no tee time required; nine-hole, par-3 course; complimentary for guests.

**Swimming.** Sensational 800,000-gallon, half-acre pool with twelve waterfalls, meandering grottos, three whirlpools, swinging rope bridge, and 45-foot waterslide; only the smaller of the two pools is heated; open 24/7; no lifeguard; pool games include diving for tokens, cannonball contests, water volleyball tournaments; dive-in family movies every Saturday night in the summer months, weather permitting.

**Tennis.** Twelve tennis courts: eight clay (Har-Tru) and four hard (Deco-Turf II), five of which are lighted (call the Racquet Club at 407-239-1944 to reserve a court); court fees complimentary to guests. Two outdoor racquetball courts; pro shop; instructional packages for all levels, round robins, teen camps, racquet stringing, rentals, and ball machines.

**Volleyball.** Two courts: one sand court located at the beach and another court near the Racquet Club; water volleyball in grotto pool.

## WORK, MOVE, SOOTHE

**Business center.** Accessible twenty-four hours; staffed Monday through Friday, 7 a.m. to 7 p.m., and Saturday and Sunday 8 a.m. to 4 p.m.; computer, Internet, fax, copier, office supplies, secretarial services.

**Car rental.** Hertz Rent a Car in lobby.

**Child care.** Camp Hyatt for outside children's activities; open daily from Memorial Day to Labor Day 9 a.m. to 6 p.m., and weekends only the remainder of the year for children ages five to twelve; twenty-four-hour notice required; call (407) 239-1234 for reservations.

Another facility, the Childcare Center, offers arts and crafts, an outside play area, sand sculpting, volleyball, movies, Pitch 'n' Putt Golf, magic shows, nature walks, and tennis; open Sunday through Thursday from 8 a.m. to 10 p.m., and Friday and Saturday from 8 a.m. to 11 p.m., for potty-trained children ages three to twelve; arrangements can be made for a private in-room sitter with a twenty-four-hour advance notice.

**Hair salon.** The Salon at Grand Cypress open daily 9 a.m. to 5:30 p.m.; full range of salon services for men and women including pedicures, manicures, cut and color, facials, waxing, body polish.

**Fitness center.** Located behind grotto waterfall; Hyatt StayFit gym is outfitted with individual LCD screens in the Life Fitness treadmills, ellipticals, and Lifecycles; weight resistance machines; free weights; men's and women's locker rooms each with sauna and steam room; open 24/7; complimentary for guests; personal training and massage available by appointment; the YogaAway program offers guests in-room, on-demand yoga on your television for a fee.

## GO

Complimentary shuttle service within the resort is available 24/7, including service to the Villas of Grand Cypress Golf Club and all recreational facilities. Very intermittent shuttles to Disney's four theme parks, Universal Orlando, and SeaWorld. I would definitely advise a rental car for convenience.

## Omni Orlando Resort at ChampionsGate

**720 rooms and 59 villas. 1500 Masters Boulevard, Champions-Gate, Forida 33896; phone (407) 390-6664, fax (407) 390-6600. Check-in 3 p.m., checkout noon. For reservations call (888) 444-6664 or your travel agent, or online at www.omniorlandoresort .com. $$–$$$$$**

**Why Stay Here?** An amazing pool and superior golfing at an unbeatable price.

**Rooms to Book.** Consider the next-door Villas at ChampionsGate, lovely accommodations just a walk away to all that the resort has to offer.

**Don't Miss.** An afternoon enjoying the resort's lazy pool.

Six miles, a twenty-minute drive, and a world away from the hustle and bustle of Walt Disney World is this destination resort sure to please. The cream marble lobby scattered with Oriental rugs and touches of black and gold is an exquisite and sophisticated first impression. The real plus here is a Mediterranean-style resort surrounded by 1,200 acres of wetlands, two Greg Norman–designed golf courses, and a fifteen-acre recreational area. Since this is a convention resort, you'll find about 75 percent of the guests are convention attendees during the week; on the weekend are leisure travelers.

In addition to hotel accommodations are luxurious two- and three-bedroom condos at the next-door Villas at ChampionsGate, which shares all resort facilities with the Omni just a quick walk away.

### REST

**Guest rooms.** While nothing much has changed since the resort's opening in 2004, the well-appointed guest rooms still look nice and fresh with only the need to upgrade the old-style, oversized TVs. Soft green, gold, and splashes of blue accent 406-square-foot guest rooms rich with contemporary cherry wood furnishings. Either one king with an easy chair or two double beds are appointed with cream-colored diamond weave spreads topped with a pale blue knit cotton throw blanket and plaid and floral pillows. Relax in a comfy dandelion-colored easy chair with ottoman. There's also a small work desk and a bamboo-trimmed armoire holding a flat-screen TV and minibar. Baths have a black marble vanity with a single sink, bath/shower combination, lighted makeup mirror, Institute Swiss bath products, and thick towels. Pluses include triple sheeting, soft down pillows, pillow-top mattresses, bathrobes, full-length mirror, on-demand movies, laptop-size electronic safe, iron and ironing board, and two phones with dual lines, one a cordless. There is, however, no room balcony. A $16 per day resort fee includes in-room coffee for the coffeemaker, daily newspaper delivery, complimentary local and 800 calls, high-speed and wireless Internet access, an on-request turndown service, use of the fitness center, self-parking, all recreational facilities, and transportation to the Walt Disney World theme parks. Premier Rooms are the same size as a standard guest room with either two doubles or a king, but come with views of the golf course, pools, or the surrounding countryside, some with small balconies. *CARA'S TIP:* The Omni's second-floor guest rooms are pet-friendly for animals up to twenty-five pounds with a $50 non-refundable fee.

**Suites.** On the resort's sixteenth floor are two 2,100-square-foot presidential suites, the Presidential and the Omni Suite, each with identical floor plans but with different decor. In both you'll find balconies running the length of the suite with sweeping views of the golf course, pools, and the surrounding area. Off the marble foyer are a pantry kitchen and half bath. The living area in the Presidential Suite, decorated in gold and moss green with butter yellow and cherry accents, offers a sleeper sofa, two easy chairs, coffee table, entertainment center with a 42-inch flat-panel TV, and eight-person dining table. Off the dining area, French doors lead to a large office with desk and chaise with another set of French doors that open to a striking master bedroom with four-poster king bed, easy chair and ottoman, and entertainment center; in the Presidential there's an Asian touch in the bedding with a cherry blossom motif and cherry tinted bolsters and pillow; the Omni Suite has a nautical decor. The stylish marble and granite master bath has double sinks, whirlpool tub, shower, makeup mirror, and vanity. A standard room can be added to make a two-bedroom, two-and-a-half-bath suite.

Eight Florida suites, all with the same decor, have 1,200 square feet with one bedroom and one and a half baths. Like the presidential suites, the carpeted foyer opens on either side to a pantry kitchen and half bath. Soft gold, blue, and green tones decorate the living area where you'll find a sofa sleeper, easy chairs, coffee table, entertainment center with a 42-inch plasma TV, balcony, and a six-person dining table. Pocket doors open off the dining area to the standard size master bedroom with king bed, easy chair, desk, bamboo entertainment center, and balcony with views of the golf course and pools. The master bath has black granite countertops with double sinks, cream-colored marble floors, small whirlpool tub, shower, and makeup mirror. A standard room with two double beds can be added to make a two-bedroom, two-and-a-half-bath suite. *CARA'S TIP:* Ask for the Key Largo Suite, Room 250, where the balcony is extra deep.

Executive Suites, at 865 square feet, have a cream chenille sleeper sofa (beginning to look quite tired), two sea blue easy chairs, small coffee table, entertainment center, and two-person table. Pocket doors separate the living area from a standard size bedroom with king bed and balcony. The bath, larger than a standard size, opens into both the bedroom and entry hall and has three small areas off a narrow hallway: a tub and separate shower, a commode area, and a single-sink vanity. You'll find a balcony off both the living area and bedroom, and all have a golf course view. A standard room with two double beds can be added to make a two-bedroom, two-and-a-half-bath suite.

Studio Suites are 655 square feet and have a king bed, a sitting area within the bedroom with sofa sleeper and easy chair, and a separate vanity area outside a larger bath than a regular guest room. Most have balconies and come with views of the golf course, but a few face the parking lot minus the balcony (view on request only).

**The Villas at ChampionsGate.** If room to spread out and a full kitchen are more to your liking, think about one of these villas, just a walk away from all services and recreation of the Omni. The lovely decor is very similar to that in the hotel. Off a small, natural stone foyer in the two-bedroom villas is a small den with full-size sleeper sofa and 27-inch flat-panel TV sharing a single-sink bath with the guest bedroom holding two double beds or one queen. The fully equipped kitchen has black granite countertops and stainless steel appliances with a two-person eating bar. A granite wet bar sits between the kitchen and living area next to the six-person dining table. Through a columned arch is the living area with a queen sleeper sofa, coffee table, a 42-inch flat-panel TV with DVD player, leather easy chair and ottoman, and two additional easy chairs. The master and the living area share a deep, covered balcony or patio with a four-person table. In the master bedroom is a king bed, additional TV, his-and-her closets, a marble bath with whirlpool tub, stand-alone shower, double sinks, and separate toilet area. Views are either of the small villa pool or the golf course.

Three-bedroom villas are found on the end of the building, all with golf views. They also have a small den, but with a larger kitchen, larger dining room with a six-person circular table, and larger living area with balcony or patio. The master is exactly the same as a two-bedroom; in one guest room is a queen bed and in the other either two double beds or a queen, both sharing a bath with pedestal sink and shower. Each villa has daily housekeeping, Internet access, iron and ironing board, stackable washer/dryer, and 27-inch flat screen TV in each bedroom.

In the lobby is a concierge desk and small fitness room, and outside the building entrance you'll find a pool and whirlpool. Future plans include several more villa buildings (five in all) and a lazy river-style pool. Units are individually owned, so there may be a few differences such as TVs and other amenities between villas, but all have the same standard decor.

## DINE

**Broadway Deli.** Take-away deli featuring Starbuck's specialty coffees, bagels, sandwiches (chicken, egg or tuna salad, ham, turkey, roast beef, pastrami, corned beef, Hebrew National hot dog), salads (Caesar with chicken, chef, chicken, egg, or tuna), wraps (chicken Caesar, turkey, veggie), pizza by the slice; hand-dipped ice cream, smoothies, root beer floats, milkshakes, beer, wine, and desserts.

**Croc's.** Excellent poolside bar and cafe with pool table and foosball; Mediterranean, Caesar with chicken or shrimp, citrus shrimp, or tropical fruit salads; blackened grouper, blackened chicken breast with passion fruit barbecue sauce and goat cheese, and Philly cheese steak sandwiches; Angus burger, portobello mushroom wrap, deep-fried tempura-battered crab wrap (fantastic!), lemongrass-glazed swordfish skewers, teriyaki beef skewers; *children's menu:* cheeseburger, hot dog, grilled cheese, chicken fingers, PB&J; ice cream bars, desserts; frozen and tropical drinks, wine, beer.

**David's Club.** Upscale sports bar and grill; crab and avocado tower, Kobe beef burger, walnut-encrusted grouper, double cut pork chop, sixteen-ounce rib eye steak, twin lobster tails; golf course views.

**Piper's Grille.** Golf club dining and bar with indoor and outdoor seating overlooking the course; salads and sandwiches; open from sunrise to sunset with bagpipers at sunset. Either walk from the hotel or villas or use the call button found by the hotel pool area for golf cart transfers.

**Trevi's.** Serving Mediterranean cuisine for breakfast, lunch, and dinner; indoor and outdoor dining; *breakfast:* H&H bagels, Tuscan frittata, brioche French toast, eggs Benedict, banana macadamia nut pancakes, cheddar and bacon quiche; *lunch:* flatbreads, fried grouper sandwich, turkey club panini, chicken parmigiana sandwich, Italian sausage sandwich; *dinner:* portobello mushroom crusted salmon, veal milanese, Chilean sea bass wrapped in prosciutto, soft garlic polenta and lemon oil; indoor as well as outdoor dining available.

**Zen.** Pan-Asian cuisine; sushi and sake bar; open for dinner 6 to 10 p.m. Tuesday through Sunday. (See full description in chapter 8, Dining.)

**In-Room Dining.** Available 24/7.

### SIP

**David's Club.** Upscale sports bar; single-malt scotches, cognac, wine, full bar; the Player's Lounge offers billiards, darts, and foosball; six flat-screen TVs; small cigar patio; full-service restaurant serving from 5 p.m. to 11 p.m.; bar open until 1:30 a.m.

**Lobby Bar.** Cocktail lounge with live piano music; light menu of honey Pilsner shrimp cocktail, beer battered onion rings, hangar beef steak sandwich, artichoke crab dip, club sandwich, prime beef or crab cake sliders, grilled cheese; open nightly from 6 p.m. to midnight.

### PLAY

**Arcade.** Small arcade located near Camp Omni.

**Basketball.** Lighted court.

**Children's activities and playground.** Omni Kids Bag filled with treats on arrival; children can check out a backpack filled with games for their room. Activities include arts and crafts for a fee, pool games, Wii tournaments; kids' playground near family pool.

**Fire pit.** Found between Trevi's restaurant and the formal pool.

**Golfing.** Two Greg Norman–designed eighteen-hole courses; lighted nine-hole, par-3 golf course; David Leadbetter Golf Academy. (See full description in the Golf section in chapter 6, Sporting Diversions.)

**Jogging and bicycling.** Jogging, hiking, and biking trails wind through the resort.

**Swimming.** Formal pool lined with private cabanas that hold lounge chairs, mini refrigerator, ceiling fans, robes, TV, sodas and water, fruit platter, and wireless Internet access (full-day cabana rates are $110); nearby Jacuzzi meditation garden; 850-foot Lazy River family pool with complimentary tubes for drifting; zero-entry family pool with 125-foot waterslide and interactive water playground featuring a 30-foot water tower; two hot tubs; pool concierges provide chilled towels, fresh fruit, and smoothie samples every hour on the hour; my only complaint is the need to sign out and back in for pool towels.

**Tennis.** Two lighted, clay courts with complimentary rackets and balls available at the towel hut; private lessons available.

**Volleyball.** Sand volleyball court located near family pool.

## WORK, MOVE, SOOTHE

**Business center.** Open 24/7; manned Monday through Friday 7 a.m. to 3 p.m. and Saturday 8 a.m. to noon with computer and high-speed Internet access, photocopying, fax service, notary public, secretarial and printing services, mail services.

**Car rental.** Hertz car rental on-site.

**Child care.** Camp Omni Kids Escape is an evening program with movies, video and board games, dinner, and other activities. Nightly from 5 to 11 p.m. for children ages four to twelve for $10 per hour; call (407) 390-6664 for reservations; in-room child care available.

**Hair salon.** Salon services at The Spa; highlights, cut, nails, waxing, Fijian coconut scalp treatment, and cosmetic application; call (407) 390-6664 for appointments.

**Fitness center.** An excellent fitness facility is complimentary to resort guests; Cybex strength training machines and cardio equipment; treadmills equipped with individual flat-screen TVs and headphones, recumbent and upright bicycles, elliptical and cross trainers; free weights; resort guests may use the spa locker rooms and facilities including steam, sauna, and whirlpool for no additional charge; yoga and personal training for an additional fee; open 24/7.

**Spa.** 10,000-square-foot spa with ten treatment rooms; massage, facials, body exfoliations and treatments; retail store featuring Pure Fiji, Phytomer, Jane Iredale, and SkinCeuticals; open 8 a.m. to 8 p.m.; call (407) 390-6603 for reservations. (See full description in Spas section of chapter 5, Beyond the Theme Parks.)

### GO

Complimentary scheduled transportation is provided by Mears to the Walt Disney World theme parks. Fee-based transfers available to Universal, SeaWorld, Disney's water parks, and the Orlando airport. A car is suggested for added convenience.

## Reunion Resort

**320 homes and villas. 1000 Reunion Way, Reunion, Florida 34747; phone (407) 662-1100, fax (407) 662-1111. Check-in 4 p.m., checkout 11 a.m. For reservations call (888) 418-9611 or your travel agent, or online at www.reunionresort.com. $$–$$$$**

**Why Stay Here?** Access to three of Orlando's best golf courses only available to members and resort guests.

**Rooms to Book.** Those at the Reunion Grande with easy access to the golf club and the resort's excellent restaurant and bars.

**Don't Miss.** Nibbling on tapas and savoring a cocktail at the Reunion Grande's super-cool rooftop bar while viewing Disney's fireworks shows.

A golf lover's delight, the Reunion Resort is spread over 2,300 acres and is a twenty-minute, 6-mile drive from Walt Disney World. Here you'll find a wealth of accommodations, all individually owned with very attractive standardized furnishings, all a nice alternative to the hotel rooms found at most resorts. It's the feel of a small-town community instead of a resort, with one-, two-, and three-bedroom villas or fully furnished residential homes, all with full-size kitchens surrounded by three golf courses, wetlands, a private water park complex, and more. While construction is ongoing at this huge complex, the property is so large that you really won't feel it. What you will feel is mighty special with your own personal concierge who assists you from booking through arrival and departure and is on call whenever needed, arranging tee times, spa treatments, theme-park tickets, and more. You'll love the no-tipping policy, replaced by a daily service charge, in effect throughout the resort. Because this is a cashless resort, the spa and golf courses are off limits to the public; only the restaurants are open to anyone. Another good reason to vacation at this super resort.

## REST

Accommodations here are so diverse that it's almost impossible to describe them all, but I'll try my best. All include daily newspaper and house-keeping, turn-down service, robes, and resort-wide transportation as well as high-speed Internet access. Because most, but not all, owners in the rental pool buy the standardized furnishing packages, I would highly suggest requesting a villa with one, which will ensure a beautifully decorated unit. Avoid the Towers area located very close to the extremely busy I-4 corridor.

**Reunion Grande.** This upscale, high-rise, condominium hotel has super luxurious one- and two-bedroom units, the best that Reunion Resort has to offer. The intimate lobby is decorated in a sophisticated icy blue and chocolate with travertine floors, a stone fountain, and leather chaises. The plus of staying here is its oh-so-happening rooftop pool with fireplace, poolside cabanas, tapas bar, sweeping views of the golf course and Walt Disney World fireworks, and cocktail waitresses with white go-go boots and chic dresses. There's also a fine-dining restaurant, Forte.

Reunion Grande Condos have two different color schemes according to the choice of the owner (each unit is individually owned and in the rental pool): rich reds mixed with soft greens and gold, or a relaxing spa blue, with sea green and a touch of gold, both with handsome wood fur-nishings. Full-size kitchens have beige granite countertops and stainless steel appliances.

**Seven Eagle Condominiums and Townhouses.** Close to the golf clubhouse and adjacent to the pool pavilion are these lovely accommoda-tions in two- and three-story buildings with inside entrances. Choices include either a one-bedroom condo or three-bedroom townhome.

King Premium Balcony condos are 730-square-foot, one-story units that sleep four adults offering an attractive Floridian-style, Key West decor with pistachio green and butter cream painted walls (request one with a view of the golf course instead of the interior courtyard). The small living area has a soft green queen-size sleeper sofa, four-person glass dining table, palm-motif side and floor lamps, small coffee table, gold easy chair, entertainment center with TV and DVD/CD player, and small patio or balcony with two chairs and a table. In the kitchen are granite countertops, a four-burner gas range, dishwasher, full-size refrigerator with icemaker, microwave, and enough flatware, glassware, dishes, and pots and pans to make a complete meal for four people. The king-bedded master offers outstanding comfort with a two-poster bed that is triple-sheeted and topped with a gold, pistachio, and cherry-colored floral motif spread—sleep under a soft white duvet accompanied by loads of down or foam pillows. There's also a cushioned wicker chair, a corner garden tub set within an alcove, a second TV, a second patio or stand-up balcony, and a closet with robes, iron and ironing board, and electronic safe. An adjoining bath offers gold and chocolate brown granite countertops, soft gold ceramic tile flooring, single-sink vanity, large tile shower with rain showerhead, full-length and makeup mirrors, hair dryer, and loads of soft cushy towels. Washers and dryers are available in each section of Seven Eagles.

King Standard villas are really the same as the Premium Balcony accommodations, just minus the patios and balconies.

Three-bedroom/three-bath Seven Eagle townhouses sleeping eight offer 1,986 square feet over two stories with a washer and dryer inside the unit. Downstairs is the entry and two guest rooms: one with two twin beds, an easy chair, and entertainment center, the other with a king bed, entertainment center, desk, and oversize tub that opens to the bedroom, each with a single-sink bath. They both open to a shared patio with table and chairs (again, request a unit that overlooks the golf course). Upstairs is the same as the one-bedroom condo described above.

**The Villas at Reunion Square.** Three-bedroom accommodations with exterior entrances, comfy furnishings, full-size granite kitchen with stainless steel appliances, and easy access to all that Reunion has to offer make it a good choice, particularly for those who plan to spend a lot of time at the Water Park, which is within walking distance. Just avoid the Villas

North section, which may come with some highway noise. A mix of artful fabrics in two color schemes are available: one a coral, green, and gold design in floral, plaids, and solid fabrics with coral reef motif accents; the other in shades of terra-cotta, beige, and gold with floral, plaids, and dragonfly touches. Off the foyer is a guest bedroom with one queen bed, a single-sink bath, and separate tub/toilet area. On the other side of the foyer is the second guest room with two double beds, poor lighting, and a single-sink, one-room bath. Both guest rooms have flat-panel TVs and DVD players. The full kitchen is done in black and beige granite with cherry wood cabinets opening to a five-person circular dining table and living room with sleeper sofa, coffee table, easy chairs, occasional chair, writing desk, and entertainment center with large LCD TV and Bose stereo. In the master is a king bed with fabric headboard, white duvet, entertainment center with flat-panel TV and DVD, and easy chair; the bath has granite counters, tile flooring, double sinks, separate toilet area, stand-alone shower, and tub. Other amenities include an iPod clock radio, robes, and electronic safe. Opening to both the living area and master is a patio or balcony. You'll also find a washer and dryer. *CARA'S TIP*: Request an end unit, which comes with three additional windows in the living area.

**Centre Court Ridge.** This complex offers Wimbledon or Grand Slam–themed villas next to the tennis courts, all with a golf course view, all with exterior entrances. Almost identical in layout as the Villas at Reunion Square above, all are three bedrooms, two and a half baths, but because of their lock-off capabilities, they can be offered as one-, two-, or three-bedroom units. These come in probably my least favorite decor with a neutral sporting theme that, while pleasant, isn't exactly my taste.

**Heritage Crossing.** Located near the resort's entrance are these one-, two-, and three-bedroom condominiums and townhomes. These do have the disadvantage of being very close to a fairly busy road and quite far from the Water Park and central hub.

Three-bedroom condos that can also be rented as one- and two-bedroom units have 1,352 square feet. The kitchen offers the same amenities as those in Seven Eagles but with dark granite countertops and a breakfast bar with four counter stools instead of a dining table. The adjoining living area has an olive green queen sleeper sofa, two rust-toned chairs, coffee table, entertainment center with plasma TV and DVD/CD player, and 221-square-foot balcony or patio. Off the living area is the master bedroom with its pineapple and palm tree decor featuring a rattan armoire with TV, a two-poster king bed topped with a white duvet and rich green chenille pillows, and balcony or patio. Open to the bedroom is a corner garden tub and bath with single sink and separate commode area. There are two guest bedrooms with absolutely delightful Floridian decor; one with two double beds, the other with a king bed, both with an entertainment center, and both sharing a hall bathroom with single sink and a separate shower/tub area. A washer and dryer are inside the unit.

Three-bedroom, two-level townhomes come with a whopping 1,987 square feet of space. Downstairs is the master suite and bath, kitchen with breakfast bar, living area, six-person dining table, half bath, and patio. Upstairs are two additional bedrooms that share a double-sink bath.

**Private homes.** In Homestead (the estate homes), Liberty Bluff, and Patriots' Landing areas are attractive three-, four-, and five-bedroom homes available for rent and managed by Reunion Resort, some with pools and many overlooking the golf course. Estate homes are valued at more than $1 million (even one with eight bedrooms). Each is individually decorated according to the owner's taste, but furnishings are purchased from the resort and have strict standards. Photos of the homes can be viewed online, and rental prices begin at just over $200 nightly. All are stocked with Reunion towels and bath products.

## DINE

**Clubhouse Restaurant.** Golf club restaurant serving breakfast and lunch; dining both inside and out on the terrace overlooking the putting green and driving range.

**The Cove at Seven Eagles.** Bar and grill at the Seven Eagles pool; spicy wings, coconut shrimp, deli hoagie, blackened fresh catch, hamburger, chicken tenders, Hebrew National hot dog, fruit plate, grilled chicken, cheese and red pepper quesadilla.

**Eleven.** Super-cool tapas cafe with illuminated bar located on the Reunion Grande rooftop; panoramic view of the Orlando skyline; Kobe beef sliders, ahi tuna flatbread, jumbo lump crab cakes with Yuzu beurre blanc; open evenings with changing hours; closed Tuesdays.

**Forté.** Stunning, contemporary chophouse in the Reunion Grande (See full description in Dining chapter.)

**Longboards at the Water Park.** Water Park pool bar and grill; buffalo chicken wings with blue cheese dip, calamari fritters, barbecue baby back ribs, pizza, fruit salad, Caesar salad, grilled chicken salad with roasted peppers, turkey BLT wrap, hot Italian meatball sub, all-beef hot dog, tuna salad roll, cheeseburger.

**In-Room Dining.** Order in for a nominal delivery charge from a menu of breakfast baskets, picnic or movie baskets, and late night snacks of pizza, turkey club sandwiches, and chocolate chip cookies.

## SIP

**Clubhouse Bar.** Golf club bar.

**Grande Lobby Bar.** Sophisticated lobby bar in the Reunion Grande condo hotel; wine and champagne by the glass, full bar; appetizers: sushi, steak tartare, Alsatian onion soup, Caesar salad with chicken, steak, or shrimp, chilled crustacean platter for two or four with Mexican white gulf shrimp, lobster tail, and oysters.

## PLAY

**Bicycle rentals.** Rentals as well as villa delivery and pick-up available.

**Children's activities and playground.** Children's playground located near tennis center; small activity center at the Seven Eagles Pool Bar; kid's tennis clinics available for a fee; Kid's Crew recreation program for children ages four to twelve is held at the Seven Eagles Pool, Water Park, or in the activities center and includes pool and lawn games, scavenger hunts, nature hikes, tennis, sand art, dance parties, bingo, dive-in movies, treasure hunts, arts and crafts, and more ($60 for a full day and $45 for a half day); teen socials with volleyball, movies, and games; a variety of kid's activities at the Water Park; contact (407) 662-1605 for more information.

**Golf.** Three courses: the Legacy Course, an Arnold Palmer Signature Course; the Independence Course, a Tom Watson Signature Course; and the new Tradition Course, a Jack Nicklaus Signature Course; clubhouse with restaurant and retail shop; ANNIKA Academy provides individualized golf instruction and custom fitness programs in a state-of-the-art facility. (See full description in the Golf section of chapter 6, Sporting Diversions.)

**Jogging and bicycling.** Miles of hiking and biking trails wrap throughout the property.

**Segway Tours.** Offered each Saturday from 8 to 10 a.m. with one hour of instruction and one hour adventure through the resort ($70) or Friday at 11 a.m. for a one-hour informational session and a short ride ($35); ages sixteen and up with a 250-pound maximum weight; call (407) 662-1605 for more information.

**Swimming.** The Seven Eagles Pool Pavilion has one large pool, two whirlpools, and a bar and grille; private cabana rentals. Multiple community pools are spread throughout the property. Best of all is the five-acre, multilevel Reunion Water Park, a mammoth pool complex with a 966-foot lazy river, two water slides, an interactive Splash Factory with water jets and giant water-filled bucket, zero-entry lagoon, beach volleyball, and waterfalls; rooftop pool at Reunion Grande with private cabanas.

**Tennis.** Six lighted Har-Tru, HydroGrid clay courts as well as a stadium court; professional instruction available; adult and kid's clinics; monthly exhibitions; $20 per-person court fee charge for resort guests; pro shop; men's and women's locker rooms; call (407) 662-1630 to reserve court times.

**Volleyball.** Sand beach volleyball found at the Water Park as well as a sand professional court at the tennis center.

### WORK, MOVE, SOOTHE

**Hair salon.** Salon at The Spa offers cut, color, waxing, and updos.

**Fitness center.** Complimentary fitness facility located at Seven Eagles Pool Pavilion; Life Fitness cardio equipment, free weights; yoga Monday and Thursday at 9 a.m. at Heritage Crossing; Aqua Fitness Wednesday at 9 a.m. at Seven Eagles Pool; personal training available; open 7 a.m. to 8 p.m.

**Spa.** The Spa at Reunion; wonderful boutique spa offering a full menu of services; small outdoor pool and whirlpool. (See full description in Spas section of chapter 5, Beyond the Theme Parks.)

**GO**

For inter-resort transportation take the complimentary, on-call resort tram, perfect for a trip to the water park or spa. A car rental is almost mandatory here.

## Waldorf Astoria Orlando

**497 rooms. 14200 Bonnet Creek Resort Lane, Orlando, Florida 32821; phone (407) 597-5500; fax (407) 597-5501. Check-in 3 p.m., checkout 11 a.m. For reservations call (407) 597-5500 or your travel agent, or online at www.waldorfastoriaorlando.com. $$–$$$$$**

**Why Stay Here?** Simply put, it's the most luxurious resort in Orlando.

**Rooms to Book**. A lavish Luxury Suite with views of the golf course and nature sanctuary.

**Don't Miss.** A treatment at the fantastic Guerlain spa followed by cabana time at the pool.

The first Waldorf-Astoria to be built from the ground up since its New York flagship property opened seventy-eight years ago, this new luxury resort sits right in the middle of Walt Disney World Resort. Swank and sophisticated, it has redefined local luxury in Orlando. Although not technically on Disney property, it's almost next-door to Disney's Hollywood Studios and just a five-minute drive to Downtown Disney. The reasons to love the resort are many: a Guerlain Spa, the Rees Jones–designed golf course, two divine pools, seventy-five acres of wetlands . . . the list goes on. It's certainly my pick for the most splendid resort around.

Stunningly impressive is the circular, high gloss marble lobby studded with glittering mosaic tile and an aquamarine-blue glass reception desk. Its centerpiece is a round velvet settee topped with a handcrafted replica of the New York Waldorf's signature clock. Old World with a touch of the contemporary, there are dark, rich woods and miles of marble as far as the eye can see. Though refined, expect a more casual atmosphere than the New York counterpart. This is Orlando after all.

**REST**

**Guest rooms.** As you would expect, elegant guest rooms are well equipped and feature the latest technology. Stylishly appointed, they offer crown molding, maple wood furnishings, 42-inch HD LCD televisions with BluRay DVD players and surround sound, two-line phones, iPod docking station clock radio, oversized work desk, glass lamps, heavy silk curtains with shimmery sheers, plush muted gold carpeting, and Italian marble entry halls and baths. Luxuriate in the very best beds in Orlando made with triple-sheeted Egyptian cotton linens, fluffy white down duvets and pillows, feather mattresses, and a black and white houndstooth throw. Baths feature Agraria bath products and the thickest towels imaginable with dual sink vanities, an enormous shower, amber glass tile-fronted soaking tub, and lighted makeup mirror.

Amenities include twice-daily housekeeping, evening turndown service, luxe robes and slippers, daily coffee and tea service, daily newspaper delivery, Internet access, laptop-size safe, iron and ironing board, and complimentary bottled water and shoe-shine service. In short, a tastefully designed and supremely comfortable room. The hotel does offer balconies, but only in suites (only one chair per balcony is a bit of a nuisance).

Deluxe Rooms have 448 square feet and offer a king bed or two double beds. There's a desk/bureau combination on which sits a flat-panel TV, and a seating area within the bedroom with a small sofa and chair in the king room and a chair only in the two-bedded room. Baths feature black granite vanities with a single sink, a large frameless shower as well as a separate soaking tub, but not a separate room for the commode. Views are of either the golf course or Disney, and none have balconies.

**Suites.** The 945-square-foot Deluxe Suites have a separate living area with a four-person dining table, a gold sleeper sofa and sky blue easy chair, a bureau with a large flat-panel TV, and a balcony. Within the living area is a buffet with wine refrigerator and wet bar. A king bed is found in the master along with a bureau on which sits a flat-panel TV, a work desk, and easy chair. Baths are slightly larger but similar to those in a Deluxe Room. This becomes a two-bedroom Deluxe Suite with the addition of a Deluxe Room with two double beds on the other side of the living area. Views are of the resort, golf course, or theme parks.

If you're lucky enough to be ensconced in one of the Luxury Suites, you'll enjoy a 1,460-square-foot corner beauty with a larger living area, bedroom, and master bath than the Deluxe Suite. Within the living room is a chenille sleeper sofa, sea blue easy chair and ottoman, amber glass lamps, oversized flat-panel TV, and balcony. There's also a black granite kitchen of sorts with a counter and three bar stools; while nice, it doesn't seem to serve much of a function since there's only an under-counter wine refrigerator and sink with loads of unnecessary drawer space. These suites come in one- and two-bedroom options with the second bedroom being a Deluxe Room with two beds. Views are always of the front of the resort facing the nature sanctuary, some with additional golf course views.

The one-bedroom Waldorf Astoria Suites are always corner suites and come with 1,780 square feet of space. There's an oversized bar as in the Luxury Suite, but here the living area is long and narrow and feels somewhat cramped. The only plus is a half bath strangely found off the bedroom entry instead of in the main entry hall. The bedroom is a standard size and has a king bed and a full-size bath. Even though they are smaller, I prefer the Luxury Suites because of their more open feel. The addition of a connecting Deluxe Room off the entry hall makes this a two-bedroom suite.

And then the grand dames, the resort's two Presidential Suites (one on the fourteenth and one on the fifteenth floor), both with golf course corner views, both with the same decor, and both with 3,330 square feet. The oversized living area has a four-person game table with oversized high back chairs, a ten-person formal dining table topped by double chandeliers, a full kitchen minus a stove, an elegant sitting area with a soft gold velvet sofa, an alcove office, and two terraces. A half bath with a Venetian mirror is off the living area. From the dining room, French doors open into the massive master bedroom made lovely with a king bed with white linen headboard, red and platinum accents, gold velvet settee, beige chenille sofa, easy chair, a pop-up TV found in a bureau, and another balcony. Baths have two vanities, separate shower, and whirlpool tub with a huge picture window. A second bedroom can be connected.

*CARA'S TIP*: Rooms on floor eight or above enjoy an all-encompassing view of the entire area and are on request only.

**DINE**

**AquaMarine.** Poolside restaurant; buffalo wings, Mediterranean tuna salad pita, roasted turkey sandwich, grilled chicken Caesar, cheeseburger, hot dog, Reuben sandwich; specialty drinks, wine, beer.

**The Bull & Bear Steakhouse.** Overlooking the first hole of the golf course, offerings include classic steakhouse fare and a club-like atmosphere. (See full description in chapter 8, Dining.)

**Oscar's.** Informal dining in a casual setting for breakfast and lunch; *lunch:* tuna melt, natural chicken sandwich with heirloom tomatoes, arugula and avocado on ciabatta, vegetable and portobello sandwich, pastured beef burger, sustainable market fish, open-ocean diver scallops with roasted beets and citrus.

**In-Room Dining.** New York's Waldorf Astoria was the world's first hotel to offer in-room dining and the tradition continues here with round the clock service.

**SIP**

**Bull & Bear Lounge.** Classy bar adjoining the restaurant of the same name with fine wines, single malt scotch, and specialty cocktails; appetizers from the restaurant are available.

**Peacock Alley.** Found just off the lobby area with people watching at its prime, this is where guests love to congregate. You'll fall hard for the peacock feather carpeting and the delish cocktails and small plates of nibbles like marinated olives and hummus, shrimp cocktail, warm veggie chips with yogurt-cilantro dip, smoked salmon, and cured meat and artisan cheese platter; live piano music nightly.

**Sir Harry's Lounge.** At the end of the day unwind in this gem of a lounge with its private club atmosphere; cocktails, port, single-malt scotch, beer, and wines from around the world; live piano music.

**PLAY**

**Bicycles.** Complimentary bicycles are found just outside the fitness room, perfect for a spin around the property.

**Children's programs and activities.** WA Kids offers both day and evening programs with a variety of creative and educational activities for ages five to twelve; $15 per hour or $110 per day (includes lunch); from 7 to 10 p.m. is an Astoria After Dark program including dinner and activities for $75.

**Golf.** Rees Jones–designed championship eighteen-hole course surrounded by a natural setting of palms, pines, and wetlands. (See full description in the Golf section in chapter 6, Sporting Diversions.)

**Jogging.** A brick path between the Waldorf and its sister property, the Hilton Bonnet Creek, overlooks the golf course.

**Swimming.** Put on your Gucci sunglasses and head out to your choice of swimming pools: the formal signature pool is lined with private cabanas offering chaise lounges and sofas, wireless Internet, 42-inch HD flat-panel TVs, sunscreen, refrigerator, bottled water, and bath robes; a second zero-entry pool adjoins; one whirlpool.

## WORK, MOVE, SOOTHE

**Business Center.** Twenty-four-hour with Internet access, copy, fax, teleconferencing.

**Car rental.** A Hertz Car Rental is found in the lobby.

**Fitness center.** Impressively outfitted workout room with an amazing array of equipment; Precor ellipticals as well as recumbent and upright bicycles, Cybex ellipticals, Life Fitness treadmills, Precor weight machines; free weights; cable and pulley machine; complimentary yoga, aerobics, Pilates, and water aerobics classes; personal instruction available for a fee.

**Heliport.** A heliport landing pad is found on property with services available on a request basis.

**Spa.** The Guerlain spa offers twenty-three treatment suites with additional services available at the pool cabanas. (See full description in Spas section of chapter 5, Beyond the Theme Parks.)

## GO

Regularly scheduled transfers to all four Disney theme parks provided by Mears Transportation. Private transportation can be arranged through concierge.

# Universal Orlando Resorts

With the Portofino Bay Hotel, Hard Rock Hotel, and Royal Pacific Resort, Universal has established itself as a complete and self-contained vacation destination, offering some of the most interesting resorts in all of Orlando. All are within walking distance or a short boat ride to Universal's theme parks, CityWalk, and each other; all are operated by Loews Hotels; all are AAA Four Diamond Award winners, and all are worlds apart in personality.

If rock music and contemporary guest rooms are your thing, the Hard Rock Hotel should definitely be your choice, but if gracious accommodations with a European ambience are more your style, it should be Portofino all the way. Or perhaps a tropical island ambience at the Royal Pacific is more to your liking.

A weakness of all Universal hotels is the lack of room balconies. Disney has continued to indulge vacationers with a place from which to enjoy the glorious Florida weather, but Universal hasn't mastered this lesson. One definite plus is Universal's concierge-level guest rooms, and at less than $100 more per day, they are a bargain. I believe you'll find the Universal concierge lounges more sophisticated (in particular the ones at the Royal Pacific and at Portofino Bay) than Disney's, with a higher level of service for less money and not quite as many children underfoot.

## *Why Stay at a Universal Hotel?*

On-site guests receive exceptional entitlements, such as:

- Bypassing regular lines at both parks each day of your stay. Simply present your room key to the ride attendant and be directed to the Universal Express Entrance with a wait of fifteen minutes or less.

- "First available" seating at select table-service restaurants in both parks and CityWalk (not available on Friday and Saturday or at Emeril's).

- Room charging privileges at Universal Orlando retail shops and restaurants.

- Package delivery directly to your hotel room from select retail shops.

# LOEWS LOVES PETS

Universal Orlando Resorts give pets VIP (Very Important Pet) status with the Loews Loves Pets program. Where else can your pet be given the all-star treatment during their stay? Each pet is welcomed with its own personal note from the hotel's general manager and a special amenity that includes special pet place mats with food and water bowls, special bedding, toys and treats, and a Do Not Disturb sign that lets housekeeping know that a pet is in the room. There's even pet In-Room Dining menus, puppy pagers, pet walking, and pet sitting services available.

■ Complimentary transportation by water taxi or shuttle bus to both parks and CityWalk and by shuttle bus to SeaWorld and Aquatica.

## Booking a Universal Vacation

Consider staying several nights at one of Universal's fantastic resorts for convenient access to the Universal theme parks, CityWalk, SeaWorld, and Discovery Cove, combined with a stay at Disney for one great vacation.

### PACKAGES

Call (877) 801-9720 for Universal resort packages, or your travel agent. Book online at www.universalorlando.com. And always price the Universal hotels separately by calling Loews Hotels at (866) 563-9792.

## Hard Rock Hotel

**650 rooms. 5800 Universal Boulevard, Orlando 32819; phone (407) 503-2000, fax (407) 503-2010. Check-in 4 p.m., checkout 11 a.m. For reservations call (877) 801-9720, or (866) 563-9792,**

**or your travel agent, or go online at www.loewshotels.com or www .universalorlando.com.  $$–$$$$$**

**Why Stay Here?** A hip atmosphere and a convenient five-minute walk to Universal Studios and CityWalk.

**Rooms to Book.** A roomy King Suite on the Club 7 floor.

**Don't Miss.** Renting a cabana for the day at the resort's groovy pool.

Hard Rock's motto is "love all, serve all," and serve they certainly do at one cool place to hang out in California-hip style. Luxury reigns, from the ultraslick marble lobby to the marvelous pool complex to the stylish guest rooms. Designed to look as if it were the estate of a rock star, the California mission–style resort features a cream-colored stucco exterior, clay red-tiled roofs, shaded porches supported by arched beams, wrought-iron balconies, and imposing towers. And Hard Rock's prime location within a short walk or boat ride to Universal's theme parks is certainly a major plus.

The sunken lobby will bowl you over with its panoramic views through enormous picture windows of the sparkling pool and palm-studded grounds along with distant vistas of Universal Studios. Relax in lavish seating areas of chocolate-brown leather chairs and cushy, velvet sofas scattered among towering potted palms and massive vases overflowing with opulent, fresh flowers. Glassed display coffee tables showcasing guitars from music legends are strewn throughout, while the walls are lined with scads of gold records and fascinating rock 'n' roll music memorabilia. It's a mix of pure style and star worship.

One thing you should know is that it's impossible to escape the loud rock music blasting away in every public space; more than 900 speakers are scattered throughout the property, all running seven days a week, twenty-four hours a day. Of course, the younger crowd loves it. But rest assured, from the moment you enter the hallways leading to your guest room, only beautiful silence is heard.

**REST**

**Guest rooms.** Modern without being stark, the comfortable guest rooms offer a clean, contemporary motif, one that is certainly good-looking. Standard Rooms, smallish in size at 375 square feet, come with a closet and granite minibar in the entrance hall and either two queen-size beds or a king-size bed. Rooms are outfitted with cool, whitewashed walls, chocolate brown, aqua, and lime duvets with a piano keyboard motif, chocolate brown suede bolster pillows, 32-inch flat-panel TV, and taupe carpeting suggestive of the circular pattern of a CD. White swag curtains frame the windows, and the walls hold framed black-and-white photos of rock 'n' roll legends. Novel lighting casts a soft glow throughout. Each room features a stereo with CD/MP3 player, iPod docking station, two dual-line telephones, electronic safe, minibar, iron and ironing board, robes, and coffeemaker. A single-sink vanity in sea green Corian comes with plush towels, hair dryer, scale, fun metal bath accessories, and makeup mirror, while the separate bath/toilet area contains a second sink. Added benefits include high-speed Internet and dataport access, newspaper delivery Monday through Friday, and on-demand movies. Views are of the gardens; a pool view comes at an additional charge.

Deluxe Rooms at 500 square feet (the rooms with king-size beds are smaller at 400 square feet) feature a sitting area as well as an alcove window seating area with sleeper sofa, offering that extra bit of space needed to spread out.

**Concierge rooms.** The contemporary Hard Rock's Club 7 lounge, located on the seventh floor facing the front of the hotel, features the services of a concierge desk along with complimentary continental breakfast of yogurt, sourdough and whole grain bread, New York-style bagels, fruit, pastries, muffins, cinnamon rolls, croissants, cranberry nut muffins, oatmeal, hard boiled eggs, and juice. Nonalcoholic beverages are available throughout the day with chips, pretzels, and granola bars a typical afternoon snack. Each evening brings a fun spread of appetizers that vary nightly with items such as spring rolls, Mexican tortilla salad, grilled chicken fajitas, empanadas, vegetable antipasti, mini pizzas, cobb salad, mini corndogs, chicken wings, and pot stickers along with beer and wine (Trinchero Family Cabernet, Tunnel of Elms Chardonnay, Beringer White Zinfandel). After dinner desserts such as cookies, churros, cannolis, cheesecake bites, peach cobbler with ice cream, and Rice Krispies treats as well as soda and coffee are offered. In addition to the use of a rock 'n' roll book and CD library, you'll receive daily turndown service, DVD players in your room, half-price pool cabanas, and complimentary fitness center facilities.

**Suites.** Lil' Rock Suites at 800 square feet are absolutely the greatest with two rooms: one for adults and one just perfect for kids. A tiled entry hall with a large, curtained closet and minibar leads to the parents' bedroom, featuring a king-size bed topped with a rust-colored duvet and fun tangerine accent pillows. There's also a sitting area with love seat sleeper sofa in chocolate brown suedelike chenille, easy chair, coffee table, large bureau, TV, and stereo with CD player. The children's room contains two twin beds in the same basic decor as the parents', a kid-size table and ottoman-style chairs, clothing armoire, and TV. A convenient bathroom has two areas: one with a sink and toilet and the other with a double sink in the vanity and a shower. All suites have carpeting symbolic of CDs in chocolate and taupe.

Angular shaped King Suites at 650 square feet are especially nice, with a living area featuring a soft ochre, chenille sofa bed, three easy chairs, and coffee table in addition to a four-person dining table with teal and chocolate brown leather seating. In an alcove is a king-size bed with robin egg blue duvet and accents, bureau, TV, and second closet. The bath is all in one room with single sink, shower, and toilet (no tub). Some King Suites are altered with the dining table moved to the bedroom area and in the living room a Murphy bed (preference on request only). A standard Garden View guest room can be connected to make this a two-bedroom suite.

Two Hospitality Suites are found on the bottom floor of the hotel, a perfect retreat for visiting rock stars who wish to get away from the throngs. Off the black marble foyer is a full bath as well as a large office with desk, fax machine, easy chair and ottoman, and a wall of glass over-looking the living area. The bright, airy living room has two armless beige chenille sofas, two easy chairs, sofa and coffee table, and flat-panel TV. There's also a circular dining area for six with hardwood flooring as well as a granite and wood bar seating three with full-size refrigerator. The living room opens up to a standard king bedroom with a garden view.

The 2,000-square-foot Graceland Suite is fit for a king. The giant living area has modern furnishings in neutral tones, hardwood floors topped with an area rug, a soft gold chenille sofa, easy chairs, a coffee table, an entertainment center with stereo and DVD player, a baby grand piano, silken drapes, a circular dining table for eight, kitchen, and a half bath. An office sits off to one side. The bedroom features a flat-screen TV, two-sided fireplace, king-size bed sporting a brown leather headboard and ultrasuede bedspread, corner sofa, and stereo. And then there's the bathroom. My goodness! Within the chocolate brown granite double-head shower (large enough for ten people) is a whirlpool tub that sits by a picture window overlooking the pool and parks. Other amenities include a vanity, walk-in closet, double sink, and separate bidet and toilet area. The only thing lacking here is a balcony. A standard guest room can be added to the suite if desired.

## DINE

**Emack & Bolio's Marketplace.** Ice cream and coffee spot; hand-scooped ice cream, smoothies, floats, frozen yogurt, sundaes; pastries, muffins, doughnuts, bagels; Starbucks specialty coffees.

**The Kitchen.** Open for breakfast, lunch, and dinner; "Kids Can Cook Too!" on Monday, Tuesday, Wednesday, and Thursday; Friday evening is magician entertainment, Saturday evening is character dining; *breakfast:* breakfast burrito, pecan apple pancakes, Baja eggs Benedict with avocado and enchilada cream, corned beef hash and poached eggs, custom omelets; *lunch:* chipotle turkey chili, chicken pot pie, carne asada steak pita, crab cake sandwich BLT, gyro sliders; *dinner:* New York strip with brandy demi, vegetarian stack, paella, open chicken ravioli with marsala butter, grilled BBQ rubbed salmon.

**The Palm.** Famous New York–based steakhouse featuring prime, aged cuts of beef, fresh fish, Italian specialties, and jumbo Nova Scotia lobster; dinner only; Prime Bites menu available from 5 to 7 p.m. and 9 p.m. until closing at the bar with mini broiled crab cakes, veal parmigiana sliders, prime cheese steak, Kobe beef sliders, filet mignon Capri sandwiches, and calamari fritti.

**In-Room Dining.** Available 24/7.

## SIP

**Hard Rock Beachclub.** Poolside bar and grill; full bar, tropical drinks, smoothies; tandoori chicken satay, wings, quesadillas, nachos, cobb salad, seared ahi tuna salad, chopped salad wrap, blackened mahi mahi sandwich, Cuban sandwich, blackened shrimp po' boy, burger.

**Velvet Bar.** Chill out at this hip cocktail lounge on purple velvet sofas and animal print chairs; great specialty martinis and drinks; champagne and wine by the glass; cognac, port, single-malt scotch, coffee drinks; *light meals:* chicken samosa, artisan cheeses, grilled Chinese crispy chicken salad, chicken pot stickers, pizza, Reuben sandwich, grilled mango BBQ mahi sandwich; devil's food cake, key lime cheesecake, dessert shooter; Velvet Sessions the last Thursday of every month with live rock 'n' roll music.

## PLAY

**Arcade.** Power Station offering high-tech games and pinball machines.

**Children's activities.** Loews Loves Little Kids presented by Fisher-Price® includes baby and toddler play classes with parent and child attendance, in-room baby and toddler equipment like the Aquarium Play Yard and the Aquarium Take-Along Swing, Fisher-Price welcome gifts for children under age ten, and a selection of toys available to loan for children six months to six years.

**Jogging.** Lovely pathways connect all three Universal hotels with City-Walk; maps available at the concierge desk.

**Swimming.** Luxurious pool with zero-depth entry and underwater sound system; two whirlpools, kiddie pool, and 260-foot pool slide surrounded by sand beach, massive boulders, lofty palm trees, and flowering tropical plants; poolside tented white cabanas equipped with an armoire, table and five chairs, flat-panel television, phone, wireless Internet, refrigerator with bottled water and sodas, and ceiling fan for $110 to $200 depending on the season (there are even two themed cabanas for extra fun: Yellow Submarine and Musicquarium); adjoining outside game area featuring shuffleboard and table tennis; roaming waiters serve food and drinks from the Beachclub; poolside games for children; dive-in movies Friday, Saturday, and Sunday.

**Volleyball.** Sand court next to pool.

## WORK, MOVE, SOOTHE

**Business center.** Printing, fax, copying, Internet, shipping and receiving; open 7 a.m. to 6 p.m. Monday through Friday.

**Child care.** Camp Lil' Rock; games, computers, movies, karaoke, video games, arts and crafts, and stories. Open Sunday through Thursday, 5 to 11:30 p.m., and Friday and Saturday, 5 p.m. to midnight, for children ages four to fourteen; verify hours of availability as they may change seasonally.

**Golf.** The Golf Universal Orlando program allows for preferred tee times, complimentary transportation, club rentals, and free range balls at several nearby courses including MetroWest Golf Club, Orange County National Golf Center, and Mystic Dunes Golf Club.

**Fitness center.** Workout Room; Cybex bicycles and strength training equipment, Precor ellipticals, True treadmills, free weights; men's and women's locker rooms, each with steam room and sauna; open 6 a.m. to 9 p.m.; $10 daily fee.

**Spa.** Complimentary transportation provided to Mandara Spa located at the nearby Portofino Bay Hotel; in-room or in-cabana massage can be scheduled.

### GO

A three-minute water taxi or a lovingly landscaped walkway transports you to Universal Studios, Islands of Adventure, and CityWalk. Complimentary shuttle bus service is provided to Universal, with infrequent service to SeaWorld and Aquatica.

## Portofino Bay Hotel

**750 rooms. 5601 Universal Boulevard, Orlando 32819; phone (407) 503-1000, fax (407) 503-1010. Check-in 4 p.m., checkout 11 a.m. For reservations call (877) 801-9720, (866) 563-9792, or your travel agent, or go online at www.loewshotels.com or www.universalorlando.com. $$–$$$$$**

**Why Stay Here?** An amazing Italian ambience that can't be beat.

**Rooms to Book.** A Deluxe Room on the concierge level; request a balcony on arrival.

**Don't Miss.** An evening that begins with Italian arias on the piazza followed by dinner at Bice.

It's La Dolce Vita in a Mediterranean seaside setting at this exclusive hotel. The folks at Universal have outdone themselves in designing this resort to resemble the harbor and idyllic seaside town of Portofino, the jet-setter's paradise on the Italian Riviera. The scenery is pure postcard, with colorful fishing boats bobbing in the seductively curving bay, gentle waves lapping the shoreline, and sun-bleached buildings with shuttered windows and trompe l'oeil decorative facades. A charming waterside piazza, loaded with appetizing restaurants, offers plenty of outdoor seating areas and a scattering of interesting shops. The ambience of a quaint Italian village is overwhelming as you wander the cobbled streets encountering tiny piazzas, back alleyways, sparkling fountains, lofty bell towers, and flickering iron streetlamps. And I mustn't forget the lobby, resplendent with marble floors, tiled murals, sparkling Venetian glass chandeliers, refined furnishings, and a balcony overlooking Portofino's splendid piazza.

As night falls each evening, guests gather on the piazza to hear stirring Italian arias performed by singers perched on the resort's balconies. While often booked as a convention hotel, you'll find that it actually works to your advantage since all of the meetings are out of sight, leaving the hotel feeling almost empty during the day.

**REST**

**Guest rooms.** Standard rooms here at 462 square feet offer either a garden or a bay view. From the tiled foyer enter a comfortable room with an Old World appeal including details like a four-poster, hand-painted bed sitting high off the ground, topped with a cream and moss green duvet, ruby red bolsters and throw blanket, fine sheets, and down pillows. Walls are sunflower yellow, drapery is creamy raw silk, and the Italian-style furnishings include a sea-green and cream easy chair and ottoman, large granite writing table, two mossy green chenille chairs, and 32-inch flat-panel TV. Some rooms have French doors leading to deep balconies with wrought-iron table and chairs (available only on request at check-in). Large bathrooms boast a granite-topped, double-sink vanity over which hangs a mirror lined in colorful Italian tile; the bath is a tub/shower combo. Amenities include robes, CD clock radio, a laptop-size wall safe, iron and ironing board, hair dryer, scale, Keurig coffeemaker, makeup and full-length mirrors, high-speed Internet access, DVD player, three phones with two lines, on-demand movies, and a morning *New York Times* and turn-down service (on request). These rooms come with either a king or two queen beds.

Deluxe Rooms, located on the fifth and sixth floors, are 490 square feet and come with a slightly larger sitting area with a beige chenille sleeper love seat in lieu of an easy chair, plus a larger bathroom with separate shower in addition to the bathtub. Deluxe Rooms with two queen beds have the love seat situated a bit too tight in the corner to pull out for a sleeper. I adore Room 2663 overlooking the Beach Pool and the rooftops of the resort with great sunset views. All have either a Villa Pool or Beach Pool view.

*CARA'S TIP:* Pay extra for a standard room with a bay view, and beg for a balcony at check-in.

**Concierge rooms.** Most concierge rooms are located on the fifth and sixth floor near the lounge, but if you prefer another location, your request can usually be accommodated. Extra amenities include robes, discounted cabana rentals, in-room Internet connection, free access to the fitness center, books on loan, a small CD and DVD library, turn-down service, and an efficient concierge staff. At the spacious and sophisticated Portofino Club lounge overlooking the piazza and lagoon on the third floor, you'll find a continental breakfast of juice, fresh fruit, granola, cereal, yogurt, pastries, muffins, bagels, and croissants. An afternoon service of light snacks consists of iced tea, lemonade, chocolate and yogurt-covered raisins, trail mix, and granola bars. Early evening brings fruit with cured vegetables and meats the likes of mortadello, cheese, marinated artichokes, asparagus, mushrooms, and peppers served with wine (Bohemian Highway Pinot Grigio and Merlot, Chianti Classico, and Acacia Chardonnay) and a nice assortment of beer. After dinner there are Italian pastries. Soft drinks, coffee, tea, and bottled water are always available, and so convenient are two computers with printers and complimentary Internet access.

**Suites.** Portofino Bay's Kid's Suites at 650 square feet have two standard size rooms: one in the same decor as a standard king room; the other decorated just for kids; six are in a precious Dr. Seuss theme (with vibrant polka dot carpeting and spreads, zany Seuss wall murals, and wacky, colorful furnishings) and the rest either in fun medieval royalty finery or a sailboat theme. The kid's bedroom is minus its own entry into the main hallway for safety purposes, only opening to the adult's room. They come with either a garden or a bay view.

Off the foyer of the Villa Suites is a study as well as a bathroom with single sink and shower. The living room has two deep balconies (in only three of the Villa Suites so it isn't guaranteed), chenille sofa and two easy chairs in rich gold and red, entertainment center, large granite coffee table, service kitchen, and eight-person dining table. Either one (1,110 square feet) or two bedrooms (1,600 square feet) are on each side of the living area: one a deluxe king and the other a deluxe with two queens. Views are of the bay.

Two Governatore Suites, each at 2,300 square feet, offer a single-sink half-bath off the foyer and a massive living area overlooking the piazza and lagoon. Tile floors are topped by a rich area rug accompanied by two soft gold chenille sofas adorned with cherry red pillows, two easy chairs, an ottoman-style coffee table, and stand-up balcony the length of the room. The columned dining room with stand-up balcony seats ten and near it is a service kitchen. You'll also find a luxurious office perfect for those times when work is a must. The oversize master features gold and red fabrics, a settee, sofa, easy chair, coffee table, entertainment center, and floor-to-ceiling picture windows; its lovely granite bath comes with a walk-in closet, separate toilet and bidet, huge vanity, double sinks, enormous whirlpool tub with mosaic tiles, and a regal separate shower. Definitely a WOW! A queen deluxe guest room connects off the dining room.

The fantastic Presidente Suite is one floor above the Governatore's Suite and is very similar only with 2,765 square feet of lavishness. The decor is the same, but it comes with the addition of a wonderful, deep balcony overlooking the piazza and lagoon with lounge chairs and table, the office is larger with a TV and stereo, and the living room has a gas fireplace. Up to three additional guest rooms can be connected, making it perfect for a family gathering.

**DINE**

**Bice.** Portofino Bay's trendsetting Italian restaurant; dinner only. (See full description in Dining chapter.)

**Gelateria/Caffe Espresso.** Specialty coffees; pastries, bagels, muffins, cereal, and juice in the morning; the best gelato around; banana splits, sundaes, milk shakes; open 6 to 11 a.m. and 4 to 10 p.m.

**Mama Della's Ristorante.** Old-World, hearty Italian food; dinner only; festive atmosphere of Mama Della's home; outdoor seating available on piazza. (See full description in Dining chapter.)

**Sal's Market and Deli.** Delightfully authentic Italian deli; antipasto, excellent brick-oven pizza, paninis, a plethora of salads; cheesecake, cannoli, tiramisu; specialty coffees, wine; additional seating on piazza.

**Splendido Pizzaria.** Caesar salad, fried calamari, fried cheese ravioli, shrimp cocktail, nachos, brick-oven pizzas, salads, burgers, hot dogs, buffalo chicken tender sandwich, vegetable burger, grilled grouper sandwich, wrap sandwiches; specialty drinks and smoothies; adjacent to Beach Pool.

**Trattoria Del Porto.** Family-style restaurant serving breakfast and lunch daily; dinner hours and opening days change seasonally; hand's on kid's cooking on Sunday and Monday night, Italian buffet on Friday and Saturday night, character dinner (Scooby Doo and Woody Woodpecker) on Thursday and Friday night; outdoor seating available on piazza; *breakfast:* buffet as well as a la carte items such as frittatas, steak and eggs, Belgian waffles, whole grain and nut griddle cakes, smoked salmon and bagel, panetone French toast; *lunch:* chop salad, grilled sustainable salmon filet with new potato piquillo pepper hash, organic open faced tomato-arugula omelet, shrimp pappardelle pasta, vegan portobello bolognese; *dinner:* Key West line-caught yellow tail snapper, oven seared roasted natural half chicken with creamy potatoes, roasted chicken penne pasta with Vidalia onions and Italian sausage, grilled beef tenderloin filet with twice baked potato.

**In-Room Dining.** Available 24/7.

## SIP

**Bar America.** Elegant bar with a relaxing atmosphere and martinis, fine wine, grappa, cognac, and single-malt scotch; *appetizers:* smoked salmon, shrimp cocktail, flatbread pizza, antipasto platter.

**Bice Bar.** Classy bar in Bice restaurant serving up cocktails and wine along with a full menu, piano music, and Italian movies; indoor and outdoor seating.

**Splendido Poolside.** Beach Pool bar.

**The Thirsty Fish.** Family-friendly bar on the piazza; wine, cocktails, bellinis, cognac, single-malt scotch, port, sherry; food service from Sal's Market and Deli; live music and outdoor seating on the piazza.

## PLAY

**Arcade.** Located adjacent to Beach Pool.

**Bocce Ball Court.** Located near the Villa Pool.

**Children's activities and playground.** Loews Loves Little Kids presented by Fisher-Price® includes baby and toddler play classes with parent and child attendance, in-room baby and toddler equipment like the Aquarium Play Yard and the Aquarium Take-Along Swing, Fisher-Price welcome gifts for children under age ten, and a selection of toys available to loan for children six months to six years. Playground located by the children's pool.

**Jogging.** Lovely pathways connect all three Universal hotels with City-Walk; maps available at the concierge desk.

**Swimming.** Mediterranean-style Beach Pool with Roman aqueduct–style waterslide, waterfall, kiddie pool, and two whirlpools; secluded Hillside Pool at end of East Wing; Villa Pool encircled by tall cypress trees; cabanas available at the Villa and Beach Pools with table and four chairs, chaise lounges, wireless Internet, ceiling fan, refrigerator stocked with soft drinks and water, and fruit bowl; dive-in movies Saturday night, weather permitting.

### WORK, MOVE, SOOTHE

**Business center.** Computer rentals, packaging and shipping, fax and copy service; open Monday through Friday, 7 a.m. to 6 p.m., and Saturday, 9 a.m. to 3 p.m.

**Car rental.** Hertz Rent-A-Car desk located just off main lobby.

**Child care.** Campo Portofino; arts and crafts, video games, movies. Open Sunday through Thursday, 5 to 11:30 p.m., and Friday and Saturday, 5 p.m. to midnight for children ages four to fourteen; reserve twenty-four hours in advance; verify hours of availability as they may change seasonally. Call Kid's Nite Out for children under the age of four at (407) 828-0920.

**Golf.** The Golf Universal Orlando program allows for preferred tee times, complimentary transportation, club rentals, and free range balls at several nearby courses including MetroWest Golf Club, Orange County National Golf Center, and Mystic Dunes Golf Club.

**Fitness center.** Cybex and Life Fitness cardio equipment and strength training machines, free weights, coed whirlpool, steam room, sauna, and locker facilities; all treadmills, upright bicycles, and stair climbers offer individual TV monitors; $10 per day or complimentary for the duration of the day with a spa treatment; open 6 a.m. to 10 p.m.

**Spa.** Mandara Spa; massage, facials, body and hydrotherapy treatments; manicures, pedicures, salon services, scalp and hair treatments. (See full description in Spas section of chapter 5, Beyond the Theme Parks.)

**GO**

A walking path near the hotel's west wing connects Portofino Bay with the Hard Rock Hotel, Universal Studios, Islands of Adventure, CityWalk, and the Royal Pacific Resort, or take a lovely, convenient boat ride leaving from the dock located bayside. Complimentary shuttle bus service is provided to Universal, with infrequent service to SeaWorld and Aquatica.

## Royal Pacific Resort

**1,000 rooms. 6300 Hollywood Way, Orlando 32819; phone (407) 503-3000, fax (407) 503-3010. Check-in 4 p.m., checkout 11 a.m. For reservations call (877) 801-9720, or (866) 563-9792, or your travel agent, or go online at www.loewshotels.com or www .universalorlando.com. $$–$$$$$**

**Why Stay Here?** Gorgeous public rooms in a South Seas setting.

**Rooms to Book.** If children are in your party you must book a Jurassic Park–themed Kid's Suite on the seventh floor with club amenities.

**Don't Miss.** Dinner at Emeril's Tchoup Chop, one of Orlando's loveliest dining rooms.

The Golden Age of travel in the 1930s South Pacific is the setting of this exotic resort. From a bamboo footbridge suspended above a tropical forest and a cooling stream, you'll enter the stunning lobby filled with hundreds of flowering orchids, lofty potted palms, exotic wood carvings, and Asian-style batik and rattan furnishings. A picturesque glassed courtyard is centered around a sparkling reflecting pool surrounded by hand-carved Balinese stone maidens and elephants. A soothing lobby lounge is the perfect spot for drinks and sushi, and out back beyond the resort's famous pool is a sparkling lagoon where a vintage floatplane is beached. It's simply a tropical paradise.

**REST**

**Guest rooms.** Although rooms here don't quite live up to the deluxe standards of the Hard Rock and Portofino Bay hotels, the rates are so reasonable (this is Universal's least expensive resort) and the public areas so charming, I thought this hotel needed to be included. With only 335 square feet, guest rooms have rattan beds topped with white duvets, bamboo fabric shams, a mango-hued bolster, and a floral and bamboo motif throw in a tropical palette of aqua, melon, and kiwi. Bedding is triple-sheeted with soft down pillows, but with too-firm mattresses. Other additions include sisal-style carpeting, a palm-frond ceiling fan, rattan and cane furnishings, and bamboo touches. The only unattractive aspects are the dark, dreary porcelain tile in the entry and the scuffed entry doors. You'll also find an iPod docking station alarm clock radio, Keurig single-cup coffeemaker, and 32-inch flat-panel TV. Those with a king-size bed offer the addition of either an oversized easy chair or a small sleeper sofa. A metal bamboo-patterned wall screen divides the gold and black granite vanity area from the sleeping area. In it you'll find a single sink with non-lighted makeup and full-length mirrors, hair dryer, scale, and Bloom bath products; a separate toilet and tub area is decorated with somewhat dated gold ceramic tile. Amenities include high-speed Internet access, laptop-size electronic safe, iron and ironing board, two dual-line telephones (one cordless), robes, on-demand movies, minibar, and daily *New York Times* newspaper delivery on request. One complaint is the thin connecting doors that allow just about everything to be heard in the next room. *CARA'S TIP:* There are only two types of views here: standard and water. Standard views overlook the highway or the front of the hotel (request a room in Tower 1 with lovely views of the elaborate tropical gardens and a waterfall). Water views face the resort's beautiful pool and the Universal parks in the distance. Alas, none of the rooms, including suites, have balconies.

**Concierge rooms.** Concierge rooms and suites on the seventh floor come with access to the spacious Royal Club (albeit with a view of the highway), well worth the extra charge. Begin your day with a continental breakfast of mini-muffins, croissants, donuts, hot cinnamon rolls, pastries, toast, bagels, fruit, juice, oatmeal, and cereal. Beverages and light snacks such as fruit, granola bars, nuts, trail mix, and cookies are offered throughout the day. In the evening you'll find a small but great selection of offerings—the likes of potato salad, cheese, pasta salad, salmon with bok choy and teriyaki rice, sushi, spring rolls, conch fritters, chicken wings, ahi tuna, guacamole and salsa with chips, and crudités with dip—along with complimentary beer and Bulletin Place and Beringer wine with bar drinks costing $5; for children there are PB&J sandwiches and cookies. After dinner are desserts such as carrot cake, make-your-own strawberry shortcake, dessert shooters, Oreo cream puff and coconut cream pie, cheesecake, brownies, and cookies, along with coffee and nonalcoholic beverages. Also included are the services of a very nice concierge staff, complimentary fitness room privileges, discounted pool-side cabanas, DVD players, turndown service, and robes.

**Suites.** Only those suites on the seventh floor come with club level amenities. Kid's Suites at 670 square feet have a super-fun Jurassic Park themed bedroom for the children including two twin beds with raptor cage headboards, dinosaur wall mural, metal desk and chair, photos of the filming of *Jurassic Park,* a wall-mounted 32-inch flat-panel TV, and DVD player. The parents room is decorated in standard decor with king-size bed, table with two chairs, dresser, occasional chair with ottoman, flat-panel TV, and closet. The bathroom is part of the parent's guest room. The kid's bedroom is minus its own entry into the main hallway for safety purposes, only opening to the adult's room. Many have a view of the pool, but request one in Tower 1 which overlooks the resort's waterfall and tropical jungle, perfect for Jurassic immersion.

King Suites are 670 square feet and feature a king bed in the standard guest room with the addition of a separate living area with a sleeper sofa.

Hospitality Suites with 1,005 square feet come with a large living area holding a sleeper sofa, flat-panel TV with stereo and DVD player, rattan easy chairs, large desk, butler's pantry, bathroom with single sink and shower, and eight-person dining table. Attached is a standard guest room with two queen-size beds; a second king bedroom can be added for a total of 1,340 square feet.

The resort's 1,340-square-foot Presidential Suites called the Captain's Suites are smaller than comparable suites at other resorts, but what they lack in size is more than made up in their wonderful island style. Along with an up-close view of the pool and parks, the living room has stylish wicker and rattan furniture, a cushy cream-colored sofa, six-person dining table with bamboo chairs, kitchen, half bath, 42-inch flat-panel TV, stereo, and DVD player. There's a great office with a TV, full-size desk, and easy chair with ottoman. The delightful bedroom comes with sea grass furnishings, a white duvet with red accents, and walls of sea grass wallpaper and hand-carved wood. You'll also find another flat-screen TV, king-size bed, easy chair, and ottoman. The bathroom features a small TV, walk-in closet, above-counter double sink in a granite vanity, whirlpool tub, shower, vanity desk, and separate toilet/bidet area. A standard guest room with two queens can connect to this suite if desired. The seventh-floor Captain's Suite has a bamboo four-poster bed and club access; the sixth-floor suite, while virtually the same, has no club access and a standard king bed.

## DINE

**Bula Bar and Grille.** Poolside eatery and bar; *appetizers:* creamy shrimp and spinach dip, fish tacos, Asian chicken salad, chimichurri steak wrap, chicken sandwich with smoked gouda and guacamole on Hawaiian sweet-bread, grilled mahi mahi salad, vegetarian burger, turkey burger on brioche; specialty tropical drinks, beer, wine.

**Emeril's Tchoup Chop.** Contemporary Asian/Polynesian cuisine in a stunning setting; lunch and dinner. (See full description in Dining chapter.)

**Island Dining Room.** One of Orlando's better casual family restaurants open for breakfast, lunch, and dinner; character meals on Monday, Tuesday, and Saturday evenings; Friday night seafood buffet and Saturday night Tastes of the Pacific with a bamboo steamer basket station, catch-of-the-day, and more, both with strolling musicians and hula dancing; *breakfast:* grilled steak and eggs, Belgian waffle, custom omelet, Tahitian French toast a l'orange, Hawaiian pancakes with toasted coconut, pineapple, and roasted macadamia nuts; *lunch and dinner:* big-eye tuna sliders, vegan portobello bolognese, Palmetto Creek Farms all natural grilled pork with guava BBQ glaze, roasted turkey club on seven-grain bread, Cuban sandwich; children's buffet nightly and Bali-style play area.

**Jake's American Bar.** Fun, atmospheric bar with food from 2 to 11 p.m. and drinks until 2 a.m.; karaoke Thursday and Sunday, live music Friday and Saturday night; great outdoor porch with waterfall views; specialty and tropical drinks, full bar; Wisconsin cheddar and broccoli soup, control tower onion rings, grilled chicken quesadilla, BBQ ribs with guava glaze and chipotle cream, veggie Cuban sandwich, Hawaiian pizza, chopped Waldorf salad, club sandwich, hickory smoked salmon, Wisconsin four cheese baked macaroni.

**Wantilan Luau.** Saturday and Tuesday night at 6 p.m. (additional show Friday night in summer) with native dances and stories; tropical fruit, green salad, ahi poke salad, lomi lomi chicken salad, kim chi Napa cabbage slaw, pit-roasted suckling pig, roasted South Pacific wahoo, teriyaki chicken breast, soy marinated beef flank steak with fried yucca; white chocolate macadamia nut pie, tropical-fruit cake, chocolate banana cake; mai tai, beer, wine, nonalcoholic beverages; *children's menu:* PB&J sandwich, chicken fingers, pizza, macaroni and cheese. Call (407) 503-3463 for reservations.

**In-Room Dining.** Available 24/7.

### SIP

**Orchid Court Lounge & Sushi Bar.** Sophisticated lobby lounge and sushi bar open nightly from 5 to 11 p.m.; cocktails, sushi, sashimi, seaweed salad; *desserts:* tempura cheesecake, ginger crème brûlée, chocolate mousse martini; *breakfast:* specialty coffees, pastries, bagels, croissants, English muffins, warm cinnamon rolls, yogurt, cereal, fruit, juice.

### PLAY

**Arcade.** Game Room adjacent to the pool; high-tech games, pinball machines, and old-school machines.

**Beach.** A pleasant beach with lounge chairs facing the lagoon; beach volleyball.

**Children's activities and playground.** Loews Loves Little Kids presented by Fisher-Price® includes baby and toddler play classes with parent and child attendance, in-room baby and toddler equipment like the Aquarium Play Yard and the Aquarium Take-Along Swing, Fisher-Price welcome gifts for children under age ten, and a selection of toys available to loan for children six months to six years. Pool games like sunken treasure and water balloon toss, hula hoop contests, relay and potato sack races, sand castle building, tug of war; playground located by the children's pool.

**Jogging.** Lovely pathways connect all three Universal hotels with City-Walk; maps available at the concierge desk.

**Swimming.** One of Royal Pacific's best assets is its tropical, 12,000-square-foot Lagoon Pool with zero-depth entry; two whirlpools, kiddie pool; 4,000-square-foot "ocean liner" interactive water play area with water cannons, lifeboats, water curtains, and squirters; sandy beach area; water volleyball, shuffleboard, table tennis; rustic poolside cabanas with private patio, TV, phone, wireless Internet, ceiling fan, lounge chairs, fruit bowl, and refrigerator with water and soft drinks ($125 for a full day); torch-lighting ceremony every Friday and Saturday; dive-in movies Friday and Saturday at dusk weather permitting.

**Volleyball.** Sand court on the beach.

### WORK, MOVE, SOOTHE

**Business center.** Fax, printing, copying, Internet, shipping and receiving, office supplies; open Monday through Friday, 7 a.m. to 7 p.m., and Saturday 9 a.m. to 4 p.m.; closed Sunday.

**Car rental.** Hertz Rent-A-Car desk located just off main lobby.

**Child care.** The Mariner's Club; movies, computer, arts and crafts, video games. Open Sunday through Thursday 5 to 11:30 p.m.; Friday and Saturday 5 p.m. to midnight for children ages four to fourteen. Reservations should be made twenty-four hours in advance by calling (407) 503-3235; verify hours of availability, as they may change seasonally.

**Golf.** The Golf Universal Orlando program allows for preferred tee times, complimentary transportation, club rentals, and free range balls at several nearby courses including MetroWest Golf Club, Orange County National Golf Center, and Mystic Dunes Golf Club.

**Fitness center.** The Gymnasium; Life Fitness and True treadmills and ellipticals, Life Fitness recumbent and upright exercise bicycles, free weights; men's and women's locker rooms, each with steam and sauna; coed whirlpool; massage and in-cabana poolside massage available; open 6 a.m. to 8 p.m.; $10 daily fee for fitness center use.

### GO

A walking path connects the resort to Islands of Adventure, Universal Studios, and CityWalk, or take the convenient boat ride. Complimentary shuttle bus service is provided to Universal, with infrequent service to SeaWorld and Aquatica.

# Other Notable Resorts Near Universal

The 500-acre Grande Lakes Orlando Resort consists of sister properties, the JW Marriott and the Ritz-Carlton. They share all their marvelous facilities with each other and are connected by a convention center and a fantastic spa. Although its location just off John Young Parkway seems out of the way, Walt Disney World is only fifteen minutes away, Universal ten minutes, and SeaWorld and Discovery Cove just down the road. Nearby is Rosen Shingle Creek with two AAA Four Diamond award winning restaurants.

## JW Marriott Orlando Grande Lakes

**1,000 rooms. 4040 Central Florida Parkway, Orlando 32837; phone (407) 206-2300, fax (407) 206-2301. Check-in 3 p.m., checkout 11 a.m. For reservations call (800) 576-5750 or your travel agent, or go online at www.grandelakes.com. $$–$$$$$**

**Why Stay Here?** A great lazy river pool, amazing golf course, and easy access to some of Orlando's best restaurants.

**Rooms to Book.** One with a lake view.

**Don't Miss.** The resort's guided canoe Eco Tour on lovely Shingle Creek.

A bubbling fountain centers the JW Marriott's elegant, Spanish-Moorish-style lobby, and miles of marble continue throughout the public areas and into the guest rooms. While I wouldn't exactly call this hotel true luxury, it does come with the benefits of the amenities of the adjoining Ritz Carlton, impeccable grounds, an excellent golf course, and a fair price. But beware! This is a major convention hotel, and you'll certainly feel the effects if your travel plans coincide with a large group. Double-check when making reservations to see whether a convention is planned during your stay, and if so, think about planning for another time. A new low-rise Marriott Vacation Club is next-door to the JW, but not situated so that it mars the views of the lake and golf course.

Perhaps the resort's best feature is its Lazy River Pool, similar to the Yacht and Beach Club's Stormalong Bay. The JW Marriott shares all facilities with the Ritz-Carlton, which translates into access to the fabulous spa and fitness center, the Ritz-Carlton Golf Club, and the Ritz's luxurious pool and grounds. What a deal! It's like getting double the pleasure for your money.

## REST

**Guest rooms.** The 420-square-foot guest rooms are quite comfortable and newly restyled with warm cherry wood furnishings. A seafoam blue sofa and leather headboard are mixed with sea green accents that blend nicely with the white bed duvets topped with a soft green and white bed runner. Triple sheeting, loads of soft feather pillows, and upgraded mattresses make for a restful night. Sheer gold and silver drapery lends a shimmery feel to the room. Atop a bureau is a 32-inch HD LCD TV, nature sound alarm clock, minibar, and laptop-size safe with power source. Other amenities include Nirvae bath products, weekday newspaper delivery, iron and ironing board, hair dryer, coffeemaker, robes, high-speed Internet access, three telephones (one of them mobile), and on-demand movies. Lovely marbled bathrooms come with a tub, separate shower, and single sink. There are two types of guest rooms: those with king-size bed, a small sofa bed, coffee table, and dark brown rattan easy chair, and ones with two double beds and an easy chair. Both are furnished with an ample work desk. Seventy percent of rooms come with a balcony (on request only), but don't expect full-size ones—it's standing room only for guests.

CARA'S TIP: Lakefront Rooms come with a view of the pool and lake with the golf course in the distance. But beware the so-called Garden View Rooms that actually have a view of the highway and parking lot.

**Suites.** Doors lead into the living area as well as the bedroom and bathroom from the foyer of the 840-square-foot Executive Suites. Separated from the living room with a curtained French door is a large guest room with king-size bed, easy chair, 32-inch HD LCD TV on top of a bureau, and, balcony. The living area features a sleeper sofa, easy chair with ottoman, coffee table, 37-inch LCD TV atop a bureau, minibar, electronic safe, desk, and another standing-room-only balcony. The bath is similar to those in a standard guest room. With the addition of a standard guest room on the other side of the entry hall, these suites can become two-bedroom.

Grande Suites are 1,275 square feet and have a living area with sofa and four easy chairs, six-person dining table, an alcoved office, and a standard-size guest room.

The one-bedroom, 2,100-square-foot Presidential Suite is embellished with lovely rose and moss green hues. The bedroom has a king-size bed, easy chair, and entertainment center with a huge sitting area and a bathroom with double sink, whirlpool tub, and giant-sized separate shower. The enormous living room holds two sofas, easy chairs, a coffee table, an entertainment center, an eight-person dining table, a kitchen, and a half bath off the foyer. The suite has three small balconies with standing room only.

## DINE

**Citron.** Billed as an "American brasserie"; breakfast buffet or a la carte menu such as three egg or egg white omelet, Harris Ranch petite filet and poached eggs, French toast, eggs Benedict with Canadian bacon or house cured salmon; *lunch:* 4X4 onion soup (four types of onions and four types of cheese), chop-chop salad with shrimp and avocado, Maine lobster roll, egg salad sandwich, pulled pork sandwich, Angus chuck burger, thin crust pizza; *dinner:* Harris Ranch filet with butter poached lobster, slow smoked baby back ribs, lamb porterhouse, lobster mac 'n' cheese; weekend buffet brunch.

**Primo.** Executive Chef Melissa Kelly, a James Beard award-winner, oversees this superb restaurant; dinner only. (See full description in Dining chapter.)

**Café Bodega.** Grab 'n' go with organic snacks and chocolates, grilled pizza, salads, homemade root beer.

**The Sushi Bar.** Lobby sushi and sashimi bar.

**Starbucks.** Espresso, cappuccino, soft drinks; pastries.

## SIP

**Lobby Lounge.** Cocktails, wine, and sake from noon to midnight; sushi, sashimi, burger, club sandwich, pizza, and dessert served from 5 to 10 p.m.; fire pit just outside with outdoor service.

**Quench Bar and Grill.** Pool bar; wine, beer, tropical drinks; cayenne Gulf shrimp, grilled chicken taco salad, grilled lemon pepper grouper sandwich, veggie burger, turkey club wrap, chicken Caesar wrap, blackened grouper salad, grilled chicken sandwich with pepper jack cheese and roasted red peppers, burger, shrimp wrap; *children's menu:* burger, chicken fingers, hot dog, grilled cheese, PB&J sandwich.

## PLAY

For additional Play, see the subsequent entry for the Ritz-Carlton Orlando Grande Lakes, which shares all facilities with the JW Marriott.

**Arcade.** Located on lower level near pool.

**Basketball.** Located at tennis courts.

**Bicycles.** Surrey and single-passenger bicycles available for rent.

**Children's activities and playground.** Playground located outside game room; arts and crafts, basketball shootouts, horseshoes, outdoor bowling, pool games, ceramics, tie dye tees, sand art, campfire s'mores and movies.

**Jogging.** A 1.3-mile path winds around the resort.

**Scuba.** Certified divers lead complimentary Saturday afternoon supplied air snorkeling and scuba lessons in the Lazy River pool for ages eight and up.

**Swimming.** Lazy River heated pool, a kids' wonderland, offers a quarter mile of winding delight along with waterfalls, five lagoon pools, and whirlpool; tube and float rentals; dive-in movies Saturday evenings, weather permitting.

**Tennis.** Three championship lighted courts located in front of the hotel open 7 a.m. to 10 p.m.; tennis clinics offered every Saturday, Tuesday, and Thursday mornings for a fee.

**Volleyball.** Complimentary sand court located lakefront near the pool.

## WORK, MOVE, SOOTHE

For additional services see the subsequent entry for the Ritz-Carlton Orlando Grande Lakes, which shares all facilities with the JW Marriott.

**Business center.** FedEx Kinko's with computer workstations, fax, copier, office supplies, shipping services, high-speed Internet; open 24/7 with attendant on duty Monday through Friday from 7 a.m. to 7 p.m.; up to twenty copies and incoming faxes are complimentary at the front desk.

**Car rental.** A Hertz Rent-A-Car desk is in the lobby area.

## GO

Shuttle service is available to all four Walt Disney World theme parks for $18 round-trip per person with Mears Transportation (two-hour advance notice necessary); shuttles to Universal Orlando and SeaWorld are complimentary. A car rental here is a must for convenience.

## Ritz-Carlton Orlando Grande Lakes

**584 rooms. 4012 Central Florida Parkway, Orlando 32837; phone (407) 206-2400, fax (407) 206-2401. Check-in 3 p.m., checkout 11 a.m. For reservations call (800) 241-3333 or your travel agent, or go online at www.grandelakes.com. $$–$$$$$**

**Why Stay Here?** One of Orlando's most sophisticated resorts with the best concierge lounge around.

**Room to Book.** A roomy Executive Suite with two balconies overlooking the lake and the golf course.

**Don't Miss.** A reservation at the Ritz-Carlton spa in a VIP Suite along with a spa lunch served on the suite's elegant balcony.

Welcome to paradise! A calm refuge in the middle of a sea of theme parks, this sophisticated and elegant resort is a destination in itself. If you feel like heading to the theme parks, great. If not, don't worry! You really won't feel you've missed much, so engrossed you'll be in the resort's luxurious spa, its full-service fitness center, the ornate pools, a Greg Norman–designed eighteen-hole golf course with a unique Caddy-Concierge Program, and Normans, the resort's signature restaurant. If you're looking for a new, contemporary look so often found in today's resorts you won't find it here where the style is Old World.

You know you've come to the right place as you enter the limestone and marble lobby, a study of understated luxury. Throughout the public areas are sofas and easy chairs in soothing fabrics of sea blue, mossy green, buttercup yellow, and delicate rose hues, floors covered in Oriental rugs, and walls of original oil paintings. The level of service is fantastic—you'll understand what I mean when every staff member, from the housekeepers to the top echelon, always passes with a greeting.

The grounds are sumptuous, perfectly manicured with rose gardens and palm trees, bocce ball courts, and a palazzo-style pool overlooking the resort's lake and golf course. And who can resist the Mediterranean-style spa, located between the Grande Lake's two hotels, one of the most deluxe and undoubtedly the largest in the Orlando area. Its forty luxurious treatment rooms will make you giddy, along with a 4,000-square-foot private lap pool, a Carita Institute and Salon, a spa cafe, and a 6,000-square-foot workout facility. Just a walk-through is enough to soothe your fragile nerves. Soft, gentle music wafts down the halls, with each darkened treatment room more extravagant than the last. And in the fitness area, each treadmill, elliptical rider, and stair-climber is outfitted with its own TV monitor and headphones as well as in-machine fans that cool you throughout your routine.

**REST**

**Guest rooms.** In these plush, 490-square-foot beauties, you'll find so-soft feather beds topped with snow white duvets, triple-sheeted Frette linens, and feather pillows. Sophisticated floral motif dust ruffles and accent pillows complete the picture. Furnishings include a buttercup yellow easy chair with ottoman (only in rooms with a king-size bed), golden blond desk, and armoire. Creamy white marble bathrooms with subtle leafy green wallpaper have double sinks, a tub as well as a bit-too-small shower, and a separate room for the toilet. Each guest room has a 5-foot-long balcony, and, as you might expect, is well equipped with Internet access, a 32-inch LCD TV, on-demand movies, electronic safe large enough for a laptop computer, coffeemaker, iPod docking station clock radio, minibar, CD and DVD players, multiline telephones, and iron and ironing board. Extra amenities include complimentary shoe shines, plush robes and slippers, Bulgari bath products, lighted makeup mirror, twice-daily housekeeping service, and a daily *New York Times.* Upon returning to your room in the evenings, you'll find the bed turned down, slippers on the floor beside it, and the radio softly playing in the background. Views are either of the front of the hotel and the highway in the distance or perhaps the inner courtyard (referred to as a garden view), the lake and golf course (lake view), or the pool, lake, and golf course (lake front).

*CARA'S TIP:* A major room renovation is scheduled to begin in late 2010. While still luxe, the guest rooms are starting to look a bit behind the times so a fresh new look might be just the ticket.

**Concierge rooms.** Guests of the twelfth and fourteenth floors as well as all suites bask in the lap of luxury at the Ritz-Carlton Club, a keyed-access fourteenth-floor lounge with spectacular views of the surrounding area. There's even a large balcony, a perfect spot from which to watch the sunset. A "your wish is my command" policy is in full force here regarding the unbelievably accommodating staff, who go so far as to shake up a James Bond–style martini just for the asking. With such diverse food and beverage choices, you could just about skip restaurant meals. Mornings begin with a friendly greeting along with fresh fruit, cottage cheese, bagels, oatmeal, cold cuts, frittata, smoked salmon and garnishes, cheeses, cereal, hot and cold pastries, yogurt parfait, and hard-boiled eggs—in short, plenty to start your day off right. Lunch is quite extensive with three flavors of iced tea, cheeses, crudités, cold soup and salads, mini-sandwiches (ham, tuna, chicken salad, vegetarian roll-up), hummus, and a nice variety of mini-desserts. Evenings bring a buffet of Asian slaw, sea bass with peppers, pork bruschetta, roast duck with eggplant, and more. And be sure not to miss the after-dinner cordials, more wine and champagne, and desserts to die for, including biscotti, macaroons, chocolates, pots de crème, fruit and chocolate fondue, tiramisu, and madeleines. From lunch until closing, premium and sparkling wines flow freely. You'll also find an assortment of beverages, a cappuccino machine, and an open bar. Wine choices include a Steven Kent Chardonnay and Cabernet, Beringer White Zinfandel, Saddleblock Pinot Noir, and Francois Montand Champagne. And if you still have an appetite, here's the clincher—an always filled-to-the-brim "humidor," with a variety of addictive homemade cookies. This is one concierge lounge where your money is more than well spent and all for around $120 more per night than a standard room. I really think it's Orlando's best bargain.

**Suites.** The 960-square-foot Executive Suite doesn't even feel like a hotel room; it's more like a stylish apartment—spacious and luxurious with Frette linens, down pillows and comforters, and feather beds (of course, all of these items are standard in all guest rooms). The large separate bedroom holds a king-size bed, desk, easy chair with ottoman, and walk-in closet. The impressive marble bathrooms, of which there are two (one is a half bath), and the spacious living room are a welcome indulgence. In the living area are a bureau entertainment center with 37-inch LCD TV, sofa, coffee table, easy chairs, and wet bar. Perhaps the most difficult decision is choosing which of the suite's two balconies you want to loaf on. All come with Bose speakers, Bose wave radios, and CD and DVD players (a selection of DVDs is available from the resort's library). Executive Suites can become two-bedroom suites with the addition of a standard guest room on the opposite side of the living room. All have views of the lake and golf course.

Kids Suites are basically an Executive Suite with an additional connecting guest room outfitted especially for children. Absolutely precious is the regatta decor, which includes twin beds, kid-size table and chairs, a padded window seat in place of balcony doors, a TV with DVD player, and an assortment of fun toys and games.

The penthouse-level Ritz-Carlton and Presidential Suites are exactly the same configuration at 2,400 square feet but with different color schemes. The one-bedroom Ritz-Carlton Suite is decorated in a soft lemon, peach, and green palette, and the Presidential Suite is adorned in a richer rose hue, both with traditional fabrics. A new look is needed here with the carpeting and fabrics starting to look tired so inquire if renovations have been completed before booking one of these suites. Enter from a large marble foyer into a living room furnished with two sofas, easy chairs, coffee table, desk, wall-mounted 37-inch LCD TV, and eight-person dining table. You'll also find a half bath, a very small service kitchen, and balconies running the length of the suite overlooking the resort's pool and golf course with fantastic views outward to the surrounding area. The large bedroom contains a four-poster bed (the Ritz Carlton Suite has a bit of Asian touch to it), a huge sitting area with sofa, TV, and desk as well as walk-in closet with vanity table. An immense white marble bathroom has an oversized whirlpool tub just begging for a bath time soak, double sinks, stand-alone shower, and separate toilet area. In the Ritz Carlton Suite is a wheelchair-accessible roll-in shower.

**DINE**

**Bleu.** Atypical pool grill serving wonderful updated appetizers, sandwiches, salads, and desserts; flatbread, Bahamian jerk chicken quesadilla, coconut shrimp, guava BBQ shrimp salad, crab cake sandwich, snapper tostados; views of the lake and golf course from a covered or open-air patio; frozen drinks and cocktails great for sunset viewing; also services the pool area.

**Fairways Pub.** Dining at the golf clubhouse; Maine crab and corn chowder, fried calamari, Caesar salad with blackened shrimp, jumbo lump crab cake salad, crispy chicken wrap with caramelized onion and provolone, grilled vegetable sandwich, Florida grouper with preserved lemon tartar sauce, dry rubbed and smoked Black Angus strip loin served on a sourdough hoagie roll with Muenster cheese, fried onions, and chipotle pepper mayonnaise; open 11 a.m. to 5 p.m. with cocktails until dusk.

**Normans.** The resort's premier restaurant, featuring the New World cuisine of Norman Van Aken; dinner only. (See full description in Dining chapter.)

**Vitale Spa Café.** The spa's eatery offers Vietnamese chilled shrimp summer roll, blue crab and asparagus salad, oriental chicken or Caesar salad, whole wheat grilled chicken and avocado wrap, open-faced grilled snapper sandwich, Black Angus sirloin burger, sesame-crusted seared tuna, bento box with your choice of one protein (poached salmon, grilled snapper, filet mignon, etc.), and three side salad options (oriental glazed mushrooms, Indian three-bean salad, citrus and hearts of palm, quinoa salad, soba noodles, etc.); chocolate crème brûlée, warm pear puff pastry, cinnamon ice cream and apricot coulis.

**Vineyard Grill.** Casual restaurant serving breakfast, lunch, and dinner; *breakfast:* buffet and a la carte items such as frittatas, cinnamon raisin French toast, house smoked salmon and garnishes, petit filet mignon with eggs; *lunch:* grilled salmon and cobb salads, Black Angus sirloin burger, swordfish melt, filet mignon sandwich, pan-roasted red snapper with lump crab; *dinner:* butter poached Maine lobster, bronzed snapper with pineapple rum glaze, lamb two ways (double cut and braised osso bucco), seven-ounce filet mignon with Gruyère cheese and polenta cake; elaborate and very popular Sunday champagne brunch with interactive cooking stations and live music.

**In-Room Dining.** Available 24/7.

## SIP

**Lobby Lounge.** Lovely and relaxing lobby lounge serving cocktails and light meals from 11 a.m. until closing; French onion soup, artisanal cheeses, ground sirloin burger, chicken quesadilla, buffalo style chicken tenders, Florida crab cake; traditional afternoon tea daily from 2 to 4 p.m. with a Peter Rabbit tea offered for children (reservations recommended on weekends by calling 407-393-4060); excellent live entertainment Saturday through Wednesday 8 p.m. to midnight.

**Normans Salon.** Sophisticated cocktail lounge within Normans restaurant; premium wine and champagne, martinis, beer, brandies; full restaurant menu available.

## PLAY

For additional Play, see the previous entry for the JW Marriott Orlando Grande Lakes, which shares all facilities with the Ritz-Carlton.

**Adventure Course.** Multi-level structure of poles, cables, and platforms with twenty-five unique traversing and climbing elements; rock climbing wall, 600-foot zip line, and a 40-foot Giant's Swing; choose your own personal level of challenge; various packages are available to those over age ten.

**Bicycles.** Available near the pool area.

**Bocce court and shuffleboard.** Located near the Villa Pool on the Da Vinci Lawn.

**Children's activities and playground.** Children's check-in desk in the lobby; playground located near the kiddie pool; Ritz Kid's open play, arts and crafts, Frisbee toss, scavenger hunts, pool relay races; Grande Lakes Junior Adventure Course for guests above the age of five with thirteen unique climbing and traversing elements including a mini swing and a 120-foot mini zip line.

**Fishing and eco-tours.** Grande Lakes Outfitters offers private fly-fishing instruction, two-day fly-fishing seminars, First Time Flyer three-hour seminars, and 18 Holes of Bass Fishing on the golf course's private ponds, all with professional guides; private guided eco-tours by canoe or kayak on Shingle Creek; open to outside visitors; call (407) 393-4060 to reserve.

**Golf.** Greg Norman–designed course set on the headwaters of the Florida Everglades; 11,000-square-foot clubhouse with retail store and restaurant; innovative Gold Caddy-Concierge Program (see full description in the Golf section of chapter 6, Sporting Diversions, for details).

**Swimming.** Gracious Romanesque-style main pool and whirlpool surrounded by palm trees and cushy lounge chairs; lake- and pool-side cabanas available for rent complete with TV, refrigerator stocked with soft drinks and water, fruit plate, and ceiling fan; private outdoor lap pool and whirlpool at the spa (open only to spa guests); dive-in movies on Saturday evenings.

## WORK, MOVE, SOOTHE

For additional services see the previous entry for the JW Marriott Orlando Grande Lakes, which shares all facilities with the Ritz-Carlton.

**Business center.** Fax, photocopying, shipping, high-speed Internet access, personal computers, and laser printers; located on the lower level next to the convention area; 24/7 access with attendants on duty Monday through Friday 7 a.m. to 7 p.m. and Saturday 7 a.m. to 5 p.m.

**Child care.** Ritz Kids for children ages five to twelve offers a variety of programs including arts and crafts, dive-in pool parties, outdoor adventures, dinner and a movie, fish feeding, lady bug release, surrey bike rides, Wii tennis tournament, limbo contest, cookie decorating, and more; open daily noon to 10 p.m.; youth program also available for older children; nanny service by licensed and bonded professionals can be arranged with a twenty-four-hour advance notice.

**Fitness center.** Complimentary to resort guests; 6,000-square-foot facility; dry saunas, steam rooms, and specialty showers (extra fee for those not paying for a spa treatment); fabulously equipped with free weights and Life Fitness resistance training equipment, and outfitted with individual TV monitors in all cardiovascular equipment including Precor and LifeFitness elliptical cross trainers and Star Trac Pro recumbent bicycles and treadmills (with individual fans); fitness classes such as yoga, Pilates, core classes, body conditioning, fun boot camp, and spinning available for an additional fee; open daily 5 a.m. to 10 p.m.

**Hair and nail salon.** Carita Salon, located within the spa building, for cut, styling, shampoo and conditioning, blow-drying and sets, scalp and hair reconstructive treatments, coloring and highlighting, mustache and beard trims, manicures, pedicures, tips and acrylics, sculptured nails, silk and fiberglass wraps.

**Spa.** 40,000-square-foot facility with forty treatment rooms; men's and women's areas offering locker rooms, relaxation lounges, dry sauna, aromatic steam rooms, showers, and verandas; retail store; private spa pool available only to spa guests; call (407) 393-4200 for reservations and information. (See full description in Spas section of chapter 5, Beyond the Theme Parks.)

**GO**

Shuttle service is available to all four Walt Disney World theme parks for $18 round-trip per person with Mears Transportation (two-hour advance notice required); shuttles to Universal Orlando and SeaWorld are complimentary. A car rental here is a must for convenience.

## Rosen Shingle Creek

**1,500 rooms. 9939 Universal Boulevard, Orlando, Florida 32819; phone (407) 996-9939, fax (407) 996-9938. Check-in 3 p.m., checkout 11 a.m. For reservations call (866) 996-6338 or your travel agent, or online at www.rosenshinglecreek.com. $$–$$$$$**

**Why Stay Here?** Well priced, comfortable rooms, an award-winning golf course, and two of Orlando's better restaurants, Cala Bella and A Land Remembered Steakhouse.

**Rooms to Book.** One with VIP Lounge privileges, a bargain at only $50 more per night.

**Don't Miss**. A treatment at the lovely Spa at Shingle Creek.

Close to Universal Orlando and SeaWorld and only a ten-minute drive to the airport, this resort has a prime position on Shingle Creek, the headwaters of the Everglades. Completely surrounded by the Shingle Creek golf course and a 230-acre natural environment are luxurious accommodations, a super spa, and three pools. Reasonable room rates, two AAA Four Diamond Award winning restaurants, and the pristine golf course make this a resort to consider on your next trip to Orlando.

A somewhat austere lobby is outfitted with loads of creamy marble and stone, lofty wood-beamed ceilings, iron chandeliers, an oversize birdcage populated by native birds, and scattered seating areas, one with a fireplace. Come prepared for a large convention crowd, but because the convention facility is in a separate building, you won't see signs of it in the resort lobby. Holidays and summer are great, both low convention times perfect for families.

## REST

**Guest rooms.** Large, comfortable rooms at 436 square feet have an Old-World feel, handsomely outfitted with carved cherry wood furniture, soft lemon-colored walls, and, on the thirteenth and fourteenth floors, lofty ceilings with crown molding. Your sleep will be restful in what the hotel dubs a Creek Sleeper Bed. Pillows are soft, sheets are luxe, and beds are topped with a white duvet, firebrick red accents, and teal and gold-striped dust ruffle. Other details include a large work desk, a bureau with a 32-inch flat-screen TV, and color photos of the resort's nature areas. King-bedded rooms have a sofa, and rooms with two double beds an easy chair and ottoman. In the bath are handsome chocolate and beige granite countertops (in a height more appropriate for men) with a single sink; the tub and toilet area are separate. I love the Citrus & Cedar bath products, the same used in the resort's spa.

Amenities include high-speed Internet connection, hair-dryer, iPod docking station clock radio, digital movies, electronic laptop-size safes, two telephones, robes, iron and ironing board, mini-refrigerator, and Keurig one-cup coffeemaker. Alas, none have balconies. Views always include a vista of the golf course since it surrounds the resort, but half the resort offers a view of the parking lot (but also the SeaWorld fireworks), and the other half a view of the pool. Views are on request only. I like the corner rooms, which give you two additional windows, allowing in plenty of light.

**Concierge rooms.** There is not a concierge floor per se, but the VIP Lounge on the fourteenth floor is a nice retreat. Overlooking the pool and golf course with a very small balcony, it offers sweeping views of the surrounding area. For $50 more per night, a sure-to-please concierge staff as part of the deal, and with complimentary valet parking, fitness center access, and in-room Internet, it's one of Orlando's better bargains. There's even use of a laptop within the lounge—just ask at the concierge desk.

Morning continental breakfast consists of cereal, toast, pastries, mini muffins, bagels, yogurt, fruit, juice, and a self-serve cappuccino machine. In the evenings are typical catering-style appetizers like crudités and dip, cheese and crackers, and two hot dishes such as coconut shrimp, spring rolls, pot stickers, crab cakes, fried chicken fingers, fajitas, mini beef Wellington, teriyaki beef, and sundried tomato and feta in phyllo. For drinks there's a refrigerator stocked with Perrier and sodas, and honor bar cocktails, wine, and beer for a nominal charge. After dinner are chocolate petit fours with ganache, red velvet cake, and key lime tartlets.

**Suites.** With 159 suites there is no shortage of upscale accommodations here. The foyer of the Executive Suite is set apart by arches leading to a living/dining room combination with sofa, coffee table, two easy chairs, flat-panel TV, six-person dining table, queen Murphy bed, and full bath with shower and single sink. In an alcove near the dining table is a great granite bar with three high-back stools, microwave, sink, and small refrigerator. A standard guest room is just off the dining/bar area. The addition of more standard guest rooms makes these suites a one-, two-, or three-bedroom.

Three impressive Presidential Suites are all two-bedroom and 1,744 square feet, but each has a different, distinctive decor: The Hammock Suite (overlooking the front of the hotel) has a spa feel with shades of soothing blues and beige with palm motif bedding; the Ibis Suite (overlooking the pool) has a baby grand piano and shades of florals and terracotta; and the Everglades Suite (overlooking the front of the resort) has a pool table, masculine decor, a carved living room ceiling, and leather and chenille furnishings in rich tones. Each has a marble foyer off of which is a half bath. The open living/dining area is roomy with two sofas, two easy chairs, coffee table, second seating area with two chairs around the flat-panel TV, an eight-person dining table with large chandelier, and a granite bar set in an alcove. The master is king bedded with whirlpool tub and separate shower; the second bedroom has two queen beds and a larger-than-standard open bath with bidet, tub, separate shower, and double sinks.

### DINE

**Café Osceola.** Open for breakfast, lunch, and dinner; *breakfast:* buffet and a la carte items such as eggs and corned beef hash, eggs Benedict, smoked salmon and bagels, breakfast quesadilla, wild blueberry stack; *lunch and dinner:* grilled mojo shrimp salad, steak and cheese wrap, turkey and avocado wrap, Caribbean spiced swordfish with mango glaze, chicken or beef fajitas, penne with chicken, shrimp, wild mushrooms, spinach, tomatoes, and a creamy Boursin sauce; *nightly themed buffet:* Monday is Caribbean, Tuesday is Taste of Asia, Wednesday is Italian, Thursday is Southern Barbecue, Friday is a Seafood Buffet, Saturday and Sunday is All-American Prime Rib.

**Cala Bella.** Fine dining Italian bistro; open nightly from 5:30 to 10 p.m. (See full description in Dining chapter.)

**Cat Tails Pool Bar and Grille.** Bar and outdoor restaurant servicing the pool area; chips and salsa, conch fritters, spicy chicken nachos, pizza, Caesar salad with shrimp or jerk chicken, buffalo chicken salad, fruit plate, turkey club wrap, burger, fish tacos, hot dog.

**Clubhouse Grille.** Golf club restaurant with indoor and outdoor options; open for lunch only; cigar shrimp, baked spinach and Gruyère, southwest chicken salad, buffalo chicken salad, fish and chips, pesto grilled chicken breast sandwich, crab cake po' boy, blue cheese peppercorn burger, blackened prime rib open-faced sandwich with mushroom and provolone, Reuben wrap.

**18 Monroe Street Market.** Twenty-four-hour self-service deli (grill open 6:30 a.m. until midnight) with indoor and outdoor seating; *breakfast:* croissant breakfast sandwiches, fried egg sandwich, breakfast wrap in a flour tortilla, sausage biscuit, scrambled eggs, grits, oatmeal, potato cakes; *lunch and dinner:* hand-tossed pizzas, paninis, hot subs, lasagna, penne with marinara and meatballs or sausage, stromboli, black bean chili, hot and cold deli sandwiches and wraps; bakery with pastries, cookies, brownies, cakes, cannoli; mini convenience store with wine, beer, snacks, sundries, prepared sandwiches, and salads. Creek Ice Creamy here serves Haagen-Dazs ice cream, sorbet sippers, milk shakes, floats, and sundaes.

**A Land Remembered Steakhouse.** High-end classic steakhouse within the golf clubhouse; open nightly for dinner. (See full description in Dining chapter.)

**Smooth Java.** Starbuck's specialty coffees, smoothies; sandwiches, salads, fruit, fresh pastries, bagels, muffins; beverages, juice.

**In-Room Dining.** Available 24/7.

**SIP**

**Bella's Bar.** Hopping bar within Cala Bella restaurant with live piano music on weekends, cocktails, excellent wines by the glass, port, cordials, cigars; Cala Bella appetizers and desserts; open from 5 p.m. to midnight.

**Cat-Tails Pool Bar & Grille.** Small pool bar serving cocktails and the 18 Monroe Street Market menu (see above).

**Headwaters Lounge.** Convention center lounge. Specialty drinks, martinis, margaritas, mojitos, beer, wine, single-malt scotch, cognac; appetizers served after 5 p.m. of spinach dip and chips, peel-and-eat shrimp, loaded chicken nachos, conch fritters, fried calamari, spicy wings, salads, sandwiches and wraps, burger, fish tacos.

**A Land Remembered Bar.** Classy bar just off the restaurant serving great wines by the glass, several types of margaritas, and a full bar list. Appetizers include oysters, frog legs, crab cakes, sushi, steak tartare, warm brie and portobello mushroom, shrimp cocktail, ahi tuna, and flatbreads.

**Osceola Bar.** Tiny bar just outside of Café Osceola.

**PLAY**

**Arcade.** Nice-size arcade is located downstairs near the fitness center.

**Golf.** The Shingle Creek Golf Club; Brad Brewer Golf Academy for private lessons and Academy programs. (See full description in the Golf section of chapter 6, Sporting Diversions.)

**Fishing.** A fishing dock is located on the waterway near the tennis courts. Pick up a pole at The Spa ($10 for three hours); catch and release.

**Jogging.** Two jogging and nature trails: one skirts the golf course and the other leads to Shingle Creek where you may spot alligators, mallard ducks, owls, egrets, river otters, osprey, and blue heron; the only caveat is the highway noise.

**Swimming.** Three pools with absolutely no shady areas and little foliage: a lap pool, a family pool with a whirlpool and kiddie pool, and an adult pool with whirlpool; adult pool offers cabana rentals with lounge chairs, fan, bottled water, and fruit ($75 per day).

**Tennis.** Two lighted courts. Tetherball and horseshoes near tennis courts.

**Volleyball.** Sand volleyball court near tennis courts.

## WORK, MOVE, SOOTHE

**Baggage Airline Guest Service.** The same program offered at Walt Disney World resorts with the same airlines participating; airline check-in service allows passengers to receive a boarding pass and check in their luggage from the lobby; $10 charge per person; bags must be checked three to twelve hours prior to the flight, which eliminates flights before 9 a.m. from using this service.

**Business center.** Open Monday through Friday 7 a.m. to 7 p.m., Saturday and Sunday 8 a.m. to 5 p.m.; Internet, copies, fax, office supplies and rentals, shipping, computer and printer usage.

**Car rental.** Enterprise Rent A Car desk in hotel lobby.

**Child care.** Swamp Camp for children ages four to fourteen; indoor and outdoor play; computer center, play stations, cooking lessons, arts and crafts, science projects, movies, board games, hula hoop, ring toss, limbo contests. Open Thursday 5 to 11:30 p.m., Friday, and Saturday 5 p.m. to midnight with extended days and hours in busy season. In-room childcare, nannies, and mother's helper service available through Kid's Nite Out.

**Fitness center.** True treadmills, ellipticals, cardio bikes; Smith Machine and Paramount strength training equipment; free weights; $10 fee per day or $20 length-of-stay; personal training available by appointment; open from 6 a.m. until 10 p.m.; use of steam, sauna, and whirlpool are included in fee.

**Spa.** The Spa at Shingle Creek; massage, facials, body treatments, manicures, pedicures, salon services, makeup. (See full description in Spas section of chapter 5, Beyond the Theme Parks.)

## GO

Complimentary shuttles to Universal Orlando theme parks and CityWalk. Transportation to Disney theme parks for a fee.

# THE VERY BEST OF THE WALT DISNEY WORLD THEME PARKS

Newcomers often think Walt Disney World is comparable in size to California's Disneyland, with the Magic Kingdom being first and foremost in their minds. Most never envision a complex twice the size of Manhattan with four theme parks spread out over 30,000 acres. Yes, the Magic Kingdom, completed in 1971, was the first theme park at Walt Disney World. But three more parks followed in succession, beginning with Epcot a decade later. Twice the size of the Magic Kingdom, it was a totally different concept—an education in technology and innovation, other lands and cultures. Disney's Hollywood Studios followed in 1989, and with it came the glamour and glitz of show business. Then came the Animal Kingdom in 1998, conveying the theme of unity and harmony among all living creatures. Each park is unique and wonderful and offers its own brand of enjoyment with new additions and attractions constantly in the works.

# General Information

First I'll go over what you need to know about getting into and around the parks. Then I'll examine the best of each park. Walt Disney World features such a wealth of attractions that most people don't have enough time on a vacation to experience them all. That's why I've narrowed down the field for you and have chosen to feature the attractions that are, in my expert opinion, the very best each park has to offer. You'll find important information on only the best attractions and dining, the most anticipated special events, and the most memorable entertainment, plus loads of tips for making your vacation an exceptional one.

## *Disney Theme Park Admission*

There are many options available in Disney theme park passes, beginning with a Magic Your Way base ticket. Choose the number of days you wish to purchase and then start considering the many choices available to you. Purchase tickets by calling (407) WDW-MAGIC or (407) 939-6244, by going online at http://disneyworld.disney.go.com/tickets-passes, by visiting a Disney retail store, or by consulting a Disney specialist travel agent. No matter which ticket plan you opt for, children age two or younger get in free. The following are your ticket options:

**Magic Your Way Base Ticket.** Choose the number of days you'll need, allowing entrance to one theme park each day. Base Tickets are offered for as many as ten days. Tickets expire fourteen days after first use. You'll save with each extra day added.

**Park Hopper Option.** Allows park-hopping privileges for a flat rate of $52 regardless of the number of days.

**Water Parks Fun & More Option.** Includes one admission per day to your choice of Typhoon Lagoon, Blizzard Beach, DisneyQuest, Disney's Oak Trail Golf Course (advance reservations required), or ESPN Wide World of Sports for a flat rate of $52.

**No Expiration Option.** Allows the freedom to return to Walt Disney World anytime in the future and take advantage of unused days on your Magic Your Way Tickets, which would normally expire fourteen days after first use ($18 for two-day tickets, $24 for a three-day, $52 for a four-day,

$73 for a five-day, $84 for a six-day, $115 for a seven-day, $152 for an eight-day, $178 for a nine-day, and $209 for a ten-day ticket).

**Theme Park Annual Pass.** Unlimited access to all four Disney theme parks as well as complimentary parking and an array of discounts for 365 days. If you plan to return within a year, this is the way to go. You may even consider this type of pass for shorter stays simply to receive the great savings available to Annual Pass holders; only one person in your party must have an annual pass to obtain the discount. If you make an annual trip to Disney, you should plan your return trip a few weeks shy of the expiration date of your pass and your park admission will already be paid. At press time Annual Pass rates were $489 for adults (age ten and up) and $432 for children ages three through nine.

**Theme Park Premium Annual Pass.** Same as the Annual Pass but also includes Blizzard Beach, Typhoon Lagoon, Disney's Oak Trail Golf Course (advance reservations required), and DisneyQuest. At press time Premium Annual Pass rates were $619 for adults (age ten and up) and $546 for children ages three through nine.

## FASTPASS

FASTPASS is a free computerized service offered to all visitors as a way of reducing time spent waiting in line. Here's how it works. As you approach a FASTPASS attraction, you'll see two time clocks on display: one estimating the wait time in the normal line, the other the return time for the FASTPASS being issued at the moment. If the normal wait time is less than thirty minutes, by all means get in line. If not, just insert your park pass in one of the machines located at each individual FASTPASS attraction and receive a ticket printed with a designated one-hour window in which you may return and enter a special line with little or no waiting.

In most cases, only one FASTPASS at a time can be issued. To find out when you can receive another FASTPASS ticket, look on your current FASTPASS. Each person must have a FASTPASS to enter the line and must show it to the cast member (Disney's name for park employees) at the beginning of the line and the cast member waiting at the boarding area. There is usually no need to use FASTPASS for the first hour or so after the park opens, but it is a good idea to pick one up right away for one of the big attractions if you wish to ride it more than once later in the day. Note that on the most popular attractions, particularly in the busier seasons, those seeking a FASTPASS late in the afternoon may find there are none left for the remainder of the day.

## Touring Advice

Much ado is made of exactly how to approach each park and in what direction and order to tour. I think a bit of planning is necessary, and I have outlined a suggested touring plan for each theme park in the appendix. However, it does take the fun out of your vacation if you're tied down to a crazy, high-speed timetable. During very slow times of the year, determine which attractions are the most desirable in each park, and simply see each one as you encounter them.

In the busier seasons be in place at rope drop and head immediately to the most popular rides in the park. In the Magic Kingdom this means Splash or Space Mountain; in Epcot it's Test Track and Soarin'; at Disney's Hollywood Studios the biggies are Toy Story Midway Mania!, Tower of Terror, and Rock 'n' Roller Coaster; and at the Animal Kingdom move quickly to the Kilimanjaro Safaris or Expedition Everest. When you're finished with these attractions, pick one or two of the more popular rides and knock them off. After that you'll have lost your edge on the latecomers, so simply explore each attraction as you come to it, utilizing FASTPASS when necessary.

At the very least plan a loose itinerary for each day and make Advance Dining Reservations for any full-service restaurants. Find out before leaving home the park hours for the days of your vacation and what special events might be happening during your stay by going online at http://disney world.disney.go.com or calling (407) 824-4321. The worst thing you can do is wake up each morning and then decide what you want to do that day; that's best left for free days when you plan to just relax by the pool (speaking of free days, try to schedule one at some point in the middle of your trip to ease sore feet, unwind, and just enjoy). Failure to plan at least a bit could mean losing out on that great restaurant your friends told you about or missing a special show like Cirque du Soleil because it's totally booked. Of course, don't plan so stringently that there's no spontaneity in your day, no time to smell the roses. This is Disney after all.

The best advice I can give is to come during the slower times of the year (see chapter 1, Planning Your Trip, for details) by avoiding holiday weekends (except for maybe Labor Day and Veterans Day) and the height of summer. Of course, that may not be possible for those tied down to school schedules. I shouldn't admit it, but I took my children out of school during slower seasons, worrying about the extra homework later. It was well worth it!

### "Rider Swap" Program

Disney extends this option to parents with small children at all attractions with a height restriction. Just advise the cast member on duty upon entering the line. Your entire party will wait in line as usual until you reach the loading area. Then one adult rides while the other stays behind with the child. When the first adult returns, the second adult rides without delay.

## The Magic Kingdom

Most people's image of Disney is encompassed in a mere 107 acres of pure enchantment. Walt Disney World's first theme park is a kid's fantasy of marvelous, themed lands created to charge the imagination of young and old alike. Around every corner is a vision bound to take the breath away, one that's guaranteed to draw you back time and time again. Cinderella's Castle, the park's visual magnet, hits you square in the face as you walk under the train station and into a world of make-believe with all the glory of Main Street spread out before you and that fairy-tale castle at the end.

One big piece of news is an expanded Fantasyland opening sometime in 2013. Details includes the Be My Guest Restaurant located in the new Beast's Castle as well as quick-service fare at Gaston's Tavern. Meet and greet Disney princesses in Sleeping Beauty's cottage, Belle's village, and Cinderella's country chateau; there will even be an expanded Pixie Hollow featuring Tinker Bell and her fairy friends. And an Under the Sea with Ariel ride and expanded Dumbo attraction offering double the capacity promise to be huge hits. Get ready for the time of your life!

# Magic Kingdom

1. Walt Disney World Railroad
2. City Hall
3. Main Street Vehicles
4. Town Square Exposition Hall
5. Guest Information Board
6. Swiss Family Treehouse
7. Jungle Cruise
8. Pirates of the Caribbean
9. The Enchanted Tiki Room
10. The Magic Carpets of Aladdin
11. Frontierland Shootin' Arcade
12. Country Bear Jamboree
13. Splash Mountain
14. Walt Disney World Railroad
15. Big Thunder Mountain Railroad
16. Tom Sawyer Island
17. Liberty Square Riverboat
18. The Haunted Mansion
19. The Hall of Presidents
20. Peter Pan's Flight
21. "it's a small world"
22. Ariel's Grotto
23. Mickey's PhilharMagic
24. Dumbo the Flying Elephant
25. Cinderella's Golden Carousel
26. Snow White's Scary Adventures
27. Fairytale Garden
28. The Many Adventures of Winnie the Pooh
29. Mad Tea Party
30. Walt Disney World Railroad
31. Tomorrowland Speedway
32. Space Mountain
33. Walt Disney's Carousel of Progress
34. Tomorrowland Transit Authority
35. Astro Orbiter
36. Stitch's Great Escape!
37. Buzz Lightyear's Space Ranger Spin
38. Monster's Inc. Laugh Floor
39. Dream Along With Mickey

## Park Basics

### GETTING THERE

Those driving to Walt Disney World should take I–4 to exit 64 and then follow the signs to the Magic Kingdom.

### USING WALT DISNEY WORLD TRANSPORTATION

**From the Bay Lake Tower, Grand Floridian, Polynesian, and Contemporary Resorts:** Board the monorail and disembark at the park's entrance. Take the boat launch from the Grand Floridian, Polynesian, and the Wilderness Lodge to the Magic Kingdom's dock. You can also walk a short path from the Contemporary and Bay Lake Tower.

**From the Wilderness Lodge and Villas:** Take the Wilderness Lodge boat to the Magic Kingdom dock or use bus service.

**From other Disney Resorts, Disney's Hollywood Studios, and the Animal Kingdom:** Board the bus marked Magic Kingdom.

**From Epcot:** Take the monorail to the Transportation and Ticket Center (TTC), and then transfer to either the ferry or the direct monorail to the Magic Kingdom.

### PARKING

Cost is $14 per day; free to Walt Disney Resort guests and Annual Pass holders. Keep your receipt, good for parking at the Animal Kingdom, Epcot, and Disney's Hollywood Studios for that day only.

Because of the beautiful obstacle of the Seven Seas Lagoon, parking at the Magic Kingdom is a bit different than the other three Disney theme parks. Park in the lot, make a note of the section and aisle, and board the tram to the Transportation and Ticket Center. From there, take the ferry or monorail to the park entrance. If the monorail line is long, the ferry will be quicker. If riding the monorail, make sure you board the one departing for the Magic Kingdom, not Epcot.

### OPERATING HOURS

Open 9 a.m. to 7 p.m. or 8 p.m. with extended hours during holidays and busy seasons. Call (407) 824-4321 or log on to http://disneyworld.disney.go .com for updated park hours along with parade and fireworks information.

Get a jump on the crowds by arriving about 45 minutes early, allowing plenty of time to park, ride the monorail or ferry, buy tickets, and be one of the first to hit the big attractions. I recommend heading straight to Splash or Space Mountain.

## FASTPASS ATTRACTIONS

- Big Thunder Mountain Railroad
- Buzz Lightyear's Space Ranger Spin
- Jungle Cruise
- The Many Adventures of Winnie the Pooh
- *Mickey's PhilharMagic*
- Peter Pan's Flight
- Space Mountain
- Splash Mountain
- Stitch's Great Escape!

See the introduction to this chapter for FASTPASS details.

## PARK SERVICES

**ATMs.** Six cash-dispensing ATMs are located in the park: just outside the turnstiles on the right, next to the locker rentals, next to City Hall, in Fantasyland near the Pinocchio Village Haus restrooms, near the Frontier Shootin' Arcade, and in Tomorrowland Arcade. An additional machine is located at the TTC.

**Baby Care Center.** An infant facility found next to the Crystal Palace at the castle end of Main Street is outfitted with changing tables, high chairs, and a room for nursing mothers. Disposable diapers, bottles, formula, and baby supplies can be purchased. All restrooms throughout the park are outfitted with changing tables.

**First aid.** The First Aid Center is located at the end of Main Street next to Crystal Palace.

**Guest Relations.** City Hall, just inside the park entrance on the left, houses Guest Relations, where a knowledgeable staff is ready to assist with dining, ticket upgrades, messages for separated parties, information for guests with disabilities, and international guests.

**Guests with disabilities.** A guide for guests with disabilities is available at Guest Relations. Guests with mobility disabilities should park adjacent to the Entrance Complex (ask at the Auto Plaza for directions). Wheelchairs and ECVs are available for rent. Most restaurants and shops are accessible to guests with disabilities, although some quick-service locations have narrow queues with railings (ask a host or hostess for assistance). Companion-assisted restrooms are located at First Aid, the lower level of Cinderella's Royal Table, Pirates of the Caribbean, Splash Mountain, near the Pinocchio Village Haus in Fantasyland, to the right of Space Mountain, and at the TTC East Gate.

Over half of the attractions provide access through the main queue while others have auxiliary entrances for wheelchairs and service animals along with as many as five members of your party. Certain attractions require guests to transfer from their wheelchair to a ride system. Parade routes and some shows have designated viewing areas on a first-come, first-served basis.

Braille guidebooks, assistive listening devices, and audiotape guides are available at City Hall for a $25 refundable deposit. Handheld captioning receivers are available for a $100 refundable deposit. Reflective captioning is provided at many theater-type attractions and video captioning at some attractions. With a seven-day notice, a sign language interpreter will be provided at live shows on Monday and Thursday. For more information call (407) 824-4321 or (407) 827-5141 (TTY).

**Lockers.** Lockers are located at the TTC as well as on the right as you enter the turnstiles. The cost is $7 per day, plus a $5 refundable key deposit for a small locker, and $9 plus a $5 key deposit for large lockers. If you're park-hopping, keep your receipt for a locker at the three other Disney theme parks for no extra charge.

**Lost and Found.** Located at City Hall near the entrance or call (407) 824-4245.

**Lost children.** Locate lost children at the Baby Care Center next to the Crystal Palace at the castle end of Main Street. Go to City Hall after operating hours.

**Package pickup.** Located at Station Break underneath the Main Street Railroad Station. Allow three hours for delivery. Disney resort guests may send packages directly to their hotel for next-day arrival.

**Pet kennel.** A kennel, operated by Best Friends Pet Care, is located next to the TTC. For reservations and information call (407) 824-6568. Proof of vaccination is required.

**Strollers and wheelchairs.** Rentals are located under the Main Street Railroad Station. Single strollers are $15 per day, double strollers $31, and wheelchairs $10. Electric convenience vehicles are $45 inclusive of a $20 refundable deposit. Rental units must be returned to the original rental location to receive a security deposit refund. If you're park-hopping, keep your receipt for a same-day replacement at the three other Disney theme parks and Downtown Disney.

## The Lay of the Land

The compact Magic Kingdom consists of six bewitching lands accessed by five bridges leading from a central hub in front of Cinderella's Castle. Travel down Main Street to reach the hub from the front entrance. Moving counterclockwise around the hub, you first encounter the bridge to Tomorrowland. The second and third bridges take you to Fantasyland, the fourth crosses under the castle to Liberty Square and Frontierland, and the fifth brings you to Adventureland.

## The Very Best Attractions in the Magic Kingdom

### SPACE MOUNTAIN

Located in Tomorrowland, a 180-foot, conical-shaped "mountain" is one of the most popular attractions in the park, a cosmic roller coaster shooting through the darkest depths of the solar system. Load into six-person shuttle transporters and blast into orbit, plunging through a dark interior of sparkling comets, shooting stars, and glowing planets. Look closely to spot the other coaster ripping around on the second track. New enhancements include an interactive queue area, a smoother and quieter ride, new sound effects, and a darker interior. The somewhat slow (28 mph) ride holds only small drops and no loops or twists; it's just the darkness that makes it such a thrill. **Minimum height 44 inches (3 feet, 8 inches).**

**Not recommended for expectant mothers, those with back or neck problems, or those prone to motion sickness. FASTPASS. 2½-minute ride.**

CARA'S TIP: This is the second most popular ride in the park (Splash Mountain being the first), and lines can sometimes be extremely long. Come first thing in the morning or before park closing. And hang onto your valuables or risk losing them in the deep, dark vastness of space.

**THE MANY ADVENTURES OF WINNIE THE POOH**

Board giant "hunny" pots to travel through the Hundred Acre Wood with Pooh and his friends Piglet, Tigger, Eeyore, Owl, Kanga, and Roo. In Fantasyland, giant storybook pages relay the tale of a blustery day while sailing and bouncing through a Pooh dream sequence, rain and more rain, and at last a celebration. "Hooray!" Adults and children alike will be lulled into the delights of A. A. Milne's captivating stories accompanied by delightful music. **FASTPASS. 3½-minute ride.**

CARA'S TIP: Expect long lines and remember to use FASTPASS if necessary.

**MICKEY'S PHILHARMAGIC**

This 3-D attraction located in Fantasyland is a delightful winner! Even though Mickey's name is featured in the title, the mischievous Donald Duck steals the show as he takes visitors along on a wild ride through Disney animated movies, interacting with the largest cast of Disney characters ever in a single 3-D movie. You'll see Ariel, Aladdin, Jasmine, Lumiere, Simba, Peter Pan, Tinker Bell, and more, all accompanied by popular Disney music and fun in-theater effects of squirting water and delicious aromas. Shown on one of the largest seamless projection screens in the world (150 feet long and 28 feet high), it's an attraction kids as well as kids-at-heart will absolutely adore. **FASTPASS. 10-minute show.**

**PETER PAN'S FLIGHT**

This is one of the most endearing attractions in Fantasyland, sure to steal your heart. Though old-fashioned and certainly not a thrill a minute, you'll find it hard to resist "flying" with Peter Pan, Wendy, and the boys to Never Never Land. On gently soaring pirate ships, your adventure begins in the

# CHARACTER GREETING SPOTS IN THE MAGIC KINGDOM

The pointing Mickey glove on your guidemap will help you find the following locations:

- An assortment of Disney characters in Main Street Square throughout the day.
- *Alice in Wonderland* characters near the Mad Tea Party attraction in Fantasyland.
- Ariel's Grotto in Fantasyland where the mermaid herself is on hand for photos and autographs.
- *Winnie the Pooh* characters at Pooh's Playful Spot in Fantasyland.
- Buzz Lightyear in Tomorrowland.
- Peter Pan near Tinker Bell's Fairy Treasures in Fantasyland.
- A variety of characters in front of the Castle Forecourt Stage intermittently throughout the day.
- Aladdin and Jasmine in Adventureland near the Magic Carpets of Aladdin.
- Captain Hook, Mr. Smee, and Captain Jack Sparrow near the Pirates of the Caribbean ride in Adventureland.
- Characters from *The Princess and the Frog* are found in Liberty Square.

Darling nursery, "and off we go," flying over the twinkling lights of London with Big Ben and the London Bridge standing out against a starry, moonlit night (definitely the best part of the ride). Next stop Never Never Land, where far below are glistening waterfalls, glowing volcanoes, sunning mermaids, an Indian Village, the Lost Boys, and Captain Hook's ship. All the

# PARTY ON!

*By Mike Scopa*

Throughout the year Walt Disney World offers special parties at the Magic Kingdom that require special admission; regular park admission does not grant access to the park on party night. Discounts are available on selected nights for Annual Passholders and Disney Vacation Club Members. On party nights the Magic Kingdom closes at 6 p.m. and "reopens" at 7 p.m. Guests receive special wrist bands allowing access to the party.

Here are some important guidelines for party guests:

Order tickets as far in advance as you can to insure you get the date you want.

A day or two before the party, visit Guest Services and ask for a party brochure to become familiar with the event happenings.

On party day, to get the full party experience have dinner no later than 5:30 or 6 p.m.

Limit your attraction touring. Party entertainment and party happenings should take precedence over attraction touring.

Plan on seeing the later parade when the crown has thinned out.

Note entertainment times for parades and fireworks. Those times will dictate how you tour the park.

The longtime favorite parties are Mickey's Not So Scary Halloween Party (MNSSHP), which runs from September through October, and Mickey's Very Merry Christmas Party (MVMCP), which runs from November through December.

Mickey's Not So Scary Halloween Party offers guests a Halloween experience unlike any other. The park takes on an eerie atmosphere with fog, spooky music, and haunting silhouettes on Main Street USA. Many guests dress up in their Halloween costumes when attending.

MNSSHP offers guests special entertainment in the form of a Villains Mix and Mingle experience in front of the castle, the famous "Boo to You" parade, and an amazing fireworks spectacular known to many as "Hallo-Wishes." Also, each guest is given their own goody bag which they can use to collect treats throughout the park. That's right; guests can do their own trick or treating during the party. There are several designated spots throughout the park where the guests are given treats.

Mickey's Very Merry Christmas Party is well-loved by many guests who come over and over each year to experience the Magic Kingdom during the holiday season. Guests who attend MVMCP can expect to see some special entertainment around the park, snow on Main Street, USA, a special Christmas parade and, of course, a Christmas-themed fireworks spectacular. Guests can also look forward to cookies and hot chocolate on those nights, and will leave MVMCP filled with the Christmas spirit.

The Magic Kingdom parties are another way to add a special layer of entertainment to your Walt Disney World vacation experience.

*Mike Scopa is a co-host of the WDWTODAY Podcast and writes a regular blog, the View from Scopa Towers, for AllEars.net: http:// land.allears.net/blogs/mikescopa.*

while the movie's theme song tells us "you can fly." The sight of Wendy walking the plank is hair-raising, but of course Peter Pan saves the day. This ride is a real charmer; perfect for all ages. **FASTPASS. 3-minute ride.**

## HAUNTED MANSION

Eerie sounds, toppled fountains, unkempt grounds, and not even a hint of a smile on the faces of the creepy cast member servants cause a definite sense of foreboding on approach to this Tudor-style, redbrick mansion in Liberty Square. Enter a gargoyle-guarded Stretch Room where your "ghost host" asks all to gather tightly in the "dead" center of the room and warns that "there is no turning back." Then board a "doom buggy," your conveyance through this dusty, ghostly retreat where many terrific special effects and hair-raising sounds up the ante. You may have to ride several times to spy even half of the terrific details. New special effects and a stronger storyline have added even more mystery to this attraction. If this sounds frightening, it's not. It's nothing but fun and only the smallest of children might become alarmed. **9-minute ride.**

*CARA'S TIP:* If you're prone to allergies, don't worry; the "dust" used here is an artificial, nonallergenic material.

**BIG THUNDER MOUNTAIN RAILROAD**

In Frontierland, inside the 200-foot rocky outcropping resembling the scenery in Monument Valley is a zippy coaster ride offering visitors a

## MAGICAL MAKEOVERS

Aspiring pirates both young and old will want to reserve a place at the Pirates League at the Magic Kingdom for a true buccaneer makeover. The multi-eyed Jack is a kick—watch the surprise on others' faces when you flash them your painted eyelids. Even girls get into the act with the Empress Package including vibrant makeup and bandana, a face gem, and nail polish. Once your transformation is complete, take your photo in the "secret room." Now that you're in character, it's time to hop onboard the Pirates of the Caribbean attraction. Call (407) WDW-CREW (939-2739) for reservations.

Young girls love the Magic Kingdom's Bibbidi Bobbidi Boutique, a beauty salon that transforms them into little princesses. Offering multiple hair styles, nail color, make-up, and a total package including Disney Princess costume and photographs, it's simply irresistible. There's even a Hannah Montana look for the older set, and a Cool Dudes transformation for young boys. Call (407) WDW-STYLE or (407) 939-7895 for reservations.

peek at the mining country of the Old West. Disney rounded up an amazing assortment of old mining equipment to give a taste of the gold rush to this blast of an attraction. Board a fifteen-car "runaway" mining train led by a puffing and chugging engine for a wild journey through creepy bat caves, steaming geysers, bubbling mud pots, hazardous rockslides, rumbling earthquakes, and collapsing mine shafts. The details whip by so quickly, you'll have difficulty absorbing them all. For those who like speed but not big drops, this is your coaster; there are plenty of curves and small dips, but all in all you'll find it fairly tame and loads of rip-roarin' fun. Not recommended for expectant mothers or those with back or neck problems. **Minimum height 40 inches (3 feet, 4 inches). Children age six or younger must be accompanied by an adult. FASTPASS. 4-minute ride.**

## SPLASH MOUNTAIN

This is one ride guaranteed to put a smile on your face. Who can resist the charms of Brer Rabbit, Brer Fox, Brer Bear, and the rest of the gang, even if it culminates in one heck of a plunge? Float through Audio-Animatronics scenes from Disney's classic film *Song of the South* in a hollowed-out log, splashing and dropping through Brer Rabbit's Laughin' Place. Drift 'round the briar patch while toe-tapping music plays among the cabbages and carrots, jugs of moonshine, chirpin' birds, and croakin' frogs as you relax and bob your head to the beat. Inside the mountain Brer Fox and Brer Bear cause plenty of commotion along the way as Brer Rabbit outwits them at every turn. As you float through bayous, marshes, and caverns, all a delight to the eye with loads of colorful detail and too-cute cavorting characters, the addictive theme song "Time to Be Moving Along" plays. When the ride creeps upward, heed the doomsday warnings of a gloomy pair of buzzards ("It's turning back time" and "We'll show you a laughing place") just before the final doozy of a splashdown over a five-story waterfall and into an oversize briar patch. It's pretty tough to keep your eyes open (at least for first-timers), but try to grab a peek of the park from the top. And don't think you missed the cherished "Zip-A-Dee-Doo-Da" tune; you'll hear it on the way out. **Not recommended for expectant mothers or those with back or neck problems. Minimum height 40 inches (3 feet, 4 inches). FASTPASS. 11-minute ride.**

# THE MAGIC KINGDOM'S BEST BEHIND-THE-SCENES TOURS

Call (407) WDW-TOUR or (407) 939-8687 for reservations.

**Backstage Magic.** This seven-hour tour encompasses all four parks. Check out the Utilidors (subterranean tunnels) at the Magic Kingdom and learn about the behind-the-scenes artistic and technical creations at Epcot and Disney's Hollywood Studios. $219 including lunch at Whispering Canyon Cafe. Park admission not required. Begins at 8:45 a.m. Monday through Friday. Guests must be age sixteen or older.

**The Magic Behind Our Steam Trains Tour.** Join the Disney crew early in the morning for three hours as they prepare the trains for operation. Check out the engine cab, see the roundhouse where the trains are stored overnight, and learn about Walt Disney's fascination with steam trains. $45 plus park admission. Begins at 7:30 a.m. Monday, Tuesday, Thursday, Friday, and Saturday. Guests must be age ten or older.

**Disney's Family Magic Tour.** Put your Disney trivia knowledge to the test during this two-hour scavenger hunt. $27 plus park admission. Starts at 10 a.m. daily.

**Keys to the Kingdom.** One of the best behind-the-scenes tours offered in all of Disney. Meet at City Hall for a four-and-a-half-hour trip around the park to learn the hidden secrets and history of the Magic Kingdom. Visit three attractions, the Production Center where floats line up for the daily parade, and the Utilidors, the tunnels below the park. $65 plus park admission, including lunch. Tours depart daily at 8:30, 9, and 9:30 a.m. Guests must be age sixteen or older.

**Mickey's Magical Milestones.** This two-hour spin around the park visits attractions and special locations associated with Mickey Mouse's famous career. $25 plus park admission. Begins at 9 a.m. Monday, Wednesday, and Friday.

*CARA'S TIP:* The drop's really not as bad as it looks, so don't let it keep you from experiencing one of the best rides Disney has to offer. Parents who want to stay behind with the little ones will want to utilize the playground area just to the right of the attraction's FASTPASS distribution area.

**PIRATES OF THE CARIBBEAN**

The tune "Yo Ho, Yo Ho, a Pirate's Life for Me" will ring in your ears for hours after leaving this likable ride. Float through dripping caves and into a darkened bombardment of a Caribbean town at the merciless hands of scurvy pirates. Hundreds of shouting, singing, and grunting Audio-Animatronics buccaneers chase women (some women chase the men), pillage and burn the town, and party through the night. It may sound a bit rough, but it's quite a charmer and executed in nothing but good humor. Captain Jack Sparrow is prominently part of the theme, and you'll find music from the *Pirates of the Caribbean* movie and Jack's lifelike image throughout. **10-minute ride.**

## The Very Best Dining in the Magic Kingdom

The Magic Kingdom is certainly not known for fine dining, but sometimes it is just easier to have dinner here while waiting for the nighttime festivities to begin. Just don't expect even a touch of gourmet food.

**The Crystal Palace.** Breakfast, lunch, and dinner buffet with Winnie the Pooh characters. (See full description in the Magic Kingdom Dining section of the Dining chapter.)

**Cinderella's Royal Table.** The toughest ticket in town and perhaps the most expensive, dine high above Fantasyland in the towers of Cinderella's Castle; character breakfast, lunch, and dinner. (See full description in the Magic Kingdom Dining section of the Dining chapter.)

**Pecos Bill Café.** Best quick-service spot in the Magic Kingdom; good char-grilled burgers and such in an Old West atmosphere; quarter-pound cheeseburger, bacon double cheeseburger, chicken wrap, barbecue pork sandwich, grilled chicken salad, fried chicken breast with gravy, vegetarian burger, taco salad, chili cheese fries, great topping bar with hot skillets of onions and mushrooms; strawberry yogurt, carrot cake; children's menu: burger, mixed green salad with chicken.

## Special Entertainment

**Dream-Along with Mickey.** Gather 'round Cinderella's Castle stage for this live stage show about a Mickey Mouse dream-inspired party to which the whole cast of characters is invited. There's music, dancing, and adventurous exploits, with Maleficent stirring up trouble. However, the party guests prove that believing in your dreams is strongest of all. Check your guidemap for showtimes. **20-minute show**.

**Celebrate a Dream Come True Parade.** This wonderful afternoon parade is a huge hit with guests of all ages. Giant floats topped with scores of Disney characters—the likes of Mickey Mouse, Pinocchio, Aladdin, and more, accompanied by dancers, dancers, and more dancers. Don't miss it! **15-minute parade.**

   *CARA'S TIP:* Those not interested in the parade will find this to be a great time to ride the big-name attractions when all the crowds are elsewhere.

**SpectroMagic.** A glittering sorcerer Mickey leads this parade of dazzling Disney characters aglow with fiber optics, holographic images, and twinkling lights (more than 600,000 of them), all accompanied by Disney classic songs.

**Wishes.** What a way to end your day at this magical park! Jiminy Cricket narrates the story of how wishes come true, accompanied by Disney songs, character voices, and unbelievable pyrotechnics. While the castle constantly changes colors, you'll be wowed by 557 firing cues and 683 individual pieces of fireworks launched from eleven locations. Everyone's favorite part is the flight of Tinker Bell from the tip-top of the castle. **12-minute show.**

   *CARA'S TIP:* Although it can be seen throughout the entire park, the best spot from which to view the show is near the Walt Disney and Mickey statue in front of the castle.

## Special Events

**Mickey's Not-So-Scary Halloween.** On selected nights in September and October, Halloween is celebrated at a kid-friendly, after-hours party featuring costumed characters. The park's most popular attractions are open as well as character dance parties, trick-or-treat locations, street entertainment, Mickey's Boo to You Parade, and a special Happy

# BEST PLACES FROM WHICH TO VIEW THE WISHES FIREWORKS SHOW

- Bridge to Tomorrowland, for a prime view of Tinker Bell on her flight from the top of the castle.

- In the hub directly in front of the castle near Walt and Mickey's statue.

- The California Grill's fifteenth-floor observation deck at the Contemporary Resort (dining reservations required).

- The romantic beach at the Polynesian Resort.

- The marina or Narcoossee's Restaurant at the Grand Floridian Resort.

- The balcony of a tower guest room on the Magic Kingdom side of the Contemporary and Bay Lake Tower Resorts.

- A theme park view room at the Polynesian Resort or Grand Floridian Resort.

- From your table at Tomorrowland Terrace's Fireworks Dessert Party held every night at the Magic Kingdom where you can enjoy Wishes from an exclusive viewing area along with a plethora of desserts. Call 407-WDW-DINE for reservations.

HalloWishes fireworks display. Call (407) W-DISNEY or (407) 924-7639 for ticketing information and pricing.

**Mickey's Very Merry Christmas Party.** "Snow" falls on the decorated streets of the Magic Kingdom on select nights in November and December. The park's most popular attractions are open, along with special Castle Dream Lights, enchanting parades, Christmas shows, character greetings, holiday family portraits, cocoa and cookies, and a presentation of the Wishes fireworks with a holiday twist. Call (407) W-DISNEY or (407) 924-7639 for ticketing information and pricing.

# Epcot

Although its founder died in 1966, the Walt Disney Company brought Walt Disney's dream of an experimental prototype community of tomorrow to reality in 1982, only in a much broader fashion—an atypical theme park dedicated to the resourcefulness and imagination of the American free enterprise system, a continual showcase of imagination, instruction, research, and invention, an education in technology and innovation, other lands and cultures.

Comprising 260 acres (more than twice the size of the Magic Kingdom) and divided into two parts, Future World and World Showcase, it takes almost two full days and a good pair of walking shoes to truly explore the park's full scope.

At Future World visitors encounter shining glass pyramids, choreographed fountains, shimmering steel, and unconventional landscaping. Towering above it all is Epcot's symbol, Spaceship Earth. Here visitors learn about communications, energy, health, agriculture, transportation, the oceans, space, even their imagination. If it sounds a bit like school, don't worry. Disney always manages to add its special style to the learning process, transforming it into sheer fun.

At World Showcase you'll see authentic-looking replicas of famous landmarks and buildings, typical streets overflowing with marvelous architectural detail, shops presenting the best of the world's merchandise, exotic food and wine, and captivating entertainment. Without leaving the country, or the park for that matter, behold the Eiffel Tower, stroll a Japanese garden, witness Venice's St. Mark's Square, or visit a Mexican *mercado* (market). Definitely plan to spend an evening here, when all the countries are lit with shimmering lights and the true romance of this wonderful area of the park shines through.

Strolling in a counterclockwise direction around the 1.3-mile World Showcase walkway, you'll encounter each country in this order: Canada, United Kingdom, France, Morocco, Japan, America, Italy, Germany, China, Norway, and finally Mexico. Those weary of walking can utilize the very slow Friendship water taxis that ply the World Showcase Lagoon,

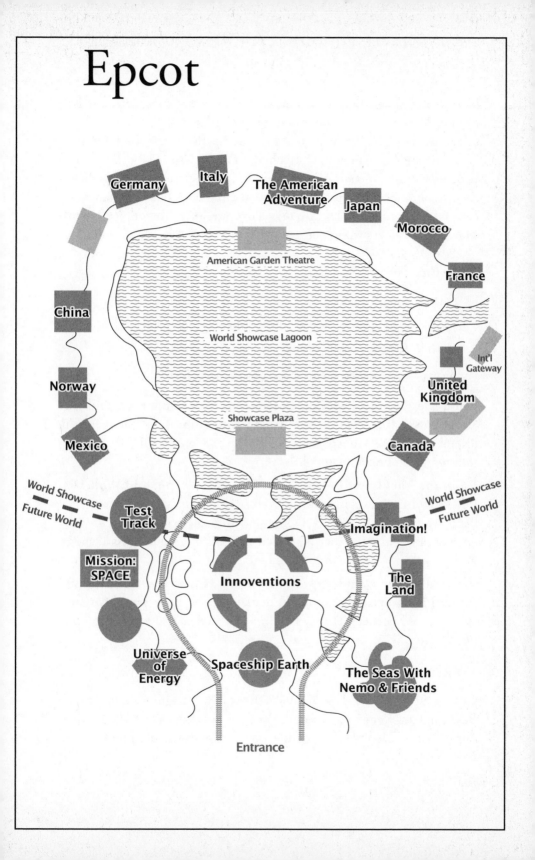

located at strategic points: two on each side of Showcase Plaza, one in front of Morocco, and another in front of Germany.

While there are plenty of attractions and activities for the little ones, Epcot's appeal is mainly to older children and adults. The draw: a huge variety of dining choices, loads of exciting entertainment, magnificent gardens, around-the-world shopping, and attractions that simultaneously entertain and educate. The grounds alone are worth the price of admission, a fact well known to horticulturists worldwide.

## Park Basics

### GETTING THERE

Those driving to Walt Disney World should take exit 67 off I-4 and follow the signs to Epcot's main entrance.

### USING WALT DISNEY WORLD TRANSPORTATION

**From the Grand Floridian, Polynesian, Contemporary, and Bay Lake Tower Resorts and the Magic Kingdom:** Board the monorail, disembark at the Transportation and Ticket Center (TTC), and then transfer to the Epcot monorail.

**From the Yacht and Beach Club, BoardWalk Inn, and Walt Disney World Dolphin and Swan:** Walk or take a boat to the International Gateway entrance in World Showcase. Although World Showcase isn't open until 11 a.m., entrance is allowed anytime after Future World opens. Park passes may also be purchased here.

**From all other Disney resorts, Disney's Hollywood Studios, and Animal Kingdom:** Board the bus marked Epcot. Boat transportation is also provided between Disney's Hollywood Studios and Epcot's International Gateway.

### PARKING

Cost is $14 per day; free to Walt Disney Resort guests and Annual Pass holders. Keep your receipt, good for parking at the Magic Kingdom, Disney's Hollywood Studios, and Animal Kingdom on that day only.

Parking is conveniently located in front of the park. Trams circulate throughout the parking area for easy transportation to the entry gate. Be sure to make a note of your aisle and section.

**OPERATING HOURS**

Future World is open 9 a.m. to 7 p.m. (The Seas with Nemo & Friends, Test Track, Mission: SPACE, Soarin', and Spaceship Earth are usually open until 9 p.m.) and World Showcase 11 a.m. to 9 p.m. Call (407) 824-4321 or log on to http://disneyworld.disney.go.com for updated park hours.

Entrance Plaza and Spaceship Earth normally open a half hour before official park opening time. To get a jump on the crowds, arrive at least thirty minutes early to allow time to park, buy tickets, purchase a snack or cup of coffee, and be one of the first to hit the big attractions. I recommend heading straight to Test Track or Soarin'.

**ENTRY GATES**

Epcot has two entrances: the main gate in front of Spaceship Earth and the International Gateway Entrance in World Showcase between the United Kingdom and France. Visitors staying at the Epcot resorts should use the International Gateway that opens at the same time as Future World. Park passes may be purchased at both entrances.

**FASTPASS ATTRACTIONS**

- Mission: SPACE
- *Captain EO*
- Living with the Land
- Soarin'
- Test Track
- Maelstrom

See the introductory section of this chapter for FASTPASS details.

## PARK SERVICES

**ATMs.** There are three: next to the stroller rentals at Entrance Plaza, on the center walkway between Future World and World Showcase, and at the America pavilion in World Showcase.

**Baby Care Center.** An infant facility is located in the Odyssey Center between Test Track and the Mexico Pavilion on the east side of the park, outfitted with changing tables, high chairs, and a room for nursing mothers. Disposable diapers, bottles, formula, and baby supplies can be purchased. All restrooms throughout the park have changing tables.

**First aid.** For minor medical problems head to the First Aid Center in the Odyssey Center located between Test Track and the Mexico Pavilion on the east side of the park.

**Guest Relations.** On the east side of Spaceship Earth is Guest Relations, where a knowledgeable staff is ready to assist with dining, lost and found, ticket upgrades, information for guests with disabilities, separated guests, and international guests.

**Guests with Disabilities.** A guidebook for guests with disabilities is available at Guest Relations. Guests with mobility disabilities can park adjacent to the Entrance Complex (ask at the Auto Plaza for directions). Wheelchairs and ECVs are available for rent. Most restaurants and shops are accessible to guests with disabilities, although some quick-service locations have narrow queues with railings (ask a host or hostess for assistance). Companion-assisted restrooms are located at First Aid, near Spaceship Earth, in Future World East opposite Test Track, in Future World West opposite the Land, and in World Showcase near the pavilions for Norway, Germany, Morocco, and the UK.

Most attractions in Future World and the ride at Norway in World Showcase provide access through the main queue, while others have auxiliary entrances for wheelchairs and service animals (service animals are not permitted on Soarin', Mission: SPACE, and Test Track) along with as many as five members of your party. Certain attractions require guests to transfer from their wheelchair to a ride system.

Braille guidebooks, audiotape guides and portable tape players, assistive listening devices, and video captioning devices are available at Guest Relations with a $25 refundable deposit. Wireless handheld captioning receivers are also available with a $100 refundable deposit. Many theater-type attractions have reflective or video captioning. With a seven-day notice, a sign language interpreter will be provided at live shows on Tuesday and Friday. Call (407) 824-4321 with any questions.

**Information Central.** Check the up-to-the-minute tip board between Innovations East and West near the Fountain of Nations for wait times and special event information.

**Lockers.** Locker rentals, $7 per day plus a $5 refundable key deposit for a small locker, and $9 plus a $5 key deposit for large lockers, are available next door to the Camera Center in Entrance Plaza and at the International Gateway entrance. If you're park-hopping, keep your receipt for another locker at the three other Disney theme parks for no extra charge.

**Lost and found.** Located at Guest Relations, or call (407) 824-4245.

**Lost children.** Locate lost children at the Baby Care Center or Guest Relations.

**Package pickup.** Purchases may be sent to the Gift Stop located just outside the main entrance as well as at World Traveler at the International Gateway for pickup at the end of the day; allow three hours for delivery. Disney resort guests may send packages directly to their hotel for next-day arrival.

**Pet kennel.** A kennel, operated by Best Friends Pet Care, is located on the left before entering the park. For information call (407) 560-6229. Proof of vaccination required.

**Stroller and wheelchair rentals.** Rentals are located on the left as you enter the park's main entrance and at International Gateway. Single strollers are $15 per day, double strollers $31. If you're park-hopping, keep your receipt for a same-day replacement at the three other Disney theme parks and Downtown Disney.

Wheelchairs are $10 inclusive of a $1 refundable deposit. Electric convenience vehicles are $45 inclusive of a $20 refundable deposit. Rented units must be returned to the original rental location to receive a security deposit refund.

## The Lay of the Land

Epcot looks a bit like a figure eight, with Future World being the northern region (shown on the guidemap at the bottom; think "upside down") and

World Showcase the southern region. Future World is composed of two concentric rings, with Spaceship Earth forming the inner circle and six pavilions the outer. The Universe of Energy, Mission: SPACE, and Test Track are located on the east side of Spaceship Earth, and Imagination!, The Land, and The Seas with Nemo & Friends are on the west side. Walkways connect Future World to World Showcase, which is made up of eleven pavilions fronted by a 1.3-mile promenade surrounding the forty-acre World Showcase Lagoon.

## The Very Best Attractions in Epcot

### SPACESHIP EARTH

Visible for miles, this symbol of Epcot comprises more than 2 million cubic feet of expanse, a silver geosphere 180 feet tall and 164 feet in diameter composed of 954 glowing panels of various shapes and sizes. Inside you'll find an attraction chronicling the story of human communications beginning with the dawn of recorded time. The slow journey to the top takes visitors through marvelous, Audio-Animatronics scenes representing humankind's quest for more efficient means of communication. Narrated by Judi Dench, you'll see Cro-Magnon storytellers, Egyptian papyrus scroll readers, ancient Greek actors, Roman couriers, Islamic scholars, even Michelangelo painting the Sistine Chapel.

Following in swift succession are the new tools and technologies of the teletype, telephone, radio, moving pictures, and television. Fun new scenes include giant-size versions of the first computers, a garage showcasing the birth of the first personal computer, and a tech tunnel. The most captivating scene is found at the top of the sphere where, in the middle of a sky thick with stars, the earth sits suspended in space. The finale utilizes touch-screens that enable guests to create their own funny vision of the future. **15-minute ride.**

*CARA'S TIP:* Lines move quickly and efficiently on this continually loading ride. Because this is the first attraction visitors encounter, lines can get lengthy in the morning. If the wait looks reasonable, go for it; if not, come back in the afternoon when most people are touring World Showcase. This attraction is usually up and running a half hour before official park opening time.

**MISSION: SPACE**

The year is 2036. You're off to Mars in an X-2 Deep Space Shuttle with a team of four—Commander, Pilot, Navigator, and Engineer. As the engines rumble, seats tilt back in preparation for countdown. Then lift-off. Wow! Experience the heart-palpitating, G-force thrill of rocketing into outer space through clouds of exhaust. As you peer out the window into a computer-generated imagery of space, panic sets in. But after the first thirty seconds or so, you'll settle down for the ride of your life with a brief sense of weightlessness, a slingshot maneuver around the moon, and one heck of a landing on Mars. What a rush!

Afterward head to the Advanced Training Lab, an interactive center featuring the popular Mission: SPACE Race with two teams of twenty competing to be the first to complete a successful mission. Minimum height 44 inches (3 feet, 8 inches). An adult must accompany children age six or younger. **This is a highly turbulent motion simulator ride and not recommended for expectant mothers or those with high blood pressure; back, heart, or neck problems; motion sickness; or other medical conditions. FASTPASS. 4-minute ride with a short preshow.**

*CARA'S TIP:* Those who want a milder alternative to this somewhat disconcerting ride may choose a less intense version of the attraction that eliminates the spinning centrifuge.

**TEST TRACK**

In a six-passenger vehicle, riders move through a series of rigorous tests normally used on prototype cars. Begin your journey with a hill climb, then a rough road test, two brake tests (one with and one without anti-lock brakes), subjection to extremes of hot and cold temperatures, and finally the long-awaited handling run. Move through hairpin turns before barreling outside onto a high-speed banking loop at more than 60 mph. It's quite a ride, not really scary but fast and absolutely loads of fun! Minimum height 40 inches (3 feet, 4 inches). An adult must accompany children age six or younger. **Not recommended for expectant mothers or those with back, heart, or neck problems. Closed in inclement weather. FASTPASS. Singles Line. 5-minute ride with a short preshow.**

*CARA'S TIP:* If you want to utilize FASTPASS (which is a great idea), don't wait until the end of the day; passes are sometimes gone by the afternoon. If you're willing to ride without other members of your party, the single-riders' line is a much quicker alternative; simply ask for directions at the entrance.

## LIVING WITH THE LAND

Explore the past, present, and future of farming on a boat tour through three diverse ecosystems: a stormy rain forest; a harsh, arid desert landscape; and the rolling American prairie, complete with an early nineteenth-century family farm. Then proceed to immense greenhouses where more efficient and environmentally friendly ways of producing food are researched and developed. You'll see plants grown hydroponically (without soil; check out the trees with nine-pound lemons); there's even a fish farm. Work is also done here in conjunction with NASA to learn how to grow crops for future space colonies. A remarkably absorbing attraction for all ages. FASTPASS. 13-minute ride.

*CARA'S TIP:* At lunchtime the overflow from the food court produces extremely long waits.

## SOARIN'

Hang glide over California in an attraction guaranteed to leave you speechless. After rising 40 feet inside a giant, 80-foot projection screen dome, you're completely surrounded with phenomenal, bird's-eye views of the Golden State. Soar over the Golden Gate Bridge, towering redwood forests, hot air balloons drifting over the Napa Valley wine country, a golf course in Palm Springs, the majesty of Yosemite, and more, ending high above Disneyland just in time for a fireworks display. Smell the aroma of the orange groves and feel the wind in your face, all the while listening to a stirring musical score. This is one fantastic ride! **Minimum height 40 inches (3 feet, 4 inches). Not recommended for expectant mothers or those with motion sickness, or heart, back, or neck problems. FASTPASS. 10-minute ride.**

*CARA'S TIP:* Don't wait until late afternoon to get a FASTPASS for this attraction; they oftentimes run out early in the afternoon. Ask for the first row; if not you'll be a bit distracted with the dangling feet above you.

## THE SEAS WITH NEMO & FRIENDS

This attraction is a winner, combining a kid-friendly ride with the fantastic Living Seas six-million-gallon aquarium filled with more than 2,000 sea creatures. The queue winds through a seashore setting that gradually transitions to a dark underwater theme before boarding your "clammobile" that slowly moves through animated projection scenes under the ocean. Nemo has wandered off from his teacher, Mr. Ray, and everyone is in search of him. Meet up with Nemo's dad and his friend Dory, check out the larger-than-life bobbing jellyfish, and even travel through a fast-moving current tunnel filled with turtles, finally ending up in front of the massive aquarium. In Sea Base, don't skip *Turtle Talk with Crush,* a fun show starring the surfer dude turtle, who interacts in a full-blown conversation with the audience. Then take your photo inside Bruce the Shark's mouth. Other attractions include fish feeds, dolphin presentations, educational talks by the research team on the Observation Deck, and, my favorite, the fascinating Marine Mammal Research Center where manatees reside.

## *THE AMERICAN ADVENTURE* SHOW

Momentous film, inspiring music, and lifelike talking, gesturing, and walking Audio-Animatronics characters weave the impressive tale of the United States of America, with Ben Franklin and Mark Twain serving as hosts; the grand finale film montage is a real tearjerker. Some adore this show while others sleep right through it; personally, I'm one of its greatest fans. **Shows every 35 minutes.**

CARA'S TIP: It's fairly easy to get a seat in this huge theater. Try to catch the *Voices of Liberty* performance in the waiting area and just watch your patriotism shoot up a few notches.

## *REFLECTIONS OF CHINA*

Behold the wonders of China in this remarkable 360-degree film narrated by Tang Dynasty poet Li Bai. In Circle-Vision, walk atop the Great Wall, enter the Forbidden City, stand in the middle of Tiananmen Square, and cruise down the mighty Yangtze River. View the modern world of Hong Kong, Macau, and Shanghai. Stunning views of rice terraces, Inner Mongolia's nomadic people, the misty Huangshan Mountains, the Gobi desert, the extraordinary Terra Cotta Warriors, and the haunting landscape of

# CHARACTER GREETING SPOTS AT EPCOT

The pointing Mickey gloves on your guidemap will help you find the following locations:

- Snow White and Dopey in Germany.
- An assortment of characters at Entrance Plaza in front of Spaceship Earth.
- Aladdin and Jasmine in Morocco along the World Showcase Lagoon.
- Aurora, Belle and the Beast, and the Aristocats in France.
- Epcot Character Spot on the west side of Innoventions Plaza for Mickey and friends throughout the day.
- Winnie the Pooh, Mary Poppins, and Alice in Wonderland at the United Kindgom's Kidcot Fun Stop.
- Mulan in China.

Guey Ling only serve to make you want more. Come prepared to stand throughout the presentation. **12-minute show.**

**MAELSTROM**

A favorite of World Showcase visitors is this watery boat ride through both real and mythical scenes of Norway's history. In your dragon-headed longboat, drift past a tenth-century Viking village and then on to a dark, mysterious forest where a hairy, three-headed troll casts a spell on your vessel, causing it to drop backward down a soggy cataract. Sail past glacier-bound polar bears, narrowly miss a plunge off the edge of a waterfall, and finally drop into a stormy North Sea. Your voyage ends with a pleasant, short film on Norway. **FASTPASS. 10-minute ride and show, including the film.**

*CARA'S TIP:* Drops are very small and of no consequence on this tame ride. If you would rather not see the film, walk into the theater and then immediately out the doors on the opposite side.

## The Very Best Dining in Epcot

**Coral Reef Restaurant.** Your table has a front-row seat of The Seas with Nemo & Friends' massive aquarium; lunch and dinner. (See full description in the Epcot Dining section of the Dining chapter.)

**Bistro de Paris.** Second-floor dining room featuring French food in an upscale atmosphere; dinner only. (See full description in the Epcot Dining section of the Dining chapter.)

**Chefs de France.** Lively French bistro serving lunch and dinner. (See full description in the Epcot Dining section of the Dining chapter.)

**Restaurant Marrakesh.** Exotic Moroccan cuisine; lunch and dinner; picture-perfect surroundings with belly dancer entertainment. (See full description in the Epcot Dining section of the Dining chapter.)

**San Angel Inn.** Unquestionably Epcot's most romantic restaurant; lunch and dinner; spicy, traditional Mexican dishes in a candlelit riverside setting. (See full description in the Epcot Dining section of the Dining chapter.)

**Sunshine Seasons**. Here you'll find prepared-to-order, fast-casual food options at several different counters.

*The Grill*: rotisserie half chicken or pork chop, grilled salmon and mashed potatoes with kalamata olive pesto; *children's menu*: chicken leg with mashed potatoes.

*Asian*: *breakfast*: breakfast croissant sandwich, oatmeal, child's French toast, platter with bacon, sausage, biscuit, and scrambled eggs; *lunch and dinner*: ginger Mongolian beef, spicy Thai chicken, vegetable and tofu noodle bowl with lime ginger broth, sweet and sour chicken; *children's menu*: sweet and sour chicken.

*Sandwiches*: Black Forest ham and salami grinder, turkey and Monterey jack cheese on focaccia with chipotle mayonnaise, oak grilled vegetable flatbread; *children's menu*: minisub sandwich.

*Soup and Salad*: Caesar salad with oak-fired chicken, seared tuna on mixed greens with sesame rice wine dressing, roasted beet and goat cheese salad with honey sherry dressing, freshly made soups include crawfish chowder, vegetable minestrone, and broccoli and Tillamook cheese; *children's menu:* macaroni and cheese.

*The Bakery:* Rice Krispies treats, croissants, Asian chocolate cheesecake, strawberry shortcake, apple caramel cake, fruit tartlets, muffins, hand-dipped Edy's ice cream, Toll-House cookies, apple flan, key lime pie, brownies.

**Tangierine Café.** Excellent quick-service cafe; shawarma sandwiches and platters (marinated, rotisserie-roasted sliced chicken and lamb); meatball platter; Mediterranean wraps of lamb or chicken; vegetarian plate (falafel, couscous, hummus, lentil salad, and tabbouleh); freshly baked Moroccan pastries; Moroccan wine, Casablanca beer, specialty coffees; *children's menu:* hamburgers, chicken tenders.

## Special Entertainment

**Illuminations: Reflections of Earth.** Each evening at closing time, crowds gather around the World Showcase Lagoon to witness Walt Disney World's most spectacular nighttime extravaganza. The story of planet Earth is told in a combination of unbelievable pyrotechnic displays, amazing lasers, stirring music, and fanciful water movement. 13-minute show.

CARA'S TIP: To avoid smoke from the fireworks, check which direction the flames in the torches are pointed and avoid that side of the lagoon. Illuminations does not cancel during inclement weather.

## Special Events

**Epcot Flower and Garden Festival.** For seventy-five days each spring, Epcot is covered in more than thirty million blooms with more than one hundred extravagant topiaries, a Pirate's Adventure Zone, a floating wonderland in East Lake, a Pixie Hollow garden just for kids, a lovely butterfly garden, and an array of amazing gardens throughout World Showcase. Special appearances by nationally recognized gardeners, how-to presentations by Disney horticulturists, kid-friendly activities and play areas, and a nightly Flower Power concert series add to the festivities. Entrance is included in the price of park admission.

**International Food and Wine Festival.** This six-week fall festival is the most heavily visited food festival in the world, attracting more than

## SPECIALTY DRINKS AT WORLD SHOWCASE

- Mango Gingerita at Joy of Tea stand in China
- Dooley's Creme Liqueur Coke float at the Rose and Crown pub in the United Kingdom
- French wine and champagne as well as Grand Marnier orange or Gray Goose Citron lemonade slushes at the Les Vins de France
- Wine tasting at Vinoteca Castello in Italy
- German wines at Valckenberg Weinkeller
- Viking coffee spiked with Kamora Coffee Liqueur and Bailey's Irish Cream at Kringla Bakery in Norway
- Margaritas at Cantina de San Angel in Mexico
- A dizzying array of seventy tequilas and a huge variety of specialty margaritas at La Cava del Tequila in Mexico
- Proscecco, bellinis, and lemoncello or grappa margheritas at Tutto Italia kiosk in Italy

one million visitors. Booths representing the cuisine of more than thirty countries line the World Showcase walkway, each one selling reasonably priced, appetizer-size food along with wine and beer. Included in the price of admission are daily cooking demonstrations by some of the countries' top chefs, book signings and meet-and-greets with celebrity authors, wine-tasting seminars, and Eat to the Beat nightly concerts with such past performers as David Cassidy, Jon Secada, Spyro Gyro, and Kool & the Gang. Avoid the weekends if you can, when the locals come out in full force.

Special themed dinners and wine seminars sold out months in advance include:

# EPCOT'S BEST BEHIND-THE-SCENES TOURS

Call (407) WDW-TOUR or (407) 939-8687 for reservations.

**Around the World at Epcot.** Learn the skills involved in operating a Segway Human Transporter, a motorized, self-balancing, personal transportation device, then head out to World Showcase for a one-hour spin. $95. Four times daily at 7:45, 8:30, 9, and 9:30 a.m. Participants must be at least age sixteen with a minimum weight of 100 pounds and a maximum of 250 pounds. Young people ages sixteen and seventeen must have a parent or guardian sign a waiver.

**Behind the Seeds Tour.** See the Living with the Land greenhouses on this one-hour journey. $16 per adult and $12 per child ages three to nine. Offered daily every forty-five minutes from 10:30 a.m. to 4:30 p.m. Book ahead or just show up the same day at the desk next to the Soarin' attraction in the Land pavilion.

**Dolphins in Depth.** A look at dolphin behavior and training with a chance to enter the water and get up close to these astonishing creatures. The three-hour program includes a souvenir photo and T-shirt. $150. Starts at 9:45 a.m. Monday through Friday. Be sure to bring a bathing suit. No swimming required. Theme park admission is neither required nor included. Guests must be age thirteen or older to participate; those ages thirteen through seventeen must have a parent or guardian participating in the tour.

**Epcot DiveQuest.** This three-hour program includes a pre-dive briefing, a talk on oceanography, and a forty-minute dive in the six-million-gallon aquarium at The Seas With Nemo & Friends. $140. Theme park admission is neither required nor included. Offered daily at 4:30 and 5:30 p.m. to all certified divers; guests ages ten and up welcome, but those ages ten through fourteen must dive with a parent or guardian. Dive equipment provided.

**Seas Aqua Tour.** A two-and-a-half-hour program in the back-stage area of The Seas With Nemo & Friends with a chance to explore the aquarium for thirty minutes using a supplied air snorkel system. $140; includes gear, T-shirt, and group photo; daily at 12:30 p.m.; theme park admission is neither required nor included. Bring a bathing suit. Available to guests ages eight and older; those ages eight through sixteen must be accompanied by a parent or legal guardian.

**Simply Segway Experience.** One-hour Segway training class using new Segway Personal Transporters; daily at 11:30 a.m.; $35; does not include a park tour.

**The Undiscovered Future World.** On this four-and-a-half-hour tour, visitors learn about the vision and history of Epcot, hear in-depth information on each pavilion (even a few peeks backstage), and take a look at the Epcot marina where the Illuminations fireworks show is put together. $49 plus park admission. Starts at 9 a.m. Monday, Wednesday, and Friday. Guests must be age sixteen or older.

**Nature-Inspired Design Segway Tour.** Three-hour backstage tour experiencing the nature-inspired designs incorporated into Epcot pavilions and attractions while riding a Segway Personal Transporter X-2; 8:15 a.m. Saturdays and Tuesdays; $124; guest must be age sixteen or older.

*Brewers' Dinners.* Sample international and domestic beers along with unique menu selections ($55).

*Sweet Sundays.* Some of the country's top pastry chefs demonstrate the preparation of three sweet delights with tastings; includes a buffet breakfast and sparkling wine ($80).

*Celebrating Family & Friends in the Kitchen.* Three-course lunch highlights preparing a meal with family and friends taught by celebrity chefs like Alan Wong, the Deen Brothers, and Cat Cora. ($110-130).

*Epcot Wine Schools.* Afternoon seminar hosted by a prestigious wine authority that concludes with a celebratory reception and a certificate of completion ($125).

*Party for the Senses.* Weekly Saturday evening extravaganza with tasting stations prepared by more than twenty-five eminent chefs along with seventy wines and beers at this party of all parties. Included is reserved seating for the Eat to the Beat Concert ($135).

*Cheese Seminars.* Learn about cheese with an expert "fromager" from the Artisanal Premium Cheese Center in New York City ($75).

*Signature Dining.* Walt Disney World signature chefs prepare a dinner along with a celebrity chef accompanied by wine ($100 to $375).

**Holidays Around the World.** Christmas is a special time at Epcot, with loads of decorations, a nightly tree-lighting ceremony with Mickey and friends, storytelling around World Showcase, and a special Illuminations holiday finale.

The Candlelight Processional, a thrice-nightly event staged from late November until the end of December at the America Gardens Theater, features a celebrity narrator, a mass choir, and a fifty-piece orchestra who together retell the story of Christmas. Entrance is included in the price of park admission. To guarantee seats for this performance, book a Candlelight Processional Lunch or Dinner Package that includes a meal at a select World Showcase restaurant and reserved general seating for the show (call 407-WDW-DINE or 407-939-3463 for reservations).

# Disney's Hollywood Studios

"Welcome to the glamour and glitz of show business." Although Disney's version of the heyday of Hollywood is certainly a rose-colored one, its entertainment value can't be beat. On the boulevards of Hollywood and Sunset, legendary Los Angeles buildings, re-created in romanticized and appealing art deco forms, literally scream excitement. It's as if the whole place is on the brink of breaking into a zany show at any minute.

The park is actually a working film and television studio with three production soundstages and a back lot. Visitors are allowed a sample of the mystery at the Backlot Tour attraction, where they're invited to watch

# Disney's Hollywood Studios

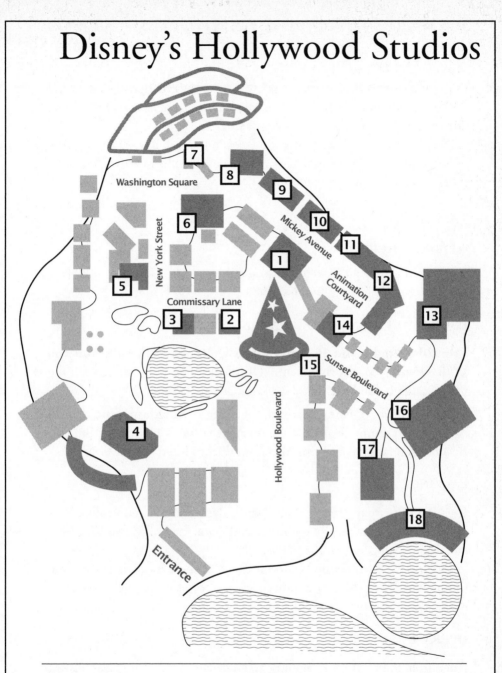

Washington Square

New York Street

Mickey Avenue

Animation Courtyard

Commissary Lane

Sunset Boulevard

Hollywood Boulevard

Entrance

1. The Great Movie Ride
2. The American Idol Experience
3. *Sounds Dangerous –*
   *Starring Drew Carey*
4. *Indiana Jones*
   *Epic Stunt Spectacular*
5. *Muppet ★ Vision 3-D*
6. *Honey, I Shrunk the Kids*
   Movie Set Adventure

7. *Lights, Motors, Action!*
   *Extreme Stunt Show*
8. Studio Backlot Tour
9. Toy Story Midway Mania!
10. Walt Disney: One Man's Dream
11. *Voyage of The Little Mermaid*
12. The Magic of Disney
    Animation
13. Rock 'n' Roller Coaster

14. *Playhouse Disney –*
    *Live on Stage!*
15. Guest Information Board
    at Hollywood Junction
16. The Twilight Zone
    Tower of Terror
17. *Beauty and the Beast –*
    *Live on Stage*
18. *Fantasmic!*

the artistic and technical processes involved in the creation of movies and television. And on the horizon is a much needed, revamped Star Tours attraction set to open in 2011 in digital 3-D.

This is a small park, one that can be seen in a full day. Because many of the shows are scheduled, check your park schedule on arrival for show-times and plan your day accordingly.

## Park Basics

### GETTING THERE

Those driving to Walt Disney World should take exit 64 off I-4 and follow the signs to Disney's Hollywood Studios.

### USING WALT DISNEY WORLD TRANSPORTATION

**From the Yacht and Beach Club, the BoardWalk Inn, and the Walt Disney World Swan and Dolphin:** Take the boat or walk the path located behind the BoardWalk Inn and the Swan.

**From all other Disney resorts, the Magic Kingdom, Epcot, and Animal Kingdom:** Board the bus marked Disney's Hollywood Studios. Boat transportation is also provided from Epcot's International Gateway.

### PARKING

Cost is $14 per day; free to Walt Disney Resort guests and Annual Pass holders. Keep your receipt, good for parking at Epcot, Magic Kingdom, and Animal Kingdom on that day only.

Parking is conveniently located in front of the park. Trams circulate throughout the parking area for easy transportation to the entry gate. Make a note of what aisle and section you've parked in.

### OPERATING HOURS

Open from 9 a.m. until an hour or so after dark. Call (407) 824-4321 or log on to http://disneyworld.disney.go.com for updated park hours.

Arrive at least thirty minutes early, allowing time to park, buy tickets, and be one of the first to hit the big attractions. I recommend heading straight to Toy Story Midway Mania!, followed by the Tower of Terror and Rock 'n' Roller Coaster.

## FASTPASS ATTRACTIONS

- *Indiana Jones Epic Stunt Spectacular*
- Rock 'n' Roller Coaster
- Toy Story Midway Mania!
- Twilight Zone Tower of Terror
- *Voyage of the Little Mermaid*

See the introduction to this chapter for FASTPASS details.

## PARK SERVICES

**ATMs.** For quick cash, two ATMs are located at the park: just outside the entrance and inside the Toy Story Pizza Planet Arcade.

**Baby Care Center.** At the Guest Relations center is an infant facility outfitted with changing tables, high chairs, a companion restroom, and chairs for nursing mothers. Disposable diapers, bottles, formula, and baby supplies can be purchased. All restrooms throughout the park are outfitted with changing tables.

**First aid.** For minor medical problems head to the First Aid Center located next to Guest Relations.

**Guest Relations.** Located just inside the park on the left is Guest Relations, where a knowledgeable staff is ready to assist with ticket upgrades, dining, messages for separated parties, and information for guests with disabilities.

**Guests with disabilities.** A guidebook for guests with disabilities is available at Guest Relations. Guests with mobility disabilities should park adjacent to the Entrance Complex (ask at the Auto Plaza for directions). Wheelchairs and electric convenience vehicles (ECVs) are available for rent. Most restaurants and shops are accessible to guests with disabilities, although some quick-service locations have narrow queues with railings (ask a host or hostess for assistance). Companion-assisted restrooms are located at First Aid; opposite the Twilight Zone Tower of Terror; at FAN-TASMIC!; on the right side of *Lights, Motors, Action!*; next to Toy Story Midway Mania!; and at Rock 'n' Roller Coaster.

Most attractions provide access through the main queue, while others have auxiliary entrances for wheelchairs and service animals along with as many as five members of your party. Certain attractions require guests to transfer from their wheelchair to a ride system. Braille guidebooks, assistive listening devices, video captioning, and audiotape guides are available at Guest Relations for a $25 refundable deposit. Many theater-type attractions have reflective or video captioning. A handheld captioning receiver is available at Guest Relations with a $100 refundable deposit. With a seven-day notice, a sign language interpreter will be provided at live shows on Sunday and Wednesday. Call (407) 824-4321 with any questions.

**Lockers.** Lockers are located at Oscar's Super Service on the right as you enter the park, available for $7 per day plus a $5 refundable key deposit for a small locker, and $9 plus a $5 key deposit for large lockers. If you're park-hopping, keep your receipt for another locker at no additional charge at the three other Disney theme parks.

**Lost and found.** Located next to Oscar's Super Service or call (407) 824-4245.

**Lost children.** Locate lost children at Guest Relations.

**Package pickup.** Purchases may be sent to the package pickup window located next to Oscar's Super Service near the Main Entrance for pickup at the end of the day. Allow three hours for delivery. Disney resort guests may send packages directly to their hotel for next-day arrival.

**Pet kennel.** A kennel, operated by Best Friends Pet Care, is located just outside the park entrance. For information call (407) 560-4282. Proof of vaccination is required.

**Strollers and wheelchairs.** Rentals are located at Oscar's Super Service on the right as you enter the park. Single strollers are $15 per day, double strollers $31. Wheelchairs are $10 inclusive of a $1 refundable deposit. Electric convenience vehicles are $45 inclusive of a $20 refundable deposit. Rented units must be returned to the original rental location to receive a security deposit refund. If you're park-hopping, keep your receipt for a same-day replacement at the three other Disney theme parks and Downtown Disney.

## The Lay of the Land

Disney's Hollywood Studios' main street, Hollywood Boulevard, leads directly to the park's central plaza, where you'll find a 122-foot Sorcerer

Mickey hat. If you're facing the hat from Hollywood Boulevard, to the right are two walkways: one branching to Sunset Boulevard and the other to Animation Courtyard. On the left is the Echo Lake area of the park that leads to the Streets of America section. Mickey Avenue and Pixar Place sit behind the Chinese theater and may be accessed via Animation Courtyard. It's a bit more confusing than the Magic Kingdom but fairly easy to maneuver.

## The Very Best Attractions in Disney's Hollywood Studios

### ROCK 'N' ROLLER COASTER

You've nabbed a special invitation to an Aerosmith concert, but it's clear across town and you're late! Disney's wildest coaster ride takes place inside a twenty-four-passenger "stretch limo" speeding down a Los Angeles freeway amid blasting Aerosmith music. Zooming past, through, and around neon Hollywood landmarks, you'll loop and corkscrew in the dark. And that's after you've accelerated to a speed of 60 mph in just under three seconds. Hold onto your hat (or anything else you might treasure) because this is pure Disney fun. **Minimum height 48 inches (4 feet). Not recommended for expectant mothers; those with back, heart, or neck problems; or those prone to motion sickness. FASTPASS. Single Rider Line. 10-minute ride.**

*CARA'S TIP*: If you'd like to sit in the Rock 'n' Roller Coaster's front seat, just ask, but be prepared for a wait, because every other daredevil around has the same idea. The chicken-hearted can take comfort in knowing that although there are three inversions on the ride, there are no steep drops.

### TOY STORY MIDWAY MANIA!

Walk through "Andy's bedroom" past oversized Crayolas, checkers, Tinkertoys, and an interactive, Audio-Animatronics Mr. Potato Head boardwalk barker. Don your 3-D glasses then board a carnival tram to embark on a 4-D virtual version of midway-style game play. Use your spring-action shooter to plug away at a series of giant-size video screens featuring virtual spinning plates, tossing cream pies, bursting balloons, and funny little green aliens as you zip through game after game, each lasting 30 seconds, each more fun than the last. Adding to the entertainment is a fourth dimension of air shots and water spritzers while Toy Story characters yell hints and cheer you along. Watch out for bonus targets and simply have a blast (no pun intended)! Don't think this is just another version of the Magic Kingdom's Buzz Lightyear attraction—you'll find Toy Story Midway Mania! way more fun. **FASTPASS. 5-minute ride.**

*CARA'S TIP*: This is now the park's most popular attraction. Head here first to avoid an hour and a half wait in line. Then pick up a FAST-PASS for later because I can guarantee you'll want to return and ride it again.

**TWILIGHT ZONE TOWER OF TERROR**

On this free-falling adventure, you'll certainly feel you've entered the twilight zone or at the very least a brand-new dimension of fright. The waiting line snakes through the crumbling grounds of the deserted, thirteen-story Hollywood Tower Hotel, with its rusty grillwork, cracking fountains, and overgrown, unkempt foliage, before proceeding through the spooky, abandoned lobby, dusty with forgotten luggage and dead flower arrangements. Step into the gloomy hotel library for a message from *Twilight Zone* TV show host Rod Serling (on a black-and-white television, of course), who relays the tale of a stormy night in 1939 when an elevator full of guests was struck by lightning and then disappeared. A bellhop invites you into a seemingly old, rusty service elevator that ascends and moves horizontally through several remarkable special effects in pitch-black space and without warning, plummets thirteen stories to the bottom. Up you go again, then down, and up, and down, during which you'll be treated to dazzling views of the park. If you can stand the thrill, don't miss this one—just be sure to ride it with an empty stomach. **Minimum height 40 inches (3 feet, 4 inches). Not recommended for expectant mothers; those with back, heart, or neck problems; or those prone to motion sickness. FASTPASS. 10-minute ride.**

*CARA'S TIP*: If you chicken out, there's an escape route immediately before entering the elevator; just ask a bellhop for directions.

### *INDIANA JONES EPIC STUNT SPECTACULAR*

In this open-air theater is a fun stunt show that allows the audience to observe the choreography of safely performed stunts and special effects—and maybe even co-star. Indiana Jones is at it again, fleeing from a 12-foot rolling ball before heading to Cairo for a street scene with audience volunteers who play along with the professionals performing a variety of flips, drops, bullwhip-cracking, and fistfights. The show's grand finale finds Indiana making a dangerous escape through a wall of flames, a barrage of gunfire, a large dousing of water, and one massive explosion; be prepared to feel the heat. Check your guidemap for showtimes. **FAST-PASS. 30-minute show.**

### LIGHTS, MOTORS, ACTION! EXTREME STUNT SHOW

Movie stunts are the highlight of this thrill-a-minute show of super-fast, high-flying stunt cars, screaming motorcycles, and crazy Jet-Skis with a cast of more than thirty. This 5,000-seat theater's 6.5-acre stage is set in a quiet French village, one that suddenly comes alive with action. Extra highlights include pyrotechnic effects, ramp jumps, high-falls, even a stuntman engulfed in flames. The premise is the filming of a European spy thriller complete with production crew, director, and stunt coordinator who show the audience the making of complex vehicle stunts including creation, design, and filming. After completion, each scene is edited with the addition of "real" actors, then shown with close-up detail on a giant video screen. The final explosion will blow you away! **35-minute show.**

### VOYAGE OF THE LITTLE MERMAID

Journey under the sea at one of Disney's Hollywood Studios' most beloved attractions. This tribute to the auburn-haired mermaid Ariel combines puppetry, live actors, animated film, and delightful music with the adorable sidekicks Flounder and Sebastian and the not-so-adorable sea witch Ursula. Favorite songs from the movie, such as "Under the Sea," "Part of Your World," and "Poor Unfortunate Souls," along with great special effects including black lights, lasers, rain showers, bubbles, and lightning make this show quite a hit with children. Besides, how often do you have the opportunity to behold a seemingly live mermaid with a flopping tail? **FASTPASS. 17-minute show.**

   *CARA'S TIP:* Don't skip this wonderful attraction simply because you don't have small children in tow. If you would like a center seat, stand back a bit when the doors open into the theater from the preshow holding room and allow about half the crowd to enter before you.

# CHARACTER GREETING SPOTS AT DISNEY'S HOLLYWOOD STUDIOS

The pointing Mickey gloves on your guidemap will help you find the following locations:

- Pixar Place across from Toy Story Midway Mania! for an assortment of *Toy Story* friends throughout the day.

- *Monsters Inc.* characters and Power Rangers on the Streets of America.

- An assortment of Disney characters throughout the day around the Sorcerer Mickey Hat.

- Meet the *Cars* at Luigi's Casa Della Tires behind Muppetvision 3-D on the Streets of America.

- An assortment of characters intermittently throughout the day in Entrance Plaza.

- The Incredibles, the stars of *BOLT*, the characters of the movie *UP*, and Mickey Mouse inside the Magic of Disney Animation.

- Prince Caspian at the Journey Into Narnia

- The Little Mermaid and Prince Eric at Voyage of the Little Mermaid

- Handy Manny, Leo, June, Annie, and Quincy outside Playhouse Disney – Live on Stage

## The Very Best Dining in Disney's Hollywood Studios

**'50s Prime Time Café.** Dine in a 1950s sitcom where Mom is your waitress and all vegetables must be consumed; lunch and dinner. (See full description in the Disney's Hollywood Studios Dining section of the Dining chapter.)

**Hollywood Brown Derby.** Re-creation of the famous Hollywood dining spot; lunch and dinner; best food and most sophisticated atmosphere in the park. (See full description in the Disney's Hollywood Studios Dining section of the Dining chapter.)

**Sci-Fi Dine-In Theater Restaurant.** Relive the drive-in of your youth at this most unusual restaurant; lunch and dinner. (See full description in the Disney's Hollywood Studios Dining section of the Dining chapter.)

## Special Entertainment

**High School Musical 3: Senior Year—Right Here! Right Now!** Dance, sing, and cheer with the Wildcats while enjoying this street show and a cast of fourteen singers and dancers. The rousing performance takes place several times a day on a traveling "rock concert" stage in front of Mickey's Sorcerer's Hat. 15-minute show.

**Block Party Bash.** This high-energy, but somewhat unexciting, interactive parade of sorts is a combination parade and stage show with several floats, rolling stages, trampoline and aerial acrobatics, scores of dancers, and giant-size props. The stars of Pixar films including Woody and the *Toy Story* gang, Buzz, Mike, Sully, and Flik are all accompanied by non-Disney-style pop tunes. Guests lining the streets are enticed to join in the fun. 15-minute parade.

**FANTASMIC!** Sorcerer Mickey's fantasies soar to new heights in the 7,000-seat Hollywood Hills Amphitheater (with standing room for another 3,000). The mouse himself orchestrates this extravaganza atop a 40-foot mountain on his lagoon-bound island. While Mickey struggles with the forces of good and evil in a series of lavish dreams and wild nightmares, guests thrill to the sight of walls of dancing water and wild, windy storms accompanied by stirring music, choreographed laser effects, and projecting flames. A favorite segment is the procession of floats representing the best of Disney happy endings, quickly followed by a bevy of Disney villains. Of course, Mickey wins out and, to the delight of the audience, a steamboat, captained by Steamboat Willie and stuffed with Disney characters, sails past in anticipation of the grand finale of water, lasers, and fireworks. Shown only two nights a week (Sunday and Thursday) except in the busiest of weeks when it increases to a nightly performance.

For guaranteed seating with less waiting, book a FANTASMIC! Dinner and Lunch Package available at Hollywood Brown Derby, Mama Melrose's, or Hollywood and Vine. Reservations can be made as early as 180 days in advance by calling (407) WDW-DINE, or (407) 939-3463. After your meal you'll receive a seat ticket in a special reserved area on the far right of the theater, making it possible to arrive only thirty minutes prior to showtime. Reservations fill up quickly, so book as early as possible. Do know that the FANTASMIC! Dinner Package requires a very early dinner time and is becoming increasingly difficult to book since the show is only twice a week. **25-minute show.**

*CARA'S TIP:* I know it sounds tedious, but it's necessary to arrive about one hour prior to snare a seat; once the theater is full, you're out of luck. If you wait until twenty minutes prior, you have a good chance of a standing-room-only spot whose only advantage is a quick dash out once the show is over. If you'd like to be among the first out of the theater, take a seat in one of the back rows (really some of the better seats; the front rows can be a bit soggy). On windy or rainy nights, the show is sometimes canceled.

## Special Events

**ESPN The Weekend.** It's the ultimate sports fan's weekend in late February with star athletes, ESPN personalities at live telecasts, and sports celebrity motorcades and chats, plus an interactive sports zone. Included in regular park admission.

**Star Wars Weekends.** For four weekends in May and June, Disney's Hollywood Studios is filled with dozens of Star Wars characters, heroes, and villains. Also celebrated is the television animated series *The Clone Wars*. There's a Hyperspace Hoopla! show with music, comedy, and dancing, autographs sessions, and motorcades. Other activities include a talk show, trivia contests, and question-and-answer sessions. For updated information visit http://disneyworld.disney.go.com/parks/hollywood-studios/special-events/star-wars-weekend. Included in regular park admission.

**Night of Joy.** On two consecutive nights in early September, some of the biggest names in contemporary Christian music perform on several stages at Disney's Hollywood Studios. Acts in 2009 included such names as P.O.D., newsboys, Kutless, Tomlin, NEEDTOBREATHE, Leeland,

Superchick, Skillet, MercyMe, Jars of Clay, Flyleaf, Family Force 5, Grits, Mandisa, and more. Call (407) W-DISNEY, or (407) 924-7639 for ticketing information and pricing.

**The Osborne Family Spectacle of Dancing Lights.** From mid-November until early January, the park's Streets of America are dusted with "snow" and lit by five million colorful "dancing" lights. It's quite a sight to see. Included in regular park admission.

## Disney's Animal Kingdom

"We inherited this earth from our parents and are borrowing it from our children." This is the important message Disney strives to convey in its environmentally conscious theme park, the Animal Kingdom. It's quite a beauty with more than four million lush, towering plants, trees, and grasses. Although the Animal Kingdom is five times the size of the Magic Kingdom, don't panic; it won't take two days to see everything. Remember, much of the land is an enclave for the animals; the rest is easily conquered in a day.

The beauty of the Oasis hits you square in the face as you enter the park, a tropical jungle of flowering plants, cooling waterfalls, and overgrown plant life thriving with a menagerie of fascinating creatures. A cool mist pervades the air amid a cacophony of chattering birds and the aroma of fragrant trees and flowers on the variety of pathways leading to hidden grottoes, rushing streams, and towering vegetation. Critters housed in replicas of their natural habitats include macaws, an iguana, wallabys, a giant anteater, sloths, African spoonbills, and swans. They are surrounded by colossal banana trees, swaying palms, massive bamboos, and flowering orchids.

After making your way through the Oasis, cross the bridge over the Discovery River into the park's central hub, Discovery Island. Here visitors congregate to wander streets filled with lampposts, benches, and storefront facades carved with folk art animals. And here, all eyes are immediately drawn to the focal point of the park, the awesome Tree of Life.

Along with the main attractions are great hidden nooks and mysterious trails just waiting to be discovered. If you see a path leading off the main walkway, by all means follow it; it may just take you to a place of sheer enchantment. Take time to explore and discover the many marvelous natural settings throughout or risk leaving a bit disappointed when you haven't grasped the true significance of this magnificent theme park.

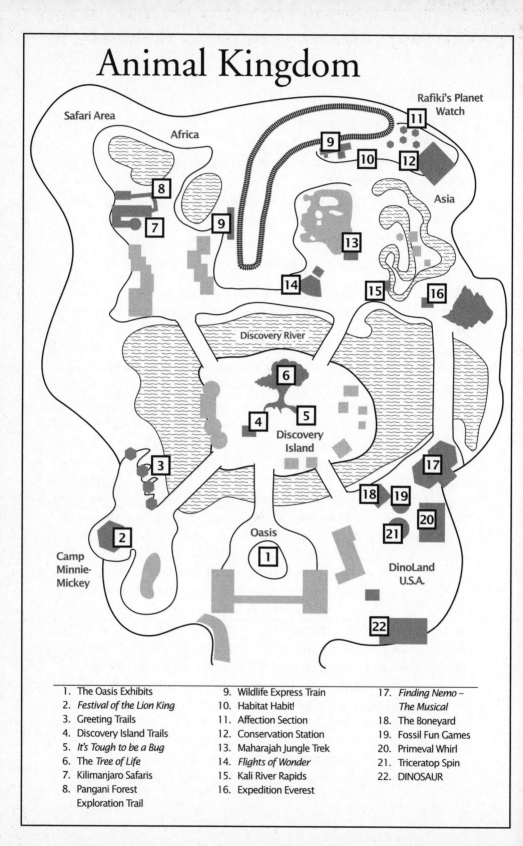

# Animal Kingdom

Rafiki's Planet Watch

Safari Area

Africa

Asia

Discovery River

Discovery Island

Oasis

Camp Minnie-Mickey

DinoLand U.S.A.

1. The Oasis Exhibits
2. *Festival of the Lion King*
3. Greeting Trails
4. Discovery Island Trails
5. *It's Tough to be a Bug*
6. The *Tree of Life*
7. Kilimanjaro Safaris
8. Pangani Forest Exploration Trail
9. Wildlife Express Train
10. Habitat Habit!
11. Affection Section
12. Conservation Station
13. Maharajah Jungle Trek
14. *Flights of Wonder*
15. Kali River Rapids
16. Expedition Everest
17. *Finding Nemo – The Musical*
18. The Boneyard
19. Fossil Fun Games
20. Primeval Whirl
21. Triceratop Spin
22. DINOSAUR

## Park Basics

### GETTING THERE

Those driving to Walt Disney World should take exit 65 off I-4 and follow the signs to the Animal Kingdom.

### USING WALT DISNEY WORLD TRANSPORTATION

**From all Disney Resorts and theme parks:** Board the bus marked Animal Kingdom.

### PARKING

Cost is $14 per day; free to Walt Disney Resort guests and Annual Pass holders. Keep your receipt, good for parking at the Magic Kingdom, Epcot, and Disney's Hollywood Studios on that day only. Parking is conveniently located in front of the park. Trams circulate throughout the parking area for easy transportation to the entry gate. Make a note of what aisle and section you have parked in.

### OPERATING HOURS

Open from 8 or 9 a.m. until around dark. Call (407) 824-4321 or log on to http://disneyworld.disney.go.com for updated park hours.

   Arrive thirty minutes early, allowing time to park, buy tickets, and be one of the first to hit the big attractions. I recommend heading straight to Expedition Everest followed by Kilimanjaro Safaris.

### FASTPASS ATTRACTIONS

- DINOSAUR
- Expedition Everest
- *It's Tough to Be a Bug!*
- Kali River Rapids
- Kilimanjaro Safaris
- Primeval Whirl

See the introduction to this chapter for FASTPASS details.

## PARK SERVICES

**ATMs.** A cash-dispensing bank machine is located just outside the park entrance, one just inside the entrance on the east side, and another in DinoLand outside of Chester and Hester's Dinosaur Treasures gift shop.

**Baby Care Center.** An infant facility located behind the Creature Comforts shop on Discovery Island is outfitted with changing tables, high chairs, and a room for nursing mothers. Disposable diapers, bottles, formula, and baby supplies can be purchased. All restrooms throughout the park are outfitted with changing tables.

**First aid.** For minor medical problems head to the First Aid Center located behind the Creature Comforts shop on Discovery Island.

**Guest Relations.** Located just inside the park on the left is Guest Relations, where a knowledgeable staff is ready to assist with general information, dining, ticket upgrades, lost and found, separated guest assistance, information for guests with disabilities, and international guests.

**Guests with disabilities.** A guidebook for guests with disabilities is available at Guest Relations. Guests with mobility disabilities should park adjacent to the Entrance Complex (ask at the Auto Plaza for directions). Wheelchairs and electric convenience vehicles (ECVs) are available for rent. Most restaurants and shops are accessible to guests with disabilities, although some quick-service locations have narrow queues with railings (ask a host or hostess for assistance). Companion-assisted restrooms are located at First Aid, Discovery Island opposite Flame Tree Barbecue, Africa in the Mombasa Marketplace, at Chester and Hester's Dinosaur Treasures in DinoLand, inside Maharajah Jungle Trek to the right as you exit the Bat House, Conservation Station at Rafiki's Planet Watch, and in Asia near Maharajah Jungle Trek. Most attractions provide access through the main queue while others have auxiliary entrances for wheelchairs and service animals along with as many as five members of your party. Certain attractions require guests to transfer from their wheelchair to a ride system. Service animals are welcome in most locations of the park.

Braille guidebooks, assistive listening devices, video captioning, and audiotape guides are available at Guest Relations for a $25 refundable deposit. The attraction *It's Tough to Be a Bug!* has reflective captioning.

With seven-day notice, a sign language interpreter will be provided at live shows on Saturday. Call (407) 824-4321 for more information.

**Lockers.** Lockers are located just outside the park entrance and just inside on the left for $7 per day plus a $5 refundable key deposit for a small locker, and $9 plus a $5 key deposit for large lockers. If you're park-hopping, keep your receipt for another locker at the three other Disney theme parks for no extra charge.

**Lost and found.** Located at Guest Relations or call (407) 824-4245.

**Lost children.** Locate lost children at the Baby Care Center or Guest Relations.

**Package pickup.** Purchases may be sent to Garden Gate Gifts for pickup at the end of the day. Allow three hours for delivery. Disney resort guests may send packages directly to their hotel for next-day arrival.

**Pet kennel.** A kennel, operated by Best Friends Pet Care, is located just outside the park entrance. Call (407) 938-2100 for information. Proof of vaccination is required.

**Strollers and wheelchairs.** Rentals are located next to Garden Gate Gifts on the right as you enter the park. Single strollers are $15 per day, double strollers $31.

Wheelchairs are $10 inclusive of a $1 refundable deposit. Electric convenience vehicles are $45 inclusive of a $20 refundable deposit. Rented units must be returned to the original rental location to receive a security deposit refund. If you're park-hopping, keep your receipt for a same-day replacement at the three other Disney theme parks and Downtown Disney.

## The Lay of the Land

The Animal Kingdom's Main Street of sorts is the Oasis, a winding series of pathways leading to the hub, Discovery Island, whose focal point is the Tree of Life. Four of the Animal Kingdom's five lands—Camp Minnie-Mickey, Africa, Asia, and DinoLand—are accessible by crossing one of the bridges sp anning the Discovery River that encircles Discovery Island. Africa, Asia, and DinoLand are interconnected by back pathways. Africa and Rafiki's Planet Watch are connected to one another by train.

# CHARACTER GREETING SPOTS AT THE ANIMAL KINGDOM

- Winnie the Pooh and Friends on Discovery Island across from Flame Tree Barbecue
- An assortment of characters like Mickey, Minnie, Pluto, and Goofy dressed in safari wear can be found at the Greeting Trails in Camp Minnie-Mickey
- Lilo and Stitch at Island Mercantile
- Characters like Jiminy Cricket, Pocahontas, Meeko, and Rafiki can be found at Rafiki's Planet Watch
- Mickey, Minnie Mouse, Goofy and more just outside the main entrance
- Thumper from *Bambi* in Camp Minnie Mickey

## The Very Best Attractions in Disney's Animal Kingdom

### IT'S TOUGH TO BE A BUG!

On the winding walkway leading to this attraction is a menagerie of wild-life, lush foliage, waterfalls, caves, and most importantly, an up-close view of the marvelous animal carvings that make up the Tree of Life. It's always twilight in the low-ceilinged waiting area underneath the tree, where chirping crickets sing Broadway tunes from such insect shows as *The Dung and I* (featuring the hit song "Hello Dung Lovers"), *Beauty and the Bees,* and *A Cockroach Line.* Flik (the star of *A Bug's Life*) is the host of this creepy-crawly 3-D movie of assorted bugs who only want humans to understand them. But much to the glee of the audience seated in the the-ater, they just can't help misbehaving. A favorite opening act is the stink-bug who accidentally lets his smelly, gaseous fumes rip into the crowd.

As the show progresses, you'll be doused with bug spray, stung sharply in the back, and showered with termite acid, all innocently achieved through special effects. Receive one final surprise as the beetles, maggots, and cockroaches exit safely ahead of you. What a great show, a highlight of the park! **FASTPASS. 8-minute show.**

CARA'S TIP: Definitely one attraction too intense for young children, particularly when Hopper, the despicable grasshopper from A Bug's Life, scares the dickens out of every child under age five. If you'd like to sit in the center of the auditorium, hang back a little in the waiting area and allow some of the audience to enter ahead of you. And try not to sit on the far sides of the theater where the 3-D effects are minimized.

### FESTIVAL OF THE LION KING

The all-important message of the continuing "circle of life" is wonderfully portrayed in this sensational stage extravaganza of Broadway-caliber song and dance. The story of the Lion King is told through a combination of elaborate costumes, wild acrobatic tumble monkeys, daring fire-twirlers, and massive Audio-Animatronics animal floats accompanied by the beat of tribal drums and jungle noise. Don't worry if you're not acquainted with the music; you'll be an expert by the time you leave. Plan your day around this don't-you-dare-miss-it show. Check your park schedule for showtimes. **30-minute show.**

CARA'S TIP: All 1,400 seats are great in this circular, enclosed theater; however, arrive early in busy season to guarantee your party a spot. The first show of the day has the least attendance and requires less of an advance arrival. Children who would like to be chosen to participate in the closing parade should try to sit in the bottom section of the bleachers.

### KILIMANJARO SAFARIS

Load into safari vehicles for your trip around Disney's 110-acre African savanna brimming with baobab trees, waterfalls, rivers, watering holes, and rickety bridges. Each excursion is different and depends entirely upon which animals decide to make an appearance. As you rumble across the authentic-looking landscape, your driver will assist in locating the wide assortment of wildlife including lions, cheetahs, warthogs, elephants, gazelles, crocodiles, wildebeests, exotic birds, giraffes, even white rhinos. Those with luck might encounter a male lion, rare because they sleep about eighteen hours a day. Some animals may come close to your vehicle, while predators and more perilous species only look as if they could from behind their seemingly invisible barriers. The calm, soothing portion of the ride ends when ivory poachers are discovered, resulting in a wild, crazy chase. Of course, in Disney fashion, the bad guy has to pay. **Not recommended for expectant mothers or people with heart, back, or neck problems. FASTPASS. 20-minute ride.**

*CARA'S TIP:* Don't run for cover during an afternoon thundershower; it's the animals' favorite time to come out for a rain bath.

## PANGANI FOREST EXPLORATION TRAIL

Many people walk right past this self-guided trail and only when it's too late find out what they've missed. Your first encounter is with colobus monkeys at the Endangered Animal Rehabilitation Center and naked mole rats at the Research Center. Then on to a beautiful aviary holding birds native to Africa, a cooling waterfall (complete with faux mist), and an aquarium overflowing with kaleidoscopic fish. Soon all visitors are drawn to a terrific underwater observation tank of swimming hippos before hitting the real highlight—lowland gorillas. You'll find a family of six on the right side of the pathway and a group of four bachelors on the other side. Take time to search for them; it can sometimes be difficult to spot them in the profuse vegetation. Experts are scattered throughout to answer questions and give short, informative talks about each exhibit.

*CARA'S TIP:* Go early after the safari or late in the afternoon when crowds are low. It can be difficult to spot wildlife from behind rows of human heads.

## EXPEDITION EVEREST

Disney's best coaster is combined with an innovative story line and a queue so interesting you tend to forget the long wait. The premise is a base camp of a trekking company, the Himalayan Escapes Tours and Expeditions, overflowing with bunks and supplies as well as a Yeti Museum filled with fascinating artifacts. Then board the Anandapur Rail Service, your transportation for an expedition to the summit of the 199-foot mountain. Ascend through bamboo forests, over teetering bridges, past waterfalls and glacier fields, then up to the snow-capped peak. The excitement truly begins when the train races forward then careens wildly backward through icy caves and dark canyons until the crazy encounter with the hulking Yeti himself! A twisting, turning escape ending in an 80-foot plunge down the mountain is your exciting conclusion. **Minimum height requirement 44 inches. Not recommended for expectant mothers or those with heart, back, or neck problems. FASTPASS. Single riders line. 4-minute ride.**

### FINDING NEMO—THE MUSICAL

A wonderful Broadway-caliber, original stage show brings the *Finding Nemo* characters to life in a combination of puppetry, live performance, and original music and lyrics. Inside an enclosed theater is a magical undersea environment with dazzling oversize puppetry (designed by Michael Curry, creator of Broadway's *The Lion King*), charming songs, and a way fun animated backdrop with special effects. The puppeteers are not hidden—you see the actor and the puppet together, making for one unusual performance. This is Disney at its best. **40-minute show.**

CARA'S TIP: Check your guidemap for showtimes and get in line early! The first show of the day is usually the least crowded and does not require such an early arrival, or consider dining at Tusker House, a buffet restaurant in Africa, that offers reserved seating for the 3:15 p.m. show to anyone booked for lunch between 1 and 1:40 p.m.; one ticket per person dining.

### MAHARAJA JUNGLE TREK

Wander the grounds of the Anandapur Royal Forest through the ruins of a crumbling palace where you'll encounter spectacular wildlife beginning with the Komodo dragon, a giant lizard (look hard because it's in there somewhere). Next are Dracula-like flying foxes and Rodrigues fruit bats with 6-foot wingspans. Then the walk's highlight—Bengal tigers roaming the grasslands, surrounded by gentle deer and blackbucks, a type of antelope. This remarkable journey ends in the Asian bird sanctuary filled with the most exotic varieties imaginable.

CARA'S TIP: Take time to gaze at the marvelous details along the trail such as walls of fading murals, flapping Tibetan prayer flags, abandoned rickshaws, and authentic-looking pagodas.

**DINOSAUR**

Face fiery meteors and voracious predators on a trip back 65 million years to retrieve a 16-foot, plant-eating dinosaur and return with it before the big asteroid hits the earth. Load into twelve-passenger, all-terrain Dino Institute Time Rovers that rock, tilt, twist, and turn as they move through a dense, dark, prehistoric forest teeming with shrieking dinosaurs, giant lizards, and massive insects. When a hail of meteors strikes, off you go on a wild ride dodging shrieking, nostril-flaring Audio-Animatronics dinosaurs until the big scream encounter with a huge carnosaurus (the only meat-eating dinosaur) who'd like you for his dinner. **Minimum height 40 inches (3 feet, 4 inches). Not recommended for expectant mothers or those with heart, back, or neck problems. FASTPASS. 4-minute ride.**

*CARA'S TIP:* This ride is pretty intense for children not only because of massive, screaming dinosaurs but also because of the scary anticipation in an extremely dark attraction.

## The Very Best Dining in Disney's Animal Kingdom

The Animal Kingdom offers some of the most visually delightful quick-service dining in all of Walt Disney World. While the food is just so-so, you'll love the dining terrace at Flame Tree Barbecue with views of Asia and the hulking Expedition Everest. Even Pizzafari offers a great screened eating porch with a tropical view. And don't forget Tusker House in Asia, offering one of Disney's best buffets.

**Rainforest Café.** Enter through a thundering waterfall to dine among screeching and roaring jungle animals; breakfast, lunch, and dinner; priority reservations advised for lunch. (See full description in the Animal Kingdom Dining section of the Dining chapter.)

**Tusker House.** Character buffet breakfast with Donald and Daisy Duck, Mickey, and Goofy with lunch and dinner offering delicious African-inspired buffet fare. (See full description in the Animal Kingdom Dining section of the Dining chapter.)

## Special Entertainment

**Mickey's Jammin' Jungle Parade.** Carousing around the Tree of Life each afternoon is an island street party procession featuring Mickey and

# ANIMAL KINGDOM'S BEHIND-THE-SCENES TOURS

Call (407) WDW-TOUR, or (407) 939-7687 for reservations.

**Backstage Safari.** On this three-hour tour, guests explore the animal housing areas, meet the keepers, and learn how the animals are cared for. Visit the nutrition center where animal food is prepared, and see the backstage area of the Veterinary Care Hospital at Conservation Station. Finish with a special tour through Kilimanjaro Safaris. $70 plus park admission. Two tours, one at 8:30 a.m. and another at 1 p.m., are offered on Monday, Wednesday, Thursday, and Friday. Guests must be age sixteen or older to participate.

**Wild By Design.** Discover how the park's designers combined ethnic art and artifacts, authentic architecture, and story line to create the Animal Kingdom park on this three-hour tour. $60 plus park admission. Starts at 8:30 a.m. Monday, Wednesday, Thursday, and Friday. Guests must be age fourteen or older to participate. Those ages fourteen or fifteen must be accompanied by a participating adult.

his gang joined by a bevy of giant rolling animal sculpture drums sounding out an energetic beat. Mickey, Minnie, Goofy, and Donald overload zany safari vehicles with their idea of exactly what should be taken on an extended vacation. They're accompanied by lofty animal puppets on stilts and rickshaws filled with lucky visitors chosen from the crowd, all adding up to one wacky parade. **15 minutes.**

CARA'S TIP: A great place to watch the parade is from the bridge between Africa and Discovery Island, quite often almost empty of people.

# 5

# BEYOND THE THEME PARKS

## Disney's BoardWalk

Inspired by the Mid-Atlantic wooden seaboard attractions of the 1930s, Disney's BoardWalk offers dining, shopping, and entertainment on the shores of Crescent Lake. Situated in back of the BoardWalk Inn and just outside of Epcot's International Gateway, it's the perfect destination for a before- or after-Illuminations dinner at the Flying Fish, or a place to party down at Jellyrolls and Atlantic Dance, two very different nightclubs. The BoardWalk is at its best in the evening hours, when all the restaurants are open and entertainment in the form of arcades, midway games, musical performers, magicians, fortune-tellers, sword swallowers, caricature artists, and more is in high gear; don't bother during the daytime, when many of the restaurants are closed and entertainment is nil. Although Jellyrolls charges a cover, there's no admission fee to walk the BoardWalk. For up-to-date information, call (407) 939-3492.

### Getting There

The BoardWalk sits in back of the BoardWalk Inn and is about a ten-minute walk from Epcot's International Gateway, a short stroll from the Yacht and Beach Club and the Walt Disney World Swan and Dolphin, and a boat ride or twenty-minute walk from Disney's Hollywood Studios. If traveling from a Disney resort during park hours, take transportation to the closest theme park and then a bus to the BoardWalk Inn. After park hours it requires a trip to Downtown Disney and then a transfer to the BoardWalk Inn; a much less frustrating choice is to either drive a car and park it at the BoardWalk Inn or simply cab it.

## Parking

Park in the complimentary self-park lot in front of the BoardWalk Inn. Valet parking is available for $12.

## Hours

Dining hours vary, with some spots open as early as 7 a.m. for breakfast and others not closing until after midnight. Shop from 10 a.m. to 10 p.m. with the exception of the Screen Door General Store, open from 8 a.m. to midnight.

## The Very Best Dining at the BoardWalk

**BoardWalk Bakery.** A good stop in the mornings on your way to Epcot or after the Illuminations fireworks; open early morning until late night; key lime tart, peanut butter cake, carrot cake, chocolate mousse cake, sugar-free cheesecake brownie, flan, eclairs, tiramisu, fruit tarts; specialty coffees, beverages, smoothies; hot ham and cheese panini, turkey, bacon, and swiss cheese multigrain sandwich; tuna salad multigrain sandwich, tomato mozzarella panini, chicken salad wrap in a whole wheat tortilla; chicken Caesar salad; *breakfast:* breakfast croissant sandwiches, yogurt, fruit.

**Flying Fish Café.** Excellent seafood in whimsical surroundings; dinner only. (See full description in Dining chapter.)

**Kouzzina by Cat Cora.** American Iron Chef Cat Cora's Greek and Mediterranean family recipes and favorites; breakfast and dinner; *breakfast:* steel cut cinnamon oatmeal with bananas and pecans, turkey-sweet potato hash, vegetable flatbread, blueberry orange granola pancakes, spinach, tomato, and feta scrambled eggs; *dinner:* cinnamon stewed chicken, fisherman's stew, pastitsio (Greek lasagna), char-grilled lamb burger, whole pan-roasted fish with braised greens, Greek olives, fennel, and smoked chili.

## Nightclubs at the BoardWalk

**Atlantic Dance.** Video DJ music of the '80s, '90s, and today; arrive at opening time and make a quick dash upstairs to the outdoor terrace for an excellent view of the Illuminations fireworks. Open 9 p.m. to 2 a.m.; guests must be at least twenty-one years old for admittance; closed Sunday and Monday. No cover charge.

**Jellyrolls.** Extremely popular dueling pianos and sing-along bar. Open 7 p.m. to 2 a.m.; guests must be twenty-one or older for admittance; $10 cover charge.

# Downtown Disney

Many changes and additions over the years have created what is now known as the very successful Downtown Disney, a combination of more than seventy scene-setting restaurants and shops. During the day it's a perfect getaway from the parks, but at night after the parks close, Downtown Disney truly comes alive.

At Disney Marketplace you'll find the largest Disney Store in the world, a boat marina, plenty of shopping, a rip-roaring T-Rex restaurant, and the volcano-smoking Rainforest Café. Pleasure Island is undergoing a major change until 2011 with its nightclubs gradually being replaced by restaurants and retail stores. And then there's the West Side, loaded with dining and entertainment venues including Wolfgang Puck Café, House of Blues, Gloria Estefan's Bongos, Cirque du Soleil, AMC Movie Theater, and DisneyQuest. It's always hopping, but those preferring a bit of peace and quiet can opt for a quiet stroll along the pleasant promenade running beside the Buena Vista Lagoon.

## General Information

### GETTING THERE

Those driving should take I-4 to exit 67 and follow the signs to Downtown Disney. Direct buses operate from all Disney resort hotels. Buses stop first at the Marketplace and then at Pleasure Island/West Side.

## PARKING

Parking here can prove difficult, particularly during busy season and weekend evenings when both locals and visitors alike jam Downtown Disney. If you're a guest of a Disney resort, consider using Disney transportation to avoid the hassle of parking. Self-parking is free; valet parking is not available.

## HOURS

Shops at Downtown Disney Marketplace are open Sunday through Thursday from 9:30 a.m. to 11 p.m. and Friday and Saturday from 9:30 a.m. to 11:30 p.m. Pleasure Island shops are open Sunday through Thursday from 10:30 a.m. to 11 p.m. and Friday and Saturday from 10:30 a.m. until midnight. Downtown Disney's West Side shops are open Sunday through Thursday from 10:30 a.m. to 11 p.m. and Friday and Saturday from 10:30 a.m. to midnight. Restaurant hours vary; see specific restaurants for exact times.

## GUEST RELATIONS

Stop here for Advance Dining Reservations, lost and found, park passes, and services for international guests and guests with disabilities, along with general information. Facilities are located at both the West Side and the Marketplace.

## ATMS

Withdraw cash from your bank account at ATMs located at House of Blues and Wetzel's Pretzels on the West Side; and across from Guest Relations, the World of Disney, and by the restrooms near Once Upon a Toy at the Marketplace.

## STROLLERS AND WHEELCHAIRS

Rentals are located at Disney's Wonderful World of Memories at Downtown Disney Marketplace and at DisneyQuest Emporium at Downtown Disney on the West Side. Single strollers are $15 per day; double strollers are not available. Wheelchairs are $10 and electric convenience vehicles are $45, plus a $100 refundable deposit. If you're park-hopping, keep your receipt for a same-day replacement at the four Disney theme parks.

## AMC Pleasure Island 24 Theatres Complex

Watch newly released flicks in loveseat-style stadium seating with THX Surround Sound and Sony Dynamic Digital Sound in this state-of-the-art, twenty-four-screen theater. Call (888) 262-4926 or (407) 827-1308 for movie listings and showtimes.

## Characters in Flight

A tethered helium filled balloon takes guests 400 feet above Disney World for a breathtaking view of the surrounding area. Holding up to thirty people at a time, prices are $16 for adults and $10 for children ages three through nine (guests under age twelve must be accompanied by an adult).

## Cirque du Soleil

The tent-shaped building overpowering the West Side of Downtown Disney is none other than Cirque du Soleil, the most talked about entertainment venue in town. Although it's sometimes described as a type of circus, it's actually a mixture of circus, dance, drama, and street entertainment, more than worth the hefty price of admission. And because of its immense popularity, think about booking your seats way in advance.

It's difficult to explain this extraordinary event. The show, entitled *La Nouba,* has more than sixty mesmerizing human performers (no animals) in outrageous costumes entertaining in the midst of exciting live music (not one syllable is uttered throughout the show) and surrealistic choreography. Witness daring, gravity-defying acts, each one more outlandish and bizarre than the next. Two showstoppers are the young Chinese girls who perform a routine with a diabolo, a Chinese yo-yo (you won't believe it!), and a trampoline finale with power men literally running up the sides of a wall. The sheer physical strength of these performers is absolutely astonishing and quite a sight to see. Tickets can be purchased up to 180 days in advance by calling (407) 939-7719, or going online at www.cirque dusoleil.com; two ninety-minute performances Tuesday through Saturday at 6 and 9 p.m.; four levels of ticket prices according to seating.

CARA'S TIP: Although some seats are better than others, there really isn't a bad seat in the house. You may want to avoid the first row of the highest tier; the wheelchair-accessible seats in front block your view a bit.

## DisneyQuest

With five floors of virtual games and interactive adventures diverse enough to entertain the entire family, this indoor theme park offers a multitude of attractions (including more than 180 video games) that can be played over and over for the single cost of admission. Become a swashbuckling pirate in a fierce battle for treasure at the virtual 3-D **Pirates of the Caribbean: Battle for Buccaneer Gold**; watch a large projection screen while paddling with motion-sensor oars on a prehistoric, white-water adventure with the **Virtual Jungle Cruise**; fly through the ancient city of Agrabah on your magic carpet in search of precious jewels in a virtual reality setting on **Aladdin's Magic Carpet Ride**; design your own thrilling roller-coaster ride with **Cyberspace Mountain**; play space-age bumper cars with **Buzz Lightyear's AstroBlaster**; or wield a light saber to fight supervillains sword-to-sword in virtual reality with **Ride the Comix**.

Upstairs, FoodQuest offers a quick bite with wrap sandwiches, Italian deli and pulled pork sandwiches, burgers, chicken nuggets, grilled chicken BLT, hot dogs, nachos, pizza, pasta, paninis, baked ziti, and salads.

Open Sunday through Thursday from 11:30 a.m. to 10 p.m. and Friday and Saturday from 11:30 a.m. to 11 p.m. Admission prices are $41 for adults and $35 for children ages three through nine; same-day reentry allowed with ticket and hand stamp. Guests age nine or younger must be accompanied by someone age sixteen or older, all of whom must pay admission.

*CARA'S TIP*: Come during the daytime on weekdays and avoid rainy days. Although DisneyQuest is mainly geared to kids and adolescents, it's a great place for quality family time. Adults traveling alone may want to pass unless they really enjoy this type of entertainment.

## The Very Best Shopping at Downtown Disney

**Art of Disney.** Disney collectibles, animation cells, sketches drawn by a Disney artist, Lenox and Goebel Disney character figurines, touch-screen ordering of Disney posters or canvas art.

**Curl by Sammy Duvall.** Surf shop for the younger generation; Quiksilver, Billabong, Roxy clothing and accessories; entire wall of flip-flops; loads of sunglasses including Oakley, Ray Ban, and Gucci; sports watches.

**Disney's Days of Christmas.** Whopper of a Disney Christmas store; Disney character ornaments and stockings; Victorian Disney character plush toys; tree skirts and toppers; Tinker Bell ornaments and accessories; have your purchases personalized on the spot.

**Goofy's Candy Company.** Cookies, fudge, Rice Krispies treats, bulk candy, a wall of jelly beans, boxed and individual chocolates, candy apples, lollipops, pastries, cupcakes, cinnamon rolls, specialty coffees, powder candy dispenser; interactive candy show kitchen.

**Hoypoloi.** Glass art; sculpture in glass, metal, bronze, and wood; Zen-inspired gifts and books; scented candles; whimsical lamps; indoor water sculptures.

**Lego Imagination Center.** Giant Lego sculptures; 3,000-square-foot outdoor play area; every Lego set imaginable.

**Once Upon a Toy.** 16,000 square feet of Disney and Hasbro toys, many of them exclusive; Lincoln Logs; Build-Your-Own Mr. Potato Head and Build-Your-Own Lightsaber stations; huge assortment of Disney CDs and DVDs.

**Pop Gallery.** Art gallery featuring original, contemporary art; high-end gifts; artists featured are Todd Warner, Markus Pierson, and Roy Barloga; limited edition Dr. Seuss lithographs.

**Sosa Family Cigars.** Fine cigars; smoking accessories; master cigar roller in action Thursday through Saturday evenings.

**World of Disney.** Largest Disney merchandise store in the world with a giant-size, spitting Stitch hanging over the entrance; 50,000 square feet crammed with just about every Disney item imaginable; elaborate displays in themed rooms including an Adventure Room with an Audio-Animatronics pirate, Create Your Own Pirate Hat, Build a Magic Wand, and Fill Your Own Treasure Chest stations; the Bibbidi-Bobbidi Boutique in the Princess Room where little princesses can be made up with royal hair topped with crowns, sparkling jewels, shimmering nail paints and makeup, a complete costume, and other magical accessories followed by a photo shoot (a boys' experience called Cool Dude offers hair styling, colored gels, and sparkles)—reservations are taken 180 days prior at (407) WDW-STYLE or (407) 939-7895.

## The Very Best Dining at Downtown Disney

**Bongos.** Cuban-themed restaurant and entertainment spot owned by Latina pop star Gloria Estefan; lunch and dinner. (See full description in Dining chapter.)

**Portobello.** Italian food in a countryside trattoria atmosphere; lunch and dinner. (See full description in Dining chapter.)

**Raglan Road.** Irish contemporary cooking served up with authentic Irish music; lunch and dinner. (See full description in Dining chapter.)

**Rainforest Café.** Follow the sound of a rumbling volcano to this popular spot; dine amid waterfalls and exotic Audio-Animatronics jungle animals; lunch and dinner. (See full description in Dining chapter.)

**T-Rex Café.** Downtown Disney's most entertaining dining spot with life-size Audio-Animatronics dinosaurs and wild meteor showers; lunch and dinner. (See full description in Dining chapter.)

**Wolfgang Puck Grand Cafe.** Four separate dining concepts in one facility: cafe for lunch and dinner; upscale dining room on second floor (dinner only); the Sushi Bar; express patio dining. (See full description in Dining chapter.)

# Water Parks

Choose from two Disney water parks, each with its own brand of entertainment. At Blizzard Beach you'll find the exhilarating 120-foot Summit Plummet slide, and at the tropical Typhoon Lagoon, there's a whopper of a surf pool and Crush'n'Gusher, a water coaster thrill ride. Both parks are beautifully themed and landscaped, and each offers something for just about everyone. And because the pools are heated in the cooler months, it's a year-round playground.

During the sizzling summer months, it's important to arrive early in the morning if you want to avoid the long lines that start forming at almost every attraction by midday; in fact, parks are sometimes filled to capacity by midmorning, and new guests are kept from entering until late in the afternoon. Weekends are the worst, when the locals add to the swell. Be sure to bring water footwear to protect tender feet from the scorching hot pavements.

Locker and towel rentals are available at both parks; life jackets are complimentary. Ice chests are allowed as long as they don't contain alcoholic beverages or glass containers (alcoholic drinks may be purchased at the parks). An adult must accompany children ages nine or younger, and all swim attire must be free of rivets, buckles, or exposed metal. Parking is free. Both parks are on a rotating schedule of refurbishment in the winter months, so check ahead.

Those that don't want to fight for a lounge chair should consider shaded premium chair space rentals available at both water parks (Polar Patios at Blizzard Beach and Beachcomber Shacks at Typhoon Lagoon) that include the personalized services of an attendant, private lockers, all-day drink mugs, cooler with bottled water, Adirondack lounge furniture, and towels. Accommodating up to six guests, the cost is $250 for a full day. Call 407-WDW-PLAY for reservations.

CARA'S TIP: In the busy summer months when the water parks are open until 8 p.m., think about arriving in mid- to late afternoon when the morning guests are beginning to depart. It's the best time to enjoy the attractions minus the crowds.

## Blizzard Beach

Disney's largest water park features the strange theme of a melting alpine ski resort in the middle of the hot Florida sunshine. The thaw has created a watery "winter" wonderland where chairlifts carry swimmers instead of skiers up a 90-foot-high mountain to slalom bobsled runs that are now thrilling waterslides. Although you'll find plenty of tame attractions, this is Disney's water park for daredevils, with wild, rushing water and death-defying slides. Upon arrival head straight for Summit Plummet to avoid huge lines later in the day.

Hours vary according to the season but are usually 10 a.m. to 5 p.m., with extended hours until 8 p.m. in summer. In cooler months the two water parks are open on a rotating basis, with one open and the other closed for refurbishment. Call (407) 560-3400 for up-to-date information.

**GETTING THERE**

Blizzard Beach is located in the Animal Kingdom area on West Buena Vista Drive. If using Disney transportation, direct buses depart from all resorts. Those driving should take exit 65 off I-4.

## THE VERY BEST ATTRACTIONS AT BLIZZARD BEACH

**Melt-Away Bay.** One-acre wave pool with "melting snow" waterfalls. Swells here are not as intense as those at Typhoon Lagoon.

**Runoff Rapids.** Those in search of a thrill-but-not-a-scare will love this attraction. Tube down your choice of three runs (one is enclosed, the others open) for a blast of a ride. To reach this attraction, go behind Mt. Gushmore to pick up a tube at the bottom of a tall flight of stairs and start climbing.

**Summit Plummet.** The king of water park attractions. From the top is a 120-foot plunge at speeds of up to 55 mph. The slide itself is a 350-foot speed trap where daredevils body slide so fast they don't know what hit them as they plummet to the bottom.

**Teamboat Springs.** One of the most popular rides in the park, this 1,200-foot attraction accommodates anywhere from three to five people per raft as it twists and turns through a fun-filled succession of rushing waterfalls.

**Toboggan Racers.** If you're looking for a challenge on this eight-lane mat slide, go headfirst down the steep slope.

## *Typhoon Lagoon*

At this beauty of a water park, you'll find a fifty-six-acre tropical fantasy-land. The premise is that a great storm swept everything in its path to a once sleepy resort town that became Typhoon Lagoon. The shipwrecked shrimp boat, *Miss Tilly,* perched atop the 95-foot-high summit of Mount Mayday, creates a ruckus every half hour when it tries in vain to dislodge itself by spewing a geyser of water high above the park. Geared toward a bit tamer crowd than Blizzard Beach, only one waterslide here is a daredevil's delight. The park's main draw is the 2.75-million-gallon wave pool that boasts some of the tallest simulated waves in the world (some as high as 6 feet tall).

Before park opening on Monday (only in summer season), Tuesday, and Friday is your chance to take surfing lessons in the huge wave pool with surfboards provided. Participants must be at least eight years old and strong swimmers. Cost is $150 per person. Call (407) WDW-SURF, or (407) 939-7873, for reservations.

Hours vary according to the season but are usually 10 a.m. to 5 p.m. with extended hours until 8 p.m. in summer. During the cooler months, the two parks open on a rotating basis with one always closed for refurbishment. Call (407) 560-4141 for up-to-date information.

## GETTING THERE

Typhoon Lagoon is located across Buena Vista Drive from Downtown Disney's West Side just off I-4, exit 67. If using Disney transportation, the bus to catch is marked Downtown Disney/Typhoon Lagoon.

## THE VERY BEST ATTRACTIONS AT TYPHOON LAGOON

**Crush 'n' Gusher.** This exciting attraction billed as a water coaster thrill ride is the only one of its kind in Central Florida. Whisk along a series of flumes and spillways, experiencing torrents of water while weaving in and out of a rusty old tropical fruit factory. Choose from three different spillways ranging between 410 and 420 feet long with a variation of slopes and turns.

**Humunga Kowabunga.** This trio of 214-foot speed slides is only for the most daring of thrill-seekers. Fly along at speeds around 30 mph, a feat for those with strong hearts. Lines can be excruciatingly long, so head for this attraction first thing in the morning.

**Shark Reef.** Pick up your snorkeling gear and prepare yourself for the bracingly cold saltwater of Shark Reef. Instructors are on hand to help guide inexperienced snorkelers as they swim through a short-but-sweet pool of tropical fish, stingrays, and harmless sharks.

**Storm Slides.** Corkscrew through 300 feet of caves and waterfalls at speeds of 20 mph. Try all three slides—each offers a different experience.

**Typhoon Lagoon Surf Pool.** This is the park's main attraction. What sounds like a typhoon warning is a foghorn announcing the impending wave soon to follow; some waves are as high as 6 feet. Separate but nearby, you'll find a lagoon made for children too small to handle the big waves.

# Spas

When your muscles are aching and your body is screaming for rest after days at the parks, soothe your jangled nerves at one of Orlando's spas. Immerse yourself in luxury with a feel-good treatment or two, guaranteed to rejuvenate and swiftly get you back on your feet and ready for another long day of walking the parks.

Disney's spas, while nice and convenient, are not exactly up to par with the Dolphin's Mandara Spa or any of the spas at the luxury resorts in the Orlando area. So expect a nice, but not ultra luxurious experience at either the Grand Floridian or Saratoga Springs Spa.

## Grand Floridian Spa

This 9,000-square-foot spa offers a nice range of treatments and packages along with an adjoining fitness center. Separate women's and men's locker rooms are equipped with whirlpools, Turkish steam baths, saunas, robes, and slippers, and within each is a not too special waiting lounge equipped with tea, coffee, and fruit. Open 6 a.m. to 9 p.m., with treatment hours from 8 a.m. to 8 p.m. daily. Guests ages ten and older are welcome in the spa, although an adult must accompany those under age eighteen. Call (407) 827-4455 for information and reservations.

**Don't leave without buying:** The Hydrating Face Polish and Yogurt Mask from the boutique's Amala line of products.

**Must-have treatment:** Two-hour Aromatherapy Massage and Body Wrap, a calming Swedish aromatherapy massage followed by warm compresses and heat while wrapped to encourage absorption of healing essential oils. Finish with a scalp massage.

### SAMPLE SERVICES

**Grand Floridian Deluxe Facial.** The beneficial effects of two masks leaves your skin feeling fresh and hydrated.

**Grand Romantic Couples Massage.** In a candlelit couples room, each person receives an aromatherapy massage.

**My First Facial.** Designed for children age twelve or younger to introduce the basics of skin care.

**Olive Oil and Salt Exfoliation/Massage.** A deep cleansing and exfoliating body scrub followed by an aromatherapy massage.

**Detoxifying Body Wrap.** A thorough body exfoliation with mineral rich sea salts, crushed olive stone, and plant essences to stimulate and cleanse the body. This is followed by a warm clay mask body wrap, which should leave you relaxed and rejuvenated.

## Mandara Spa at the Walt Disney World Dolphin

The nicest spa on Disney property. Offering creative treatments based on both East and West traditions and one of the prettiest tea lounges in all of Orlando, it's definitely a cut above the others. You'll feel worlds away from the bustling parks as you wait in a replica of a centralized "Asian Bale" around which are situated the treatment rooms—beautiful but a bit uncomfortable. Under the soothing touch of Esperanza my La Therapie HydraPeel, which uses a glycolic preparation perfect for resurfacing skin, was a winning experience, or consider trying one of the ultra interesting Eastern-style treatments such as the choreographed Balinese massage, almost too exotic to pass up. Relax afterwards in the spa's hand-carved "Meru Temple sanctuary," where hot tea and light snacks are served overlooking a garden courtyard. Consider timing your treatment to coincide with lunch since a cold, four-course spa menu with an Asian emphasis is available in the temple. The only things lacking are a sauna and whirlpool in the locker rooms; only a small steam room is to be found. A small salon and separate pedicure and manicure rooms complete the list of services. Open from 8 a.m. until 9 p.m.; call (407) 934-4772 for reservations. For more information go online at www.swandolphin.com/mandaraspa.

*CARA'S TIP*: Children ages four to twelve may enjoy two complimentary hours of fun at Camp Dolphin with any spa service lasting seventy-five minutes or more.

**Don't leave without buying:** Elemis Pro-Collagen Marine Cream, an intense anti-aging product.

**Must-have treatment:** The Elemis Aroma Spa Seaweed Massage, a deeply detoxifying treatment using sea plants and marine algae with aromatherapy to detoxify, decongest, and stimulate your body systems. A warm seaweed body mask is applied before cocooning your body in a foil wrap while your scalp and feet receive a soothing massage. The follow up is a full-body massage.

**SAMPLE SERVICES**

**Elemis Exotic Frangipani Body Nourish Wrap.** A blend of coconut and frangipani flowers is massaged into the body, then a wrap to let the ingredients absorb.

# TIPS FOR MAKING THE MOST OF YOUR SPA TIME

- Arrive fifteen to twenty minutes early. This will allow time to check in, don your robe, have a cup of tea, and prepare for your treatment. Better yet, arrive one hour early and enjoy a pre-treatment whirlpool.

- Be comfortable. It's not necessary to remove underclothing if it truly makes you uneasy; your masseuse is able to do their job either way. But if you're okay with it, you'll certainly receive a more thorough treatment with all clothing removed. Remember that only small parts of the body are exposed at one time with the rest of you well covered by a sheet or towel.

- Talk about any trouble spots before your treatment begins. Let your therapist know if you have any sensitive areas or whether you like soft or firm pressure. During your treatment let your therapist know if he or she is talking more than you care for (a good therapist will take their talking cue from their client). It's your treatment and it's essential that you receive exactly what you are looking for.

- Relax and enjoy. After just one treatment you'll more than likely be hooked on this very pleasurable experience.

**Ionithermie Cellulite Reduction Program.** Noninvasive way to detoxify your body, reduce fluid retention, and tone muscles.

**Elemis Pro-Collagen Quartz Lift Facial.** Anti-wrinkle facial proven to reduce wrinkles and improve firmness with Padina Pavonica accelerated by the electrical energy of precious minerals to re-energize cell communication.

**Nurturing Massage for Mother-to-Be.** A safe pregnancy massage with special positioning on a unique beanbag to ensure the ultimate in comfort and relaxation.

**Couples Retreat Ritual.** Indulge together with an aromatic massage side by side in a beautiful Balinese-style treatment room followed by a river-rocked rimmed hydrotherapy Jacuzzi tub. End with each receiving a facial.

## Spa at Disney's Saratoga Springs Resort

This is another choice for a respite from the hectic theme parks. Here the Adirondack stone therapy massage, using heated stones and aromatherapy oil to massage the entire body, is the best. Hydrotherapy treatments are another specialty with pressurized streams of water working deep in the muscle to help relieve tension. There are ten treatment rooms, including a couple's room, plus a small tea lounge. Each locker room has steam, sauna, and whirlpool. Within the spa is Disney's best fitness center with an exclusive line of Life Fitness and Hammer Strength equipment. Open from 6 a.m. to 9 p.m., with treatment hours from 8 a.m. to 8 p.m. daily. Call (407) 827-4455 for reservations.

**Don't leave without buying:** Mystical Forest Aromatherapy Mineral Bath Salts.

**Must-have treatment:** A four-hour Adirondack Adventure, which includes a stone massage, stone facial, and maple sugar body polish.

### SAMPLE SERVICES

**Couple's Relaxation.** One person receives a forty-five-minute aromatherapy massage while the other is in the hydrotherapy tub in the same room. Then they switch, with tea in between.

**Maple Sugar Body Polish.** A gentle exfoliation using micronized sugar and essential oils to restore the natural radiance of your skin.

**Gentleman's Facial.** Experience a deep-cleansing and exfoliating facial, leaving skin fresh and revitalized.

**Mystical Forest Therapies.** A signature treatment that combines reflexology and Swedish massage.

**Detoxifying Body Wrap.** Begin with a dry body brush and a salt exfoliation, then your body is wrapped in a detoxifying clay mask cocoon while you receive an ear and scalp massage.

## Mandara Spa at Portofino Bay Hotel

Here, fourteen treatment rooms illuminated by candles as well as two Spa Suites with a Vichy shower and hot tub offer a bit of Bali to the Orlando area. Both the men's and women's locker rooms have a sauna and steam room, but the spa's one whirlpool is coed. You'll also find male, female, and coed lounges stocked with soothing Asian touches and a couples suite offering the luxury of combining a massage with a hydrotherapy treatment. The specialty here is the Balinese service, a traditional healing system passed down from mothers to daughters. On my last visit I enjoyed a combination Balinese massage and an Elemis Visible Brillance Facial, the perfect duo. The Elemis products used are worth taking home, and I left with an absolutely glowing complexion. There's also a teen program with such offerings as a heavenly massage, fabulous fruity facial, and surfer's scrub body exfoliation.

An adjoining fitness center, complimentary with a spa treatment, has a full gym with individual TV monitors in each fitness machine. In-room or in-cabana massage is available as well. Open from 6 a.m. to 8 p.m., with personal services and salon available from 8 a.m. to 8 p.m. daily. Call (407) 503-1244 for an appointment.

**Don't leave without buying:** Elemis Skin Nourishing Milk Bath.

**Must-have treatment:** Mandara Four Hands Massage, with two therapists working on you simultaneously in synchronicity and silence.

### SAMPLE SERVICES

**Balinese Massage.** A choreographed massage combination of pressure points, acupressure, and traditional Balinese techniques.

**Elemis Aroma Stone Therapy.** Small heated stones placed on key energy points are used to massage the body.

**Elemis Exotic Coconut Rub and Milk Ritual Wrap.** Warm milk bath poured over your entire body and then a cocoon foil wrap.

**Shiatsu Massage.** This traditional Japanese pressure point massage stimulates the muscles and helps breakdown toxin build-up.

**La Therapie HydraLift Facial with Microdermabrasion.** Using the latest computerized technology and fine granules, skin is exfoliated to reveal the healthy, undamaged skin underneath, then nourished and deep cleansed to withdraw deeply embedded impurities.

## Relâche Spa at Gaylord Palms Resort

Gaylord Palms Resort's European-inspired spa has twenty-five soothing treatment rooms, a tea-and-relaxation room, and men's and women's locker rooms each with steam, sauna, and fantastic multi-head showers. Programs focus on therapies from both East and West including Ayurvedic (a holistic treatment for mind and body) and Fijian rituals. On my latest visit I had the pleasure of a treatment called the Muscle Melt whereby warmed herbal pouches are lightly pounded into the muscles and pressure points to ease aches and pains followed by a deep tissue massage with lemongrass oil; it was a nice alternative to my usual favorite, a stone massage. There's an adjoining fitness club as well as a full-service salon. Open from 8 a.m. to 8 p.m. daily. Call (407) 586-4772 for spa reservations.

**Don't leave without buying:** Something from the SpaRitual line of eco-friendly products using vegan ingredients from around the world, including many specially sourced and selected plant essences that are wild crafted or organic.

**Must-have treatment:** Ishara, a slow movement treatment beginning with hot sage towels placed on the face to help calm the mind, then a geranium scalp massage followed by the application of body herbs. After the herbs are gently buffed off, you will soak in a rose petal tub with muscle relaxing oils, followed by a very slow massage with Clary Sage vanilla oil.

## SAMPLE SERVICES

**Thai Massage**. Performed on a floor mat using compression and slow rocking movements, the therapist stretches the soft tissue while balancing the body's energy.

**Shiatsu.** An ancient Japanese treatment meaning "finger pressure," this active, rhythmic massage stimulates acupressure points along energy meridians throughout the body.

**The Gaylord Glow.** This highly active enzyme reprograms skin cells to use more energy, thereby becoming self-rejuvenating. Symptoms of aging skin, including wrinkles, loss of glow, irregular skin tones, and increased pore size are reversed and repaired.

**Secrets of India.** Traditional ayurvedic facial treatment, customized with essential oils. A facial massage focuses on the marma points (energy points) and also includes choice of relaxing dry scalp massage or Shirodhara.

**Shirodhaa.** A steady stream of oil will be dripped onto your third eye to bring inner peace to the mind and body. Enjoy a relaxing scalp massage along with a hand and foot massage.

## Ritz-Carlton Spa

Consider staying put for a day to enjoy this outstanding 40,000-square-foot, Mediterranean palazzo–style facility, an exquisite oasis of soothing perfection. Citrus is the word here, with citrus-inspired products used in the spa's forty treatment rooms, where you're lavishly pampered and indulged. Coed as well as separate men and women's lounges are stocked with fruit and citrus water, and each locker area has a whirlpool, sauna, and steam room; in the women's locker room is a pressure shower (not terribly impressive) and in the men's an ice cold plunge pool. There's even a rooftop area utilizing hammocks in treatments. Nothing can beat the unbelievable experience of the ashiatsu massage—a specially trained therapist uses bars set in the ceiling to balance while his or her feet perform deep massage. The Thai massage utilizes stretching and acupressure to rejuvenate the body, or at the other end of the spectrum a non-surgical face lift procedure offers a deep serum infusion, LED light therapy, and crystal-free microdermabrasion. For the ultimate in luxury, book one of the VIP suites offering half- or full-day programs along with a spa lunch, served on the suite's elegant balcony. Another bonus is the exclusive use of the spa's outdoor heated lap pool. I highly recommend planning a complete spa day here. Begin by sweating it out at the posh fitness center followed by a steam, sauna, and whirlpool. Then languish beside the serene spa pool, take a dip, and order lunch delivered poolside from the Vitale Spa Cafe. Schedule your treatment for mid-afternoon, relaxing in the lounge afterward.

Open from 10 a.m. to 7 p.m. daily. Call (407) 393-4200 for treatment reservations.

The 6,000-square-foot Wellness Center within the spa is phenomenal, with each Movement Studio's cardiovascular equipment sporting its own TV monitor.

The Carita Salon features stylist consultations and scalp massage, citrus manicures and pedicures, latte stone manicures, and hair extensions along with traditional hair services. The Retail Store sells Carita products, candles, casual clothing, and lingerie. And if hunger pains strike, try the Vitale Spa Café, offering healthy appetizers, sandwiches, salads, and low-fat desserts.

**Don't leave without buying:** Since you won't want to take off your oh-so-comfy spa robe, go ahead and purchase one in the retail store.

**Must-have treatment:** Ashiatsu Massage, an ancient form of body work where therapists use bars set in the ceiling to balance while their feet perform broad, deep compression to bring about a change in tight muscle tissue as well as provide deep relaxation and stimulation to the lymphatic system.

### SAMPLE SERVICES

**Eco-Rooftop Hammock Experience.** On your own private rooftop sanctuary enjoy nature and the benefits of "zero gravity" combined with massage. A fully clothed treatment, it uses cranial sacral, reflexology, and shiatsu massage while the hammock moves in a rhythmic, rocking motion. Or partake in the Eco Garden Scrub Bar, an interactive spa experience in the herb garden on the rooftop. To concoct the scrub the therapist will pick herbs according to the guest's needs, and then add Himalayan salt or ground poultice to the mixture to use in a bathing ritual or in a pedicure or body scrub treatment, leaving skin glowing and soft.

**Four Hands Massage.** Full-body Swedish massage performed simultaneously by two therapists.

**Rain Forest Stones.** Begin with a light exfoliation followed by a Vichy waterfall and an application of tropical passion fruit extracts and heated stones.

**Poultice Massage.** Using traditional herbs, the medicinal heat soaks into the muscles, releasing tightness and inducing a deep, full body relaxation.

**Deep Cleansing Organic Escape.** Purifying, anti-aging facial using pumpkin enzymes that clear skin of cellular build-up that causes clogged pores, beta carotenes to slow environmental damage, and 100 percent natural plant-based products to nourish the skin.

## The Spa at the Omni Orlando Resort at ChampionsGate

A small but lovely spa utilizing the techniques and products of the South Pacific as its inspiration. Don your robe and head to the separate men's and women's waiting/relaxation lounge (one of the better ones in Orlando) where herbal teas, fruit, and soothing music encourage lingering. There are ten treatment rooms (request one without a window) and one couple's room. Men have a sauna and whirlpool while the women have steam and a whirlpool. Lockers are stocked with a nice variety of hair products and lotions. Try the refreshing Fiji Sugar Glow body exfoliator, just the thing for me after a summer spent at skin-drying high altitude, although the promised oil massage ending was merely a quick rubdown. The body wraps here are also nice—they begin with a dry brush massage followed by an application of a tonic or serum of choice, then a warm non-confining cocoon wrap accompanied by a head and foot massage. The boutique offers a line of natural makeup products as well as a full line of the spa's exclusive products. There's also a full service salon for hair and nail care, makeup, and waxing. A menu of services is available online at www.omni hotels.com/spas/orlando/index.html. Open 8 a.m. to 8 p.m. Call (407) 390-6603 for spa reservations.

**Don't leave without buying:** Something from the Pure Fiji line in either the coconut or pineapple scent.

**Must-have treatment:** Hydrating Island Wrap where the skin is gently dry brushed, then drenched in virgin coconut, macadamia, and tropical oils, giving your body a boost of vitamins and minerals. All this plus a stone facial and scalp massage.

**SAMPLE SERVICES**

**Duet Massage.** Simultaneous massages for two in a specially designed treatment room.

**Deluxe Hydractive Facial.** Designed for mature skin using exclusive freeze-dried marine vegetable fibers that saturate the upper epidermis and provide hydration and visible results after one treatment.

**Golfer's Massage.** Designed to release toxins, relieve stress, and stimulate circulation.

**Regenerating Vitamin C Facial.** Good for all skin types, it's the perfect facial to take on the damaging effects of a toxic environment.

**Dragonfly Body Mask.** Begin with a dry brush massage followed by an application of soy clay, which decreases bumps and smoothes the skin's texture. While comfortably wrapped in a warm cocoon, you are given a head and foot massage.

## The Spa at Reunion Resort

This is one of my favorite spas in Orlando. If you are tired of the impersonal service at a traditional spa, try this boutique spa, the only caveat being you must be a guest of the Reunion Resort (how's that for exclusivity!). Housed in a charming, freestanding home, this is a totally different experience from your normal resort spa.

There are five treatment rooms including a couple's room as well as one for facials, and an inviting coed tea lounge with cushy chaise lounges, cashmere throws, snacks, and a caring staff. Locker rooms are small but well equipped with all the amenities. A private courtyard holds a small pool and whirlpool tub. Or relax on the outdoor balcony overlooking the Legacy golf course.

My latest visit included a decadent ashiatsu massage in which the therapist supported herself on bars suspended from the ceiling to provide a foot massage and the exact right amount of pressure—once you've tried it, you'll become a firm believer. Or consider one of the "green" environmentally sound and sustainable body wraps using organic products of tropical fruits combined with vitamins A and C.

Treatments are also available in the privacy of your accommodations. A two-chair salon offers cut, color, waxing, and up-dos. The spa boutique sells Pevonia Botanica products. Open daily 10 a.m. to 6 p.m.; call (407) 662-4772 for reservations. For more information go online at www .reunionresort.com/spa/spa.asp.

**Don't leave without buying:** Pevonia Botanica Dry Oil Moisturizer for silky smooth skin.

**Must-have treatment:** The ultimate anti-aging Premier Caviar Facial, a super treatment with caviar, crushed pearls and Escutox, which will exfoliate and firm leaving you with radiant skin.

## SAMPLE SERVICES

**Firming Neck & Decollete Treatment.** Utilizing the phyto-extract Kigelia Africana, restore suppleness and elasticity to your neck and bust area. Good for sun-damaged and sluggish skin.

**Warm Stone Massage.** The relaxing nature of Swedish massage and hot stones facilitates the flow of relaxation through the body, mind, and spirit.

**Reflexology.** A pressure point massage technique applied to the feet to release tension. Each point corresponds to an area of the body in which to heal. Improves circulation and reduces fatigue.

**Green Coffee Slimming Body Wrap.** Stimulates your body's ability to break down fat, increase metabolism, and eliminate water retention. Pure 100 percent micronized green coffee smoothes and enhances your skin's overall texture thus reducing cellulitic areas.

**Pampered Prince or Princess Facial.** Cleanse, tone, and mask young skin while teaching the importance of good skin care. Little ones will also receive a sample bag of products to use at home.

## The Spa at Shingle Creek

Nine treatment rooms in this delightful 10,000-square-foot spa have heated beds and the heady aroma of citrus-cedar, the spa's signature product. The staff is congenial, the robes are comfy, and I always leave with a feeling of great contentment. Small, somewhat bright, non-coed lounges each offer hot tea, citrus water, biscotti, cookies, and fruit, and both locker rooms have a small but more than adequate sauna and steam as well as a whirlpool. Consider booking a Native Creek Stone Massage—a perfect choice with exactly the right degree of oh-so-soothing pressure. Adriana used Sophia Dakar products combined with the spa's signature Citrus & Cedar line for my last facial here; my skin absolutely glowed for days. A full-service salon offers shampoo and style, haircuts, up-dos, bridal consultation, and makeup artistry. The retail store sells Sonya Dakar and Jurlique products as well as their signature Citrus & Cedar line. Open from 8 a.m. to 8 p.m. Call (407) 996-9772 for reservations and information.

**Don't leave without buying:** Something from Sonya Dakar body line.

**Must-have treatment:** A Creekside Citrus & Cedar Massage, Body Revitalizer, or Facial, the spa's signature treatments.

## SAMPLE SERVICES

**Craniosacral Therapy.** Using a very light touch, the therapist monitors the craniosacral rhythm to determine where restrictions are located, gently releasing them.

**Gentlemen's "Viro" Facial.** Deep cleansing and purifying facial designed for a man's special needs. Skin is cleansed, exfoliated, and hydrated using antioxidant-rich products to repair and revitalize sun and pollution damage.

**Custom Aromatherapy Massage.** Combines the therapeutic benefits of touch and smell with aromatic oils infused with essential oils of natural plant extracts to stimulate the body's own healing mechanisms. Choices include Breathe (eucalyptus, rosemary, and lemon), Green Tea (sweet orange, litsea cubeba, ylang ylang, black pepper, and clove), Muscle and Joint (peppermint, clove, and eucalyptus), and Rejoice (tangerine and orange).

**Calusa Cocoon.** Utilizing natural oceanic clay infused with grapefruit, eucalyptus, peppermint, and spearmint, begin with a gentle exfoliation of the entire body then a moisturizing wrap rich in vitamin E and the essences of orange, tangerine, and mandarin. Relieves stress and brings balance to your body and a sense of well-being to your spirit.

**Cypress Salt Glow.** An invigorating treatment including a gentle massage using lemon and lime essential oils. Fine sea salts provide exfoliation to remove toxins.

## Waldorf Astoria Spa by Guerlain

This exceptional spa has the true luxury of being at the Waldorf Astoria Orlando, an oasis of style. 24,000 square feet on two stories include twenty-one treatment rooms with services also available outdoors in a pool cabana. Locker rooms have a full-body shower, eucalyptus-scented steam shower (not quite hot enough), whirlpool, and separate men and women's tea room. My massage was a bit eclectic, but amazing, with a combination of a Swedish, deep tissue, and the technician's own special moves. The Impériale Massage is the signature treatment, but if you're craving deep tissue work skip this one whose emphasis is on abdominal work. Guerlain products are available on site. Open daily 9 a.m. until 7 p.m. Call (407) 597-5360 for reservations.

**Don't leave without buying:** Guerlain Exceptional Complete Care, Orchidée Impériale used in the spa's Exceptional Orchidée Impériale Treatment facial.

**Must-have treatment:** The Guerlain Impériale Massage, which includes an anti-stress cocoon followed by an Impériale Massage facilitating oxygenation and stimulating circulation. This is also offered as a four-hand treatment.

**SAMPLE SERVICES**

**Men's Skin Saver Facial.** Following exfoliation, skin is strengthened and revived with Guerlain's exclusive facial therapy and mask. An eye therapy is added to relieve congestion and to reveal youth and clarity.

**Exceptional Orchidée Impériale Treatment.** Luxurious two-hour facial treatment features two exclusive facial therapies to detoxify and invigorate, two targeted masks, and a specific eye contour treatment providing exceptional results against all signs of aging.

**5-Senses Hydrotherapy.** Sequentially controlled jets work the entire body for the ultimate release. Great before any body therapy.

**Intensive Body Therapy.** Combines an invigorating Vichy shower Body Polish, replenishing body wrap, and customized skincare concentrate therapy to sublimate the skin from head to toe.

# Wow Experiences!

Although everything at Walt Disney World and Orlando seem special, a handful of experiences really take the cake. Plan on at least one or two of the following excursions to make your stay extra unique, a memory to last a lifetime.

## Swim with the Sharks

Take the ultimate dive in Epcot's six-million-gallon indoor aquarium at the Seas with Nemo & Friends with more than sixty-five species of marine life, including sharks, turtles, eagle rays, and diverse tropical fish. With DiveQuest you become part of the show and are guaranteed calm seas and no current with unlimited visibility. Even more fun, your family and friends can view your dive through the aquarium's giant acrylic windows. Guest must be at least ten years of age and must provide proof of scuba certification to participate. Price of $140 includes a T-shirt, refreshments, dive certificate, and a dive log stamp. Call 407/WDW-TOUR for information.

At SeaWorld the Sharks Deep Dive is quite the incredible experience. From the safety of your steel cage you'll be face to face with over thirty sharks of different species in the Shark Encounter tank. Special underwater helmets provide oxygen without the need for scuba gear so scuba certification is not necessary. Price of $149 per person (ages ten and up only) includes a T-shirt. Park admission not included.

## Catch a Wave

If the ocean is a bit too intimidating, learn to hang ten in a safe and controlled environment at Typhoon Lagoon. Since lessons begin before park opening hours, guests must furnish their own transportation to the park because buses are not up and running quite so early in the morning. Cost is $150. Offered Monday (in summer season only), Tuesday, and Friday at 6:30 a.m. Participants must be at least eight years old and strong swimmers. Maximum of thirteen people per class. Surfboards provided. Call (407) WDW-SURF for reservations.

## Celebrate Your Special Day

Step aboard a pontoon boat complete with driver, bag snacks, and beverages, and for an additional charge balloons, ice cream, cake, and banner at any of the Walt Disney World marinas for an especially memorable birthday cruise around Disney's waterways. Boats carry a maximum of eight for $275 or ten for $325. Decorations are an additional $25, and cakes may be ordered from resort catering. Call (407) WDW-BDAY or (407) 939-2329 for reservations.

## Commune with Nature

Get away from the theme parks for one of Orlando's best excursions. A canoe eco-tour is led by an expert guide on Shingle Creek, the headwaters of the Everglades, where you'll see a taste of what's left of old Florida and a fast disappearing way of life. View native species in their natural habitat including alligators, turtles, blue heron, bald eagles, bobcats, and more surrounded by a canopy of moss-dripping cypress trees as you paddle along an area of astounding beauty. Head south on the creek for a more serene and, I think, more beautiful trip; north if you want to see more wildlife. Tours are conducted by Grande Lakes Outfitters based at the Ritz Carlton Resort. $80 per adult and $50 per child for a two-hour excursion. Call (407) 393-4060 to reserve, or visit www.grandelakes.com/orvis-fly-fishing-35.html.

## Get the Royal Treatment

Talk about luxury for children! Little princesses and princes dressed in all their finery can enjoy tea in the Garden View Lounge at the Grand Floridian with Princess Aurora. Enjoy sing-alongs, story-telling, and a parade, all for the princely sum of $250 (price for one child and one adult). Each little princess receives a tiara and a My Disney Girl Princess Aurora doll; little princes get a princely crown and a bear. Sorry, but children must be accompanied by an adult, who will only get tea. Reservations can be made 180 days prior by calling (407) WDW-DINE or (407) 939-3463.

Adults can participate in their own high tea here sans the tiara and all the hoopla from 2 to 4:30 p.m. with a wide assortment of teas, scones, tarts, trifle, pound cake, pâté, tea sandwiches, and, of course, champagne.

Come after 3 p.m. when tea is accompanied by live entertainment in the Grand Lobby.

## Hit the Water

For true action head to the Contemporary Resort, where waterskiing, kneeboarding, wakeboarding, and tubing are offered for $165 per hour including boat, driver, and instruction (boats carry up to five guests). Morning guided personal watercraft excursions on Bay Lake and the Seven Seas Lagoon or afternoon freestyling personal watercraft fun in a roped-off area the size of three football fields are $135 per hour per watercraft holding up to three people with a combined weight under 400 pounds (only four personal watercraft are allowed on the water at any one time). Regular parasailing packages begin at $95 per flight for a single and $170 for a tandem, including eight to ten minutes in the air and 450 feet of line. Premium packages begin at $130 for a single and $195 for a tandem, including ten to twelve minutes in the air and 600 feet of line. Participants must weigh at least a total of 130 pounds and no more than 330 pounds total weight. For reservations call (407) 939-0754.

## Hunt for Buried Treasure

Children ages four through ten board their own pint-sized ship, don their mouse-ear pirate caps, and depart the Grand Floridian's marina to sail the Seven Seas Lagoon. At each "port of call," aka the surrounding Magic Kingdom resorts, a new treasure hunt awaits with all booty divided between the adventurers. A similar Albatross Treasure Cruise can be found at the Yacht and Beach Club. $34 per child. Grub included. Call (407) WDW-DINE, or (407) 939-3463, for reservations.

## Indulge in Your Very Own Yacht

For the ultimate in luxury, charter Disney's 52-foot Sea Ray yacht, the *Grand I,* moored at the Grand Floridian's marina, perfect for pampered VIP guests. Available for a morning spin, a sunset cruise, or the ultimate viewing location for the Wishes fireworks show, it features a full salon with panoramic, wrap-around windows, three staterooms, four plasma TVs for DVD viewing, a galley, and outside deck. Your own captain and deckhand are included and the boat is large enough for up to eighteen people.

Perhaps the perfect elegant evening would include a sunset gourmet dinner onboard complete with private butler service followed by champagne while viewing the Magic Kingdom's Wishes fireworks extravaganza. If your party is a large one, you'll have to be content with appetizers and drinks since a plated dinner is available only for three people or fewer. Or consider an afternoon excursion exploring the nearby resorts on the Seven Seas lagoon and Bay Lake with a bevy of snacks to keep the appetite at bay— sail past the beaches of the romantic Polynesian and the Grand Floridian's Wedding Pavilion, check out the geyser on the shore of Wilderness Lodge, and watch the parasailing action around the Contemporary Resort. Basic cost is $520 per hour. Call (407) WDW-PLAY for reservations.

## Experience a Culinary Feast

At Victoria and Albert's Chef's Table at Disney's Grand Floridian Resort, chef Scott Hunnell prepares a feast just for you. Your table is located in the restaurant's kitchen and seats from one to ten, but it's exclusively yours once booked. Up to ten courses are served, each tailored to your tastes. If you're smart, you'll choose the wine pairings where each course is coupled with a specially chosen vintage.

## Spin Around the Wilderness.

On Disney's Wilderness Back Trail Adventure, enjoy nature on a Segway X2, a treaded model with all-terrain tires, on a two-hour trip around Fort Wilderness. Begin with a short training session, then ride along numerous nature trails and the shores of Bay Lake. Visit the stables and take a quick trip around Wilderness Lodge. Descriptions of foliage and wildlife along the way are an added benefit. $90 per person. Call 407-WDW-TOUR or (407) 939-8687 for reservations.

## Take Tea with Alice

Children simply love the Wonderland Tea Party held at the Grand Floridian Resort, hosted by *Alice in Wonderland* characters. The one-hour event includes games, storytelling, a parade through the Grand Lobby, sandwiches, and apple juice "tea." $40. Held Monday through Friday at 1:30 p.m. Strictly for children ages four through ten. Call (407) WDW-DINE, or (407) 939-3463, for reservations.

## Watch Disney's Nighttime Extravaganzas on a Fireworks Cruise

Depart from the docks of the Yacht Club and Magic Kingdom Resorts for a special viewing of either the Wishes fireworks display at the Magic Kingdom or Illuminations at Epcot. Anchoring at the perfect viewing spot facing the Magic Kingdom or under the International Gateway Bridge at Epcot, you'll settle in just minutes before the nighttime spectacular begins. There's nothing quite as magical as a view over the glistening water of Disney's best fireworks presentations. A driver, beverages, and bag snacks are included, but wine, champagne, hors d'oeuvres, cheese and fruit platters, dessert, or even chocolate covered strawberries can be ordered ahead from Private Dining, perfect for a special floating party. Boats carry a maximum of eight for $275 or ten for $325. Call (407) WDW-PLAY or (407) 939-7529.

Children love the Magical Fireworks Voyage that departs from the marina at the Contemporary Resort. Upon arrival, snacks and beverages are served, and before boarding Captain Hook and Mr. Smee join the fun for a meet-and-greet. Your onboard host is a comedic pirate named Patch who guides everyone through the unpredictable waters of the Seven Seas Lagoon while leading sing-alongs and Disney trivia games. After viewing the Wishes fireworks show, it's a surprise visit by none other than Peter Pan, ready to pose for photos and sign autographs. Offered Friday through Monday for $54 per adult and $31 per child ages three to nine. Call (407) WDW-PLAY or (407) 939-7529.

### Wet a Line

Receive private instruction, full-day fly-fishing seminars, and fly-fishing tours with Grande Lakes Outfitters, headquartered at The Ritz Carlton. Your fishing ground is the shores of twelve-acre Shingle Pond found at the headwaters of the Everglades. If you're in luck, you'll spot some of the native species like alligators, deer, wild turkey, and bobcats. $50 per hour per person for private instruction; $180 per person for three-hour Hyde drift-boat fishing (maximum four guests); $470 per person for two-day fly fishing school (maximum four guests). Open to outside visitors; call (407) 393-4007 to reserve.

At Walt Disney World choose a private guided bass fishing excursion on one of Disney's many lakes and canals. You'll fish for trophy-size catch onboard Nitro Bass Boats with a BASS expert angler and return home with a good fish tale about the one that got away. $235 (afternoon) and $275 (morning) for a two-hour trip. $455 for a morning four-hour trip. Call (407) WDW-PLAY or (407) 939-7529.

## Go Skydiving (Indoors!)

If you've always wondered what it feels like to skydive but are afraid to jump from an airplane, SkyVenture Orlando is the place for you. Experience the amazing sensation of flying, but do it on a 125 mph column of air! You'll receive classroom training with a flight instructor, don a flight suit, helmet, goggles, and other gear, then head to the tunnel to fly one-on-one with your instructor. Each person gets two flight rotations, which is equal to two real skydives. Located near Universal Orlando, flight packages begin at $44.95. For reservations and information call (407) 903-1150 or (800) SKY-FUN-1 or go to http://skyventureorlando.com.

## Soar Up, Up, and Away

Soar over Orlando at sunrise in a hot air balloon followed by a champagne toast and an all you can eat breakfast buffet at the Ramada Orlando Celebration hotel. The one-hour flight is $175 per adult; children age ten and under are free; call Orlando Balloon Rides at (407) 894-5040 or go to www.orlandoballoonrides.com for reservations and information.

# 6

# SPORTING DIVERSIONS

I f you love the outdoors, Orlando is definitely the place to head. In addition to an overabundance of theme parks, you'll also find a wealth of sporting activities—golf courses everywhere you turn, tennis courts at almost every resort, plenty of pathways for bicycling and jogging, and miles of waterways for boating and fishing. Those with a bigger appetite for adventure can even try driving a race car. The sunny Florida weather almost guarantees year-round access, with the exception of an occasional cold snap or two.

## Golf

### Disney Golf

There's certainly no lack of choice when it comes to playing a round of golf while visiting Mickey Mouse. In fact, some people have been known to never quite make it to the parks, so intent are they on playing all of Disney's eighty-one holes. Each course is designated as an Audubon Cooperative Sanctuary System and offers full-service clubhouse facilities, including pro shops, driving ranges, locker rooms, on-course beverage service, snack bars and restaurants, and equipment rentals. Golf carts at four of the five courses (all except the walking Oak Trail course) are equipped with a Global

Positioning System (GPS) featuring "smart" full-color monitors providing detailed 3-D renderings of golf holes and course features, exact distances from the golf ball to the flagstick, and tips from professionals with helpful strategies for each hole. Guests of Disney resorts receive complimentary taxi transportation and special rates. For up-to-date information and fees, visit www.golf.disneyworld.com.

**Instruction.** Available from the PGA Professional staff at any course; check your swing with video analysis. Forty-five-minute private lessons are $75 per adult and $50 for youths age seventeen and under. Reservations are essential; call (407) 938-4653.

**Tee times.** Reservations may be made by calling (407) 938-4653 or online at www.golf.disneyworld.com. Be sure to ask for any special rates at time of booking such as a two-round discounts, military rates, twilight specials, and complimentary golf club rentals.

## OSPREY RIDGE

Located between the Magic Kingdom and Downtown Disney, Osprey Ridge is a peaceful, North Carolina-style course in a remote woodland and wetland setting with holes that cut through live oak, pine, palmetto, cypress, and bay trees. Here you'll find uncharacteristically rolling Florida terrain, dramatically raised greens and tees, seventy bunkers, and nine water holes, making this Tom Fazio–designed course Disney's most challenging. *7,101 yards. Slope: 131.*

Back at the clubhouse the Sand Trap Bar and Grill offers light choices for breakfast and lunch with indoor and outdoor dining along with a full bar.

## PALM AND MAGNOLIA

Located near the Magic Kingdom within the grounds of the Shades of Green Resort (an armed forces resort on Disney property) are the first courses ever opened at Walt Disney World, both designed by Joe Lee. Part of the PGA Tour is held here each October, and the eighteenth hole of the Palm is rated as one of the toughest on the tour.

The heavily wooded Palm is one of Disney's most difficult courses, with fairways cinched by tall trees and lovely, elevated tees and greens; nine water holes; and ninety-four bunkers. *6,957 yards. Slope: 133.*

At Magnolia, the longest of all Disney's courses, wide fairways are framed magnificently by more than 1,500 magnolia trees. It too doesn't lack for challenge, with eleven holes of water and ninety-eight bunkers in the midst of large, undulating greens. Check out the sixth-hole hazard in the shape of Mickey Mouse. *7,190 yards. Slope: 133.*

### OAK TRAIL

In a corner of the Magnolia course, this nine-hole, par 36 walking course is a good choice for family fun. With its small, rolling greens, it's an ideal course for beginners; however, it does pose a few challenges for the serious golfer or a quick round of golf for those who want to get on to the parks. This course is included as part of the Water Parks Fun & More ticket option. *2,913 yards.*

### LAKE BUENA VISTA GOLF COURSE

Located in the Downtown Disney area within the grounds of Saratoga Springs is this Joe Lee–designed course in a country-club setting. Wandering through pine forests and tall cypress, this shortest of Disney's eighteen-hole courses sports small, elevated greens with plenty of bunkers, narrow fairways, and an island green on the seventh hole. This is a great place for beginners but challenging enough for the more experienced. *6,749 yards. Slope: 133.*

## Golfing Beyond Disney

The Orlando area is bursting at the seams with many excellent golf courses. In fact, there are about 175 courses within a forty-five-minute drive from downtown Orlando. Following are several great choices close to Walt Disney World.

### CHAMPIONSGATE GOLF CLUB

Surrounding the Omni Orlando Resort at ChampionsGate are two eighteen-hole courses: The International, reminiscent of the great courses in the British Isles, has hard, fast fairways and bunkers surrounded by marshes and wildlife. The bonus? Bagpipers on the tenth tee at sunset. *7,363 yards. Slope: 143.*

The National is a more traditional American-style course amidst woodlands, wetlands, and orange groves with great bunkering and difficult tee shots. *7,128 yards. Slope: 138.*

Carts are equipped with Prolink GPS Caddy Systems acting like a professional caddy with tips for skill improvement, PGA-type scoring, and food and beverage ordering capabilities. Putting green and a short play practice facility are complimentary with your round. Snack and beverage cart caters the course, and an iced towel service is a true extra. There is a 35,000-square-foot clubhouse with dining and lounge area, full-service golf shop, and locker facilities. Call (888) 558-9301 or (407) 787-4653 for information and reservations, or go online at www.championsgate golf.com.

Just steps away from the clubhouse, the David Leadbetter Golf Academy, ranked by *Golf* magazine as one of the Top 10 Best Golf Schools in the country, is headquartered on the golf course with private lessons, minischools, and retreats. Here you'll find a short-game practice facility, separate pitching area with target greens and fairway bunkers, and 30,000 square feet of chipping and putting green surfaces. With a maximum of four students per instructor, the academy has spacious classrooms fitted with V1 Golf swing analysis computer technology. Check online at www .davidleadbetter.com or call (888) 633-5323 or (407) 787-3330.

## GRAND CYPRESS GOLF CLUB

The Grand Cypress Resort boasts four Jack Nicklaus–designed golf courses: the nine-hole North, the nine-hole South, the nine-hole East, and the eighteen-hole, St. Andrews–style New Course. The North and South courses are marked by sharply ledged fairways, tall shaggy mounds, and plateau greens. The wooded East has less bunkering. And for a full round of eighteen, courses can be combined as North-South, South-East, or East-North. The New Course comes with steeper and more challenging bunkers and slopes complete with double greens, stone bridges and walls, long grassy mounds, pot bunkers as deep as twelve feet, very little water, and few trees.

At the Golf Club, located on the grounds of the Villas of Grand Cypress, the Grand Cypress Academy of Golf offers lessons under the guidance of PGA and LPGA certified professionals in a twenty-one-acre practice facility. Also available is state-of-the-art computer instruction, ModelGolf. All golf carts are equipped with the latest in GPS technology, like an electronic caddy complete with full-color illustrations of each hole, accurate yardage, key hazards, playing tips, and score keeping. Fully stocked hospitality carts travel throughout the courses, and after a long day golfers can relax at the Club, a restaurant and sports bar. Call (877) 330-7377 for information and reservations.

## REUNION GOLF CLUB

Fifty-four holes on three gorgeous courses designed by some of the greatest names in golf—Arnold Palmer, Tom Watson, and Jack Nicklaus—can be found at Reunion Resort. Since this is a cashless resort, each player must be a guest or play with a guest of the resort, an uncommon level of exclusivity.

The Legacy Course, designed by Arnold Palmer, is routed on hilly, roller coaster–type terrain with dramatic elevation changes, a mixture of natural preserve areas, wide fairways, and strategically placed bunkers. *6,916 yards. Slope: 137.*

The Independence Course, designed by Tom Watson, is a traditional parkland layout bordering a nature preserve with terrain elevations as much as 45 feet from tee to green, and a windswept, native appearance framed by grasses, azaleas, hibiscus, and camellias. *7,257 yards. Slope: 140.*

The Tradition Course, designed by Jack Nicklaus, is smooth and flowing with long horizons, elevated tees and greens, and water on nine holes. *7,300 yards. Slope: 147.*

Call 407-396-3199 for information and tee times.

Other amenities include a golf practice facility, golf pro shop, and clubhouse with restaurant. The ANNIKA Academy, a 5,400-square-foot, state-of-the-art teaching facility, blends golf and fitness in a "boutique like" school featuring small classes of seven to nine people. A modern fitness room with top-of-the-line equipment puts extra emphasis on athletic training, including cardio and core-strengthening techniques, and mental strength in regard to the game.

## RITZ-CARLTON GOLF CLUB, ORLANDO, GRANDE LAKES

This Greg Norman–designed course set on Shingle Creek, the headwaters of the Florida Everglades, is one of the most beautiful and certainly unique golf courses in central Florida. Just off the John Young Parkway about fifteen minutes from Walt Disney World and down the road from SeaWorld, guests play through a scenery of wetlands and woodlands of palms, palmettos, and oaks to three snaking finishing holes just across the lake from the resort.

The Golf Club features clinics, a driving range, a 55,000-square-foot practice tee, a 15,000-square-foot teaching tee, and a practice putting green. Amenities include a restaurant with indoor and outdoor service, a golf retail store, and locker rooms for men and women.

What really sets this course apart is its innovative Golf Caddy-Concierge Program which allows for a professional attendant to accompany each twosome or foursome on all eighteen holes. Catering to the group's every need, your caddy offers club cleaning, golf ball locating, strategy recommendations, bunker raking, divot repair, course history, and special requests such as ordering food, dinner reservations, and so on. Call (407) 393-4900 for further information and reservations. *7,122 yards. Slope: 139.*

## SHINGLE CREEK GOLF CLUB

Shingle Creek Golf Club takes its name from Shingle Creek, the headwaters of the Everglades, that meanders through the course. Surrounding the Rosen Shingle Creek resort, this David Harmon–designed course's 18-hole championship layout plays through native oaks and pines on wide, undulating fairways with hard, fast greens and interconnecting waterways. Carts are equipped with UpLINK GPS Yardage System. Back at the clubhouse there's a pro shop with the latest in golf fashion as well as clubs, bags, and accessories. Be prepared to hear some highway noise, and plan your game around the golf club's excellent A Land Remembered Steakhouse. Call (866) 996-9933 or (407) 996-9933 or visit www .shinglecreekgolf.com/golf.asp for reservations and information. *7,228 yards. Slope: 139.*

The Brad Brewer Golf Academy offers private instruction and junior lessons. For more information go online at www.bradbrewer.com or call (407) 996-3306 or (866) 996-9933.

## WALDORF ASTORIA GOLF CLUB

This new Rees Jones-designed course has the added luxury of being part of the new Waldorf Astoria, which practically sits in the middle of Walt Disney World. Using the land's natural contours and elements as it winds through a wetland preserve, this environmentally conscious course is designed with a five-tee system, bunkers reminiscent of the hazards from those a century ago, towering pine and cypress lining the fairways, and lakes dotting the course. This along with an old world, classic look. A clubhouse grill features sandwiches and salads, and you'll find a Golf Shop on site with the latest apparel and equipment. A practice facility and private lessons are available. Call 407-597-3783 or go to www.waldorf astoriaorlando.com/golf. *7,108 yards. Slope:139.*

## Miniature Golf

Miniature golf fans have four courses to play at Disney, each sporting eighteen fun-filled holes. Fees are $12 for adults and $10 for children ages three through nine; receive a 50 percent discount on a second round played the same day. Open from 10 a.m. to 11 p.m. daily, subject to weather and seasonal changes. Reservations for tee times available in person only. For more information call (407) WDW-PLAY or (407) 939-7529.

### FANTASIA GARDENS

Two eighteen-hole miniature golf courses, Fantasia Garden and Fantasia Fairways, are located across Buena Vista Drive from the Swan Hotel near Epcot, Disney's Hollywood Studios, and the BoardWalk. Play amid tutu-clothed hippos, silly alligators, and cavorting fountains ending with Sorcerer Mickey splashing guests with his mop and buckets at the Fantasia-inspired Fantasia Garden course. The more challenging Fantasia Fairways, designed as a pint-size golf course, is great for those who like a more traditional round amid sand traps, water hazards, doglegs, roughs, and lush putting greens. A limited snack bar with small arcade is on site.

### WINTER SUMMERLAND

Designed for Santa and his elves as an off-season vacation spot, this hot-and-cold, sand-and-snow miniature golf course is a kick. Sitting adjacent to Blizzard Beach, guests play either the Snow course—amid Christmas music, ice hockey rings, snowmen, ice castles, and igloos—or the Sand course, where Caribbean music plays while Santa grills turkey outside his mobile home surrounded by sand castles and surfboards. A limited snack bar is on the premises.

# Tennis

All Disney deluxe resorts, with the exception of the Polynesian and Wilderness Lodge, have tennis courts, with a professional tennis staff offering lessons at the Grand Floridian Resort. Courts can be found at the Grand Floridian (two clay), Bay Lake Tower at the Contemporary Resort (two hard), Yacht and Beach Club (one hard), BoardWalk Inn (two hard), the Swan and Dolphin (four hard), and Animal Kingdom Villas Kidani (two hard).

Serious tennis players may want to consider staying at the Grand Floridian, where Disney's Racquet Club at the Grand Floridian Tennis Center boasts two professionally maintained clay courts. Here a gazebo-style pro shop offers private lessons, play-the-professional and tennis-pro fill-in programs, and restringing services. For court information or to book tennis lessons, clinics, and private instruction, call Michael Dublin, director of tennis operations, at (407) 621-1991.

Outside of Walt Disney World consider the excellent tennis facility at the Hyatt Regency Grand Cypress Racquet Club. It features eight Har-Tru and four Deco-Turf II courts along with clinics and private and semi-private lessons. The Grand Cypress Tennis Academy offers five hours of instruction with videotaped analysis, match strategy, and play, along with a written evaluation and a guaranteed game match service. For further information and reservations, call (407) 239-1234. You'll also find three courts at the JW Marriott Grande Lakes, two at the Omni Champions-Gate, an exceptional facility with six clay courts at the Reunion Resort, and two courts at Rosen Shingle Creek Resort; all are lighted.

# Biking

Bicycles for all ages are available for rent at the BoardWalk Inn, Wilderness Lodge and Villas, the Polynesian, and the Yacht and Beach Club. At the BoardWalk Inn and the Yacht and Beach Club, bikers can pedal their way around the walkway surrounding the 0.75-mile Crescent Lake or the pathway that circles to Disney's Hollywood Studios. Wilderness Lodge guests should take advantage of the adjoining Fort Wilderness and its miles of pine forests. At the Polynesian Resort take a spin around the property on a surrey. Helmets are provided free of charge. Young people under the age of eighteen must have a signed waiver from a parent or legal guardian.

Off-property you'll find bicycles at the Hyatt Regency Grand Cypress with two bike paths, one 3.2 miles and the other 4.7 miles. The JW Marriott and the Ritz-Carlton have bicycles available for a spin around a 1.3-mile pathway encircling the resort. At the Reunion Resort are miles to explore with rentals available. At the Waldorf Astoria pick up a complimentary bicycle to explore the pathways surrounding the area.

## Jogging

Those amazing folks with enough energy to jog after traipsing through the parks day after day will be glad to know that a nice variety of pathways is to be found throughout the Walt Disney World property. Information and jogging maps are available at the front desk of each resort. At the Polynesian a path is laid out through the tropical grounds; the Grand Floridian has a pathway along the Seven Seas Lagoon; and the Wilderness Lodge offers miles of trails winding through the adjoining Fort Wilderness among pines and cypress trees. Epcot Resort guests should take advantage of the boardwalk-style walkway surrounding the twenty-five-acre Crescent Lake or the path encircling the canal leading to Disney's Hollywood Studios.

The Hyatt Grand Cypress has jogging courses ranging from 1.3 miles to 4.7 miles that wind through the extensive property. The Reunion Resort, the Omni ChampionsGate, and the Rosen Shingle Creek have miles of jogging and nature trails. The Hard Rock, Royal Pacific, and Portofino Bay Hotels are connected by attractive pathways to and from the theme parks. The Ritz-Carlton and JW Marriott resort area has a 1.3-mile path encircling the property, and the Waldorf Astoria has walkways surrounding the area.

## Boating and Waterways

With 850 acres of lakes, 130,000 feet of shoreline, 3.122 billion gallons of water, 66 miles of canals, and more than 500 watercraft, boating is a major pastime at Walt Disney World. And with some of the most incredible weather in the nation, water sports are an important draw. Most resorts as well as Downtown Disney have their own marinas with a variety of boats available for hire (see individual resort listings for specific details). Call 407-939-7529 for reservations. Boating takes place on the following waterways:

Seven Seas Lagoon, accessed from the Grand Floridian and Polynesian Resorts and connected to Bay Lake.

Bay Lake, accessed from the Contemporary Resort, Bay Lake Tower, and the Wilderness Lodge and connected to the Seven Seas Lagoon.

Crescent Lake, around whose shores sit the Epcot resorts of the Yacht and Beach Club, the BoardWalk Inn, and the Swan and Dolphin.

Buena Vista Lagoon fronting Downtown Disney.

Boating choices include Boston Whalers, a luxury yacht, pontoon boats, sailboats, and Sea Raycers.

### Boston Whaler Montauks

These 17-foot, canopy-covered, motorized boats accommodate as many as six adults and are available at the Grand Floridian, Contemporary and Bay Lake Tower, Yacht and Beach Club, Wilderness Lodge, and Downtown Disney. *Approximately $45 per half hour.*

### Luxury Yacht

For the ultimate in indulgence, charter the 52-foot Sea Ray, the *Grand I,* docked at the Grand Floridian Resort. Accommodating up to eighteen people, it includes a captain and deckhand. Food and cocktails are available at an additional charge. *Basic cost is $520 per hour.*

### Pontoon Boats

SunTracker 21-foot canopied pontoon boats holding as many as ten people are perfect for those who want a nonthrill ride around Disney's waterways. Available at the Grand Floridian, Contemporary and Bay Lake Tower, Polynesian, Yacht and Beach Club, Wilderness Lodge, and Downtown Disney. *Approximately $45 per half hour.*

### Sea Raycers

What could be more fun than renting a Sea Raycer, a two-seater minipowerboat perfect for zipping around Disney's waterways and lakes? You'll get the most bang for your buck at one of the resorts near the Magic Kingdom, where there are miles of recreation on the Seven Seas Lagoon and Bay Lake. At the Magic Kingdom resort area marinas, at least one person in the boat must have a valid driver's license (those under eighteen must bring along a parent to sign a waiver). All other marinas permit guests at least twelve years old and 5 feet tall to operate independently as long as the parent or legal guardian signs for the child. Sea Raycers are available at the Contemporary and Bay Lake Tower, Polynesian, Grand Floridian, Yacht and Beach Club, Downtown Disney, and Wilderness Lodge. *Approximately $32 per half hour.*

## Waterskiing and Parasailing

Head to the Contemporary Resort for waterskiing and parasailing action. Sammy Duvall Water Sports offers waterskiing, wakeboarding, kneeboarding, and tubing at the Contemporary Resort for $165 per hour including boat, driver, and instruction. Morning guided personal watercraft excursions on Bay Lake and the Seven Seas Lagoon or afternoon freestyling personal watercraft fun in a roped-off area are $135 per hour per watercraft holding up to three people with a combined weight under 400 pounds. Parasailing packages begin at $95 per flight for a single and $170 for a tandem, including eight to ten minutes in the air and 450 feet of line. Premium parasailing packages begin at $130 for a single and $195 for a tandem, including ten to twelve minutes in the air and 600 feet of line. Participants must weigh at least a total of 130 pounds and no more than 330 pounds. For reservations call (407) 939-0754 up to ninety days in advance.

## Fishing

Walt Disney World's stocked fishing lakes are filled with plenty of largemouth bass, perfect for the amateur as well as the seasoned angler. In fact, the largest bass caught at Walt Disney World weighed in at 14.25 pounds. Boats departing from the marinas of the Contemporary and Bay Lake Tower, Polynesian, Grand Floridian, and the Wilderness Lodge and Villas fish the waters of Bay Lake and the Seven Seas Lagoon with an experienced guide. The waterways surrounding Epcot and Disney's Hollywood Studios are your fishing holes for boats departing the Yacht and

Beach Club. From Downtown Disney angle for bass on Lake Buena Vista. No fishing license is required, and it's strictly catch-and-release.

Two-hour trips (maximum of five people) are $235 (afternoon) and $270 (mornings). Four-hour trips are $455, which includes a pontoon boat with driver and experienced guide, Zebco equipment, tackle, artificial and live bait, one-year BASS membership, and nonalcoholic beverages. Excursions may be prearranged by calling (407) WDW-BASS or (407) 939-2277, and must be made at least twenty-four hours in advance.

Guests of the Hyatt Regency Grand Cypress Resort can fish from the shores of Lake Windsong. The JW Marriott and the Ritz-Carlton at Grande Lakes offer fly fishing on private charter boats from Shingle Creek, the headwaters of the Everglades.

## Richard Petty Driving Experience

Those who dream of sitting behind the wheel of a race car can have their chance here. Lying next to the Magic Kingdom is this sometimes very loud speedway where white-knuckle rides in a NASCAR Winston Cup–style race car are offered. Each experience begins with a one-hour training session. All driving participants must have a valid driver's license and must know how to operate a stick shift. Spectators are welcome for no charge. Since the track sometimes closes due to inclement weather, it's always best to call ahead. Call (800) BE-PETTY or (800) 237-3889, or visit www.1800bepetty.com, for information.

### Getting There

With its location virtually in the parking lot of the Magic Kingdom, it's necessary either to make your way to the Transportation and Ticket Center (TTC) and take the shuttle located near the kennels or enter the Magic Kingdom parking lot (parking is free) and follow the signs, driving through the tunnel to the infield.

### Programs

#### RIDE-ALONG PROGRAM

For $109, ride shotgun at speeds of up to 150 mph for three laps around the track with an experienced driving instructor. You must be at least age sixteen to participate (riders age seventeen or younger must be accompanied by a parent or guardian). This is the only program not requiring reservations, operating on a first-come, first-serve basis.

## ROOKIE EXPERIENCE

Those age eighteen or older can drive the car themselves for eight laps around the course. That is, of course, after an introductory class out on the speedway. The three-hour program costs $449.

## KING'S EXPERIENCE

You'll feel like a king after five hours of driving eighteen laps (one eight-lap and one ten-lap session) around the speedway for the princely sum of $849. Only those age eighteen or older may participate.

## EXPERIENCE OF A LIFETIME

For $1,299, drive three ten-lap sessions, improve your skills, and maybe change careers in this half-day driving experience. Only for those age eighteen or older.

# 7

# SHOPPING

For many people, shopping is the best part of a vacation. The parks are loaded with something for everyone in just about every price range. But those who would like to bring home something minus a Mickey Mouse or Cinderella motif will want to check out Orlando's best shopping options away from the parks.

## The Florida Mall

This 260-store mall is a bit less upscale than the Mall at Millenia but just as much fun with anchors like Saks, Nordstrom (shoe heaven), Macy's, JC Penny, Dillards, and Sears. Other stores include Williams-Sonoma, Pottery Barn, Brookstone, Coach, Abercrombie & Fitch, Guess, Ritz Camera, bebe, Waldenbooks, Harry and David, MAC Cosmetics, and Sephora. Located at the corner of South Orange Blossom Trail and Sand Lake Road. From Disney take I-4 east to Sand Lake Road and go east for 4 miles. From Universal take I-4 west to Sand Lake Road. Open Monday through Saturday from 10 a.m. to 9 p.m. and Sunday noon to 6 p.m.; (407) 851-6255.

## ❧ The Mall at Millenia

If you have time for only one mall, make it this one. Close to Universal Studios and only a fifteen-minute drive from Disney, this high-end shopping experience is Orlando's best. Anchored by Bloomingdale's, Macy's, and Neiman Marcus, other shopping choices include Chanel, Tiffany & Co., Gucci, Louis Vuitton, Burberry, Hugo Boss, Cartier, St. John, FURLA, Jimmy Choo, and Cole Haan. When the shopping gets too much for you, rest your feet at one of the mall's restaurants, including P.F. Chang's China Bistro, Brio Tuscan Grill, McCormick & Schmick's, California Pizza Kitchen, Panera Bread, and the Cheesecake Factory as well as one of the hottest bars around, Blue Martini. From Walt Disney World and Universal, take I-4 east to exit 78 (right on Conroy Road). Open Monday through Saturday from 10 a.m. to 9 p.m. and Sunday noon to 7 p.m.; (407) 363-3555; www.mallatmillenia.com. Valet parking available outside the Main Entrance.

## Orlando Premium Outlets

This 110-store designer outlet mall is a gem. Here you'll find stores like Burberry, Zegna, Fendi, Dior, Hugo Boss, Salvatore Ferragamo, Michael Kors, and Barney's New York Outlet. Located at 8200 Vineland Avenue just off I-4 (exit 68 or SR535) close to Downtown Disney. Open Monday through Saturday from 10 a.m. to 11 p.m. and Sunday 10 a.m. to 9 p.m.; (407) 238-7787; www.premiumoutlets.com/outlets/outlet.asp?id=17.

## Pointe Orlando

At this totally revamped shopping center is a Regal Cinemas as well as an IMAX theater, the Improv Comedy Club, excellent dining choices including the Capital Grille, the Oceanaire Seafood Room, Tommy Bahama's Tropical Café, and Maggiano's Little Italy among others, and a small selection of shops. You'll pay to park in the general lot so if you're only dining go ahead and use the complimentary valet parking at the restaurant. Located at 9101 International Drive, it's a short drive from Universal Orlando and across the street from the Orange County Convention Center. Call 407-248-2838 or go to www.pointeorlando.com for information.

## Prime Outlets, Orlando

This large mall is Orlando's best outlet stop. Stores include Neiman Marcus Last Call, Baccarat/Lalique, Betsey Johnson, Cole Haan, Saks Fifth Avenue Off 5th, St. John Outlet, Bose Factory Store, Dooney & Bourke, Calvin Klein, Ann Taylor Factory Store, Coach, Tumi, Nautica, Kate Spade, and Stuart Weitzman. Located at 4951 International Drive, 12 miles from Disney World; take I-4 East to Exit 75A, follow it to International Drive and turn left. Open Monday through Saturday 10 a.m. to 11 p.m. and Sunday 10 a.m. to 9 p.m.; (407) 352-9600; www.primeoutlets .com/locations/orlando.aspx.

## Winter Park

This quaint village of beautiful gardens and three notable art museums is only a twenty-five-minute drive from Disney. Shop along Park Avenue in the historical district, where blocks of small boutiques, jewelry stores, and art galleries are scattered among well-known names like Pottery Barn, Williams-Sonoma, and Restoration Hardware. Relax along the way at any number of sidewalk cafes and restaurants.

The Charles Hosmer Morse Museum of American Art has an excellent Tiffany glass collection, including an exquisite Tiffany chapel interior built for the 1892 Chicago World Columbian Exposition. There's also a 12-mile scenic boat tour on the town's chain of lakes. To reach downtown Winter Park take I-4 east to exit 87 and go east on Fairbanks Avenue for 3 miles.

# 8

# DINING IN STYLE

Crispy free-range chicken with handmade cavatelli pasta, porcini bolognese, ramps, and confit tomato. Braised buffalo short ribs with parsnip-potato gratin, glazed leeks, and red wine jus. Provençal crusted double lamb chops, tian of grilled vegetables, Provence olives, and sun-dried and fresh tomato with port reduction. Swahili curry shrimp with East African curry sauce, artichokes, and coconut rice. Just a sampling of some of the incredible meals found at Walt Disney World restaurants, where a remarkable culinary transformation has taken place since the mid-1990s. Extraordinary cuisine is especially evident in such renowned dining establishments as the California Grill at the Contemporary Resort, Jiko at Animal Kingdom Lodge, Flying Fish Café at Disney's BoardWalk, and Victoria and Albert's at the Grand Floridian, many time winner of the AAA Five-Diamond Award.

Top-notch chefs are now the norm, creating exciting menus at some of the highest-rated restaurants in the country. First-rate sommeliers (almost 300 on Disney property, more than any other company in the world) have fashioned outstanding wine lists, particularly at Victoria and Albert's, California Grill, Citricos, Jiko, and the Flying Fish. In fact, Disney sells more than a million bottles of wine every year if you count the Disney Cruise Line.

Even Disney's reputation for dreadful theme park food has changed. Once just a hot dog and hamburger haven, it's now quite possible to find pleasurable choices ranging from fine dining to more-than-palatable quick-service food. Though you'll always find burgers and chicken tenders, you'll also discover restaurants with outstanding cuisine and unique ambience. My only complaint is the non-atmospherically lit dining rooms that are sometimes so bright you'll feel as if you're in the operating room. Children are always treated as special guests; almost every restaurant along with all quick-service spots offers a menu just for kids. Meals are delivered quickly, so if a speedy dinner is not your cup of tea, stretch it out a bit by ordering an appetizer only and then your entree when you are finished with that first course.

Disney certainly gets a gold star in my book for its efforts to add whole grains and healthy choices to dining menus, and in particular, the elimination of trans fats and the addition of healthy alternatives on children's and many adult menus (also implemented at both SeaWorld and Universal Orlando). Those in need of vegetarian meals will easily find at least one option in both full-service restaurants and most quick-service spots; vegetarian choices are included in the sample entrees in this chapter. Those with special needs—such as low-fat, no sugar added, low-carb, and kosher, as well as special dietary requests regarding allergies to gluten or wheat, shellfish, soy, lactose, peanuts, or other substances—will be accommodated at all full-service restaurants. Disney prefers a fourteen-day notification by calling (407) WDW-DINE or (407) 939-3463. Perhaps it would be best to do this when making your Advance Dining Reservations. Address any questions to the Allergy Hotline at (407) 824-2634. If you don't wish to order in advance, kosher meals are always available at the following quick-service locations: Cosmic Ray's Starlight Cafe in the Magic Kingdom, ABC Commissary at Disney's Hollywood Studios, Liberty Inn and Electric Umbrella at Epcot, and Pizzafari at Disney's Animal Kingdom.

Those who plan on eating all meals exclusively on Disney property should consider the Magic Your Way Dining Plan at a cost of $42 to $47 (depending on the time of year) per adult per night and $12 to $13 per child per night for ages three through nine. Included are one table-service meal of an entree, nonalcoholic beverage, and dessert; one quick-service meal including entree, dessert, and nonalcoholic beverage; and one snack per person per night such as fruit, popcorn, sodas, or ice cream. Character meals count as one full-service meal. Those who plan on dining much of the time at Disney's signature restaurants such as California Grill, Flying Fish, or Jiko, or using in-room dining should probably opt out since it is necessary to exchange two table-service meals to dine once at this type of luxury restaurant. Or purchase the Deluxe Dining Plan for $72 per adult per night and $21 per child offering three full-service meals per night, thus allowing you to pay for a quick-service breakfast or lunch on your own leaving enough credits for a signature meal each evening. Also consider that these dining plans are quite a lot of food, so if your family likes to share entrees you might be better off simply purchasing your food as you go.

As for dress code, casual is the word. Theme park restaurants are extremely informal; however, you'll find that in many resort restaurants, dress is a bit more sophisticated. Smart casual clothing is usually fine, but I have noted the dress at each restaurant outside the theme parks.

Reservations, particularly in busy season, are very important. Advance Dining Reservations are available at Disney's theme parks, resorts, and most Downtown Disney full-service restaurants 180 days in advance by calling (407) WDW-DINE or (407) 939-3463. Reservations for most restaurants can also be made online at http://disneyworld.disney.go.com/dining. Same-day reservations may be made at each park, at the restaurant itself, through Guest Relations, or by picking up any public phone in Disney and dialing *88. Those staying in a Disney concierge room or suite may make reservations through the concierge staff. Those not on a concierge floor can utilize the lobby concierge at each Disney resort. Non-Disney reservation phone numbers are listed with their full descriptions.

Should you wish to venture a bit afield to dine you'll find a wealth of admirable restaurants near Universal Studios, particularly in the area of Sand Lake Road and Dr. Phillips Boulevard. It's a bit strange that most are in shopping centers, but nevertheless you'll find Timpano Chophouse, Roy's, Seasons 52, and MoonFish in this area with Vito's Chop House, Oceanaire Seafood Room, and the Capital Grille just around the corner on International Drive. All are worth the short drive from Disney and are only a hop away from the hotels near Universal. And you mustn't forget Emeril's at CityWalk, Tchoup Chop at Universal's Royal Pacific, and Mama Della's and Bice at Universal's Portofino Bay Hotel, all commendable restaurants.

If you would like to preview the menus of many of these restaurants, go online to www.wdwluxuryguide.com. Another Web site listing Disney menus is http://allears.net/menu/menus.htm.

## Advance Dining Reservations

Advance Dining Reservations is Disney's system whereby on arrival at the designated time you'll receive the next table available for your party size. In other words, they won't save a table for you but will seat you as soon as possible, certainly before any walk-ups. This sometimes translates into a bit of a wait, but it's undoubtedly better than simply taking your chances and walking in without any sort of seating reservation.

I cannot emphasize enough how important it is to secure advance reservations; without them, you'll be spending way too much time cooling your heels waiting for a table, particularly at Epcot and the better resort restaurants where demand is high. This is especially true in the busier times of the year and for the more popular spots like Victoria and Albert's, California Grill, Citricos, and the Flying Fish, along with all character meals. For Advance Dining Reservations call (407) WDW-DINE, or (407) 939-3463, unless otherwise noted. Advance Dining Reservations may be made 180 days in advance at all Walt Disney World Restaurants.

## Dining with the Disney Characters

If you have a child in tow, at least one or two character meals are a must. These extremely popular dining spots, offered both at the theme parks and at many of the Disney resorts, are a perfect way for children to spend extra time with their favorite characters. Meals are all-you-care-to-eat, offered in one of three ways: buffet-style, family-style, or as preplated meals. Characters work the room, stopping at each table to interact with guests, pose for photos, and sign autographs (it's a good idea to pick up an autograph book for your child right away at one of Disney's gift shops). Book advance reservations early (180 days out), particularly for Cinderella's Royal Table, Restaurant Akershus Princess Storybook Dining, and Chef Mickey's by calling (407) WDW-DINE or (407) 939-3463. Characters available may vary somewhat each day.

### *Magic Kingdom*

**Cinderella's Royal Table.** Breakfast, lunch, and dinner; breakfast is a preplated meal; lunch and dinner is a family-style salad, your choice of five entrees, and dessert; Disney's most popular character meal served

# THE BEST OF THE BEST

**Best Italian:** Il Mulino at the Walt Disney World Swan, with amazing tuna carpaccio and beautiful gamberi francese (giant shrimp in creamy white wine lemon sauce), or Bice at Portofino Bay Hotel for rich braised veal shank accompanied by creamy saffron risotto.

**Best seafood:** Flying Fish at Disney's BoardWalk for their signature potato-wrapped snapper in a red wine sauce, or Todd English's Bluezoo at the Walt Disney World Dolphin, where seafood is taken to new heights. Off Disney property it's got to be Roy's on Sand Lake Road near Universal for Roy Yamaguchi's remarkable Hawaiian fusion cuisine.

**Best steak:** Shula's at the Walt Disney World Dolphin, a standout for sensational Angus steaks cooked to perfection, or the Capital Grill on International Drive for Kona-crusted dry aged sirloin topped with caramelized shallot butter.

**Best for romance:** Victoria and Albert's at Disney's Grand Floridian Resort, where you'll savor a sumptuous six-course meal served on elegant fine china to the accompaniment of enchanting harp music.

**Best for kids:** Children love T-Rex Café at Downtown Disney with giant Audio-Animatronics dinosaurs, an ice cave, and a paleontology dig. A close runner up is Whispering Canyon Café at Disney's Wilderness Lodge; come prepared for plenty of whoopin' and hollerin', and please, whatever you do, don't ask for the ketchup—unless, that is, you like a lot of attention.

**Best character meal:** Cinderella's Royal Table at the Magic Kingdom, a chance to dine in a fairy-tale castle with Disney royal characters. Or try the Crystal Palace at the Magic Kingdom for a tasty, bountiful buffet hosted by Winnie the Pooh and his friends.

**Best hip atmosphere:** Todd English's Bluezoo at the Dolphin, the coolest spot this side of South Beach, or Tchoup Chop at Universal's Royal Pacific Resort, a knock-'em-dead, Asian-inspired beauty.

**Best Disney view:** California Grill at Disney's Contemporary Resort, with its picture-perfect views of the Magic

Kingdom, the Seven Seas Lagoon, and the Wishes fireworks presentation.

**Best Disney resort restaurant:** Tough call. My favorites are the California Grill at the Contemporary Resort (just about anything on their exceptional menu is fantastic), or Victoria and Albert's at the Grand Floridian Resort (particularly the Chef's Table, where Chef Scott Hunnel oversees an eleven-course meal designed especially for you).

**Best Downtown Disney restaurant:** Wolfgang Puck's upstairs Dining Room for "Chinois" rack of lamb served with a spicy cilantro-mint sauce.

**Best Universal resort restaurant:** Tchoup Chop at the Royal Pacific Resort for wonderful Asian and Polynesian-influenced cuisine in a stunning setting, or Bice at Portofino Bay Hotel, where superb Northern Italian food is served in a sophisticated dining room.

**Best CityWalk restaurant:** Emeril's for its justifiably famous Creole-Cajun food.

**Best Epcot Illuminations view:** Rose and Crown in World Showcase's United Kingdom. Set your priority seating for about one hour prior to showtime and pray for a lagoonside table with a good view.

**Best breakfast:** Kouzzina at Disney's BoardWalk. Go for the blueberry orange granola pancakes or the delicious spinach, tomato, and feta scrambled eggs.

**Best food at the Magic Kingdom:** *Restaurant:* Crystal Palace; *fast food:* Pecos Bill Café.

**Best food at Disney's Hollywood Studios:** *Restaurant:* Hollywood Brown Derby.

**Best food at Epcot:** *Restaurant:* Bistro de Paris; *fast food:* Tangierine Café in Morocco.

**Best food at the Animal Kingdom:** *Restaurant:* Tusker House in Africa.

**Best food at Universal Studios:** *Restaurant:* Finnegan's Bar and Grill.

**Best food at Islands of Adventure:** *Restaurant:* Mythos.

high atop Cinderella's Castle with Cinderella and other Disney royal characters; all meals include a photo package with Cinderella.

**Crystal Palace.** Breakfast, lunch, and dinner buffet; Pooh, Eeyore, Piglet, Tigger.

## Epcot

**Garden Grill.** Dinner served family-style; Farmer Mickey, Chip 'n' Dale, Pluto.

**Akershus Royal Banquet Hall.** Family-style breakfast; lunch and dinner includes cold-table buffet of appetizers, your choice of six entrees, and a trio of desserts; on a rotating schedule are Disney princesses including Belle, Jasmine, Snow White, Aurora, Mary Poppins, and Ariel; also includes a photo package.

## Disney's Hollywood Studios

**Play 'n' Dine at Hollywood and Vine.** Buffet breakfast and lunch; *Playhouse Disney* characters including JoJo, Goliath, June, and Leo.

## Animal Kingdom

**Donald's Safari Breakfast.** Breakfast buffet; Donald Duck, Goofy, Mickey, Daisy Duck.

## Disney Resorts

**Chef Mickey's.** Breakfast and dinner buffet; Contemporary Resort; Mickey, Goofy, Pluto, Donald Duck, Minnie.

**Cape May Café.** Breakfast buffet; Beach Club Resort; Goofy, Minnie, and Donald Duck.

**1900 Park Fare.** Breakfast and dinner buffet; Grand Floridian Resort; breakfast: Mary Poppins, Pooh, Eeyore, Alice in Wonderland, Mad Hatter; dinner: Cinderella, Prince Charming, Fairy Godmother, Suzy and Perla, Lady Tremaine.

**Ohana.** Breakfast family-style; Polynesian Resort; Mickey, Pluto, Lilo, and Stitch.

# The Best Magic Kingdom Dining

## *Cinderella's Royal Table Fairytale Dining*

### American cuisine. Breakfast, lunch, and dinner. $$$$

Those who want to feel like a six-year-old again should definitely plan to dine in Cinderella's fairytale castle, a medieval dream with thick stone floors, shining shields, dazzling suits of armor, and resplendent banners. Up a spiral staircase is the grand dining room where through glittering leaded-glass windows is a bird's-eye view of Fantasyland. It's a great respite from the throngs below with satisfying food, where everyone is a prince or princess waited on by "royal attendants" clad in Renaissance clothing.

The restaurant's most popular meal has always been the plated all-you-care-to-eat character breakfast, worth the high price tag only if little ones are part of your vacation. There's also a character lunch and dinner featuring a family-style appetizer, your choice of six entrees, and a set dessert. All meals are hosted by Cinderella and her Disney royalty friends. To ensure a seat for these highly coveted meals, it's essential to call (407) WDW-DINE, or (407) 939-3463, at 7 a.m. eastern standard time exactly 180 days prior. Reservations are sometimes gone in a matter of minutes.

*CARA'S TIP:* If you aren't traveling with children, I suggest you spend your money elsewhere where you'll find better food at a more reasonable price. Full payment is taken at time of booking with a twenty-four-hour cancellation policy.

**Best known for:** Major Domo's Favorite Pie of prime rib in a rich cabernet sauce with mashed potatoes and sautéed vegetables topped with a light pastry.

### SAMPLE MENU ITEMS

**Preplated breakfast:** Juice, fresh fruit, pastries, scrambled eggs, bacon, sausage, French toast, potato casserole; French toast sticks for children; *healthy choice:* granola, low-fat yogurt.

**Lunch entrees:** Pasta al pomodoro with garden vegetables; pan-seared salmon with saffron crab risotto and lemon beurre blanc; herb-crusted pork tenderloin with mustard-cheese grits and cabernet sauce; focaccia sandwich; Major Domo's Favorite Pie.

**Dinner entrees:** Roasted prime rib of beef with roasted potatoes and cabernet sauce; lemon lavender chicken on mashed potatoes with wilted spinach; pork chop with bacon and mushroom ragout with red bliss mashed potatoes finished with sweet chipotle glaze; roast lamb chops with gratin potatoes and vegetable ragout drizzled with herb pesto; pan-seared salmon with grain pilaf glazed with rosemary-lemon honey; cavatappi pasta with summer vegetables, fresh tomatoes, and ricotta.

## Crystal Palace

### American buffet. Breakfast, lunch, and dinner. $$$

Winnie the Pooh and his friends Eeyore, Piglet, and Tigger are your hosts in this sunlight-drenched, conservatory-style restaurant found at the castle end of Main Street. Patio-style wrought-iron furnishings, lofty windows, and ceilings hung with baskets of greenery create an alfresco atmosphere. A surprisingly good and bountiful buffet is the fare, definitely one of the better spreads in the park. This is a popular dining choice, so make advance reservations and on arrival ask for the dining room closest to Main Street with its charming view of Cinderella's Castle. Those dining without children should avoid dinnertime when the place is at a high frenzied fever pitch.

**Best known for:** Breakfast lasagna made of waffles, pound cake, and fruit topped with custard and pastry cream.

#### SAMPLE MENU ITEMS

**Breakfast buffet:** Juice, fresh fruit; pastries, muffins, croissants, biscuits and gravy, cereal, oatmeal, sweet breakfast lasagna; breakfast meats, prime rib hash; made-to-order omelets, scrambled eggs, frittata; roasted potatoes, puff French toast, pancakes.

**Lunch buffet:** Mixed field greens with various dressings, potato salad, Mediterranean pasta salad, beef romaine and bleu cheese salad, vine ripe tomato and mozzarella, Southwest chicken salad, seedless cucumber and pickled ginger salad, Moroccan couscous and parsley salad, edamame salad, shrimp quinoa and hearts of palm salad, assorted breads, soup; wild mushroom and chicken pasta with basil asiago cream sauce, green Thai curry chicken, fruit and vegetable tofu curry, citrus-marinated flank steak, barbecue pork tenderloin; garlic smashed potatoes, stir-fried curry noodles, fire-roasted corn spoon bread, braised kale; strawberry cheese-cake, tiramisu, chocolate trifle, peanut butter cake, assorted cookies, carrot cake, key lime pie, coconut flan, make-your-own sundae bar, hot apple cobbler, banana bread pudding with hazelnut cream sauce; *children's buffet*: mac 'n' cheese, green beans, meatballs with marinara.

**Dinner buffet:** Peel-and-eat shrimp; salads the same as lunch, assorted breads; corn chowder, creamed tomato soup, fruit and vegetable tofu curry, cheese pizza, Thai-curried mussels, adobo rubbed pulled pork, rotisserie chicken, fire-roasted prime rib and herb-roasted turkey, ancho chili-rubbed salmon; garlic mashed potatoes, vegetable medley with arugula oil, ratatouille, fire-roasted corn spoon bread, broccoli tossed in puri puri and key lime ponzu, cinnamon-and-lemon-infused basmati rice; desserts and children's buffet same as lunch.

## The Best Epcot Dining

### Akershus Royal Banquet Hall

**Scandinavian cuisine at the Norway Pavilion in World Showcase. Breakfast, lunch, and dinner dining with characters. $$$$**

Those traveling with their own little princess should definitely book a meal at this fairytale dining spot. Housed in a replica of Oslo's Akershus Castle, the dining room sparkles with massive iron chandeliers, high-beamed ceilings, lovely cut-glass windows, and a friendly waitstaff clothed in traditional Norwegian dress. Disney Princesses are in attendance for all meals and may include Belle, Jasmine, Snow White, Ariel, Sleeping Beauty, and Mary Poppins. Breakfast is a standard American family-style meal, but where Akershus really shines is at lunch and dinner. Begin with a cold buffet of Scandinavian-style salads, meats, cheese, and bread. Then choose one of the delicious entrees followed by a family-style trio of desserts. The mustard-glazed seared salmon is tough to beat, but the traditional *kjottkaker,* a plate of luscious Norwegian meatballs, might be a good choice for those who enjoy adventuresome eating. It's an excellent way to sample a bit of unfamiliar fare.

CARA'S TIP: A credit card guarantee is required to make a reservation. Cancellations must be made forty-eight hours in advance to avoid a $10 per person cancellation penalty.

**Best known for:** The best Princesses character experience around.

**SAMPLE MENU ITEMS**

**Family-style breakfast:** Biscuits, cinnamon rolls, fruit, bacon, sausage, scrambled eggs, breakfast potatoes.

**Lunch entrees:** Salmon burger on a toasted onion roll with vegetable soup; grilled venison sausage served over white bean stew; open faced chicken sandwich with potato and fennel salad; traditional *kjottkaker,* ground beef and pork dumplings served with mashed potatoes and lingonberry sauce; grilled vegetable stuffed pasta.

**Dinner entrees:** Sautéed chicken breast with vegetable barley risotto; grilled pork chop with potato gratin; seared herb-dusted beef tips in a mustard brandy sauce; citrus marinated mahi mahi with mushroom vinaigrette; grilled vegetable stuffed pasta with tomato-truffle broth.

## Bistro de Paris

**French cuisine at the France Pavilion in World Showcase. Dinner only. $$$–$$$$**

Upstairs from Chefs de France is a charming belle époque dining room with an air of exclusivity that feels dressed up even if you are not. Gilded mirrors, white linen tablecloths, crimson banquettes, and billowy white drapes framing windows overlooking the World Showcase Lagoon provide the perfect setting for delicious French accents and luscious dishes prepared simply in tantalizing sauces. Favorites include Maine lobster poached with green pea gnocchis and fava beans, or a rack of lamb served with a thin onion tart with rosemary and eggplant caviar gratin. After dinner a dessert of crepe suzette prepared and flamed tableside or the perfect apple tarte with calvados while lingering over cordials and coffee is definitely my idea of a nightcap.

*CARA'S TIP:* Request a window table (most are for two) to receive a nice view of the lagoon.

**Best known for:** Epcot's most sophisticated restaurant.

**SAMPLE MENU ITEMS**

**Dinner entrees:** Salmon roasted in a dill crust with lemon beurre blanc; roasted duck breast with polenta galette, artichoke bottom, and mushroom fricassee; pork tenderloin stuffed with mushrooms, pasta gratin with truffles, forestiere sauce; grilled beef tenderloin with peppercorn sauce.

## 🌿 Coral Reef Restaurant

**Seafood at The Seas With Nemo and Friends Pavilion in Future World. Lunch and dinner. $$–$$$**

Feel like the Little Mermaid in this one-of-a-kind, softly lit dining room of tiered leather banquettes lined with shimmering blue mosaic tiles. Dominating the restaurant and just a trident's throw away from all seats is the six-million-gallon aquarium rife with coral reefs and sea creatures. A garlicky Caesar is a nice starter with whole Romaine leaves and crispy sourdough croutons, but most can't resist the creamy, but very rich, signature lobster soup. An entrée salad of super fresh sautéed trout served atop arugula, cannellini beans, and delicate cherry tomatoes with a tart vinaigrette is astonishingly tasty—in fact, it's one of the best dishes I've had at Disney. The seasonal catch is always a nice choice (red snapper was the option on my last visit) served with risotto and a celery-root nage finished with rich truffle oil. Personally, I think the view of the aquarium alone is worth the price of a meal.

**Best known for:** Creamy lobster soup and a side of pepper jack cheese grits.

### SAMPLE MENU ITEMS

**Lunch entrees:** Apricot-braised beef short ribs and barbecue glaze with crushed Yukon gold potatoes; pan-seared tilapia served with a roasted white and green bean salad tossed in a tomato vinaigrette; lobster ravioli with tomatoes, olives, capers, and shaved parmigiano-reggiano cheese; seared chicken breast served over spaetzle finished with applewood-smoked bacon chicken broth; wild mushroom lasagna with a rustic tomato ragout.

**Dinner entrees:** Pan-seared seasonal catch with wild mushroom and scallop risotto with celery root nage finished with parsley-truffle oil; roasted Scottish salmon with leek fondue, orecchiette pasta, and red wine reduction; grilled New York strip with roasted potatoes, watercress, and tomatoes tossed in caramelized shallot vinaigrette; seared golden tile fish with roasted wild mushrooms, pearl onions, and a red wine reduction.

## Les Chefs de France

**French bistro cuisine at the France Pavilion in World Showcase. Lunch and dinner. $$$–$$$$**

This restaurant models itself on all that's right about the French bistro, transporting you to the Paris of your dreams. In a fun and festive atmosphere, white-aproned waiters with romantic accents bustle about the glass-enclosed veranda-style restaurant. Begin with classic dishes like flawless onion soup crusty with bubbly gruyère, or perhaps the not-too-rich lobster bisque. Outstanding crepes filled with smoked chicken strips, peppers, and onions topped with a light Basquaise sauce or the best quiche Lorraine this side of the pond are great lunch entrée choices. For dinner you should indulge in the grilled tenderloin of beef with a black pepper sauce accompanied by a lovely potato gratin and fresh green beans followed with the perfectly quintessential dessert of yummy profiteroles, puff choux filled with ice cream and drizzled with chocolate sauce.

*CARA'S TIP:* The lunch menu is less expensive; however, the ambience is nicer in the evening. A veranda table for the fireworks is relaxing, but don't expect a perfect view.

**Best known for:** Filet au Poivre Noir, grilled tenderloin of beef with black pepper sauce and potato gratin.

### SAMPLE MENU ITEMS

**Lunch entrees:** *Croque monsieur,* the classic French toasted ham and cheese sandwich, served with a green salad; salad Niçoise; zucchini, eggplant, and tomato lasagna; broiled salmon served on mixed cabbage with cubed apple and corn salad; beef short ribs braised in Cabernet with pasta, pearl onions, and mushrooms.

**Dinner entrees:** Broiled salmon, tomato béarnaise, ratatouille; traditional French cassoulet with braised lamb, pork sausage, bacon, and white beans; roasted breast of duck and leg confit in a spicy honey sauce, French green beans, sweet potatoes; baked macaroni with cream and gruyère cheese.

## Restaurant Marrakesh

**Moroccan cuisine at the Morocco Pavilion in World Showcase. Lunch and dinner. $$$–$$$$**

The soul of Morocco is certainly captured in one of World Showcase's best dining venues. With the feel of a lavish sultan's palace, its lace-like walls, carved columns, and graceful arches are interspersed with vibrant mosaic tiles and a lofty inlaid ceiling. Agreeable waiters in colorful silk clothing and fez hats work the two-tiered dining room around the hip-wiggling belly dancer and Middle Eastern musicians; it's even more entertaining when members of the audience get involved. The Moroccan cuisine is extremely appetizing with its many exotic spices and delicate accompanying couscous that's part of each meal. Choosing a dish is difficult, so take a crack at one of the combination meals offering a little of everything. But you won't go wrong ordering the *couscous m'rouzia fass* made savory with the addition of fall-apart tender braised beef spiked with caramelized onions, raisins, honey, and almonds. Finish up with a cup of rich Moroccan coffee. This is one of the best and certainly the most authentic attempts in Epcot to re-create the atmosphere of international dining.

*CARA'S TIP:* This is usually an easy place to dine without advance reservations.

**Best known for:** The belly dancing and spicy cuisine.

**SAMPLE MENU ITEMS**

**Lunch and dinner entrees:** Marrakesh Royal Feast (family-style meal with a sampling of appetizers, entrees, and dessert from the entire menu); roasted lamb shank in natural juices; shish kebab of tenderloin of beef served with hummus; lemon chicken (braised half chicken seasoned with garlic, green olives, and preserved lemons); Mediterranean seafood platter of shrimp ragout, broiled salmon, and seafood bastilla.

## San Angel Inn

**South-of-the-border cuisine at the Mexico Pavilion in World Showcase. Lunch and dinner. $$$–$$$$**

Okay, okay, so it's not the best Mexican food to be found, but this restaurant gets extra points for its stab at romantic ambience where it's perpetual nighttime alongside the inky Rio del Tiempo (River of Time). Begin with the fresh, somewhat spicy guacamole, or perhaps the tasty sopa Azteca, Mexico's traditional tortilla soup made with pasilla peppers. If you like

rich food the *pollo a las rajas,* grilled chicken breast served over red peppers, an overload of onions, chile poblano, chorizo, and melted cheese,
fits the bill. Meat and seafood dishes are prepared in a variety of piquant
sauces; however, the *cochinta pibil,* slow cooked pork in achiote seeds,
beer, garlic, red onions, and orange juice, which is one of the chef's recommendations, is a somewhat bland version of what is normally an exceptional dish. Those not used to spice may be in for a bit of a surprise—a
pleasant one, I hope—however, not all dishes are prepared with chiles
(your waiter can recommend a dish without the heat). Skip the boring
bread pudding and go for the creamy flan or one of the great desserts to be
had at the kiosks around World Showcase. If you're in luck, the fabulous
Mariachi Cobre will be performing during your meal.

**Best known for:** The romantic atmosphere.

**SAMPLE MENU ITEMS**

**Lunch entrees:** Ensalada Mexicana, mixed greens with grilled chicken,
avocado, cheese, and cactus strips with pico de gallo; green chicken enchi-
ladas topped with sour cream, cheese, and onions topped with a green
tomatillo sauce; grilled beef tenderloin served with chilaquiles (layers of
fried corn tortilla and green tomatillo sauce, topped with fresh cheese,
sour cream, and onions).

**Dinner entrees:** Mahi mahi à la Veracruzana (grilled fish fillet prepared
with capers, olives, bell peppers, onions, and tomatoes); beef tenderloin
tips sautéed with onions and chile Guajillo sauce served over corn torti-
llas, black beans, and cheese; mole poblano, grilled chicken breasts with
classic sauce of spices and a hint of chocolate.

## Tutto Italia

**Italian cuisine at the Italy Pavilion in World Showcase. Lunch
and dinner. $$$–$$$$**

With an obligatory grouchy maitre d' and flirty waiters, Disney has finally
scored higher marks with a fairly good Italian spot. The decor is one of
glittering chandeliers and walls of murals depicting ancient Rome, defi-
nitely an Old World ambience. I know that every Italian restaurant west
of the Tiber claims its lasagna is fabulous, but here it's the truth; Tutto
Italia's is superb with a meaty ragu and a creamy béchamel. A bufala salad

with ripe tomatoes and fresh basil is perfectly dressed with virgin olive oil and the creamiest fresh mozzarella imaginable. And the Grand Antipasto served family style with an assortment of meats, cheeses, and peppers is a definite winner. The chicken cutlet Milanese is tender, crispy, and moist topped with tangy arugula and shaved fennel, but fish dishes seem to fall flat with seemingly not-so-fresh offerings. While the pasta primavera is tasty, it's a bit heavier than your normal recipe with the inclusion of a rich, creamy sauce. Now if you really want *great* Italian and don't mind a fifteen-minute walk outside of Epcot's International Gateway, then head over to the Walt Disney World Swan instead where Il Mulino's food is a definite step above.

**Best known for:** Lasagna al Forno, their best entrée.

**SAMPLE MENU ITEMS**

**Lunch entrees:** Baked spinach potato gnocchi, fontina, Parmesan, mozzarella, gorgonzola; linguini with clams, cherry tomatoes, garlic, parsley; pan roasted pork chop, oregano, black olive, tomatoes; spaghetti with veal meatballs and pomodoro sauce; veal scaloppini alla caprese with tomatoes and mozzarella.

**Dinner entrees:** Oven roasted rack of lamb, herb crusted, red wine sauce; breaded filet of sole, lemon, caper relish; baked salmon filet over fagiolini beans with a fresh tomato relish; veal and Chianti ravioli, Parmesan cheese, sage butter, roasted tomato; black squid linguini pasta, shrimp, spicy tomato sauce.

# The Best Disney's Hollywood Studios Dining

## '50s Prime Time Café

**American cuisine. Lunch and dinner. $$**

Pass through a time warp into a 1950s family kitchen where guests dine while watching *Leave It to Beaver* and *Topper* on black-and-white TVs sitting on the counter between the toaster and the blender. Linoleum floors, Formica tables, pull-down lamps, plenty of knickknacks, and windows covered in venetian blinds and tacky drapes are accompanied by a menu of savory renditions of good old American comfort food. The only thing missing is the sliced white bread. "Mom" herself is your server, making sure everyone in the "family" observes good manners. No fighting at the table! No throwing spitballs! Mustn't forget to eat your vegetables! Our "mom" told us to set our own table; she didn't do chores. Stick with the old-fashioned basics for the best results. And remember, it's the atmosphere that counts here, not the cuisine. Check out the adjoining Tune-In Lounge for an appetizer and a drink complete with glowing ice cubes before settling in for dinner.

**Best known for:** Great golden fried chicken.

**SAMPLE MENU ITEMS**

**Lunch entrees:** Traditional meat loaf; roasted pepper stuffed with whole grains and smoked ratatouille; old-fashioned pot roast; chicken pot pie; stacked sandwich with your choice of ham or turkey on multigrain bread; fried beer battered fish sandwich.

**Dinner entrees:** Grilled boneless pork loin glazed with peppered mushroom gravy with mashed potatoes and green beans; char-grilled butcher tender steak with red wine sauce and sautéed mushrooms, cheddar scalloped potatoes; olive oil poached salmon served with sweet peas, brown rice pilaf, and a dill cream sauce.

## Hollywood Brown Derby

**Contemporary American cuisine. Lunch and dinner. $$$–$$$$**

The best food at Disney's Hollywood Studios is to be found at the illustrious Brown Derby, perfectly re-created right down to the collection of celebrity caricatures hanging on just about every square inch of wall space. It's sheer 1930s Hollywood glamour, seen everywhere from the rich mahogany walls and furnishings to the sway of potted palms. Massive cast-iron chandeliers, crisp white tablecloths, snug ruby red banquettes, and derby-shaped art deco lamps all set the mood for a sentimental waltz through the heyday of Hollywood. A light choice for lunch is the grilled Atlantic salmon that sits atop a salad of baby spinach, cannellini beans, and heirloom tomatoes tossed with a smoky warm bacon vinaigrette and a splash of Meyer lemon aioli. I do wish the chef would make the meltingly tender braised boneless short rib appetizer a full-blown entrée, with its creamy whipped parsnips and tender baby beets. You really can't go wrong with any of the fish dishes, but I particularly like the pan-fried grouper with lemon-butter sauce. Vegetarians as well as non-vegetarians will love the spicy noodle bowl spiked with coconut-crusted tofu, edamame, snap peas, bok choy, and shiitake mushrooms in a red curry broth. The wine list is exceptionally good for a theme park, with many types available by the glass. Of course, there's always the famous Brown Derby cobb salad, so finely chopped the lettuce resembles parsley. But frankly, I only need a slice of the fabulous grapefruit cake to be blissfully happy. *CARA'S TIP:* Your server won't mind providing you with the recipe for the cobb salad and grapefruit cake; just ask.

**Best known for:** Brown Derby cobb salad.

**SAMPLE MENU ITEMS**

**Lunch entrees:** Hijiki-crusted ahi tuna cobb salad seared rare with mizuna, palm sugar cucumbers, pickled daikon, flavored soy and wasabi sauces; fresh egg linguini pasta with shrimp, Cedar Key clams, and cremini mushrooms tossed in a light herb truffle cream; grilled rib eye steak with arugula, crispy sweet onions, gorgonzola, red bliss potatoes, and oven-dried tomato vinaigrette; citrus and herb marinated breast of chicken with oil saffron infused Israeli couscous, and a Meyer lemon aioli.

**Dinner entrees:** Sterling Silver pork tenderloin with white cheddar mustard spaetzle, swiss chard, onion–pomegranate relish, and cider jus; char-grilled twelve-ounce rib eye with herb-roasted fingerling potatoes, cremini mushrooms, cipollini onions, and cabernet syrup; pan-roasted duck breast and venison sausage with crimson lentils, natural reduction, and Fresno chili jam.

## Sci-Fi Dine-In Theater Restaurant

**American cuisine. Lunch and dinner. $$–$$$**

Anyone lonesome for the drive-ins of their youth will go mad for this place. Load into sleek, 1950s-era convertibles to watch B-movie sci-fi and horror trailers, and waiters who carhop the darkened, starlit theater. Speaker boxes hang on the side of your car and, of course, popcorn and hot dogs dance on the screen during intermission. One gladly overlooks the so-so food for the ambience; who cares when *Godzilla* is your entertainment!

*CARA'S TIP:* If you want to be seated more quickly, let them know you're willing to sit at one of the picnic tables instead of in a car. Stop in during non-prime hours for dessert and soak up the surroundings in one of Disney's best themed restaurants.

**Best known for:** The atmosphere; certainly not the food.

**SAMPLE MENU ITEMS**

**Lunch entrees:** Reuben sandwich; smoked St. Louis-style ribs basted in BBQ sauce; seared marinated tofu with mango glaze and fresh vegetables; Angus chuck burger; beef and blue salad, sliced steak with a wedge of iceberg lettuce topped with blue cheese dressing, tomatoes, and bacon.

**Dinner entrees:** Shrimp bow tie pasta with artichoke hearts, kalamata olives, baby spinach, and feta; butcher steak with a red wine glaze and seasonal vegetables; Italian grilled chicken sandwich with bruschetta topping served on a kaiser roll.

# The Best Animal Kingdom Dining

## *Rainforest Café*

**American cuisine at the Entrance Plaza. Breakfast, lunch, and dinner. $–$$$$**

Dine among the beasts of the jungle surrounded by crashing waterfalls, lush tropical foliage, dripping vines, and giant aquarium tanks while being bombarded with thunderstorms and noisy Audio-Animatronics wildlife. Although the atmosphere outweighs the food, it certainly is a delightful place, one that should definitely be on your Disney agenda. If you'd like a sampling of the ambience without a meal, stop for a drink at the cafe's Magic Mushroom to sip on specialty drinks, smoothies, juice, and coffee under a towering toadstool roof. An outside-the-park entrance allows dining without admission to the park.

*CARA'S TIP:* Advance Dining Reservations are taken and are highly recommended for lunch. Breakfast service begins a half hour before park opening time. Mammoth portions require either a big appetite or the need to split an entree.

**Best known for:** Audio-Animatronics jungle beasts.

**SAMPLE MENU ITEMS**

**Breakfast entrees:** Tonga toast (baked cinnamon French toast surrounded by fresh strawberries, bananas, and walnuts); eggs Benedict; Mexican-style breakfast pizza topped with scrambled eggs, tomatoes, cilantro, red, green, and poblano peppers, and Jack and cheddar cheese; top flat iron steak served with scrambled eggs and breakfast potatoes; cranberry Belgian waffle.

**Lunch and dinner entrees:** Sweet and sour stir-fry; pot roast; cobb salad; China island chicken salad with toasted sesame seeds, red cabbage, rice noodles, and scallions; pastalaya pasta of shrimp, sautéed chicken breast, bell peppers, onions and Andouille sausage tossed in a hot and spicy Cajun sauce and served over linguini; a full rack of slow-roasted spareribs basted with barbecue sauce, served with coleslaw and fries; portobello mushroom burger topped with roasted red peppers and Monterey jack cheese; Monsoon Grill, a mix of macadamia crusted snapper, shrimp scampi, and Caribbean coconut shrimp.

## Tusker House

### African cuisine in Africa. Breakfast, lunch, and dinner. $$$

One of Disney's better buffets, Tusker House offers a hefty variety of healthy fare, an emphasis on whole grains, and many vegetarian choices, all with an African twist. A wild assortment of savory desserts is served in tasting portions perfect for trying a bite of everything. Accompany your meal with a nice glass of South African wine. Breakfast is a popular character meal with Donald, Daisy, Mickey, and Goofy.

**Best known for:** The Animal Kingdom's best lunch choice.

**SAMPLE MENU ITEMS**

**Character breakfast buffet:** Fresh fruit, cereals, oatmeal, mealie pap, biscuits and sausage gravy, scrambled eggs, oven-roasted Yukon gold potatoes, bacon, sausage, vegetable frittata, ham and cheese frittata, spiced corned beef hash, cheese blintzes, beef bobotie quiche, yam casserole, carved rotisserie honey-glazed ham, warm cinnamon rolls, warm banana-cinnamon bread pudding with vanilla sauce, muffins, whole-grain breads, turnovers, cheese-filled danish, apple danish, croissants.

**Lunch and dinner buffet:** Apple endive and walnut salad with blue cheese crumbles, Caesar salad, tomato and cucumber salad with fresh mint and yogurt dressing, curried rice salad, lentils with golden raisins, green bean and onion salad, fresh fruit, hummus, tabbouleh, cold cuts and cheeses, whole grain breads and rolls, chocolate mango bread, mealy corn bread, lavash; vegetable samosas, couscous with roasted vegetables, spiced vegetable and tofu tandoori, peri peri baked salmon, saffron-infused root vegetables and cabbage, seafood stew with tamarind BBQ sauce, orzo pasta with feta cheese and spinach, spiced rotisserie chicken, oven roasted potato wedges, red skinned mashed potatoes, spit roasted beef top sirloin, Kenyan coffee BBQ pork loin, curried chicken; coconut

# DISNEY RESORTS' BEST RESTAURANTS

- California Grill, perched high atop the Contemporary Resort with its picture-perfect views of the Magic Kingdom.

- Citricos at the Grand Floridian Hotel, featuring innovative Mediterranean cuisine.

- Flying Fish at Disney's BoardWalk, specializing in seafood and everything whimsical.

- Victoria and Albert's at the Grand Floridian for a special evening of romance and fantastic food.

- Artist Point at the Wilderness Lodge for exceptional Pacific Northwest cuisine.

- Bluezoo at the Walt Disney World Dolphin for great seafood in a hip setting.

- Jiko at the Animal Kingdom Lodge, an atmospheric restaurant with an African flair.

- Il Mulino for great Italian food in a sophisticated setting.

macaroons, lemon bars, pecan chocolate tart, passion fruit tart, chocolate volcano cake, carrot spice cake, baklava, banana cinnamon bread pudding, cookies, cinnamon rolls; *children's buffet*: create-your-own PB&J sandwich, corn dog nuggets, chicken drumsticks, macaroni and cheese, roasted corn medley, green beans, and mashed potatoes.

## The Best Walt Disney World Resort Dining

The best dining experiences in the "World" are to be found at Disney's deluxe resorts. Back in 1996, the California Grill set the pace when it opened to rave reviews with an ever-changing menu of New American cuisine. One by one the deluxe hotels launched a new breed of dining venues offering innovative cuisine and superior wine lists, one of which, Victoria and Albert's, boasts a AAA Five-Diamond Award rating, the only such restaurant in central Florida.

### Artist Point

**Pacific Northwest cuisine at the Wilderness Lodge. Dinner only; resort casual dress. Open daily 5:30 to 10 p.m. $$$–$$$$**

The rustic, U.S. National Park theme of the Wilderness Lodge continues where the intoxicating aroma of cedar wafts among the expanse of fat ponderosa pine columns, vaulted ceilings, and Old West murals. Oversize windows overlook sparkling Bay Lake and the hotel's enchanting courtyard of giant boulders and cascading waterfalls; on pleasant evenings request a table on the outdoor terrace. The decor does, however, take a backseat to the Pacific Northwest cuisine of fresh seafood and game meats. I could make a meal of several of the starters such as the divine, but rich, smoky portobello soup or perfectly braised Penn Cove mussels in a fragrant fennel broth. Entree greats include the ever-popular cedar plank roasted salmon topped with ever-changing glazes as well as a terrific buffalo sirloin with tasty goat cheese polenta. Fish entrees vary according to season (you're in luck if Alaskan halibut is available), but most are accompanied by a marvelous fire-roasted corn, fava bean, caramelized onion, bacon, and corn hash. A bottle from the exclusively Pacific Northwest list is a must. Berry cobbler here is always a hit, but if the warm heirloom apple tart with buttermilk ice cream and candied pecans is offered it might possibly take priority.

*CARA'S TIP:* Before dark ask for a view of Bay Lake. After dark ask for one of the tables that sit off to right side of the restaurant with views of the resort's illuminated waterfall. It makes all the difference to move out of the central area's hustle and bustle. Then take a romantic post-dinner walk through the property to the edge of Bay Lake and wait for the geyser to erupt (every hour on the hour until 10 p.m.).

**Best known for:** Cedar plank roasted salmon.

**SAMPLE MENU ITEMS**

**Dinner entrees:** Pan-seared free range chicken breast with faro wheat, brussels sprouts, and Pedro Ximénez reduction; seared day boat scallops with olive oil crushed potatoes, baby fennel, Niçoise olives, grape tomatoes, and corn "cappuccino"; potato-chive pot stickers with edamame, spinach, and soy vinaigrette; butter-poached wild boar tenderloin with wild mushroom goat cheese bread pudding, fava beans, and huckleberry au jus.

## Boma

**African-inspired buffet at the Animal Kingdom Lodge. Breakfast and dinner; casual dress. Open daily, 7:30 to 11 a.m. and 5 to 10 p.m., open at 4:30 p.m. Friday and Saturday. $$$**

The essence of Africa is potent beneath Boma's circular thatch roof, where hearty foods prepared with an African flair (and a dash of American cuisine for the picky eater) are the fare. Even if you're just a bit adventuresome, you'll like this most interesting of Disney buffets. Earthy tones are dominant in the appealing but noisy dining room filled with hardwood chairs adorned with fanciful African-style designs and green leather booths topped with kraal fences. Breakfast is quite good, with plenty of great American favorites along with delicious African specialties like bobotie, a custard made with ground lamb. Evenings the place comes alive with tables laden with a bountiful spread of African soups and stews, savory wood-roasted meats, and an entire section (or pod) of meatless dishes, all served in a lively buffet setting. It's the perfect place to try a different and exciting cuisine.

*CARA'S TIP:* If you're in luck, you'll be around during breakfast or late in the evening when the African staff sing rhythmic songs from their homelands.

**Best known for:** Tasty wood-roasted meats.

**SAMPLE MENU ITEMS**

**Breakfast buffet:** Orange juice or Frunch (a blend of lemonade, pineapple, guava, papaya, and orange juices); fresh and dried fruit; pastries, brioche, cereal, oatmeal, quinoa porridge, pap (an African cornmeal dish), pancakes, waffles, breakfast pizza; carving station with roasted ham and cured pork loin, bacon, sausage; made-to-order omelets, scrambled eggs; roasted potatoes with peppers.

**Dinner buffet:** *Salads:* watermelon rind, chicken with chili cilantro, Moroccan seafood, curry cucumber, spinach and beet, and pasta; *soups:* chicken corn porridge, smoked tomato, chicken pepper pot, curried coconut seafood stew; *main dishes:* Durban spiced roasted chicken, pepper steak, grilled seafood, wood-roasted meats; *sides:* macaroni and cheese, sweet potato pancakes, vegetable lentil kofta, braised greens, saffron rice; *desserts:* zebra domes (ganache-covered chocolate-coffee mousse), Simba paw prints (brownies), chocolate mousse crunch, banana bread pudding, fruit tarts, carrot cake, strawberry cheesecake, pecan pie; *children's buffet:* fried chicken wings, spaghetti and meatballs.

## California Grill

**Californian cuisine at the Contemporary Resort. Dinner only; resort casual dress. Open nightly, 5:30 to 10 p.m.; lounge open 5:30 to 11:30 p.m. $$$–$$$$**

This sensational restaurant should be at the top of every visitor's list to Walt Disney World. I am a view fanatic, and this drop-dead-gorgeous setting on the fifteenth floor of the Contemporary Resort enjoys Disney's best—period. From its lofty heights diners can see the Magic Kingdom, the sparkling Seven Seas Lagoon, and, best of all, the Wishes fireworks. An inventive approach to seasonally focused food including sustainable fish is this restaurant's claim to fame. That along with their sensational desserts can only be topped by more than one hundred wines available by the glass from the exceptional list. And while great sushi and sashimi might be the last thing one would expect at Walt Disney World, here only the best is served. First course choices are among my favorite dishes, in particular the Vietnamese-style lobster and shrimp cakes accompanied by

a tasty melon relish, fresh lime, and tangy mint. I normally don't order vegetarian as my main entree, but on my last visit I dined on wild mushroom,
spinach, and fontina cheese whole wheat vegetarian ravioli swimming in
a rich broth; absolutely phenomenal, the icing on the cake being heady
shavings of black truffles. Other great choices include the ever-present
grilled pork tenderloin with a zinfandel glaze accompanied by renowned
goat cheese polenta, or I'm sure you'll be more than content with whatever version of salmon is on the menu. It's a kick to watch the kitchen
action from the dining room, and the cocktail lounge has some of the best
vistas of the Magic Kingdom in the house. Procuring a window seat can
be tough, but don't be discouraged; time your meal around the fireworks
and head outside to the super observation platform for a bird's-eye view
of the extravaganza.

*CARA'S TIP:* Reservations here go quickly, so plan ahead. Check-in is
on the second floor where you'll then be escorted upstairs. Reservations
require a credit card number at the time of booking with a $20 per person
cancellation fee for no-shows or cancellations within twenty-four hours
of the reservation.

**Best known for:** Disney's best views along with an intriguing menu and
wine list.

**SAMPLE MENU ITEMS**

**Dinner entrees:** Spiced tuna with sweet potato purée, mustard greens,
red wine braised beef rib ravioli, natural reduction; seared ostrich filet
with buttery potato purée, wild mushrooms, globe carrots, fig and honeyed
port reduction; pan-roasted Florida black grouper fillet with "stir-fry" vegetables, sticky rice, ginger-soy-hijiki broth; Palmetto Farms crispy chicken
with apple glazed pork, parsnip purée, golden beets, and natural jus; day
boat scallops with blue hubbard squash and bacon gratin, baby brussels
sprouts, apple cider-veal reduction.

## 🌿 *Citricos*

**Contemporary Mediterranean food at the Grand Floridian Resort.
Dinner only; resort casual dress. Open nightly, 5:30 to 9:30 p.m.
$$$–$$$$**

An ambitious, ever-changing menu delivers innovative Mediterranean cuisine with admirable results. Combined with a sophisticated, contemporary dining room and exhibition kitchen reminiscent of the California Grill, this is a not-to-be-missed spot. Starched white linens, rich silk curtains, mosaic tiles, and swirling wrought iron are enhanced by immense windows affording views of the charming resort courtyard and, for a few tables, the Magic Kingdom fireworks in the distance. Almost large enough for an entree, everyone favorite appetizer is the lemony sautéed shrimp peppered with feta and tomatoes. Though everyone raves about the hearty braised veal shank signature entree, the question is how to resist the intensely flavored boneless short ribs in a delicate blood orange demi-glace accompanied by oh-so-creamy cheese polenta. For dessert it's the warm chocolate banana tart, a certain winner. A *Wine Spectator* Restaurant Award winner, its more than 200 selections of international offerings shine in every category, making its wine list possibly the best in "the World." A small cocktail counter within the restaurant is a nice choice for before-dinner drinks with a view of the exhibition kitchen. And for special occasions the Chef's Domain, a small private dining room seating up to twelve, is a perfect option for an up-close view of the kitchen in action ($650 minimum per party).

**Best known for:** Tender braised veal shank.

**SAMPLE MENU ITEMS**

**Dinner entrees:** Pan-seared coho salmon, fingerling marble potatoes, brussels sprouts tossed with applewood-smoked bacon and violet mustard cream; Tanglewood Farms roasted chicken breast with pappardelle pasta, wine-braised artichokes, grape tomatoes, basil pesto, and a chardonnay broth; seared tofu with zucchini, tomatoes compote, mushrooms, and lentils; filet Sicilian, oak grilled with sweet Vidalia onions, quattro formaggio crushed potatoes, and veal glace; Berkshire pork two ways: pork tenderloin and braised pork belly with herbed gnocchi, heirloom apples, swiss chard, and Madeira broth.

### *Flying Fish Café*

**Seafood at the BoardWalk. Dinner only; resort casual dress. Open 5:30 to 10 p.m. $$$–$$$$**

Contemporary yet whimsical, this restaurant will absolutely delight the senses with its flying fish mobiles, sparkling sea blue mosaic floors, cloud-painted ceiling, and golden fish scale pillars. As fanciful as it might be, the food, however, is serious. An open kitchen creates a bit of drama with flaming preparations on an open pit wood-fired grill; the perfect place to watch is from a seat perched in front of the action, which can be requested on arrival. The garlicky Caesar salad, which was a favorite, now is prepared with less crispy young romaine leaves, although the great Parmesan crisp and tangy dressing is still alive and well. Crab cakes have a bit too much filler for my taste but come with a tasty red pepper coulis and ancho chili remoulade. Order the fabulous clam chowder instead, nice and light with just a touch of cream spiked with super fresh, plump clams. A pumpkin seed–coated tripletail special with fall vegetables was mind-bogglingly delicious; the restaurant's signature fish, potato-wrapped red snapper, while commendable, should come with a warning label of "super rich." If its steak you're yearning for, the excellent New York strip served with wilted greens and sauce foyot (a version of béarnaise sauce) is delectable, particularly with a robust red from the restaurant's *Wine Spectator* Restaurant Award winning list.

**Best known for:** Potato-wrapped red snapper with creamy leek fondue and red wine butter sauce.

### SAMPLE MENU ITEMS

**Dinner entrees:** Oak-grilled Maine diver scallops with pumpkin, sage, mascarpone, and pecorino-laced risotto, and proscuitto di parma cracklins; butternut squash and Midnight Moon chevre ravioli, Farmer Lee's root spinach, sunchokes, honshemeji mushrooms, sunchoke-porcini crema, and amaretti crumbles; oak-grilled North Atlantic Bay of Fundy salmon, wilted rainbow chard, roasted winter root vegetables, Florida citrus aioli, and crispy capers; smokey citrus and fragrant pepper-spiced yellowfin tuna loin, saffron potatoes, piquillo peppers, roasted fennel, tiny tomatoes, chorizo and saffron-vegetable nage.

## Il Mulino New York Trattoria

**Italian cuisine at the Walt Disney World Swan. Dinner only; smart casual dress. Open daily, 5 to 11 p.m. $$–$$$$**

First opened in New York's Greenwich Village more than twenty-five years ago, this restaurant offers the best Italian on Disney property. It's Abruzzi-style Italian food in a trendy, contemporary setting with fashionable lighting, leather seating, exposed brick, and wood floors. Glass partitions section off the kitchen as well as smaller, more intimate nooks, but I prefer the open, more lively dining area.

Meals begin with a complimentary antipasti plate of sliced Cacciatorini sausage, sautéed marinated eggplant, and an assortment of breads, but go lightly on this and savor an order of arancini, succulent rice balls stuffed with ground meat perched on a bed of tasty marinara. Caprese salad here comes with a bit of a twist—creamy, fresh buffalo mozzarella and oven-dried tomatoes with the addition of capers and roasted peppers all sprinkled with extra virgin olive oil and aged balsamic. The restaurant's specialty is the sea bass, but better by far is the sumptuous salmon sautéed in garlic and olive oil with an overabundance of wild mushrooms, fennel, spinach, onions, and al dente broccoli rabe. A surprisingly great *costolette di maiale,* a thick pork chop cooked pink in the middle, is topped with mounds of chopped mushrooms and spicy cherry vinegar peppers. And if you crave fabulous shrimp but don't mind intensity, the *gamberi francese* fits the bill with its lightly battered, giant, succulent shrimp swimming in a bed of creamy white wine lemon sauce. An impressive international wine list boasting a *Wine Spectator* Award of Excellence is heavy on Italian vintages.

*CARA'S TIP:* Those traveling with small children should take advantage of the two hours of complimentary child care at Camp Dolphin (one child per adult entree). Valet parking is complimentary when dining at Il Mulino.

**Best known for:** Branzino, seared sea bass cooked with cherry tomatoes, pancetta, and white wine.

## SAMPLE MENU ITEMS

**Dinner entrees:** Baked cannelloni stuffed with meat and spinach served with a cream and tomato sauce; meat tortellini and peas in a cream sauce; pappardelle with tomato basil sauce; fourteen-ounce grilled boneless rib eye with fried onions and chianti sauce; herb crusted European-cut chicken breast served with escarole and red wine; single cut veal chop with sage and garlic over a bed of potatoes.

## Jiko—The Cooking Place

**Contemporary cuisine with an African flair at the Animal Kingdom Lodge. Dinner only; smart casual dress. Open daily, 5:30 to 10 p.m. $$$–$$$$**

Jiko richly deserves kudos for its innovative and consistently great cuisine, seductive atmosphere, and all–South African wine list. The lovely dining room is furnished with massive mosaic tile columns surrounded by floor-to-ceiling windows, blue leather banquettes, honey-colored walls, and gleaming wood floors. Soft, contemporary lighting shaped in the guise of bird wings hangs from a rich, blue ceiling, giving the feeling of open space.

Giant, twin clay ovens draw the eye to the open kitchen where an eclectic blend of creations, prepared with an African flair in terms of spices and ingredients, is turned out in attractive presentations. The food veers towards the exotic, but you almost can't go wrong with anything on the menu. If the restaurant's stunning "tamales" are offered, go ahead and order them or you'll be wishing you had when you spy them on another's table; forget the typical variety because these truffled sweet potato mash and goat cheese gems are wrapped in delicate maize and served in an open husk. Move on to the moist chermoula-roasted Tanglewood chicken made savory with preserved lemons, roasted garlic, and kalamata olives, or, if you love the taste of fall-off-the-bone short ribs, Jiko's version is tantalizing.

For an after-dinner treat try the somewhat different chocolate-crusted pistachio crème brûlée. In the tiny, adjoining Cape Town Lounge and Wine Bar, knowledgeable bartenders are happy to convey the finer points of the *Wine Spectator* Award–winning, all–South African list, one of the largest in North America.

**Best known for:** Oak-grilled filet mignon with macaroni and cheese and red wine sauce.

**SAMPLE MENU ITEMS**

**Dinner entrees:** Roasted lamb loin with herbed couscous, sun-dried cherries, and red curry sauce; grilled swordfish with crisp mealie pap, asparagus, and tomato-pancetta vinaigrette; Swahili curry shrimp with East African curry sauce, artichokes, and coconut rice; seared maize pudding with chakalaka and basil buerre blanc; grilled Berkshire pork loin with braised cabbage, smoked bacon, and crispy potatoes.

## Narcoossee's

**Seafood at the Grand Floridian Resort. Dinner only; resort casual dress. Open daily, 5:30 to 10 p.m. $$$–$$$$**

Views of Cinderella's Castle and the Magic Kingdom fireworks, anyone? If so, this is the place for you. Nestled on the shores of the Seven Seas Lagoon, this two-level restaurant offers a pleasant if not exciting nautical ambience and an inventive North American seafood menu. A good start to your meal are butter-soft Prince Edward Island mussels served with garlicky toast in a liquorish pastis broth. There is always a variety of wriggling-fresh, seasonal fish choices, and my excellent flounder arrived with a crispy crab crust and a rich Meyer lemon sauce. Beef lovers will delight in the sensational filet mignon with a creamy potato gratin and a green peppercorn brandy sauce; others should consider the steamed whole Maine lobster, always a clever choice if you're prepared to spring for the high price tag. And a side of "loaded" mashed potatoes is a welcome treat with any dish. The almond crusted cheesecake is a pleaser with its blueberry sauce, but I still prefer the key lime crème brûlée that has had a permanent place on the menu as long as I can remember.

For a perfect culmination of your evening, step outside to the restaurant's wraparound deck or the adjoining boat dock for prime fireworks viewing. Then stick around for an after-dinner drink in the bar and a performance of the Electrical Light Parade.

*CARA'S TIP:* Request a window table with a view of Cinderella's Castle on arrival. The best strategy is to time your meal around the fireworks, moving outside to the deck or the adjoining boat dock for a great view.

**Best known for:** Always-on-the-menu key lime crème brûlée, and fresh, imaginative seafood.

### SAMPLE MENU ITEMS

**Dinner entrees:** Tanglewood Farms chicken breast, "loaded" mashed potatoes, spinach, and bacon vinaigrette; autumn vegetables, grilled tofu with olive caponata, sweet onion risotto, braised fennel with tomato vinaigrette, and roasted autumn squash with apple gastrique; crispy whole yellowtail snapper, basmati rice, charred haricots verts, and soy-lime vinaigrette; surf & turf, twin medallions of filet mignon, butter-poached rock lobster tail, potato gratin, broccolini, and choron sauce; grilled Loch Duart salmon, Laughing Bird shrimp risotto, brandy-truffle reduction, and pancetta.

## Sanaa

**African and Indian cuisine at Disney's Animal Kingdom Villas. Lunch and dinner; casual dress. Open daily, 11:30 a.m. to 3 p.m. and 5 to 9 p.m. $$–$$$**

This charmer of a restaurant has the advantage of full-length picture windows overlooking the resort's savanna, something not available next door at Jiko. Woven basket light fixtures, cement flooring, adobe walls, thatch ceilings, krall fencing, tree trunk posts, and shield chair backs add up to a unique and colorful setting. And for once there's somewhat subdued lighting, one of my Disney pet peeves. At Sanaa you will find a variety of tastes all vibrating with unusual spices woven into the small but interesting menu. Start with a red curry pulled duck sitting on a bed of whole grains topped with a light curry sauce. The healthy and sustainable fish dish option alters between wild salmon, halibut, and artic char depending on availability and is prepared in a light brothy curry bath with a bed of fresh vegetables accompanied by scallops and perfectly plump shrimp. Uncommonly spiced sides include sautéed green beans that have a touch of sweetness or a healthy five-grain pilaf. Or choose two of three small dishes (tender short ribs, luscious green shrimp curry, or tangy red chicken curry) with the curries tasting very different and a bit superior to their typical Asian counterparts (less sweet in a thinner broth). A must-try dessert is the incredible chai cream—very unusual and quite addictive.

   *CARA'S TIP:* Arrive early and request a table facing the wall of windows overlooking the resort's savanna. While you wait, have a drink in the restaurant's tiny gem of a bar.

**Best known for:** Great views of the resort's savanna.

**SAMPLE MENU ITEMS**

**Lunch entrees:** Grilled Angus chuck burger wrapped in naan bread with minted greens and cucumber-yogurt raita; grilled lamb kefta wrapped in naan bread; grilled pork chop glazed with ginger and pickled lime sauce; club sandwich on multigrain bread; tandoori chicken wrapped in naan bread.

**Dinner entrees:** Sustainable fish with shrimp and scallops served with seasonal vegetables in a light curry broth; tandoori chicken or shrimp with choice of basmati rice or five-grain pilaf; vegetarian sampler with choice of two: paneer cheese and spinach, stewed lentils, spicy cauliflower, onions, tomatoes, and mint; chicken with red curry sauce; shrimp with green curry sauce.

## Shula's Steakhouse

**Steaks at the Walt Disney World Dolphin. Dinner only; business casual dress. Open daily, 5 to 11 p.m. $$$–$$$$**

This handsome restaurant's theme, based on the Miami Dolphins' 1972 undefeated season, is depicted in attractively framed black-and-white pictures embellishing the rich wood-paneled walls. The dimly lit, dark-hued interior is comfortably outfitted in elegant cherrywood, loads of shiny brass, cushy high-backed chairs, leather banquettes, and white linen–covered tables. The menu is short on fuss and long on prime ingredients, but the presentation—printed on a football (yes a football!) along with a tray of raw meat explained in detail (a la Morton's)—seems a bit of cheesy overkill. But you don't have to be a quarterback to enjoy the sensational Angus beef steaks, unbelievably tender and cooked to perfection, accompanied by mouthwatering sourdough bread. The double baked potato studded with aged white cheddar and chives or the crab macaroni and cheese are the best sides, but avoid the beefsteak tomato salad, which can be overripe and tasteless. Order a bottle from Shula's outstanding California wine list, winner of the *Wine Spectator* Award of Excellence, to round out the evening ending with a decadent chocolate soufflé.

*CARA'S TIP:* Those traveling with small children should take advantage of the two hours of complimentary child care at Camp Dolphin (one child per adult entree). Be sure to reserve ahead and enjoy time on your own. Valet parking is complimentary when dining here.

**Best known for:** Monster-size forty-eight-ounce porterhouse.

**SAMPLE MENU ITEMS**

**Dinner entrees:** Steak Mary Anne, beef tenderloins prepared in a creamy rich butter sauce; twelve-ounce filet mignon; twenty-four-ounce porterhouse; thirty-two-ounce prime rib; twenty-two-ounce lamb loin chops; four- to five-pound lobster surf and turf; herb-crusted chicken breast; jumbo lump crab cakes; ten-ounce Florida snapper.

## Todd English's Bluezoo

**Contemporary seafood at the Walt Disney World Dolphin. Dinner only; business casual dress. Open daily, 5:30 to 11 p.m.; raw bar and lounge open daily, 3:30 to 11 p.m. $$$–$$$$**

You really must plan an evening at Todd English's dreamy outpost at the Walt Disney World Dolphin. It's worth the cost of dinner simply to check out this stunning, underwater-like fantasyland adorned with air bubble light fixtures, gauzy swaths of silver-blue organza curtains, and carpeting mimicking an expanding drop of water. Seductive seating of chocolate brown leather booths interspersed with mango orange chairs completes the picture.

The menu, as captivating as the surroundings, is fresh, inventive, and ultramodern. Meals here begin with a basket of savory house-made bread such as onion foccacia, sourdough, whole grain, or black olive. A good starter is something from the raw bar accompanied by a choice from the extensive and sophisticated international wine list. It's hard not to love the amazingly fresh sashimi here, but I can't pass up the irresistible tempura *haricots verts* served with truffle aioli as an appetizer. A New England clam chowder with salt-cured bacon is another treat—lighter than most and bursting with flavor. Perennial favorites include the tender miso-glazed Chilean sea bass with warm sesame spinach, or the Cantonese fried lobster tossed in a sticky soy glaze. But if it's pasta you're wanting, there is usually a daily choice; ours was a lobster fidelini in a somewhat spicy cream sauce, nice if not a little heavy on the fennel. A king salmon dish might have been too bland if not for its savory bacon-clam ragoût topping. On a subsequent visit I was surprised with a super-flavorful, Cajun-style swordfish rubbed with spicy seasonings sitting atop a delish tasso and rock shrimp–spiked risotto surrounded by plump littleneck clams. And then there's dessert: warm chocolate cake with a ganache center crowned with maracaibo chocolate cream pudding and a side of peanut ice cream or the sinful mai tai banana cream tart with rich roasted pineapple and a rum flambéed sorbet. Heaven!

*CARA'S TIP:* For a light meal and cocktails, head to Bluezoo's divine lounge. Those traveling with small children should take advantage of the two hours of complimentary child care at Camp Dolphin (one child per adult entree). Be sure to reserve ahead and enjoy your time alone. Valet parking is complimentary when dining here.

**Best known for:** Dancing Fish, fresh market fish whole-roasted on a rotisserie.

**SAMPLE MENU ITEMS**

**Dinner entrees:** Berkshire hefeweizen-brined pork loin, apple kraut, German potato salad, apple mustard glaze; Florida grouper, black truffle spaetzle, black radish, black truffle vinaigrette; Lone Peak beef tenderloin, parsnip, organic marble potatoes, brussels sprouts, agro dolce; dancing fish with smoked paprika rub, fingerling chorizo hash, green olive, orange, saffron; heritage half chicken, seasonal mushrooms, macaire potato, truffle chicken jus.

## Victoria and Albert's

**American cuisine with classical influences at the Grand Floridian Resort. Dinner only; reservations mandatory; jackets for gents (tie optional) and dinner attire for women policy. Call (407) 939-7707 for reservations. Open daily with two seating times: 5:45 to 6:30 p.m. and 9 to 9:45 p.m.; July and August one seating daily, 6:45 to 8 p.m. $$$$**

Fine dining in a stunning setting combined with virtually flawless service sets Victoria and Albert's apart. Awarded the AAA FiveDiamond for ten years running and the *Wine Spectator* Best of Award of Excellence year after year, this is Disney's true gastronomic temple. Here the china is Wedgwood, the silver Christofle, the linen Frette, and crystal Riedel. A seasonal prix fixe menu including six sumptuous courses, all small, is served by an ultra-professional waitstaff, while a harpist performs. Over the course of two and a half hours, indulge in one exemplary dish after another, every morsel with its own distinct flavor, no one ingredient overwhelming another—food here is simply a work of art. Non carnivore-eaters will swoon over the six-course vegetarian menu, a rare find.

My latest meal began with each of us choosing a different appetizer, mine a tasty peeky-toe crab and asparagus salad, and my husband's choice duck accompanied by a savory mix of golden and red beets. We both followed with *poulet rouge* with spring morels and fresh English peas. You may choose any of the vegetarian courses as an option, and if a variety of the handmade gnocchi happens to be an offering please don't miss it.

Next came the just-in-season Alaskan king salmon accompanied by tiny French lentils, delicate corn, and a subtle saffron foam. Also tender shrimp with bok choy and a light coconut emulsion. Then the star of the evening, a faultless tender lamb en croute with tomato-lamb jus, as well as veal tenderloin with braised veal cheeks stuffed in Burgundy-poached succulent sweet breads, both strokes of genius.

And then there were the desserts! Vanilla bean crème brûlée with white chocolate gelato, and a marvelous combination of Tanzanian chocolate pyramid, Hawaiian Kona chocolate soufflé, and Peruvian chocolate ice cream and puff pastry. We chose to split one wine pairing, with each glass of wine only two ounces, more than adequate particularly after the before-dinner champagne we enjoyed in the concierge lounge.

An even more exclusive dining experience is to be had in the Queen Victoria's Room. Behind closed doors just off the restaurant's main dining room are four tables overseen by the the restaurant manager, Israel Perez. Ten courses and French *gueridon* service, a rolling cart that moves from table to table, assures customized service with each and every course.

Those seeking a truly special evening should book the chef's table set in an alcove in the kitchen, a spot perfect for an up-close, behind-the-scenes look at Disney's top chef in action. The most outstanding meal around, up to thirteen spectacular courses are served, each more fantastic than the last, all overseen by the brilliant Chef de Cuisine Scott Hunnel. I can't recommend it highly enough and beg you to consider adding the wine pairing to make this a meal of a lifetime.

*CARA'S TIP:* Children under ten are not allowed, so be sure to pre-book a sitter.

**Best known for:** The only AAA Five-Diamond restaurant in central Florida.

## SAMPLE MENU ITEMS

**Appetizers and first course:** Maine lobster with watermelon, radish, kohlrabi, and vanilla aioli; Colorado buffalo with fennel, olives, artichokes, and sherry vinaigrette; Maine diver scallops with Zellwood corn and chorizo sauce; wasabi soy marinated king salmon with bok choy and soybeans; wild turbot with toasted capers and Meyer lemon.

**Entrees:** *Poulet rouge* with mushroom-truffle ragout and English peas; duck breast, sausage, and confit with salsify and delicate squash puree; Kurobuta pork tenderloin and belly with baby beets and sherry-bacon vinaigrette; Niman Ranch lamb with cannelloni bean cassoulet; Marcho Farms veal tenderloin with marble potatoes and sauce soubise; Australian Kobe beef tenderloin with smoked garlic potato puree (additional $33).

**Desserts:** Meyer lemon and blood orange purse with blackberry violet sherbet; Tanzanian chocolate pyramid with Szechuan truffles and pomegranate; Hawaiian Kona chocolate soufflé; caramelized banana gâteau; vanilla bean crème brûlée; Grand Marnier soufflé.

**Vegetarian menu:** Butternut squash cream soup and root vegetable flan; hearts of palm and fennel salad with garbanzo beans, beets, and Manni olive oil; mushroom tortellini with trumpet royal, hedgehog mushrooms, and tableside black truffles; handmade potato gnocchi with vegetable ratatouille and aged balsamic; braised red cabbage with mustard spaetzle and petite French lentils.

## The Wave

**Healthy American cuisine at the Contemporary Resort. Breakfast, lunch, and dinner; casual dress. Lounge open noon until midnight. $$–$$$**

This interesting new lobby floor restaurant at the Contemporary Resort featuring regional, organic, and sustainable offerings is a nice addition to Disney's roster. Described as American cuisine with world flavors, it's a good choice for a reasonably priced, health-conscious meal.

After a peek at the restaurant's adjoining Star Trekish, glowing blue bar, it's a bit of a letdown to see the somewhat simple dining area. Curtained-partitioned banquettes hug the wall while tables fill the floor area. Chair backs and the copper ceiling, both with a wave motif, emphasize the name of the restaurant.

Skip the bread-filled crab cake appetizer and choose instead the mixed green salad, this one exceptional with the unusual addition of spaghetti squash, edamame, flax seed, and baby mozzarella. Lunch sandwich offerings are served on multigrain bread with a side of excellent roasted red potatoes—the grilled chicken sandwich with arugula, tomato, and goat cheese is the best. Both lunch and dinner menus offer a sustainable fish entree; a cilantro pesto wild salmon perched atop a delectable medley of corn, edamame, and green beans was nicely done with a beautiful pink center. Better yet, it was absolutely scrumptious. The pork tenderloin entree tends to be on the dry side so request a juicier portion for complete satisfaction. Vegetarians will delight in the vegetable stew with whole grains and a nice assortment of seasonal vegetables in a light broth. Desserts are small-bite trios—go for the Decadent Flavors with tastes of lemon cornbread with vanilla panna cotta, blueberry compote with yogurt gelato, and chocolate mousse with salted caramel sauce.

Breakfast is one of Disney's most interesting with pancakes, waffles, and French toast all made with multigrain. Breakfast cocktails made from a combination of fruit juices, a Ribose energy supplement, and organic vodka are for the truly brave, but those preferring alcoholic beverages after sunset will enjoy whole-leaf Pyramid teas and shade-grown organic Columbian coffee.

The Wave's wine list features all screw caps from the Southern Hemisphere including Argentina, Chili, New Zealand, Australia, and South Africa with about fifty selections by the glass. And don't neglect the restaurant's lounge, a winner with a large bar lit by twinkling lights, booth seating in the glowing blue cocktail lounge, and trendy cocktails (including antioxidant choices) as well as organic draft beer. A nice appetizer menu fills in during evening hours including lettuce wraps, crab nachos with black bean salsa, and miso marinated fresh fish and edamame salad as well as other interesting options. All in all, not Disney's best restaurant, but a nice choice for a low-key, wholesome meal. Something to think about after days of overindulgence at Walt Disney World.

**Best known for:** The daily sustainable fish served over edamame stew.

## SAMPLE MENU ITEMS

**Breakfast entrees:** Multigrain waffle with fruit compote and a splash of açai juice; eggs Benedict served with a choron sauce; spinach, tomato, and onion omelet; multigrain pancakes; spinach, tomato, and feta cheese scrambled eggs.

**Lunch entrees:** Mediterranean tuna salad, herb-crusted seared ahi tuna with green beans, potatoes, roasted red peppers, and olive toast; classic Reuben sandwich grilled on grain bread; Angus chuck bacon cheeseburger served on a multigrain roll; vegetarian sandwich with grilled tofu, zucchini, eggplant, roasted red pepper, and herb goat cheese served on grain bread; spice-crusted chicken salad with local greens, apples, and crispy polenta croutons.

**Dinner entrees:** Braised lamb shank with bulgur wheat–lentil stew and red wine sauce; grilled beef tenderloin cabernet jus, white bean mash, and locally grown teardrop tomatoes; linguini with Florida littleneck clams and rock shrimp with chunky tomato broth; cinnamon-rubbed grilled pork tenderloin with spoon bread, wilted rainbow chard, and corn nectar.

## *Yachtsman Steakhouse*

**Steak at the Yacht Club Resort. Dinner only; resort casual dress. Open daily 5:30 to 10 p.m. $$$–$$$$**

An atmospheric setting of white linen–topped tables, red leather chairs, and walls of framed pictures depicting the cattle drives of the Old West makes up for the loud hubbub of this bustling but pleasant dining room. Although steaks here are tender, I don't consider them remarkable, with the specialty being the New York strip with a flavorful brandy peppercorn sauce and a first-rate white cheddar potato gratin. Non-carnivores will be content with the fish choices, such as wild salmon with smoked bacon, corn nectar, and crushed avocado, or Florida grouper with jumbo lump crab and crab butter sauce. An herb-crusted rack of lamb is made nice and rich with an olive-cabernet reduction. Crisp-fried calamari and lobster bisque make for good starters, and yummy sides of creamed spinach and truffled macaroni and cheese are worth the calories. The international wine list, strong on California selections, is a *Wine Spectator* Award of Excellence winner.

# ORLANDO COUNTER SOCIETY

Fine dining in Orlando used to take place at a table. Not so now. In many of the city's restaurants, the best seats in the house are to be had at the counter, where a front-row perch overlooking the kitchen action along with food and drink is the order of the day.

## JIKO

Nab one of eight counter seats facing the kitchen's giant, twin clay ovens at one of Disney's most exciting restaurants. Nosh on the Taste of Africa, a trio of dips with soft, house-made naan, then move on to my favorite, the chermoula-roasted Tanglewood chicken served with yummy goat cheese potatoes.

## CALIFORNIA GRILL

This may be the most difficult ticket in town, but Disney's legendary dining mecca located high atop the Contemporary Resort offers two seats at the kitchen counter, four in front of Yoshie's sushi counter, and two facing the pastry counter (*yum!*). You can request your preference upon arrival, but nothing is guaranteed. Try to time your meal to see the Magic Kingdom fireworks from the restaurant's observation deck afterward.

## EMERIL'S

In front of the restaurant's exhibition kitchen are the eight seats of the Chef's Food Bar. Pick from the enormous wine display, then kibitz with the chefs and catch the up-close action of this exciting restaurant.

## TCHOUP CHOP

At this gorgeous restaurant's ten-seat Food Bar, guests may order off the regular menu or choose the $32, three-course Chef's

Tasting Menu. But those in the know pick their choice of an off-the-menu five-, six-, or seven course tasting menu that provides them with a better sampling of the restaurant's famous cuisine.

## FLYING FISH

Serious food devotees adore the whimsical surroundings at this Disney BoardWalk restaurant, but a lucky few can observe the creativity center stage at eleven seats around the bustling open kitchen with it's open-pit wood-fired grill. Dining choices include some of Disney's most inspired seafood or even sizzling steaks. Like California Grill, the counter is only by request upon arrival.

## CALA BELLA

Rosen Shingle Creek's signature restaurant serves Italian bistro fare in a lovely Tuscan atmosphere. Three counters seating four allow ringside views of the buzzing presentation kitchen where friendly waiters and a forthcoming chef will keep you entertained for hours.

*CARA'S TIP:* Ask to sit in the circular dining room overlooking Stormalong Bay, the Yacht Club Resort's incredible pool, as well as distant views of Epcot's Illuminations fireworks.

**Best known for:** Twenty-four ounce center-cut porterhouse with fresh cut fries and roasted garlic butter.

## SAMPLE MENU ITEMS

**Dinner entrees:** Twenty-ounce bone-in rib eye with fried onion and red wine butter; New York strip steak with peppercorn brandy sauce and potato gratin with Diamond white cheddar; roasted free-range chicken breast with wild mushroom risotto and truffle jus; filet mignon with mashed potatoes and red wine sauce; potato and leek ravioli bell pepper ragout, goat cheese fondue, and buttered spinach.

# BREAK FOR LUNCH

Because all of Disney's best resort restaurants are open only for dinner, here are some great lunchtime options away from the theme parks:

- Kona Café at the Polynesian Resort, just a monorail or boat ride away from the Magic Kingdom, for Pan Asian food overlooking the lobby's tropical profusion. Try the Asian chicken chop salad or the brothy Asian noodle bowl.

- Whispering Canyon Cafe at the Wilderness Lodge, a boat ride away from the Magic Kingdom, for wood-smoked skillets of ribs, chicken, and sausage or perhaps a pulled pork sandwich. At lunchtime the hootin' and hollerin' is at a minimum.

- The Wave at the Contemporary Resort, only one monorail stop away from the Magic Kingdom, where healthy, whole-grain options and a relaxed atmosphere are on the menu. Choose the fresh, sustainable fish on a bed of luscious corn and edamame stew.

- Grand Floridian Café, a boat or monorail ride from the Magic Kingdom for super salads and oversize sandwiches, not to mention a chance to check out Disney's flagship resort. If you're not dieting, try the Grand Sandwich, an open-faced hot turkey and ham wonder topped with rich Boursin cheese sauce and fried onion straws.

- Fulton's Crab House at Downtown Disney, where fresh seafood is served in a docked Mississippi riverboat. Good choices include a lump crab club sandwich or a cold seafood platter with king crab legs, seared tuna, shrimp, scallops, clams, and mussels served with cocktail and remoulade sauces.

- T-Rex at Downtown Disney for roaring dinosaurs, ice cave dining, and a fantastic, fun atmosphere that can't be beat. Try the tomato basil soup followed by yummy tribal fish tacos.

# The Best Downtown Disney Dining

## Bongos

**Cuban cuisine at Downtown Disney's West Side. Lunch and dinner; advance reservations sometimes taken the same day at (407) 828-0999; casual dress. Open Sunday through Thursday, 11 a.m. to 10:30 p.m., and Friday and Saturday, 11 a.m. to 11:30 p.m. $$–$$$$**

While certainly not the best Cuban you'll eat in this world, I've added this restaurant for its fun atmosphere and lively crowd. Easily spotted by its three-story pineapple, this cafe is one of Downtown Disney's most defining landmarks. A rose-colored version of 1950s Havana, it features soaring palm tree columns and walls glowing with glittering mosaics representing things Cuban: Latino music, tourism, and Bacardi rum. Sip on a mojito, Cuba's classic cocktail, while relaxing on conga drum stools at the bamboo bar (one of three). In the dining room, whopping platters of decent Cuban food are served with mounds of white rice and black beans. Vaca Frita, a savory concoction of citrus and garlic-marinated and roasted flank steak topped with grilled onions, is their most flavorful dish served with super sides of chimichurri sauce, garlicky yucca, and *moros* (rice and black beans). And on weekend nights the place goes *loco* courtesy of a Ricky Ricardo–style band blasting out pulsating music for dance floor revelers.

**Best known for:** Pollo Asado, a slow-roasted half chicken marinated in lemon, garlic, and white wine tomato Creole sauce.

**SAMPLE MENU ITEMS**

**Lunch and dinner entrees:** *Ropa vieja,* shredded beef in a light tomato sauce with onion and peppers; *churrasco,* tenderized skirt steak grilled and served with a side of chimichurri sauce; *zarzuela de mariscos,* sautéed lobster, shrimp, scallops, calamari, fish, baby clams, and mussels in Creole sauce; *arroz con pollo,* chicken breast served on a bed of yellow saffron rice; *masitas de puerco,* deep-fried pork chunks marinated in Cuban mojo served with grilled onions and moro rice.

## *Portobello*

**Italian cuisine at Downtown Disney's Marketplace. Lunch and dinner; call (407) WDW-DINE, or (407) 934-8888, for advance reservations; casual dress. Open daily 11:30 a.m. to 11 p.m. $$–$$$$**

A new chef and the transformation into an Italian countryside-style osteria have done wonders to improve this dining spot that for a few years was in a downhill decline. My favorite addition to the revamped menu is the assortment of antipasto available in small plates or as part of larger tastings. The paper thin crusts of the pizzas here are magnificent with a smoky flavor from the wood-burning ovens, and I adore the tangy wood-smoked trout spiked with capers, artichokes, and kalamata olives in a lemon butter sauce accompanied by crispy roasted potatoes sometimes served as a lunch special. Thankfully, old standards like the rigatoni calabrese with Italian sausage, olives, mushrooms, tomatoes, and escarole (a dish I fell in love with on my first visit here more than twenty years ago) are still around. Another new favorite: a chicken meatball pasta with perfect al dente orecchiette pasta in a light, flavorful broth speckled with spinach and oven-dried tomatoes topped with two giant-sized meatballs. On pleasant evenings ask to dine on the outdoor patio overlooking the lake.

**Best known for:** Menu items prepared in their wood burning oven.

### SAMPLE MENU ITEMS

**Lunch entrees:** Wood oven, pesto marinated chicken with fontina sandwich; linguini with clams in a white wine sauce; baked ricotta and spinach-filled crepes with tomato basil sauce; gulf shrimp with black linguini, garlic, tomatoes, and asparagus; bolognese beef and pork ragu with spinach tagliatelle; wood oven vegetarian sandwich with fresh mozzarella; *quattro formaggi* pizza with mozzarella, gorgonzola, parmigiano, fontina, and sun dried tomatoes.

**Dinner entrees:** Trattoria flat iron steak Parmesan-encrusted with roasted tomatoes and arugula; veal milanese breaded chop with baby arugula, shaved fennel, and red onion; grilled chicken with caramelized shallots and roasted potatoes; grilled Florida snapper, garlic spinach, and grilled lemon; bucatini thick noodles with tomato, guanciale, garlic, chile pepper, and olive oil; farfalle with wood roasted chicken, asparagus, snow peas, parmigiano cream sauce, and diced tomatoes.

## Raglan Road

**Irish food and music at Downtown Disney's Pleasure Island. Lunch and dinner; call (407) WDW-DINE for priority seating or online at raglanroadirishpub.com; casual dress. Open daily, lunch 11 a.m. to 3 p.m., dinner 3 to 11 p.m., bar menu served all day; traditional Irish music 6 p.m. until midnight (except Sunday). $$–$$$**

It's easy to imagine you're in the heart of Dublin at Raglan Road. While not luxury dining, it certainly can count as perhaps Disney's most entertaining dining spot. Come in for a drink, for a snack, or for a meal . . . whatever, just don't miss this terrifically fun place. Antique bars and Victorian furniture, Irish lighting, and wall coverings add to the great ambience, but the biggest draws are the musicians who provide authentic entertainment interspersed with Irish dancing. A shepherd's pie is a bit unusual in that it uses prime ground beef and lamb as filling with a bit of mashers on top, but the dish's best attribute is its savory gravy. Or the pan-sautéed then roasted salmon topped with a crispy, thin layer of smoked salmon and a maple glaze is always a good bet. Pints all around are the favored drink, but flights of whiskey as well as beer are a fun way to try out several different varieties.

**Best known for:** Fantastic Irish music and the fish and chips.

**SAMPLE MENU ITEMS**

**Lunch entrees:** Deep dish smoked haddock quiche with potato, leeks, and Dubliner cheese; Guinness sausage served with roasted balsamic red onion and tomato chutney on olive bread; triple decker Maine lobster with avocado, boiled egg, cilantro, lemon juice, and crisp Parma ham on toast; 5 oz. strip-loin served with balsamic roasted onions and tomato chutney on an olive loaf; St. James Irish smoked salmon blinis with a chive creme fraiche.

**Dinner entrees:** Ten-ounce sirloin topped with Irish whiskey glaze; whole lemon sole lightly sautéed in lemon butter; oven-roasted loin of ham with a Irish mist glaze served with braised cabbage and creamed potato; Guinness beef stew; chicken and sage banger with roasted carrot and potato mash; portobello mushroom cap burger filled with Dubliner cheese.

## T-Rex

**American food at Downtown Disney's Marketplace. Lunch and dinner; call (407) WDW-DINE or (407) 828-8739, for reservations; casual dress. Open Sunday through Thursday 11 a.m.–11 p.m., and Friday and Saturday 11 a.m. until midnight. $$–$$$**

From the folks that brought you Rainforest Café, their new concept is definitely a one up. From under the skeletal remains of a 125-foot-long argentinasaurus, enter a prehistoric world. Clouds of volcanic steam and the continual roar of giant Audio-Animatronics dinosaurs and wooly mammoths are occasionally interrupted by earth-shattering meteorite showers that get the entire place in an cosmic uproar. It's a great experience for kids, but even adults find it loads of fun. Parents actually encourage the kids to go dig in the dirt here because there's a children's fossil pit where a set of replica T-Rex bones is buried. Better yet, the food isn't half bad. Tribal Tacos are a healthy choice with grilled fish, grainy corn tortillas, and a yummy avocado cream sauce, or try the Red Earth Rigatoni with sausage, caramelized onions, and mushrooms in a rich red wine tomato cream sauce. The restaurant's velvety tomato basil soup can be added to any entree for a few dollars. Don't be surprised to find yourself chuckling at the smoking drinks that continually arrive at surrounding tables. For dessert the Meteor Bite, warm donut holes served with chocolate and caramel sauces, is the thing, but the Chocolate Extinction is one smoking (and I'm not kidding here) giant-size dessert that you may not be able to resist.

CARA'S TIP: The ice cave is the best dining room, flooded with changing purple and blue light, or the Shark Bar and Coral Reef dining area, topped with a giant octopus whose arms and tentacles move and sway with the action (request the jellyfish table for a larger party). The Geo-Tech Room has lots of action going on with its Kitchen of Fire surrounded by live flames. Avoid the back part of the restaurant where you'll find the less exciting Fern Forest and Sequoia Room.

**Best known for:** Roaring Audio-Animatronics dinosaurs and wild meteorite showers.

**SAMPLE MENU ITEMS**

**Lunch and dinner entrees:** Butter cracker and Parmesan crusted mahi mahi topped with gulf shrimp and lemon shallot butter; Parmesan crusted shrimp with linguini tossed in a pomodoro cream sauce; braised pork shank served with potato gnocchi sautéed with wild mushrooms, carrots, peas and demi-glace; rotisserie chicken salad sandwich with tarragon, celery, onions, toasted almonds, and mayonnaise served on a croissant; steak and cheese sandwich with sautéed onions, peppers, and mushrooms, topped with melted Monterey jack and Swiss cheeses on a toasted hoagie roll; massive mushroom ravioli simmered in a rich lobster cream sauce with roma tomatoes and fresh spinach.

## Wolfgang Puck Grand Café

**Contemporary cuisine at Downtown Disney's West Side. Lunch and dinner downstairs, dinner only upstairs; casual dress downstairs and smart casual upstairs; call (407) WDW-DINE, or (407) 938-9653, for advance reservations. Open Sunday and Monday 11:30 a.m. to 10:30 p.m.; Tuesday through Thursday 11:30 a.m. to 11 p.m.; Friday and Saturday 11:30 a.m. to 11:30 p.m.; upstairs dining begins daily at 6 p.m. $$–$$$ (downstairs); $$$–$$$$ (upstairs)**

Long known for its innovative cuisine, savory thin-crust pizza, and inventive pasta, the food here is always delicious and one of Downtown Disney's better dining bets. It's a four-restaurant complex featuring the Sushi Bar, a downstairs cafe with additional seating on the glass-enclosed patio, a Wolfgang Puck Express, and an upstairs dining room serving an ever-changing menu of fusion cuisine in a more formal, sophisticated atmosphere. With so many choices it's hard to decide which delectable dining venue to choose.

With its bold, contemporary design and energetic atmosphere, the downstairs cafe serves up Wolfgang Puck's specialties, such as wood-fired pizzas, fresh hand-tossed salads, zesty pastas, savory sandwiches, and decadent desserts (the carrot cake is the best). I'm torn between my two favorite entrees: the macadamia nut–crusted breast of chicken with a zesty papaya marmalade in a creamy light mustard sauce, or Grandma Puck's fettucini in the tastiest bolognese sauce ever (the addition of Alfredo sauce is the secret). Another great pasta choice for those who enjoy something on the light side is the rigatoni with Tuscan vegetables spiked with cherry tomatoes, mushrooms, and spring peas in a brothy, slightly spicy tomato sauce. Too bad a lack of decent wine choices by the glass almost forces you to pay for a bottle.

Upstairs, the Dining Room, created after the fashion of Wolfgang's famous Spago, offers white linen, bone china, fine wineglasses, subdued lighting, and a nice view from many tables of Downtown Disney and the lagoon. The noise level here can be irritating, but the service is exceptional. Two great starters include an organic baby beet, arugula salad adorned with Humboldt Fog goat cheese and crunchy toasted pistachios, or the pan seared scallops with braised lamb shoulder, made fabulous with the side of mascarpone polenta. A salmon entree was a disappointment—the much anticipated buckwheat noodles were overcooked and overwhelmed with a miso plum sauce, the salmon was farm raised, and not enough spice for my taste buds. But the high note is the ever-present "chinois style" rack of lamb spiced with a cilantro mint vinaigrette accompanied by creamy garlic mashed potatoes.

**Best known for:** Wolfgang's famous wood-fired pizzas.

### SAMPLE MENU ITEMS

**Café lunch and dinner entrees:** Four-cheese pizza; pumpkin ravioli with brown butter, port wine glaze, toasted pine nuts, aged Parmesan, and fried sage; grilled flat iron steak with truffle butter; center cut filet of salmon, pan roasted with garlic whipped potatoes, asparagus, and basil butter sauce; Asian hoisin barbecue ribs with crisp Asian slaw and spicy honey mustard dressing.

**Dining Room entrees:** Steamed seasonal fish Hong Kong style; lobster risotto; spicy beef goulash, braised beef with sautéed spaetzle; charbroiled beef filet with lobster crushed potatoes; hormone free Berkshire pork wienerschnitzel with warm potato salad, baby mache, and mustard caper sauce.

# ORLANDO FOR THE WINE AFICIONADO

There's an amazing array of restaurants in the Orlando area with truly impressive wine lists. Here are the best of the lot:

- **Victoria and Albert's at Disney's Grand Floridian Resort.** The diverse and quite extensive array of wine is also available in pairings with a glass served for each of six courses ($60 more per person).

- **Jiko at Disney's Animal Kingdom Lodge.** The most exclusive South African wine list in the country with the addition of a rich Reserve list.

- **Citricos at Disney's Grand Floridian Resort.** An acclaimed global list with the menu suggesting an accompanying wine for every item.

- **Artist Point at Disney's Wilderness Lodge.** An exclusive Pacific Northwest wine list, even boutique wines, with many available by the glass.

- **Vito's Chop House on International Drive.** With almost 1,000 labels, this is a wine lover's dream of a restaurant.

- **Capital Grille on International Drive.** Rightly proud of its off-the-charts list, it boasts more than 5,000 international and domestic bottles of wine. A "Captain's List" of rare wines features superb older vintages as well as small vineyard productions from around the world.

- **California Grill at Disney's Contemporary Resort.** One hundred California wines are offered by the glass accompanied by spectacular views.

- **The Wave at Disney's Contemporary Resort.** An entire list of screw cap wine from the Southern Hemisphere is the exceptional offering here.

# The Best Restaurants Near Disney

## *The Bull & Bear Steakhouse*

**Steaks at the Waldorf Astoria Orlando. Dinner only; call (407) 597-5500 for reservations or at www.opentable.com; smart casual dress. Open daily, 5 to 9:30 p.m. $$$–$$$$**

Not surprisingly, the dining room decor at the Waldorf Astoria's signature restaurant is sensational. Here the theme is old money from the dark mahogany and rich leather banquettes to the starched white tablecloths, gleaming goblets, and stellar service. A stylish and roomy bar is the place to begin where fine wine and high end cocktails are on the menu. For dinner there are quite a few hits and only a few misses: misses include the Caesar salad with it's unconventional and somewhat strange dressing, an uninspiring iceberg wedge salad, and over-garlicky creamed spinach; hits are the outstandingly tender prime Angus beef steaks, the exceptional pan-roasted Scottish salmon with a sweet yet zingy mustard glaze, the creamy butter mashed potatoes, and quite exquisite desserts. The berry tart with a thin, crispy crust got my attention as did the hot beignets, while others thought the vanilla bean cheesecake pushed the sugar-coated envelope.

*CARA'S TIP:* Those wanting a view should ask for a table in the glassed-in front room with vistas of the golf course.

**Best known for:** Prime Angus steaks and impeccable service.

**SAMPLE MENU ITEMS**

**Dinner entrees:** Colorado lamb; Heritage pork rib chop; herb roasted chicken with garlic confit and preserved lemon; lobster Newberg; cold water lobster tail; broiled diver scallops; fourteen-ounce Delmonico-cut rib eye; ten ounce American Kobe flat iron steak; twenty-ounce bone-in New York strip; twenty-four ounce porterhouse.

## *Hemingway's*

**Seafood at the Hyatt Regency Grand Cypress Resort. Dinner only; call (407) 239-3854 for reservations or at opentable.com; smart casual dress. Open Tuesday through Saturday 6 to 10 p.m. $$$–$$$$**

A lovely waterfall greets you on arrival at Hemingway's, where several small dining rooms adorned with brass hurricane lanterns and vases of fresh orchids are surrounded by long, narrow windows overlooking the lush grounds of the Hyatt Regency. The Key West atmosphere is enhanced by great food and welcoming waiters. Start with the tempura-crusted fried calamari, or the cold water oyster shooters with tomato water and vodka. You can't go wrong with the delicate crab cakes, the best in town, composed of only prime crabmeat and a smidgen of filler, or the exquisite lobster-crusted sea bass with a delicate yellow tomato emulsion. There's even a Kobe beef rib eye for meat lovers with the addition of a Boursin cheese crust (just in case it isn't rich enough already!). Everything is perfectly prepared, nothing overcooked, and most simply but tastily seasoned. Finish with the Dessert Shooter Sampler, or, for a throw-back to the sixties, the Key Lime Baked Alaska. After dinner retire to the adjoining Hurricane Lounge, the restaurant's cozy lounge.

*CARA'S TIP:* The front room is not as nice as the back two dining areas that overlook the giant boulders forming the waterfalls above the resort's fantasyland pool. Try to make it before dark to enjoy the view.

**Best known for:** Maryland-style crab cakes.

**SAMPLE MENU ITEMS**

**Dinner entrees:** Duet of lobster tails, butter poached with truffled angel hair pasta; mahi mahi with lump crab tomato fondue; filet mignon, applewood smoked bacon, lobster macaroni and cheese; herb-basted diver scallops, creamy shrimp risotto, smoked tomato vinaigrette; Alaskan king crab legs, lemon herb butter; shrimp ravioli, white truffled foam, sweet corn emulsion.

## Old Hickory Steakhouse

**American cuisine at the Gaylord Palms Resort. Dinner only; call (407) 586-1600 for reservations; smart casual dress. Open daily, 5:30 to 10 p.m. $$$–$$$$**

The setting alone is worth the price of a meal here, but the outstanding food makes it tops on my list. Dine in a rustic hideaway in the Everglades area of the Gaylord Palms Resort perched above a misty faux swamp filled with the sound of croaking frogs and the flash of fireflies. Soft lighting

# ORLANDO'S CELEBRITY CHEFS

Las Vegas isn't the only city with celebrity chefs. Several notable Orlando restaurants hold that claim to fame.

- Normans at the Ritz Carlton Grande Lakes features Chef Norman Van Aken's "new world" cuisine, a fusion of Latin and Caribbean recipes in a divine setting. Tried and true favorites include filet of Key West yellowtail on a "belly" of garlicky mashed potatoes and the roasted pork Havana with 21st-century mole served with golden Haitian grits.

- Primo at the JW Marriott Grande Lakes is Chef Melissa Kelly's outpost of her famed Maine restaurant featuring home grown and organic vegetables with an Italian twist. Try favorites such as sautéed scaloppini of pork saltimbocca in a sage infused mushroom-Madeira jus, and don't miss Orlando's best dessert, Primo's zeppole, hot Italian donuts tossed in cinnamon and sugar.

- Bluezoo at the Walt Disney World Dolphin is Todd English's stunning version of a hip seafood restaurant with the bonus of a fabulous raw bar, "dancing" rotisserie roasted fish, and miso glazed sea bass.

- Emeril Lagasse boasts two restaurants in Orlando, both at Universal Orlando, and both something to write home about. At Emeril's Orlando you'll find Lagasse's signature New Orleans cuisine, and at Tchoup Chop a bold twist to Asian Pacific food.

- Wolfgang Puck brings his creative cuisine to Downtown Disney. Downstairs the Cafe offers all Wolfgang's favorites such as wood-fired gourmet pizza, Austrian-inspired classics like wienerschnitzel and spicy beef goulash, and pumpkin ravioli. In the more formal upstairs Dining Room are Spago creations like the much-lauded "chinois style" lamb rack or an Austrian three-course tour.

- Roy Yamaguchi, the pioneer of Hawaiian fusion cuisine, has an outpost of his Roy's restaurant on Sand Lake Road in Orlando. Here you'll find exciting seafood in creative sauces and Roy's renowned signature dishes like blackened ahi, macadamia nut crusted mahi mahi, and melting hot chocolate soufflé.
- Cat Cora, of *Iron Chef* fame, has opened Kouzzina at Disney's BoardWalk featuring family Mediterranean recipes. Try the delicious fisherman's stew or the already famous lamb burger.

permeates the restaurant's interior, but the top tables are those outside on the deck. Service is warm and professional, and the chef seems to know that a good restaurant needs more than just great atmosphere—course after flawlessly prepared and plated course is nothing but perfection.

Don't eat too much of the fabulous sourdough bread with its accompanying sundried tomato and kalamata olive spread in order to save room for even better things to come. For starters, opt for the rich warm pear gorgonzola tart of flaky layers of phyllo, sweet pears, and tangy gorgonzola topped with vinaigrette-tossed frisee and crispy bits of bacon. Those with an adventurous personality really should try the alligator lasagna, something certainly not found on most menus, with its rich, dark sauce spiked with alligator tenderloin. As for steak, I believe some of the best to be had in Orlando can be found here in the tenderloin of American buffalo or the grass-fed filet, both tasting like a steak really should, juicy and tender with a slightly earthy flavor. Order yours with the jumbo lump crabmeat gratinée topping for a true over-the-top meal. Less to my liking is the wild mushroom-crusted ostrich, definitely an acquired taste. An opulent wine choice is the Château Lassegue, St. Emillion Grand Cru.

If steak isn't your thing, there's plenty more to round out the menu, including lobster tail, rack of lamb, sea scallops, a daily fish, even venison medallions with huckleberry sauce. And for true decadence try the lobster mac 'n' cheese. A selection of international artisanal cheeses is a wonderful way to end the meal, but you must, and I mean *must* opt for the most perfect Grand Marnier soufflé this side of Paris.

**Best known for:** The sixteen-ounce certified Black Angus naturally aged prime center-cut New York strip steak.

## SAMPLE MENU ITEMS

**Dinner entrees:** All steaks are served with your choice of béarnaise, au poivre (my favorite), Bordelaise, or diabolo sauces; twenty-four-ounce porterhouse steak; surf and turf of beef tenderloin and lobster tail; twenty-one-ounce bone-in rib eye steak; rack of lamb; sea scallops with apple cider reduction; twin medallions of venison with huckleberry sauce; lobster served with drawn butter and lemon; boneless free-range chicken with citrus Chablis sauce.

## Zen

**Pan-Asian cuisine at the Omni Orlando Resort at Champions-Gate. Dinner only; call (407) 390-6664 or online at www.open table.com; smart casual dress. Open Tuesday through Sunday, 6 to 10 p.m. $$–$$$$**

Cool and sophisticated, this hip restaurant at the Omni ChampionsGate Resort is just a twenty-minute drive from Walt Disney World. Although the restaurant labels itself as pan fusion, the food is a slight gourmet twist on Chinese standards with the addition of a great sushi and sake bar. A glam dining room, it's filled with Asian photography, bamboo centerpieces, rice paper screens, contemporary black furnishings, bamboo curtains, and Japanese lanterns. Food may be ordered a la carte, but the Zen Experience is the way to go, offering a tasting-size portion of more than twenty menu items: sweet corn with chicken soup or hot and sour soup is followed by the best part of the meal, an appetizer sampler of crispy chicken spring rolls, sweet potato tempura, crispy scallops with spicy mayonnaise, salt-and-pepper calamari, Hunan dumplings, and more. Entree portions begin with small platters of Szechwan orange beef, General Tso chicken, stir-fry lobster in ginger sauce, cashew salmon, sweet and sour pork, sautéed shrimp in a black pepper sauce, and the list goes on. Believe it or not, it's also accompanied by sides of asparagus, Szechwan green beans, tofu, and fried or steamed rice. Those with smaller appetites should consider the excellent crispy duck served with crepes, hoisin sauce (request a bit of tongue-searing chili be added for additional zing), and a side bowl of thinly julienned cucumber and scallions—just ask that it not be overcrisped for optimal flavor. End your whopper of a meal with an unusual dessert, fried banana cheesecake.

**Best known for:** The Zen Experience.

**SAMPLE MENU ITEMS**

**Dinner entrees:** Crispy aromatic Szechwan duck served with crepes, spring onion, and cucumber; seafood bird nest with shrimp, scallops and lobster; eggplant with hot garlic sauce; salt-and-pepper shrimp; sautéed shrimp, black pepper, crisp spinach; lo mein with vegetables, pork, chicken, or shrimp; Szechwan style beef tenderloin with onion.

## The Best Universal Orlando Dining

### Finnegan's Bar and Grill

**Irish food at Universal Studios. Lunch and dinner; call (407) 224-3613 for reservations. $–$$$**

Although Lombard's Landing is considered the premier restaurant at Universal Studios, stop here for a pint, better food, and a bit of live entertainment. The casual, boisterous surroundings of an Irish pub make this the favored establishment for partygoers. Roost around an aged, dark-paneled bar with a pint in hand, reveling in the live music (not necessarily Irish) amid old family photos and memorabilia. A full pub menu—consisting of hearty, traditional Irish food along with some American choices—is served in the bar as well as in the adjoining, more serene dining room of scuffed flooring, wooden booths, dingy pressed tin ceilings, and vintage sports memorabilia.

**Best known for:** Great Cornish pasties and a yard of ale served in a glass so tall you'll need to stand up to drink it.

**SAMPLE MENU ITEMS**

**Lunch and dinner entrees:** Celtic chicken club salad; shepherd's pie; North Atlantic baked cod fish; corned beef and cabbage; bangers and mash; Guinness beef stew; corned beef, sautéed onions, and Swiss cheese served on a pretzel roll; steak sandwich topped with sautéed peppers and onions; gardenburger.

## *Mythos Restaurant*

**Contemporary American cuisine at Islands of Adventure. Lunch (dinner only in busier seasons); call (407) 224-3613 for reservations. $$**

Inside this stone sea cave of a dining room are dreamlike, undulating rock walls interspersed with bubbling streams and fountains, carved ironwork railings, and red velvet chairs and banquettes. The food is exceptional by park standards, certainly worth a gold star in Universal's crown. You'll never go wrong trying the excellent Cedar Plank Salmon accompanied by rich-tasting mashers and crisp asparagus. Or even the basic burger here is wonderful, char-grilled and giant-sized with a slab of cheese and crispy applewood smoked bacon adorning each one.

**Best known for:** Cedar Plank Salmon with citrus butter.

**SAMPLE MENU ITEMS**

**Lunch and dinner entrees:** Daily pizza special; tempura shrimp sushi; crab sliders; baby spinach salad with fresh blueberries, hard cooked egg, blue cheese crumbles, and hot bacon vinaigrette; chicken and wild mushrooms with imported penne pasta; risotto of the day; buffalo barbecue fried chicken wrap; chicken a'la Oscar with lump crab, mashed potato, chef's vegetables, and a duo of sauces.

# The Best CityWalk and Universal Resort Dining

## *Bice*

**Italian food at Portofino Bay Hotel. Dinner only; call (407) 503-1415 for reservations or online at www.opentable.com; business casual dress. Open daily 5:30 to 10 p.m. $$$–$$$$**

Everything about this place says good taste with its combination of modern chic and understated elegance. Refined Northern Italian comfort food, starchy white linens, frescoed ceilings, live piano music, massive floral arrangements, contemporary wood and marble flooring, soft lighting, and Johnny-on-the-spot service adds up to one stellar experience. *Primi piatti* dishes of delicate ravioli stuffed with braised beef short rib and spinach in a mushroom marsala sauce, or the excellent spinach and ricotta tortellini swimming in a luscious butter and sage sauce prove to be excellent beginnings. Or splurge by ordering the whole lobster perched on a bed of greens and vegetables tossed with a tangy shallot vinaigrette. The standout dishes are fall-apart osso bucco with creamy saffron risotto and, on a lighter note, an Italian seafood chowder, simple, memorable, and startlingly fresh. When the weather's nice, choose alfresco dining on the romantic terrace overlooking the piazza and bay.

**Best known for:** Braised veal shank with saffron risotto.

**SAMPLE MENU ITEMS**

**Dinner entrees:** Pappardelle with mozzarella cheese and fresh basil in a tomato cream sauce; tagliatelle with mixed mushrooms, sweet peas, and proscuitto in a creamy sauce with truffle oil; pan-seared salmon with grilled scallop stuffed with crabmeat and served in a brandy lobster sauce; oven roasted rack of lamb with pesto mash in a port wine demi-glaze; grilled beef tenderloin with grilled portobello mushroom and gorgonzola demi sauce; prosciutto and sage-wrapped chicken breast with sautéed seasonal vegetables.

## Emeril's

**Contemporary New Orleans cuisine at CityWalk; lunch and dinner; call (407) 224-2424 for reservations or online at www .opentable.com; business casual dress. Open daily, 11:30 a.m. to 2 p.m. and 5:30 to 10 p.m. (Friday and Saturday until 11 p.m.) $$$–$$$$**

Reminiscent of the New Orleans warehouse district, this vibrant dining spot is comprised of exposed pipe, stone walls adorned with contemporary art, sleek hardwood flooring, a circular slate bar, and a two-story wine wall boasting a *Wine Spectator* Best of Award of Excellence.

The beautifully presented and innovative Cajun-Creole cuisine explodes with flavor and creativity. I can never resist starting with the smoked wild and exotic mushrooms in a home-cured tasso cream sauce over angel-hair pasta, but for something a bit lighter and screaming with flavor pick New Orleans' traditional dish of barbeque shrimp. The spinach salad is another great starter with crispy bacon, toasted pine nuts, goat cheese, dried cranberries, and a sherry-herb vinaigrette. If the filet au

poivre, made delicious with green peppercorns, is on the menu it's a definite, sided with divine mashers. The house specialty, andouille-crusted
red snapper, is not one of my favorites—there's just too much going on at
once with no one flavor standing out.

The best seats in the house are in the Julia and Tchoupitoucas Room,
a glass-enclosed space facing CityWalk, or the coveted counter seats
perched in front of the exhibition kitchen. But the real secret is the
upstairs Cigar Room, an intimate three-table nook perched high above
CityWalk; just request it when making your reservations. This is one restaurant that will leave you yearning for another night and yet another
terrific meal. It is simply the best.

*CARA'S TIP:* Although no one would raise an eyebrow, you won't
feel comfortable in park clothes. If you must come without changing, try
perching at the bar for your meal (the easiest way to eat without a reservation). At lunchtime, use CityWalk's valet parking and have the restaurant
validate your ticket (good for up to two hours).

**Best known for:** Andouille-crusted Texas redfish in a Creole meunière
sauce.

## SAMPLE MENU ITEMS

**Lunch entrees:** White truffle flatbread, confit baby portobello mushrooms, diced chives and shaved Gruyère cheese; herb-dijon crusted
Atlantic salmon, endive, white asparagus, artesian mixed greens, and
citrus-herb vinaigrette; build-your-own burger (all-natural beef, turkey,
or portobello mushroom) with truffle *pommes frites;* roasted chicken with
buttermilk-chive mashed potatoes and collard greens.

**Dinner entrees:** Chili glazed rotisserie half duck, wild mushroom bread
pudding, wilted rapini and red currant reduction sauce; quail two ways
(rock shrimp and andouille stuffed with smoked quail jus and fresh thyme
marinated breast), confit onion-spinach salad with sunnyside up quail
egg; seared Chilean sea bass, fall squash-English pea risotto, porcini
mushroom-red wine butter, apple-sage chutney, and shaved black summer truffles; cast iron–seared fourteen-ounce milk-fed veal chop, herb,
garlic, and soy roasted seasonal mushrooms, prosciutto wrapped white
asparagus, and port wine poached fig reduction.

## 🌿 Emeril's Tchoup Chop

**Contemporary Asian-Polynesian cuisine at the Royal Pacific Resort; dinner only; call (407) 503-2467 for reservations or online at www.opentable.com; business casual dress. Open daily 5:30 to 10 p.m. (Friday and Saturday 5:15 until 11 p.m.) $$–$$$$**

Think Pacific Rim with Emeril's flair in a drop-dead gorgeous setting. Begin with a mai tai (the best I've had outside of Hawaii) at the restaurant's superchic bar while gazing in awe at the contemporary Polynesian setting of massive cast-glass chandeliers, a Zen-inspired water wall, and the restaurant's centerpiece, a dreamy zero-edge river rock reflecting pool filled with lotus blossoms. What's more, the food is terrific! And the kitchen, under the directions of a new chef direct from Roy's Orlando, has kicked it up a notch or two. Try the delectable, cone-shaped, wasabi cured lomi lomi salmon napoleon layered with avocado, tomatoes, and crème fraîche with crisp wontons for scooping. Beer-braised short ribs are fall-apart tender painted with a cabernet reduction, and the caramelized onions mixed in with the mashed potatoes as an accompaniment are a stroke of genius. Giant-sized seared scallops are plump and tender and, once again, the side dish reigns with an amazing roasted-corn risotto that's sweet, creamy, and most unusual. And everyone's favorite dessert is the somewhat stiff but oh-so-tasty banana cream pie topped with chocolate shavings and caramel sauce. Personally I'd go for a slice of the warm pineapple upside down cake served with caramelized ginger ice cream, or the baby ice cream sandwiches made with yummy white chocolate macadamia nut cookies and dabs of dulce de leche.

*CARA'S TIP:* Self-parking (a bit of a walk) is free. Valet parking is $5 at the Pacifica Ballroom Entrance next to the restaurant. Both require a stamped ticket from the restaurant. Request one of the booths surrounding the reflecting pool.

**Best known for:** One of Orlando's most beautiful restaurants with fantastic food as a bonus.

### SAMPLE MENU ITEMS

**Dinner entrees:** Smoked sea salt grilled filet of beef tenderloin, garlic potatoes, green peppercorn sake reduction sauce; roasted Maple Leaf

# A NIGHT ON THE TOWN

Heavily concentrated around International Drive is a wealth of fun lounges and wine bars for evening entertainment, some relaxing and laid back, others filled with locals and tourists alike.

**Blue Martini.** Wealthy hipsters keep the cocktails flowing at this very popular local hangout in the Mall at Millenia where there are more than thirty martini choices, live entertainment, a very local crowd, and small plate meals. 4200 Conroy Road in Orlando.

**ICEBAR Orlando.** This bar on International Drive is certainly an unusual concept. The 27-degree Chill Lounge is made of floor-to-ceiling ice including the furniture. For $20 per person slip on a thermal cape and gloves for a 45-minute time period (the non-ice part of the bar is free), which includes a Grey Goose vodka drink or a non-alcoholic drink for those under twenty-one (guests of all ages are welcome). 8967 International Drive.

**Grand Cru.** It's a retail shop in the day and wine bar by night. Offerings include about ten wines by the glass or just choose a bottle for retail price off the shelf and add a reasonable $3 corkage. Small plate offerings like artisanal cheeses, flat bread, chips with gorgonzola, and shrimp wrapped in jalapeno jack cheese and bacon will curb your hunger. 7730 West Sand Lake Road.

**The Grape.** A very purple space at Pointe Orlando on International Drive offers 120 wines for tasting as well as wine flights and bottles. An extensive small plate, salad, and sandwich menu adds to the fun. Don't leave without trying the delectable chocolate fondue. 9101 International Drive.

**Press 101 Sandwich & Wine Bar.** An elegant ladies-who-lunch sandwich shop by day and a wine bar by night with a menu of salads, sandwiches, and flatbreads. 7600 Dr. Phillips Boulevard.

**Vines Grille and Wine Bar.** At this original Restaurant Row wine bar, come for a glass of wine with appetizers, then move to the small but sophisticated dining room offering dry-aged prime beef, American Kobe steak, wild caught fish and seafood, all-natural chicken, lamb and Kurabuto pork accompanied by locally grown organic produce. Nightly jazz performances makes this one of the most enjoyable spots around. 7533 W Sand Lake Road.

**Fuego by Sosa Cigars.** Mellow out at this tiny spot at Downtown Disney where patrons sip on martinis and puff away on fat cigars. Also available are wine, cocktails, beer, and coffees.

**Raglan Road.** This entertaining pub at Downtown Disney is a winner with live Irish music and dancing and a full menu of Irish specialties (avoid Sundays when the band takes a breather).

Farms duck breast, pastrami confit duck leg, bok choy, bell peppers, sweet onion, steamed rice and spicy basil sauce; garlic grilled black tiger shrimp on Chinese style noodle cake with a lemongrass infused wild mushroom crèma; pepper grilled yellowfin tuna steak, wild mushroom-pea tendril stir fry, charred scallion ginger reduction; Moo Shu–style vegetable plate with tempeh, assorted stir fry vegetables, sesame pancakes, and vegetable fried rice; herb broiled Ashley Farms free range chicken breast, kimchee fried rice, Chinese hot mustard teriyaki sauce.

## Mama Della's Ristorante

**Italian cuisine at Portofino Bay Hotel. Dinner only; call (407) 503-3463 for reservations; casual dress. Open daily, 5:30 to 10 p.m. $$–$$$$**

Dine well at this highly underrated restaurant on Old World, hearty Italian food presented in the festive atmosphere of Mama Della's home. Mama herself roams the restaurant, which is decorated in gaudy, flowery wallpaper and mismatched chairs, encouraging guests to "eat, eat." Who can resist beginning with *fontina fritto,* fried aged fontina cheese served with oven roasted tomatoes, or the plump mussels with roasted garlic in a white wine sauce. While excellent strolling musicians entertain, feast on a rustic dish of eggplant napoleon with complex layers of breaded eggplant, buffalo mozzarella, oven dried tomatoes, baby spinach, and shiitake mushrooms sitting atop a pool of red pepper coulis—a surprise in every bite. Or perhaps the succulent *bisteca alla florentina* with caramelized onions and yummy wilted greens. An excellent Italian, French, and California wine list is another plus with many good choices by the glass. There's lovely outdoor dining on the piazza, great on a balmy night.

**Best known for:** *Frutti di mare* with grilled shrimp, scallops, and corvina with roasted tomato sauce, linguini, spinach and garlic.

**SAMPLE MENU ITEMS**

**Dinner entrees:** Lasagna made with traditional béchamel and meat sauce; veal medallions with lemon caper sauce; sliced chicken with cappellini, Italian bacon, sun-dried tomatoes, Parmesan, and spinach; spaghetti with veal and sirloin meatballs with sauce bolognese; seared wild river steelhead trout almondine with citrus butter sauce and mascarpone polenta.

## The Best Restaurants Near Universal
### Cala Bella

**Italian cuisine at the Rosen Shingle Creek Resort. Dinner only; call (407) 996-3663 for reservations; casual resort dress. Open daily 5:30 to 10 p.m. $$$–$$$$**

Rosen Shingle Creek's signature restaurant is elegantly edgy with high arched ceilings, rough hewn beams, low lighting, and touches of Tuscany. A 2010 AAA Four Diamond Award winner, meals begin with an outstanding sun-dried tomato tapenade accompanied by an addictive gorgonzola flatbread. Dinner might start with a rich arugula and gorgonzola salad topped with yellow tomato vinaigrette, chopped Mission figs, and sweet candied pecans, or perhaps a half-order of a super creamy risotto, perfectly finished with fennel-spiked sausage and sweet caramelized onions. The roasted eggplant with tender shrimp is made tasty with fresh basil, ripe tomatoes, and pungent grilled lemon. Combining classic with cutting edge, the crispy-skinned red snapper is cooked Sicilian style with an outstanding sauce of crushed tomatoes, olives, capers, and a bit of chili spice; and the lamb chops are doused in herbs then roasted perfectly pink with a rich rosemary scented marsala sauce. Singles should grab a seat ringside at one of three presentation counters facing the kitchen where friendly waiters and a communicative chef fill you in on all the details.

**Best known for:** Marinated herb-roasted lamb chops with pickled garlic and shallots with rosemary minted marsala.

### SAMPLE MENU ITEMS

**Dinner entrees:** Grilled Tuscan veal chops with warm tomato olive vinaigrette; seafood pescatore with lobster tail, littleneck clams, mussels, shrimp, and scallops braised in a spicy saffron tomato broth served with pappardelle; asiago chicken with sun-dried tomatoes, fried wild mushrooms, asiago cheese, and Chianti reduction; orecchiette with pan-seared diver scallops, fire-roasted tomatoes, kalamata olives, fresh spinach, and lobster butter; pappardelle with Five Diamond Harris Ranch prime New York strip and tomato ragu.

## The Capital Grille

**Steakhouse at 9101 International Drive in Orlando. Lunch and dinner; call (407) 370-4392 or online at www.capitalgrille.com for reservations; business casual. Open for lunch Monday through Friday, 11:30 a.m. to 3 p.m., for dinner Sunday through Thursday, 5 to 10 p.m., Friday and Saturday until 11 p.m. $$$–$$$$**

Superb steaks in an upscale steakhouse setting are the claim to fame of this growing and popular national chain found at Pointe Orlando on International Drive. The noise level is unfathomably loud, but deep mahogany wood and soft leather booths create an old-school ambience that's hard to beat. Just don't expect the hush-hush of a private club—this place is high energy, always bustling in the evenings with tourists and locals alike. Service is almost overly attentive, but it's unpretentious and quite nice for a change.

It's almost mandatory to begin with the garlic butter sautéed calamari tossed with hot cherry peppers and a squeeze of lemon, a definite twist on a normally ho-hum appetizer. Or if not, the French onion soup could possible be the best on the planet. Then a chopped salad or fat, crisp wedge of iceberg topped with tangy blue cheese dressing and crisp bacon keeps the ball rolling. Although the dry aged, flame-licked chops here are choice, not prime, they are quite remarkable, but pricey, cooked to perfection and tender as can be. I still believe that the super rich, Kona crusted dry aged sirloin topped with caramelized shallot butter is perhaps the best choice. Big appetites should opt for the filet Oscar crowned with lump crabmeat and béarnaise. Those preferring seafood have several great choices, the best being the seared swordfish with lemon butter sauce. And don't miss the creamed spinach. For a sweet ending the coconut cream pie topped with fresh whipped cream and drizzled with caramel is rich but definitely worth the calories. Remember that splitting appetizers, sides, even entrees, is the smart thing to do since everything on the menu is super-sized. Lunch is a lighter option; on my last visit a superb grilled shrimp chopped salad with seven types of vegetables, olive vinaigrette, and Parmesan croutons was exactly what I was looking for. And a daily special of king crab salad with remoulade was unforgettable.

The mammoth wine list, a *Wine Spectator* Best of Award of Excellence, is off the charts with more than 5,000 international and domestic bottles of wine. A "Captains List" features superb older vintages as well as small vineyard productions from around the world.

**Best known for:** Kona crusted dry aged sirloin with caramelized shallot butter.

## SAMPLE MENU ITEMS

**Lunch entrees:** Grilled tuna steak salad with basil and roasted red pepper vinaigrette; Maine lobster salad; lobster and crab burger; roasted half chicken with secret red rub spices; dry aged sirloin steak.

**Dinner entrees:** Dry-aged twenty-four-ounce porterhouse; filet Oscar served with steamed asparagus spears, colossal lump crab, drizzled with housemade béarnaise; double cut lamb rib chops; dry aged steak au poivre with a Courvoisier cream sauce; veal chop with Roquefort butter; broiled fresh lobster; sushi-grade sesame seared tuna with gingered rice.

# ORLANDO'S BEST SUNDAY BRUNCHES

- Vineyard Grill at the Ritz-Carlton offers a spectacular champagne brunch (not offered in the summer months) with interactive cooking stations, live music, and unlimited champagne.

- La Coquina at the Hyatt Regency Grand Cypress is rightly famous for its seasonal champagne brunch. Head down to the kitchen to choose from a dozen entree choices along with groaning tables filled with cheese, sushi, caviar, eggs Benedict, waffles, and more, or made to order entrees, finishing with a huge assortment of desserts. That along with unlimited champagne. Not available in the summer months.

- Villa De Flora at the Gaylord Palms. With over one hundred items to choose from, this Sunday spectacular features an assortment of egg dishes including an omelet station, waffles and French toast, salmon cakes, coq au vin, fresh salads, roasted pork and prime rib carving station, boiled shrimp, chocolate fondue, cookies and ice cream, cakes, strawberry shortcake, and tarts.

- House of Blues at Downtown Disney. Head here for a New Orleans style gospel brunch featuring inspiring music along with an eat-your-fill of down-home cooking including jambalaya, red beans and rice, cheese grits, biscuits and gravy, chilled prawns with cocktail sauce, and more.

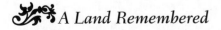 A Land Remembered

Steakhouse at Rosen Shingle Creek. Lunch and dinner; call (407) 996-3663 for reservations; resort casual. Open daily for dinner, 5:30 to 10 p.m. $$$$

If you want to break away from the oftentimes great but found everywhere chain steakhouse, try this upscale gem at Rosen Shingle Creek's clubhouse. The deluxe digs are not your typical boisterous steakhouse; here there's peace and quiet in stylish Western-style surroundings overlooking the resort's golf course. At this AAA Four Diamond Award winner, you'll feast on remarkable steak, seafood, and more with super service as a bonus. Begin with one of the sampler platters, served either chilled or hot. The cold platter features such delicacies as a somewhat spicy steak tartare, lemon myrtle encrusted ahi tuna seared rare, steakhouse sushi prepared with prime rib topped with horseradish and truffle sauce, and giant shrimp cocktail simmered in Gator Drool beer with a trio of dipping sauces. The hot platter's cornmeal-crusted oysters on a bed of rich and creamy spinach-cheese fondue is phenomenal, accompanied by frogs' legs topped with a mango-rum glaze, no-filler crab cakes with a red chili pepper glaze, and creamy warm brie with earthy portobello mushrooms. The gator stew with white beans is interesting but a bit strange; more to my liking is a phenomenal grilled hearts of romaine salad topped with creamy artisan goat cheese and dressed in an unusual palm sugar vinaigrette.

Now I know you are asking how in the world there could possibly be room for anything else, but with food this inspiring you must move on. An organic Harris Ranch Prime Black Angus bone-in rib eye is marvelously tender and flavorful, served with a choice of sauce, the sauce Diane or the au poivre being the best. There are several seafood choices for non-meat lovers including a divine cold-water lobster tail. A side of caramelized Vidalia onions or sautéed wild mushrooms are great accompaniment choices, but do not neglect to order the baked sweet potato mash with honey butter. The best dessert on the menu is the crispy-crusted, warm bread pudding, this one made with port wine reduction topped with rum raisin ice cream and crème anglaise—yum!

A well-rounded wine list offers plenty in all price ranges—I enjoyed a reasonably priced Lyeth Meritage but a $520 bottle of Chateau Margaux '01 from the restaurant's "Rare and Endangered Species" list of allocated, limited production, large format wines would have done nicely as well.

**SAMPLE MENU ITEMS**

**Dinner entrees:** Lamb Tequesta, dry rubbed with roasted garlic, stone ground mustard; spit roasted free range chicken, tangerine and thyme butter; braised short ribs, garlic mashed potatoes; Chiefland porterhouse smothered with Vidalia onion gravy; châteaubriand for two, twenty-ounce prime filet carved tableside, béarnaise sauce, garlic mashed potatoes, wild mushrooms, grilled asparagus; cedar plank & broiled fresh catch of the day with roasted cipollini onion and chive butter.

## MoonFish

**Seafood, steaks, and sushi at 7525 West Sand Lake Road. Dinner only; call (407) 363-7262 for reservations; business casual. Open Sunday through Thursday, 4:30 to 10:30 p.m. and Friday and Saturday until 11 p.m. $$–$$$$**

Locals flock to this happening restaurant on Sand Lake Road for fish fusion with an Asian accent and oversize portions of excellent food. Brick and dark wood walls lined with booths, crisp white tablecloths, and a bustling open kitchen are what you'll find in the main dining room; don't get delegated to the cramped dining area off the bar or you'll leave unhappy. Most everything is pretty darn fabulous, but it seems like half the plates that leave the kitchen are topped with sizzling steaks and a side of lobster tail. Don't bother ordering the seafood cocktail appetizer, really a ceviche that is a bit too sweet and not quite spicy enough. Instead opt for the crispy almond fried lobster tails, something that you definitely won't find on your run-of-the-mill menus, or perhaps the delicately flavored fried green tomatoes. If you want to work for your dinner, the crispy whole fish is quite dramatic and delicious in a sweet-sour sauce with loads of bones. Entrees are a la carte, so share one of the giant sides like blue cheese mashed potatoes, wok-steamed ginger veggies, delicious creamed spinach, or oak-grilled asparagus, and forget the forgettable house salad. Desserts are super-sized; consider ordering one for the entire table. The aquarium-themed bar is great if you just want to stop in for super sushi and a cocktail.

**Best known for:** Hong Kong sea bass steamed in dry sherry and served over sautéed fresh spinach, accompanied by a honey soy drizzle.

### SAMPLE MENU ITEMS

**Dinner entrees:** Bamboo steamer of lobster tail, king crab, fish, shrimp, and steamed fresh vegetables; Hawaiian style double chicken breast;

MoonFish bouillabaisse; Oscar mignon (blue crab, soft shell crab, asparagus, and hollandaise); Shanghai duck breast (sesame, soy, ginger, pineapple marinade); wok-fried soft shell crab; crispy Szechuan yellowtail snapper.

##  Normans

**Contemporary New World Cuisine at the Ritz-Carlton Grande Lakes. Dinner only; call (407) 393-4333 or online at www.open table.com; resort casual. Open Sunday through Thursday, 6 to 10 p.m. and Friday and Saturday, 6 to 10:30 p.m. $$$$**

For fine dining in ultrasophisticated surroundings, head to celebrity chef-restaurateur Norman Van Aken's outpost at the Ritz-Carlton Grande Lakes Resort. The seductive, octagonal dining room is accented by caramel-hued marble walls and floors, lofty windows covered in dreamy raw silk drapery, leather banquettes in warm black and chocolate brown, and iron chandeliers with Venetian glass shades. Service is attentive and the food divine in this AAA Four Diamond award-winning restaurant, and the exciting menu consists of an extraordinary fusion of Caribbean, Southern U.S., Latin American, and Asian cuisines. For starters the creamy cracked corn chowder is always available, but I prefer the yucca-stuffed crispy shrimp, in particular the accompanying sour orange mojo and habanero tartar sauce. Norman's signature dishes are here: grilled pork Havana in mole sauce, and the oh-so-popular Key West yellowtail in citrus butter sauce. Or consider one of the excellent ever-changing seasonal entrees; a delectable Florida black grouper "a la Veracruzana" was a clear winner spiked with olives, capers, and tomatoes. Those with smaller appetites may want to consider a light meal in the adjoining cocktail salon where anything can be ordered off the regular menu. Whatever you choose, you really can't go wrong here at one of the best dining spots in Orlando.

**Best known for:** Pan-cooked fillet of Key West yellowtail on a "belly" of garlicky mashed potatoes with citrus butter.

### SAMPLE MENU ITEMS

**Dinner entrees:** Bacon wrapped free range breast of chicken, corn pudding, black eyed peas, piquillo pepper mojo; harrisa grilled salmon, confit beets, cooling cucumber froth; roasted free range chicken, sweet corn cake, zucchini, poblanos; beef two ways, grilled rib steak, *vaca frita* *"Cubana,"* chipotle cipollini, Hen of the Woods mushrooms; "Mongolian" marinated and grilled veal chop, Chinese eggplant, and Thai fried rice.

## The Oceanaire Seafood Room

**Seafood at 9101 International Drive, Orlando, Forida 32819. Dinner only; call (407) 363-4801 for reservations or online at www.opentable.com; business casual dress. Open Sunday through Thursday, 5 to 10 p.m.; Friday and Saturday, 5 to 11 p.m. $$$– $$$$**

A comfortable and friendly dining room is a kick-back to the 1930s when glamorous ocean liners plied the seas and supper clubs were the thing. An art-deco look of shiny wood flooring, chrome and wood paneling, red curved banquettes, potted palms, and white tablecloths is accompanied by brilliant seafood and a never-ending menu that can be a bit bewildering. The BLT Salad is a good start to the meal with yummy buttermilk bacon dressing; however, request about half of the dressing be eliminated. Or go with the thick and flavorful chowder chunked full of tender clams. If you like giant-size starters share the Grand Shellfish Platter with towering mounds of super-fresh shrimp, crab, lobster, and oysters.

A generous seafood selection varies nightly according to what is fresh and available from around the world. Entrees include a broiled amberjack prepared a la "Black and Bleu," scrumptiously grilled on a bed of caramelized onions and topped with crusty Roquefort cheese; or lobster thermidor that's irresistible. You might simply choose your favorite fish and have it either broiled; sprinkled with sea salt and grilled with virgin olive oil and lemon; or "dirty" with Cajun spices. Super sides of olive oil fried hashed brown potatoes spiked with bacon, or tasty green beans with bacon-sherry sauce should be shared. Great endings include a fun baked Alaska flamed tableside, or choose the massive chocolate caramel brownie served with two scoops of ice cream, accompanied by boats of caramel and fudge.

*CARA'S TIP:* Valet parking is free during restaurant hours.

**SAMPLE MENU ITEMS**

**Dinner entrees:** Fish and shellfish cioppino; grilled Mexican black grouper with mushroom ragout; black tiger shrimp scampi with traditional garlic butter; crispy fried fisherman's platter with scallops, shrimp, oysters, and whitefish over salt and vinegar fries; fresh Alaskan king crab clusters; pan-seared whole Mediterranean bronzini with Italian olives, leeks, tomatoes, herb butter, and wine.

## Primo

**Contemporary Mediterranean cuisine at the JW Marriott Grande Lakes. Dinner only; call (407) 393-4444 for reservations or online at www.opentable.com; smart casual dress. Open daily, 6 to 10 p.m. $$$–$$$$**

JW Marriott's signature restaurant is quite the star. Executive chef Melissa Kelly, a James Beard Foundation award winner, is passionate about seasonal, organic produce and believes in offering it in the ever-changing, Mediterranean-influenced menu. A bountiful garden, just outside the restaurant door, testifies to that policy. Italian-style decor and a bustling, copper-clad, open kitchen make for a pleasant atmosphere where diners are seated at cherry red banquettes or comfortable tables in the dimly lit space. A rustic antipasto platter is enough for two and changes according to what's fresh and seasonally available. A gorgonzola lover's roasted beet salad tossed with fresh garden greens, three types of baby beets, gorgonzola vinaigrette, and maple toasted walnuts is superb. Exquisitely light pillows of gnocchi spiked with generous chunks of rich lobster were one of the best dishes I've had in eons as was an outstanding wild king salmon with a light lemon burrida accompanied by tiny Pemaquid mussels and buttery clams.

I'm still reeling from the dessert of hot zeppole, Italian donuts tossed in cinnamon and sugar, crispy on the outside, moist on the inside, accompanied by an espresso float with chocolate and vanilla gelato. Phenomenal! Service is extremely efficient and delightfully friendly. Don't get relegated to the side dining area, an uninteresting, almost windowless space that seems like an afterthought. Instead, ask for the softly lit main dining room surrounded by floor-to-ceiling windows or the candlelit terrace.

**Best known for:** Scallopine of Niman Ranch pork saltimbocca in a sage-infused mushroom-Madeira jus with prosciutto and olive oil mash.

**SAMPLE MENU ITEMS**

**Dinner entrees:** Pan Roasted Port Clyde halibut atop a buttercup squash risotto, pumpkin seed pesto, warm black trumpet mushroom, and petite green salad with parsley sauce; wood grilled grass fed New York strip steak, braised local beef and horseradish potato cake, salad of spicy cress and roast beets; grilled organic chicken breast stuffed with house-made hot Italian sausage served with eggplant Parmesan, lemon and olive oil braised garden escarole; Ells Farm lamb two ways (braised shoulder and grilled leg), flageolet beans, rosemary and tomato gratin, baby spinach; sweet anise sausage, spinach, and wild mushroom stuffed quail, wilted Tat soi, dijon and fines herbes gnocchi in a Parmesan brood.

## Roy's

**Hawaiian fusion cuisine at 7760 West Sand Lake Road. Dinner only; call (407) 352-4844 for reservations or online at www .roysrestaurant.com; business casual dress. Open daily, 5:30 to 10 p.m. $$$–$$$$**

Roy Yamaguchi originated Hawaiian fusion cuisine in Honolulu and has spread his worldwide dining experience to a stretch of West Sand Lake Road near Universal. This is no tacky tiki lounge with drinks in coconut shells or Don Ho look-alikes; only a sleek, contemporary dining room washed in soft amber light attracting a stylish crowd of in-the-know locals. The best starters are a wonderfully fresh ahi poke salad and the crunchy lobster pot stickers. Although beef is on the menu, go for one of the many fresh fish choices, always cooked just so and set off by delectable sauces. If you simply can't decide, try one of the trios—we enjoyed the hibachi grilled salmon (the best of the lot) with a ponzu sauce, the blackened island ahi, and the crispy Hawaiian style misoyaki butterfish (a little salty). My favorite remains the spinach-and-gorgonzola-topped fish that changes weekly accompanied by a Maryland blue crab chardonnay sauce. End with the restaurant's signature chocolate soufflé or the moist pineapple upside-down cake.

**Best known for:** Roy's original blackened island ahi with spicy soy mustard butter, and the melting hot chocolate soufflé with vanilla bean ice cream.

## SAMPLE MENU ITEMS

**Dinner entrees:** Roasted macadamia nut–crusted mahi mahi with lobster cognac butter sauce; sea salt grilled New York strip, *pommes frites,* and smoked gouda cream; peppercorn mélange crusted salmon, roasted baby beets, kale, and Riesling leek reduction; sweet 'n' sour chicken, Calrose rice, and black Mandarin dragon sauce; thyme crusted tiger shrimp, butternut squash risotto, asparagus, and edamame.

## *Seasons 52*

**New American cuisine at 7700 West Sand Lake Road. Lunch and dinner; call (407) 354-5212 for reservations; smart casual. Open for lunch Monday through Friday 11:30 a.m. to 2:30 p.m. and Saturday and Sunday continually serving from 11:30 a.m.; dinner nightly 5 to 10 p.m.; Friday and Saturday until 11 p.m. with flatbreads and desserts served in the lounge one hour after dinner ends. $$–$$$**

This still-buzzing restaurant offers fresh food low in calories (nothing is over 475 calories) with prices gentle on the pocketbook. The handsome, Frank Lloyd Wright–chic dining room is a happening spot, but on balmy nights the outdoor veranda with views of Little Sand Lake beckons. Just a few of the terrific appetizers—such as any of the incredible, super-thin flatbreads on the menu (I particularly like the grilled steak and crimini mushroom choice dotted with creamy blue cheese) or goat cheese ravioli in a light broth with tomatoes and basil—could make a meal, but don't stop there. A lunchtime spinach salad tossed with ripe Anjou pears, blue cheese, and toasted pine nuts, and an appetizer such as the cheesy chicken chili relleno prove to be the perfect combination. Good entree picks are the cedar plank salmon (go for the organic Scottish salmon over the Atlantic choice for a $5 surcharge) or the mesquite-smoky pork tenderloin served over soft herbed polenta with a nice sherry glaze. The under-100-calorie minidesserts served in shot glasses offer just a few bites of perfection. The only improvement could be in re-training the somewhat young and uppity seating hostesses.

For a simpler dining choice sit in the bar and order up a few small plates, pick a glass of wine from the more than sixty choices, and enjoy the live piano music.

**Best known for:** Cedar planked salmon and the luscious low-cal minidesserts.

**SAMPLE MENU ITEMS**

**Lunch entrees:** Oak-fired western buffalo burger with guacamole, spicy chili sour cream, and roasted pepper salsa; roasted market vegetable sandwich with three cheeses on grilled ciabatta; tiger shrimp penne pasta and market vegetables sautéed in a lemon-basil sauce with Parmesan cheese; lemongrass salmon salad with mesclun greens, grilled pineapple, jícama, and sesame dressing; caramelized sea scallops grilled and served with roasted asparagus and sundried tomato pearl pasta.

**Dinner entrees:** Char crust filet mignon with garlic mashed potatoes, fresh vegetables, and tamarind sauce; grilled rack of New Zealand lamb with red bliss potatoes, asparagus, balsamic red onions, and dijon sauce; caramelized sea scallops grilled and served with roasted asparagus and sundried tomato pearl pasta; grilled boneless rainbow trout with parsley new potatoes, fresh roasted vegetables, and broiled lemon; Fieldale Farms all-natural chicken with pearl onions, mushrooms, broccoli, and Lundberg organic wild rice; tiger shrimp penne pasta and market vegetables sautéed in a lemon-basil sauce with Parmesan cheese.

## Timpano Chophouse & Martini Bar

**Italian steaks, seafood, and pasta at 7488 West Sand Lake Road. Lunch and dinner; call (407) 248-0429 for reservations or online at www.opentable.com; smart casual dress. Open for lunch daily, 11:30 a.m. to 4 p.m.; dinner Sunday through Wednesday, 4 to 11 p.m. (Thursday through Saturday until midnight). $$–$$$$**

There are several good reasons to come to this retro-swank throwback to a Manhattan-style, 1950s supper club: first of all for a great martini, second for dreamy Frank Sinatra music, and last but not least for top-notch food in a wonderfully nostalgic atmosphere. Tourists comingle with smartly dressed locals in this restaurant of rustic wood floors, black leather booths, white linen tablecloths topped with butcher paper, and a poised and professional staff. A great starter is a sizzling skillet of roasted mussels in a satisfying citrus glaze with garlic, rosemary, and drawn butter. Those whose waistline can afford it should try the tower (and I mean tower!) of crunchy, beer-battered onion rings accompanied by dipping sauces. Even though they specialize in chops, I really don't think they are the restaurant's forte—too charred on the outside, a distraction from the flavor. At lunch go for one of the fun Rat Pack "Lunch Boxes" (an American twist on the bento box) with a variety of four mini-course combinations ending with a mini dessert. Pasta is a winner here, especially the delicate lobster ravioli served with plump shrimp in a rich, roasted tomato sauce, but my favorite entree is the crispy roasted salmon served on sautéed artichokes and spinach with a mustard cream sauce. A variety of frozen cheesecake "lollipops" served on a dessert tree are a fun ending to a good meal. Whatever you do, stop in to wash down your serious meal with a playful cocktail at the restaurant's intimate Starlight Lounge, the most seductive bar around with live music Tuesday through Saturday from 6:30 p.m. until 1 a.m.

**Best known for:** Grilled ahi served rare with tomato-basil vinaigrette.

### SAMPLE MENU ITEMS

**Lunch entrees:** Herbed roasted chicken breast flatbread with sundried tomato pesto, blue cheese, and fresh mozzarella; turkey club panini; lasagna bolognese; shrimp fra diablo fettuccini, asparagus, goat cheese, pine nuts, and spinach, tossed in a spicy rosa sauce; chicken marsala.

**Dinner entrees:** Shrimp oreganata served with spaghettini and a cream sauce with lemon, fresh oregano leaves, and Padano Parmesan; rock shrimp and lobster ravioli, fire-roasted plum tomato sauce, and sweet basil topped with sweet shrimp; veal marsala with mushrooms, Marsala wine, herbs, and diced tomatoes; seafood cioppino; sixteen-ounce organic grain-fed veal chop; sixteen-ounce double bone pork chop; eight-ounce dry aged hand cut filet; twenty-ounce bone-in rib eye (all chops available either "Al Forno" with creamy peppercorn sauce or "Al Balsamico").

## Vito's Chop House

**Steakhouse at 8633 International Drive. Dinner only; call (407) 354-2467 for reservations; smart casual dress. Open Sunday through Thursday, 5 to 10:30 p.m., and Friday and Saturday 5 to 11 p.m. $$–$$$$**

Ignore the fact that it's located on tacky International Drive and plan an evening at Vito's, a sophisticated steakhouse with an Italian flair and loads of ambience. Melt into one of the red leather banquettes to enjoy the intimate dining room decorated with exposed brick and cases of wine. Excellent service is provided by tuxedoed waiters who present enormous and succulent aged steaks and impeccably fresh, perfectly prepared seafood. And with almost 1,000 labels, the blockbuster wine list (*Wine Spectator's* Best of Award of Excellence winner many years in a row) is a dream come true.

Order a *frito misto* to start, a giant platter of tender fried scallops, mussels, squid, fish, and shrimp accompanied by garlic aioli and fried capers, enough to be shared with several people. Known best for their grilled, thick pork chops topped with an assortment of sweet and hot peppers, other favorites include a lean and flavorful 2½-inch-thick veal chop and a colossal twenty-four-ounce prime rib eye. Feast on great sides of potatoes rapini smashed and then pan-sautéed with bacon and broccoli rabe, or perhaps creamed spinach, fried green tomatoes, or fresh oak-grilled vegetables. Better bring a hungry friend or two along to share one of Vito's colossal desserts (it is hard to resist the chocolate cake as big as a serving platter, but it is a bit of overkill). Just as rich but oh-so-heavenly is the grilled peaches caramelized with brown sugar and peach schnapps with pound cake and vanilla bean ice cream.

**Best known for:** Thirteen-ounce filet mignon stuffed with gorgonzola.

## SAMPLE MENU ITEMS

**Dinner entrees:** Twenty-four-ounce bone-in prime rib eye; the ultimate surf and turf of a fifty-ounce porterhouse with a one-and-a-half-pound lobster; thirty-two-ounce Tuscan porterhouse seasoned with garlic and herbs; linguine and clam sauce en papillote; king salmon cedar plank roasted in a wood-burning pit; lobster fra diablo, twin lobster tails fried and placed atop linguine and then topped with marinara and an assortment of peppers.

# 9

# UNIVERSAL ORLANDO

Just 12 miles north of Walt Disney World is this whopper of a destination composed of two side-by-side theme parks, Universal Studios and Islands of Adventure; a dining, shopping, and entertainment venue, CityWalk; and three themed resorts where a few nights of pampering could only add to your vacation experience. Universal's rapid expansion has certainly given Walt Disney World a run for its money, and what it lacks in magic it more than makes up for in its certain brand of frenzied, high-speed intensity. Although Disney has the edge in service, attractions, and plain old customer satisfaction, the compact Universal Orlando is a great two- or three-day excursion.

With more thrill rides at Islands of Adventure theme park than Walt Disney World will probably ever have, a trip here is a must if you have a teenager or coaster addict in your party. Although it will never live up to the Magic Kingdom in the eyes of small children, Universal does have fascinating child-oriented areas in each theme park. Low-key adults love the working studio aspect of Universal Studios and are simply wowed by the creativity invested in Islands of Adventure. And with the new Wizarding World of Harry Potter at Islands of Adventure, time spent here is almost mandatory.

## Getting There

From the airport take Highway 528 west (the Bee-Line Expressway) then I–4 east to exit 75A, Universal Boulevard, and follow the signs. From Walt Disney World take I-4 east to exit 75A and follow the signs.

## Parking

Parking is $14 per day, $18 for preferred parking closer to the main entrance (although it is still a five- to ten-minute walk), $22 for valet parking, and free to Preferred and Premier Pass holders. Instead of wide-open lots like those at Walt Disney World serviced by a shuttle, Universal Studios, Islands of Adventure, and CityWalk all share two gigantic high-rise parking facilities. The result is quite a jam-up in the mornings; more-experienced people or simply more people (believe it or not, many times only one person is moving all those cars along) directing traffic could certainly improve matters. From the parking lot proceed on long walkways (some of which are moving sidewalks) to CityWalk and then either straight ahead to Islands of Adventure or to the right for Universal Studios. Either way it is about a ten- to fifteen-minute walk to the parks from your parking space. No trams are available.

## Operating Hours

Both parks operate 365 days a year. They normally open at 9 a.m. and close at 6 or 7 p.m., with extended hours during holidays and busy season. For special events parks may close as early as 4 or 5 p.m. Go online to www.universalorlando.com or call (800) 837-2273 for up-to-date operating hours and information.

## Basic Universal Orlando Reference Guide

**Alcohol.** Alcohol is sold at both parks and CityWalk.

**Child Swap Program.** Available at most attractions is a child-swap area allowing parents to take turns staying with a child while the other parent rides without losing their place in line.

**Pets.** A day kennel, located in the parking structure, is $15 per day. No overnight boarding. Guests must provide food as well as return at least once a day.

**Loews Loves Pets.** Guests of the Portofino Bay, Hard Rock, and Royal Pacific Hotels can have their pets in the room. Offered are special pet menus, pet walking and sitting services, and pet amenities. A veterinarian certificate no more than ten days old is required, and no more than two pets are allowed per room. A one-time $25 cleaning fee is assessed.

**Smoking.** Smoking is permitted in designated areas only.

**Transportation to Universal.** From the airport use the same town car, limousine, and shuttle services as for Disney for a slightly lower fee. From Walt Disney World either take a taxi, or for $18 round-trip per person utilize Mears Transportation shuttles (407-423-5566), or pay around $50 one way for private transfers. From the Universal resorts, board the convenient water taxi or bus shuttle to reach the parks and CityWalk.

**Universal Express Plus.** An extra fee lets you bypass the regular line one time for each park attraction that participates in the program. You can prepurchase your Universal Express Plus Passes online at www.universalorlando.com/tic_express.php. Prices are based on the date of your visit. Only a limited quantity of Universal Express Plus Passes are offered and, if you wait, they may not be available at the gate on the day of your visit. The Universal Express Program is available as a free benefit to resort guests staying at the Royal Pacific Resort, Hard Rock Hotel, and Portofino Bay Hotel.

**VIP Tours.** For $120 per person, a Universal guide will take you and as many as twelve people from different parties on a non-exclusive five-hour tour with no wait in line on at least eight major attractions. A 1-Day/2-Park seven-hour VIP tour is $180.

For a true splurge, opt for the $1,600 (per tour group up to twelve persons) private Exclusive VIP Tour, an eight-hour behind-the-scenes tour of the park of your choice, with front-of-the-line access to the rides of your choice. A 1-Day/2-Park Tour is $2,000 and a 2-Day/2-Park Tour is available for $3,000. Park admission is not included, but valet parking, the opportunity for private character meet-and-greets, a VIP gift bag, and priority seating at restaurants are part of the deal. Call (407) 363-8295 or e-mail to viptours@universalorlando.com for information and reservations. Reservations must be made at least seventy-two hours in advance.

# Universal Studios Florida

This one-hundred-acre theme park based entirely on the movies is actually a working motion picture studio with more than one hundred back lot locations and excellent attractions. Here you'll find realistic facades and sets intermixed with an array of rides and live shows including stage sets and props, film production, mind-blowing pyrotechnics, even tornado reenactments. Its immense appeal to adults sets it apart from many of Orlando's other theme parks, but child-oriented features in Woody Woodpecker's Kidzone will certainly charm the little ones. However, realize that many attractions outside this area can be intense and not appropriate for small children.

## *Park Services*

**ATMs.** Six automated teller machines are located at the park: one just outside to the right of the main entrance, two just inside on the right, one near Animal Actors on Location, one near *Revenge of the Mummy,* and one in the San Francisco/Amity area near Lombard's Landing.

**Baby facilities.** A nursing room and companion restroom are located at Family Services. Diaper-changing facilities are available in all restrooms.

**Dining reservations.** Make same-day dining reservations for Lombard's Landing and Finnegan's Bar and Grill at the dining kiosk in Production Central. If you'd like to plan ahead, call (407) 224-3613.

**First aid.** First-aid stations are located across from Beetlejuice's Graveyard Revue as well as at Family Services just inside the main entrance.

**Guest Services.** Located just inside the park entrance on the right is the place for information, special dining assistance along with guides for guests with disabilities, assistive listening devices and captioning services, and foreign currency exchange.

**Guests with disabilities.** Guests with disabilities may park in a special parking area; ask for directions at the toll plaza. All attractions, shopping and dining facilities, and restrooms are wheelchair accessible; however, several rides require the ability to transfer from the wheelchair to the

# Universal Studios Florida

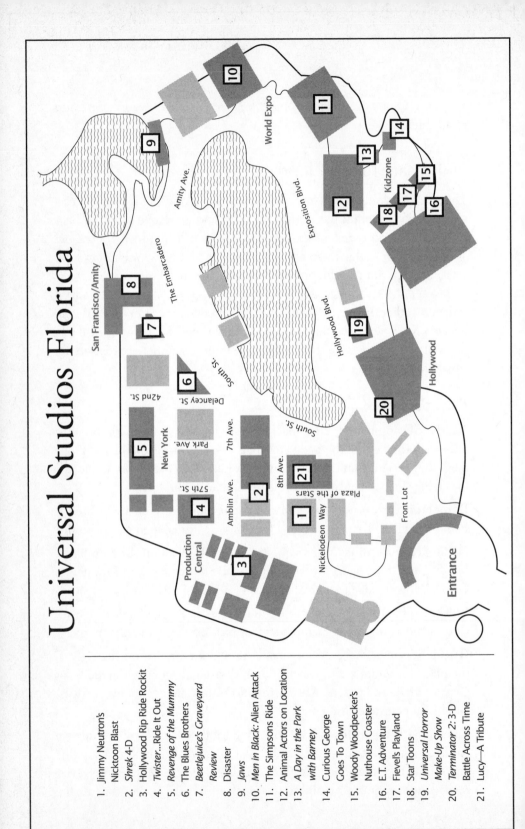

1. Jimmy Neutron's Nicktoon Blast
2. Shrek 4-D
3. Hollywood Rip Ride Rockit
4. Twister...Ride It Out
5. Revenge of the Mummy
6. The Blues Brothers
7. Beetlejuice's Graveyard Review
8. Disaster
9. Jaws
10. Men in Black: Alien Attack
11. The Simpsons Ride
12. Animal Actors on Location
13. A Day in the Park with Barney
14. Curious George Goes To Town
15. Woody Woodpecker's Nuthouse Coaster
16. E.T. Adventure
17. Fievel's Playland
18. Star Toons
19. Universal Horror Make-Up Show
20. Terminator 2: 3-D Battle Across Time
21. Lucy—A Tribute

ride's seating (check the guidemap for details). A companion restroom is located at Family Services. Interpreted "live action" shows are available daily; check your park map for show schedules and the "interpret" sign next to show times. Closed captioning, assistive listening devices, a guidebook for guests with disabilities, and attraction scripts are available at Guest Services. Guide dogs are allowed in the park.

**Locker rental.** Located on both the right and left sides of the Front Lot; $8 for a small locker and $10 for a large locker per day. Additional lockers are located outside the *Men in Black* and *Revenge of the Mummy* attractions for $2 per hour, with the first forty-five minutes free.

**Lost and found.** Located at the Studio Audience Center just inside the main entrance.

**Lost children.** Look for a lost child at Guest Services.

**Package pickup.** Purchases may be sent to the It's a Wrap gift store for pickup before leaving the park. Registered guests of Loews Universal hotels may have purchases sent directly to their rooms.

**Stroller and wheelchair rentals.** On your left as you pass through the turnstiles are stroller rentals for $13 single and $21 double; upgraded strollers called "kiddie cars" with a kid steering wheel and cup holders rent for $16 and $24 respectively; wheelchairs are $12 and ECVs are $45 (with a $50 refundable deposit). Call (407) 224-6350 at least forty-eight hours in advance for ECV reservations.

**Universal Orlando Vacations Services.** The place for ticket upgrades, hotel and dining reservations, movie tickets for Cineplex at CityWalk, and special event passes. Located on the left as you enter the park.

## The Lay of the Land

The Universal Studios layout can be a bit confusing. Just beyond the park's main entrance you'll encounter a wide boulevard with attractions on either side making up Production Central. Branching off to the right are four main streets leading to the other areas of the park: New York, San Francisco/Amity, World Expo, Woody Woodpecker's Kidzone, and Hollywood, all of which partially encircle a large lagoon.

## The Very Best Attractions at Universal Studios

### SHREK 4-D

Picking up where the first *Shrek* movie left off, Shrek, Princess Fiona, and Donkey depart on a honeymoon adventure with plenty of mishaps along the way. If you're not familiar with the movie, don't worry; it will be recapped in the silly preshow. Now, don't expect to see your typical, run-of-the-mill 3-D film; this one adds an extra dimension of awesome special effects. You can see, hear, and really feel what the characters are experiencing from seats that move along with the action. Get ready for lots of laughs with squirts of water, creepy-crawly things under your rear end, and more. Unquestionably this show one-ups any other 3-D theme park movie around. Those with back, heart, or neck problems or families with small children may want to take advantage of the stationary seats available. **12-minute show.**

### REVENGE OF THE MUMMY

Located in Universal's New York area is this super attraction featuring a combination flat-track and dark coaster with loads of special effects and mind-games. After working your way in line through a tomblike setting, board your "mine car" and blast off through scene after scary scene; you'll even travel backward and rotate 180 degrees, encountering ghouls, mummies, walls of scarab beetles, and fog and flame effects along the way. If it makes you feel any better, there are no loops or big dips, just speed. Just as you think this hair-raising ride is almost over, think again—the mummy doesn't let you off that easily! It certainly plays with your mind; you'll find yourself close to freaking out at every turn. Don't miss this unique attraction, one of Orlando's best. **Minimum height 48 inches (4 feet). Not recommended for expectant mothers or those with heart, back, or neck problems. 3-minute ride.**

*CARA'S TIP:* If you don't mind riding without other members of your party, go for the singles line, a process used to fill empty seats, which will greatly cut your time in line. Carry-on bags are not allowed; use the free (for the first forty-five minutes) lockers out front to store your gear.

## *TWISTER*: RIDE IT OUT

In the waiting area for this hair-raising attraction is film footage of actual twisters wreaking their devastation. Move inside a soundstage to view clips of *Twister* narrated by stars Helen Hunt and Bill Paxton, who relay many of the frightening experiences they encountered during the filming of the movie. Walk through the set of a twister-ripped house where another video explains the logistics of some of the more intense portions of the film. Then on to the grand finale, a re-creation of a scene set in a small Midwestern town, one in which visitors will actually feel the power of a five-story twister. The wind and pelting rain build and darkness and cold descend as the funnel cloud approaches. The entire set begins shaking as trees tear apart, power lines fall, a gas tank explodes, and a drive-in movie screen, truck, and cow go flying through the air. Just a small testimony to the majesty and mystery of nature. **15-minute attraction.**

*CARA'S TIP*: Rated PG-13 due to the intensity of the twister demonstration. Those in the back and immediate front get the wettest, although no one actually gets drenched. If you stand too far to the side, you might not get the full effect of the wind and rain—which can be a good or bad thing, depending on your taste for thrills.

## HOLLYWOOD RIP, RIDE, ROCKIT

Begin by picking out a soundtrack from huge LED screens in the queue line that will serenade you during your ride. Then board one wild and crazy coaster! Snaking above CityWalk with a track looping outside the park, this knock-out attraction tops out at 167 feet with riders hitting 65 miles per hour, soaring straight into the sky with six near-misses and a record-breaking loop. All this without over-the-shoulder or leg restraints with only a single waist belt to hold you in! Color changing LEDs, concert lighting, and special effects bump it up just a few more notches. Your ride is outfitted with video cameras so when it's all over and you return to normal you can edit your taped ride and take it home in the form of a music video or even email it to a friend. **Minimum height 51 inches (4 feet, 3 inches). Not recommended for expectant mothers, those with heart, neck, and back problems, and those susceptible to motion sickness. 2-minute ride.**

### MEN IN BLACK: ALIEN ATTACK

The MIB training facility is searching for several good agents to protect Earth from the galaxy's evil aliens in this interactive, video-game thrill ride. Two six-passenger cars depart together and meet up again several times as they speed through New York streets and alleyways, playing laser tag along the way, blasting away at as many lifelike aliens as possible. The team that creams the most extraterrestrial creatures is the winner. Look up, down, and sideways for the little green guys: in trash cans, Dumpsters, hot dog stands, and upstairs windows, on top of buildings, and hanging from lampposts; there's even a baby alien in a carriage. Zip, tilt, and spin as your score builds. What makes this ride interesting is that contestants find themselves in battle with the other vehicle as well as the aliens themselves, who react when they are shot and even shoot back; when your vehicle is zapped, it goes into a 360-degree spin. The last creature you encounter is a 50-foot-wide, 30-foot-tall alien bug. **Minimum height 42 inches (3 feet, 6 inches); children between 42 and 48 inches (4 feet) tall must be accompanied by an adult. Not recommended for expectant mothers, those with heart, neck, and back problems; and those susceptible to motion sickness. 5-minute ride.**

*CARA'S TIP:* If you don't mind riding without other members of your party, go for the singles line, a process used to fill empty seats, which will greatly cut your time in line. Carry-on bags are not allowed; use the free (for the first forty-five minutes) lockers out front to store your gear.

### THE SIMPSONS RIDE

The Simpsons family is vacationing at Krustyland, and what an adventure it is! After a funny preshow, board an oversized roller coaster car that rises in front of an 80-foot Omnimax domed screen and off you go on a simulated wild chase through Krustyland, through spoof scenes of Orlando including a killer whale tank, a Pirates of the Caribbean attraction, and a crazy rollercoaster. If you are the least bit susceptible to motion sickness avoid this ride like the plague. **Minimum height 40 inches (3 feet, 4 inches). Not recommended for expectant mothers or those with motion sickness, dizziness, claustrophobia, heart, back, or neck problems. 6-minute ride.**

### *TERMINATOR 2*: 3-D BATTLE ACROSS TIME

You're on a tour of Cyberdyne's corporate headquarters when, during a briefing on the new SkyNet program, John Conner and his mother, Sarah, from *Terminator 2* seize the video screen. They're here with a warning that SkyNet's newest scheme is a threat to the human race and must be destroyed before it destroys us. Only five minutes remain to get out before the building is obliterated. The video is quickly stopped and the ditzy tour guide smoothes over the interruption by escorting visitors into the huge Cyberdyne theater.

Then slip on your special glasses and be prepared to watch one of the best 3-D shows around. The original stars of *Terminator 2* appear on giant screens along with 8-foot Cinebotic T-70 Soldiers and stunt actors. Fantastic 3-D special effects and colossal explosions accompanied by loads of smoke and a rocking theater will leave you reeling. I guarantee your mouth will be hanging open when it's all over. **Expectant mothers or those with heart, neck, or back problems may sit in stationary seats. 20-minute show.**

*CARA'S TIP:* Rated PG-13 and a pretty darn intense show for young children due to loud and startling noise. All seats are decent, but hang back a little and enter the doors on the right to sit front and center. At one point all the seats in the theater jerk abruptly; people with back or neck problems may want to sit this one out.

## The Very Best Dining at Universal Studios

**Monster's Café.** Saturday afternoon fiends from baby boomers' childhoods are glorified here at this special counter-service cafe for monster movie fans; purchase your frightfully decent grub in Frankenstein's lab and proceed to your preference of monster dining rooms; chopped chef's salad, chicken Caesar salad, penne primavera, spaghetti bolognese, wood-oven pizza, rotisserie chicken; devil's food cake, deep-dish apple pie, strawberry shortcake, butterscotch chocolate parfait, fresh fruit cup.

**Finnegan's Bar and Grill.** Irish pub dining with live entertainment; lunch and dinner. (See full description in the Universal Orlando Dining section of the Dining chapter.)

**Lombard's Seafood Grille.** Seafood is the specialty here in a San Francisco warehouse setting; lunch and dinner; bay shrimp cobb salad, mahi

mahi sandwich, grilled Asian chicken wrap, popcorn shrimp roll, shrimp pasta primavera, fried shrimp, catch of the day.

**Richter's Burger Co.** Good burgers complete with all the trimmings; single and double hamburger, grilled chicken sandwich, gardenburger, chili cheese fries, toppings bar; shakes, apple pie, fruit cup, chocolate chip cookies.

**Mel's Drive-In.** Authentic-looking 1950s-style burger joint a la *American Graffiti*; bright vinyl booths, curved picture windows, vintage jukebox; counter service instead of gum-smacking waitresses; burgers, chicken "fingers," grilled chicken sandwich, grilled chicken salad, onion rings, chili cheese fries; shakes, root beer floats.

## Special Entertainment in Universal Studios

**Blues Brothers.** This hopping street show on the corner of Delancey Street in Universal Studios' New York really gets the crowd rocking. Jake and Elwood Blues sing and dance accompanied by a piped-in soundtrack, a talented sax player, and a one-woman showstopper with an Aretha Franklin–like voice. The Blues Brothers' renditions of "Soul Man," "Everybody Needs Somebody to Love," even "Rawhide," all sung in the movie *The Blues Brothers,* entertain the hand-clapping crowd.

## Special Events

**Mardi Gras.** Each Saturday night late winter into early spring, experience the festivity of New Orleans with parades, live concerts, New Orleans bands, tons of beads, and Cajun food. Past performers include KC & the Sunshine Band, the Village People, Pat Benatar, Kelly Clarkson, and Barenaked Ladies. Included in the price of admission.

**Rock the Universe.** For two nights on a weekend in early September, the latest in contemporary Christian music is on the agenda. Requires purchasing a separate ticket.

**Halloween Horror Nights.** Experience your favorite rides and attractions along with a spooky evening on selected nights during September and October. This is a very popular event for teens and adults, featuring eight haunted houses, Scare Zones such as Asylum in Wonderland and Fractured Tales, the comedic Bill and Ted's Excellent Halloween Adventure

Show, almost 500 jack-o'-lanterns, and scream-inducing ghouls and monsters roaming the park. The party extends to both parks. Young children are encouraged not to attend. No costumes allowed. Requires purchasing a separate ticket. Call (407) 22-HORROR, or (407) 224-6776, or go online at www.halloweenhorrornights.com.

**Holiday Festivities.** The park is merry with plenty of Christmas decorations, a Macy's holiday parade with floats and giant helium balloons direct from New York's Macy's Day Parade, a tree lighting ceremony, carols, Santa Claus sightings, and a Blues Brothers Christmas Show. A Day in the Park with Barney comes with a special Christmas show.

# Islands of Adventure

When Islands of Adventure opened in 1999, it was an immediate hit, with more state-of-the-art attractions and amazing thrill rides than any other park in Orlando. Totally different from its next-door sister park Universal Studios, it's worth the price of admission simply for a glimpse of its six distinctive islands, each more imaginative and outrageous than the next. Everywhere the eye rests, there's a barrage of zany color and immense creativity.

Although the park has something for every age, it's a sure lure for coaster junkies and the teenage set. Many of the attractions have height restrictions; however, with Seuss Landing and Camp Jurassic, there's plenty to keep the little ones happy. If roller coasters are not your thing, you'll be more than thrilled with the variety of attractions for the tamer crowd. And with the new Wizarding World of Harry Potter area, this is definitely the park of the moment.

## Park Services

**ATMs.** Three automated teller machines are located at the park: just outside the park's entrance, on the right after entering the park next to the restrooms, and near the Spider-Man attraction.

**Baby facilities.** A nursing facility and companion restroom are located in First Aid. Diaper changing facilities are available in all major restrooms.

# Islands of Adventure

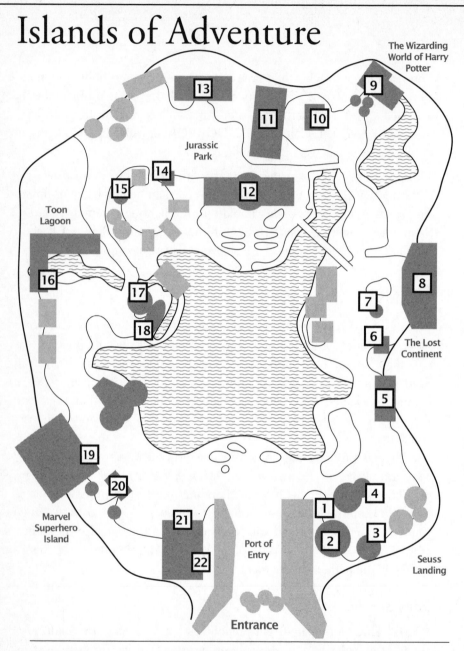

The Wizarding World of Harry Potter

Jurassic Park

Toon Lagoon

The Lost Continent

Marvel Superhero Island

Port of Entry

Seuss Landing

**Entrance**

1. If I Ran the Zoo
2. *The Cat In The Hat*
3. One Fish, Two Fish, Red Fish, Blue Fish
4. Caro-Seuss-el
5. High in the Sky Seuss Trolley Train Ride
6. Poseidon's Fury
7. The Mystic Fountain

8. The Eighth Voyage of Sinbad
9. Dragon Challenge
10. Flight of the Hippogriff
11. Harry Potter and the Forbidden Journey
12. Jurassic Park Discovery Center
13. Jurassic Park River Adventure
14. Pteranodon Flyers
15. Camp Jurassic

16. Dudley Do-Right's Ripsaw Falls
17. Popeye and Bluto's Bilge-Rat Barges
18. Me Ship, *The Olive*
19. The Amazing Adventures of Spider-Man
20. Doctor Doom's Fearfall
21. Incredible Hulk Coaster
22. Storm Force Accelatron

**Dining reservations.** Make same-day dining reservations at Vacation Services on your left as you enter the park. If you would like to plan ahead, call (407) 224-3613.

**First-aid stations.** Located near the Eighth Voyage of Sinbad in the Lost Continent and at Guest Services to the right of the main entrance.

**Guest Services.** Located on the right-hand side of Port of Entry in the Open Arms Hotel building for information, special dining assistance, guides for guest with disabilities, assistive listening devices and captioning services, and foreign language maps.

**Guests with disabilities.** Special parking areas for guests with disabilities are available; ask for directions at the toll plaza. All shops, dining facilities, attraction queues, and restrooms are wheelchair accessible; however, many rides require the ability to transfer from the wheelchair to the ride's seating (check the guidemap for details). Wheelchair-accessible restrooms are located throughout the park, and companion-assisted restrooms can be found at First Aid. Interpreted "live action" shows are available daily; check your park map for show schedules and the "interpret" sign next to show times. Closed captioning, assistive listening devices, a guidebook for guests with disabilities, and attraction scripts are available at Guest Services. Guide dogs are allowed in the park.

**Lockers.** Located on the left upon entering the park; $8 for a small locker and $10 for a large per day. Lockers are also located at the entrance to Incredible Hulk, Jurassic Park River Adventure, and Dragon Challenge for $2 per hour, with the first forty-five minutes free.

**Lost and found.** Located at Guest Services.

**Lost children.** Locate lost children at Guest Services.

**Strollers and wheelchairs.** Located on the left as you pass through the turnstiles are stroller rentals for $13 single and $21 double; upgraded strollers called "kiddie cars" with a kid steering wheel and cup holders rent for $16 and $24 respectively. Wheelchairs rent for $12 and ECVs for $45 (with a $50 deposit). Call (407) 224-6350 at least forty-eight hours in advance for ECV reservations.

## When to Come and What to Wear

Because of the popularity of this park with local teenagers, avoid the weekends. And this is one park that requires a bit of forethought in park attire. If you plan on riding Popeye and Bluto's Bilge-Rat Barges, you will, and I repeat, *will* become thoroughly soaked. Depending on where you sit, Dudley Do-Right's Ripsaw Falls and Jurassic Park River Adventure can cause quite a drenching. Come wearing fast-drying clothing, water foot-wear of some sort, and in cooler months perhaps a rain poncho to remain somewhat dry. A change of clothing (easily stowed in a locker) might also be helpful. And remember, if you're a coaster fan, flip-flops cannot be worn on Dragon Challenge.

## The Lay of the Land

This park is laid out in a more traditional fashion than Universal Studios. A main street, Port of Entry, leads from the entrance and dead-ends into a large lagoon, with the islands arranged in a circular fashion around it. Moving clockwise, you'll first find Marvel Super Hero Island, then Toon Lagoon, Jurassic Park, the Wizarding World of Harry Potter, the Lost Continent, and finally Seuss Landing.

## The Very Best Attractions at Islands of Adventure

### THE AMAZING ADVENTURES OF SPIDER-MAN

This remarkable attraction was the first to combine 3-D film, special effects, and moving vehicles. Board your twelve-passenger, state-of-the-art "scoop vehicle," actually a 3-D simulator that moves along a track and rotates 360 degrees, for the ride of your life. You'll scream with delight at each encounter with Spider-Man and his foes as they spring onto the hood of your car in amazing 3-D, causing your vehicle to gyrate and pitch off to the next crazy commotion. Move through more than a dozen New York scenes, plowing through warehouses, dropping below the streets to the city sewers, and flying above towering skyscrapers. Feel the heat of mind-boggling 3-D explosions accompanied by state-of-the-art sound (each vehicle has its own proprietary system) offering intense audio along with the excitement of the ride. The most remarkable scene is the 400-foot simulated drop (pure illusion but scary just the same). Don't worry, Spider-Man plans on catching you in his net at the bottom. **Minimum**

**height 40 inches (3 feet, 4 inches); children 40 to 48 inches (4 feet) tall must be accompanied by an adult. Not recommended for expectant mothers, those with back or neck problems, or those prone to motion sickness. 5-minute ride.**

*CARA'S TIP:* If you want to save huge amounts of time, use the singles line; just don't expect to ride in the same vehicle with your party. Ask to sit in the front seat. This is an intense ride for young children; even though there are no actual drops, it certainly feels as if you're falling at a high rate of speed.

### HARRY POTTER & THE FORBIDDEN JOURNEY

Not yet open at press time, this signature attraction is rumored to be quite the scene stealer in the Wizarding World of Harry Potter land. Housed in a replica of Hogwarts Castle, riders will be swept up into the details of the blockbuster movies and the books, putting themselves into the amazing life of a wizard. This is guaranteed to be the most popular park attraction so head here first thing.

### INCREDIBLE HULK COASTER

An eruption of gamma rays from the studio of Bruce Banner (better known as the Hulk) launches you straight up from a near standstill to a whip-lashing 40 mph in just two seconds on this green giant of a steel coaster. Immediately roll into a gut-wrenching 128-foot, zero-G dive, accompanied by a feeling of weightlessness and an adrenaline rush beyond belief, straight down toward a misty lagoon. With speeds of up to 60 mph, loop through inversion after giant inversion and twice underground before you finally come to a halt on this unbelievable monster. This is one of America's most thrilling rides and not to be missed if you are a fan of big, bad coasters. **Minimum height 54 inches (4 feet, 6 inches). Not recommended for expectant mothers or those with heart, back, or neck problems. 2-minute ride.**

*CARA'S TIP:* You can't possibly hold on to your valuables; make use of the short-term lockers located at the attraction entrance, free for the first forty-five minutes. If you'd like to ride in the front seat be ready for a long wait. To save huge amounts of wait time, use the singles line; just don't expect to ride in the same row as the rest of your party.

## POPEYE AND BLUTO'S BILGE-RAT BARGES

This is perhaps the funniest barge ride you'll ever have the pleasure of encountering. You can't help but get entirely soaked on this absolutely hilarious attraction as you swirl and twist over white-water rapids in twelve-passenger circular rafts accompanied by the tooting and bellowing of boat horns, renditions of "Blow the Man Down," and Popeye's theme song. Sail through scenes of Popeye and Bluto fighting for Olive Oyl's love while water swirls close to your knees. You'll rendezvous with a squirting, giant octopus and ride through Bluto's Boat Wash for a good cleaning. Of course, Popeye saves Olive Oyl in the end but is none the drier in the process. Don't miss this enjoyable attraction, even if you have to wear a rain poncho to keep dry. **Minimum height 42 inches (3 feet, 6 inches); children 42 to 48 inches (4 feet) tall must be accompanied by an adult. Not recommended for expectant mothers. 5-minute ride.**

*CARA'S TIP:* Place your valuables in the watertight containers located in the center of the raft, and make sure the snaps are tightly shut. You must wear footwear to ride, so come prepared in fast-drying shoes or water sandals; even if you prop your feet off the floor, they'll still get soaked from above.

## JURASSIC PARK RIVER ADVENTURE

This ride brings you gently into the middle of a lost world and then roughly lets you out. In oversize, twenty-five-person rafts, travel deep into the lush rain forest of Jurassic Park as you float past gentle five-story-tall dinosaurs (some of the largest Audio-Animatronics in any theme park) who ignore the passing traffic as they breathe, roar, and munch on plants. Soon, however, the sweetness turns to fighting when visitors come across the more aggressive breeds (even a few that spit!), particularly a nasty T. rex that forces the raft into the Raptor Containment Area, where a few hairs might rise on the back of more than one passenger's neck. The only way out of this mess is up and over, and by over I mean by way of a pitch-dark, 80-foot, very steep plunge at speeds of 50 mph ending in a tremendous splash guaranteed to douse each and every person in the boat. And if this attraction wasn't wet enough there are now additional opportunities to get wet with new water surges that surprise around every corner. **Minimum height 42 inches (3 feet, 6 inches); children 42 to 48 inches (4** feet) tall must be accompanied by an adult. Not recommended for expectant mothers or those with back or neck problems or medical sensitivity to dizziness and fog or strobe effects. 6-minute ride.

*CARA'S TIP:* Use the short-term lockers, free for the first forty-five minutes, for loose articles or valuables. To the right of Thunder Falls Terrace Restaurant is a walkway leading to a great splash zone and observation spot where the chicken-hearted can watch as others drop down the final descent. If you want to save huge amounts of wait time, use the singles line; just don't expect to ride in the same vehicle with your party.

### DRAGON CHALLENGE

Rethemed to fit the new Wizarding World of Harry Potter, you'll notice as you board either one of these two terrifying roller coasters, named Chinese Fireball and Hungarian Horntail—surprise! surprise! Your feet dangle free. On the world's first inverted, dual-track, near-miss coasters, two dragons are in a dogfight and you're along on the back of one for the battle. As you loop and twist along, you'll swear your feet almost touch those of the opposite dragon as it goes roaring by (supposedly they're only a scant foot apart). Ride one first and then the other for comparison; they are two different experiences. This ride is not for the fainthearted. **Minimum height 54 inches (4 feet, 6 inches). Not recommended for expectant mothers or those with heart, back, or neck problems. Flip-flop footwear not permitted. 2-minute ride.**

*CARA'S TIP:* If waits are short, it won't be necessary to go all the way back to the entrance to ride the other coaster; just look for an opening on the way out for the turnaround to the second coaster. Daredevils should try for the front row in order to get a clear shot of the oncoming train. Use the short-term lockers (free for the first forty-five minutes) for loose articles or valuables. If you want to save huge amounts of wait time, use the singles line; just don't expect to ride in the same row as the rest of your party.

### THE CAT IN THE HAT

Anyone who's ever enjoyed Dr. Seuss's book *The Cat in the Hat* will love this amusing ride. Sit on powder-blue sofas and ride, spin, and swoop along to the hilarious story of the famous cat that comes to visit two children home alone for the day. Your journey includes the Cat along with the naughty Thing One and Thing Two and the tormented family goldfish who tries but fails to keep order while the parents are away. Every creature and object moves, flies, and bounces along to the frenzied beat of the crazy narration. Laughingly move through scene after scene of this celebrated children's book and be enchanted with the re-creation of a simply great story. **Children under 48 inches (4 feet) tall must be accompanied by an adult. Not recommended for expectant mothers, those with back or neck problems, or those prone to motion sickness. 3-minute ride.**

## The Very Best Dining at Islands of Adventure

Islands of Adventure has many creative dining areas, many with delightful views, offering plenty to eat besides the typical hot dog and burger meals.

**Confisco Grille.** Full-service restaurant serving a character breakfast buffet with Thing One, Thing Two, Spider-Man, and others (Thursday through Sunday only), lunch, and dinner; Greek salad; hot pressed Italian panini open-faced turkey sandwich smothered in gravy; penne puttanesca with Italian sausage, kalamata olives, and fried pepperocinis, tossed in a vodka tomato cream sauce; pad thai; mixed grill of chicken, Italian sausage, and smoked bacon; hickory smoked barbecue ribs.

**Three Broomsticks.** Not open at press time, this new restaurant in the Wizarding World of Harry Potter will offer traditional British fare.

**Mythos.** Sea cave dining room offering the best food in the park; lunch (and dinner only in busy seasons). (See full description in the Universal Orlando Dining section of the Dining chapter.)

## Special Events

**Grinchmas.** For most of December, the back lot is transformed into the Christmas town of Whoville, featuring the Grinch, real snow, wintertime activities, and a live stage show, *How the Grinch Stole Christmas*. Included in the price of admission.

# CityWalk

With the demise of Downtown Disney's Pleasure Island's nightclub themed area, CityWalk remains the most viable option to club hop in the Orlando area. It's also a nice alternative to park food for day-trippers and a sparkling mirage of twinkling lights, fun if not luxurious dining (unless you count Emeril's), so-so shopping, and unique and happening nightclubs for evening partygoers (come prepared for a young, local crowd). The thirty-acre complex, conveniently positioned between Universal Studios and the Islands of Adventure, is a definite lure for those making their way to and from the parks, and the picturesque lagoon running through it offers an opportunity for a boat ride to the Universal resort hotels, where even more dining and entertainment possibilities exist.

## CityWalk Basics

### ADMISSION

There's no charge to enter CityWalk; however, there is a $7 individual cover charge at each club. If you plan to party in several spots, consider the CityWalk Party Pass for $12, allowing unlimited entry for one night to all clubs (excluding Hard Rock Live). Any Universal Multiday Pass comes with a CityWalk Party Pass. The $15 CityWalk Party Pass and Movie buys unlimited one-night club admission plus a movie at Universal Cineplex. Purchase a Meal and Movie Deal for $21 to receive dinner at one of several CityWalk restaurants and a movie.

### PARKING

Parking is $14 during the day, and $3 between 6 and 10 p.m.; valet park for $12 for under two hours or $22 for anything more.

## Blue Man Group

You either love this show, or you just won't get it. Personally I think if you don't have a twentysomething along you'll be part of the latter group. Here is the premise: three bald blue guys combine mad drums, crazy antics such as cramming as much Captain Crunch into their mouths as possible, wild live music, audience participation, crazy improv, and an ending that is such a waste of paper that trees are wailing. I think bizarre is the best way to describe it. Housed in a specially created, 1,000-seat theater accessible from both CityWalk and Universal Studios, tickets can be tough to come by so plan ahead. Call 407-BLUE-MAN (407-258-3727) or visit www.universalorlando.com/shows/blue_man_group_tickets.aspx# for tickets and information.

## Universal Cineplex Movie Theater

When you weary of walking and are ready to relax, head here for your choice of twenty extra-large screens of entertainment including an IMAX. Along with stadium seating and high-backed rocking seats are wine (so bad it's undrinkable) and beer at the refreshment stand.

## Dining at CityWalk

### RESERVATIONS

Call (407) 224-3613 for priority seating or stop by the CityWalk Information kiosk on the walkway in front of the movie theater.

### THE VERY BEST FULL-SERVICE RESTAURANTS AT CITYWALK

**Emeril's.** CityWalk's best dining spot, a spin-off of the hot New Orleans' restaurant. (See full description in the CityWalk and Universal Resorts Dining section of the Dining chapter.)

**NBA City.** Good food and a nonstop barrage of NBA championship highlights. In the upstairs SkyBox Lounge are twenty TV screens and a view of CityWalk along with a full bar and menu items; pizza, grilled mahi mahi sandwich, Cajun stuffed chicken, sesame crusted salmon with a ginger soy glaze, chicken bleu cheese pasta, jambalaya, maple glazed pork chop.

**Pastamoré.** Excellent thin-crust pizzas baked in a wood-fired oven and flavorful, creative pastas and wood-roasted and grilled meats; chicken marsala, oak-grilled chicken and creamy Alfredo pesto penne, rib eye steak topped with caramelized onions and mushroom butter, salmon Provençal, baked lasagna, seafood fra diavolo.

## The Very Best Nightlife at CityWalk

**Bob Marley—A Tribute to Freedom.** There's "no worries, mon!" in this replica of Bob Marley's Jamaican home; two levels face an open-air courtyard holding a gazebo-shaped bandstand and dance floor; live reggae on tap every evening along with Red Stripe beer; appetizers and light meals: jerk chicken dip, Jamaican curried fish stew, plantain crusted corvina, fried red snapper in a Red Stripe tempura batter, Jamaican-style ahi in a Caribbean brown sauce with rice and peas, herb seared leg of lamb with scotch bonnet mashed potato.

**CityWalk's Rising Star.** Karaoke club where you take center stage with a live band (Tuesday through Saturday), backup singers, and a host; full bar, martinis, coffees, specialty drinks, wine, beer, champagne; buffalo wings, quesadillas, sliders, potato onion web, fried banana caramel cheesecake.

**The Groove.** DJ-driven techno music and occasional live bands; five bars and three specialty lounges spread over two stories; hopping dance floor, terrific sound system, and special effects.

**Hard Rock Live.** Live entertainment arena; big names, local bands, and live comedy; can be configured as either a large rock concert venue accommodating more than 3,000 or converted to an intimate nightclub setting. Ticket prices vary; purchase tickets at Hard Rock Live box office, by calling (407) 351-5483, through Ticketmaster, or online at www.hardrocklive.com.

**Pat O'Brien's.** Replica of the world-famous New Orleans watering hole; three bars: fun Piano Bar where the concept of dueling pianos originated, laid-back Main Bar with its neighborhood gathering place atmosphere, and the romantic, candlelit courtyard with flaming fountains and famous Hurricane drinks; light meals: crawfish nachos, po' boy sandwich, gumbo, crawfish étouffée, jambalaya, muffuletta sandwich, beignets, bread pudding.

**Red Coconut Club.** Tropical club catering to an older crowd that seems to be having trouble finding its niche; DJ and live music with everything from Sinatra to R&B to disco; full bar with signature martinis, premium cocktails, and wine; small dance floor and palm-fringed balcony overlooking CityWalk; three cheese chicken quesadillas, coconut fried shrimp, vegetarian spring rolls, crab rangoon, chorizo empanadas, mini beef fillets with cilantro sauce, orange ginger teriyaki chicken.

# 10

# OTHER NEARBY THEME PARKS

## SeaWorld

This first-rate marine park's 200 acres of fun are certainly worth a day away from Mickey. If you think Shamu is the only show of real interest here, think again. Show after show and exhibit after exhibit lead you through the fascinating world of marine life and its connection with humankind. And it's all done at a more laid-back pace, a welcome respite from the breakneck speed of Walt Disney World and Universal's theme parks. With a bit of planning and lots of speed walking, it's possible to go from one show to the next with a short break for lunch, although that doesn't leave much time for seeing the continuous exhibits, many of which are even better than the live shows. If time allows, plan two days for a relaxed tour of the park and all it has to offer.

### *Getting There*

From Disney take I-4 east to exit 71. From Universal take I-4 west to exit 72 (Beeline Expressway/FL-528/Airport), then once on the Beeline, take the first exit (International Drive). At the traffic light turn left (you'll be driving on International Drive). At the second light turn right onto Central Florida Parkway. SeaWorld's entrance is on the right-hand side of Central Florida Parkway.

## Operating Hours

Open at 9 a.m. with closing times varying according to the season. Call (888) 800-5447 for up-to-date information or go online at www.seaworld.com.

## Park Services

**ATMs.** Seven automated teller machines are scattered throughout the park: just outside and just inside the main entrance, across from Stingray Lagoon, across from Terrors of the Deep, across from Penguin Encounters, in the Games Area near Shamu's Happy Harbor, and next to Mango Joe's.

**Baby care services.** The Baby Care Center is located in Happy Harbor between the First Aid Station and the Swishy Fishies ride. Provided is a nursing mother's room, restrooms with "Tiny Toilets," baby changing stations, and a children's play area with toys. You'll also find a microwave, bottle warmer, juice, cereal, snack items, diapers, wipes, and other baby care items for purchase. An additional nursing area is located at the Guest Assistance Center near Penguin Encounter.

**Dining.** Make dining reservations at the Information counter at the front of the park or call (888) 800-5447.

**First aid.** Two locations: behind Stingray Lagoon and in Shamu's Happy Harbor.

**Guest relations and information counter.** Just past the entrance gate is an information booth with guidemaps and guest information. Make reservations for dining and behind-the-scenes tours, and look for lost children and lost articles here.

**Guests with disabilities.** Parking for guests with disabilities is located near the main entrance. All exhibits and attractions are accessible through the main entrance for guests in wheelchairs. All restrooms, restaurants, and gift shops are accessible to guests in wheelchairs, and companion-assisted restrooms are located near the main entrance next to Exit Gifts, at the Friends of the Wild Gift Shop, in the Village Square across from Polar Parlor, at the Baby Care Center in Happy Harbor, at SeaFire Inn, at Voyager's Restaurant, and at Shark Encounter. Guide dogs are permitted. Sign language interpreters for live shows are available for the hearing-impaired with at least a one-week notice; call (407) 363-2400 for reservations. Guides for guests with disabilities and in braille are available at the

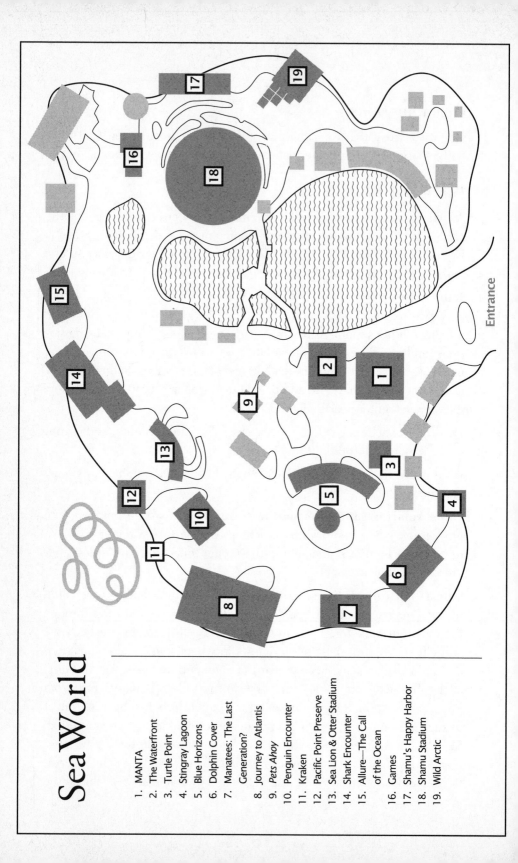

# SeaWorld

1. MANTA
2. The Waterfront
3. Turtle Point
4. Stingray Lagoon
5. Blue Horizons
6. Dolphin Cove
7. Manatees: The Last Generation?
8. Journey to Atlantis
9. Pets Ahoy
10. Penguin Encounter
11. Kraken
12. Pacific Point Preserve
13. Sea Lion & Otter Stadium
14. Shark Encounter
15. Allure—The Call of the Ocean
16. Games
17. Shamu's Happy Harbor
18. Shamu Stadium
19. Wild Arctic

Entrance

information booth at the park. Assistive listening devices for many of the live shows are available at Guest Services, with a $20 refundable deposit. Call (800) 432-1178 for more information or download an accessibility guide at www.seaworld.com/assetrepo/documents/orlando/may%20 2009%20internet%2072r.pdf.

**Lockers.** Located just inside the main gate, in Shamu's Happy Harbor, and near Kraken; available for $7 to $10 per day depending on the size.

**Parking.** $12 per day; free for Platinum Passport holders. Preferred parking for $20 within easy walking distance to the entrance. Valet parking is $25. Rows 1 through 37 are within walking distance; all others serviced by tram.

**Pet kennels.** Located outside the main gate next to the tram stop for a daily fee of $6. Proof of vaccination required.

**Quick Queue.** Enjoy unlimited access through express entrances to all major rides and shows for a fee that varies according to the season ranging from $14.95 to $29.95.

**Soak zones.** Some of the live shows have clearly marked soak zones. Avoid them if you wish to stay dry and/or are carrying expensive camera equipment. Believe it when you're warned that you'll get wet; you may even get soaked, and that's with ice-cold salt water.

**Stroller and wheelchair rentals.** Single strollers rent for $14, doubles $18.50, wheelchairs $10, and ECVs $45.

**VIP Tours.** The Standard VIP Tour gives front-of-the-line access for you and other participants for $100 to $125 per person (depending on the season). Just for private groups, an Elite VIP Tour, available for up to twelve people, which also includes a penguin encounter and lunch at Shark's Underwater Grill, is $250 per person. Call (800) 406-2244 for reservations and information.

## The Very Best Attractions at SeaWorld

### JOURNEY TO ATLANTIS

Travel on water as well as high-speed rails in a special-effects battle between good and evil at this one-of-a-kind attraction. Riders are lured by sirens into the Lost City of Atlantis where, with the use of lasers and holographics, they encounter hundreds of special effects and several surprises along the way, including two steep and wet drops, one of which is totally unexpected. Pump up your heart for the final 60-foot plummet and be prepared for a good soaking. **Minimum height 42 inches (3 feet, 6 inches); guests 42 to 48 inches (4 feet) tall must be accompanied by an adult. Not recommended for expectant mothers or those with heart, neck, and back problems. 6-minute ride.**

### KRAKEN

A legendary sea monster held in captivity by the sea god Poseidon is released in all its fury at the longest, tallest, fastest, and only floorless coaster in Orlando. All that's holding you in are your bench and shoulder harness. Ascend to the top of the steepest drop in central Florida before plunging 149 feet (fifteen stories) to the bottom at speeds of 65 mph. You'll find yourself upside down seven times and underwater three times before shooting through a tunnel and immediately screeching to a halt. It's so fast you won't know what hit you. **Minimum height 54 inches (4 feet, 6 inches). Not recommended for expectant mothers or those with heart, neck, or back problems. 3½-minute ride.**

### MANTA

Find out what it's like to skim and fly like a manta ray on the world's only flying coaster. This mind-boggling attraction has the distinction of putting guests horizontally, head first and face-down on the back of a giant manta ray. After walking the queue filled with marine life aquariums of sea dragons, octopus, schools of fish, and 300 rays, harness up in a prone position and soar through the air with four sweeping inversions as you skim along the top of the lagoon throwing out a 14-foot high spray of water. You'll top out at 56 miles per hour with drops up to 113 feet. Need I say more? **Minimum height is 54 inches (4 feet six inches). 2½-minute ride.**

### BELIEVE

An inspiring show in a state-of-the-art theater that reveals the close connection between trainers and SeaWorld's killer whales. Suspended above the whale pool are four massive 10- by 20-foot LED screens that when brought together form a super giant screen for close-ups of the whales underwater, above water, even aerial views. Listen to the screams of astonishment echoing throughout much of SeaWorld as the audience watches the whales propel their trainers around the pool, riding them 30 feet in the air, leaping and diving as they perform an absolutely remarkable show.

Members of the audience who choose to sit in the designated soak zone will indeed get drenched throughout the show. You'll roar laughing as the mind-changing audience runs up the stadium steps to higher and drier ground when they realize the true power in the tails of these huge creatures. The after-dark show, seasonal Shamu Rocks, is performed to rock 'n' roll music. **25-minute show.**

*CARA'S TIP:* Think twice before seating young children in the soak zone. The water that hits the audience can be quite powerful and could intimidate an adult, much less a small child. A major advantage that might possibly overshadow the soaking is the spectacular underwater view of the whales through the glass-walled tank from the lower seats. Even though the stadium holds 6,000 people, don't show up at the last minute and expect to find a seat.

## BLUE HORIZONS

Take an adventure into a young girl's dreams where an amazing cast of divers, bungee jumpers, and aerialists interacts with bottlenose dolphins, false killer whales, and beautiful soaring birds. A lovely set design, brilliant costumes, and an original contemporary score combine to make this one of SeaWorld's best shows. You can't help but love these gentle creatures who steal your heart away as they vault as high as 25 feet while the crowd squeals with delight. Come prepared for plenty of tail splashing in the lower seats. **25-minute show.**

*CARA'S TIP:* Show up thirty minutes prior to showtime to ensure yourself a seat at this very popular show.

## *CLYDE AND SEAMORE TAKE PIRATE ISLAND*

In a live show with a loose plot involving pirates, a treasure map, and a search for gold, Clyde and Seamore, two of SeaWorld's cleverest resident sea lions, entertain while slipping and sliding through their antics as they mimic their way around the stage. A sneaky sea otter only adds to the fun.

# SEAWORLD PARK TOURS AND INTERACTIVE PROGRAMS

Call (800) 327-2424 or go online at http://4adventure.com/swf/special_programs_home.aspx to reserve. For Sharks Deep Dive call (800) 406-2244 or book online. Once inside the park, reservations may be made at the Guided Tour Counter.

**Animal Shows and Photo Tour.** Seven-hour experience with inside access to the park's animals and their shows. See Believe, Blue Horizons, and Clyde and Seamore Take Pirate Island with reserved seating. At the end of each show have your photo taken with the animal stars. Also meet a penguin and have lunch poolside with Shamu. Admission not included and is required. Adults from $125 and from $100 for children.

**Behind the Scenes Tour.** See what happens behind the scenes at SeaWorld on this ninety-minute tour. Discover how the animal experts care for rescued manatees and sea turtles. Interact with a shark, explore a polar bear den, and touch a penguin. Admission is not included and is required. Adults from $30 and from $20 for children.

**Beluga Interaction Program.** Learn about mysterious beluga whales before changing into wet suits and getting into the water to touch, feed, and communicate with them through hand signals. Open to guests ten years of age and older. Park admission is not included and is required. $149.

**Dolphin Spotlight Tour.** One-hour walking tour backstage at Blue Horizons to see what it takes to care for and train the animal stars. Then participate in a training session and touch a dolphin. Admission is not included and is required. Adults from $50 and from $40 for children.

**Marine Mammal Keeper Experience.** Eight-hour program designed for those interested in the care, feeding, rescue, and rehabilitation of SeaWorld's animals. Work alongside marine mammal experts, interacting with and caring for dolphins, sea lions, walruses, whales, and manatees. $399 including lunch, T-shirt, souvenirs, and seven-day pass to SeaWorld. The program begins at 6:30 a.m. for up to three guests per day; only those age thirteen and older may participate.

**Penguin Spotlight Tour.** One-hour walking tour behind the scenes at the Penguin Encounter exhibit. Discover what it takes to care for these unique birds, see a puffin up close, and interact with penguins. $40 for adults, $30 for children. Park admission is not included and is required. Children under eighteen must be accompanied by an adult.

**Sharks Deep Dive.** Two-hour program immersing guests into the fascinating world of the shark. The program begins by exploring shark physiology, conservation, and myths. Then don wet suits and an underwater helmet, allowing participants to breathe and communicate without scuba equipment, before entering a shark cage smack dab in the middle of more than thirty sharks and thousands of fish. $149. Program requires park admission and includes a souvenir T-shirt. Must be ten years or older.

And if you're in luck, a 2,000-pound walrus will put in an appearance, making the entire show worth the wait. (Be careful, it spits!) **25-minute show.**

### PETS AHOY

Worth a bit of planning, this comically entertaining live show set in a harborside village features one hundred animals, including dogs, cats, birds, rats, even a potbellied pig. Considering that most have been rescued from local animal shelters, you'll be amazed at their skillful performance in a variety of fun skits and tricks. You'll see cats walking tightropes, pigs driving cars, dogs jumping rope, and ducks flapping their way across the stage. All in all, one cute act. **25-minute show.**

*CARA'S TIP:* Arrive early to avoid being shut out of this small theater.

## SHARK ENCOUNTER

This is definitely SeaWorld's best exhibit, fear-inspiring yet fascinating. Begin your exploration by traveling on a moving sidewalk through an amazing underwater clear acrylic tunnel surrounded by tropical fish and moray eels. Look closely at the reef for eels that love to find cozy hiding places. If you're in luck, one might swim slowly over your head.

Proceed to individual tanks filled with scorpion fish, barracuda with razor-sharp teeth, poisonous puffer fish, lionfish with its toxic spines, and sea dragons with leaflike appendages. Then on to the best part of the exhibit, the shark tunnel. Fifty sharks swim around you, a sight guaranteed to raise the hair on the back of your neck. The accompanying ominous music only adds to the tension. Oftentimes as you move through the tunnel, a sawfish will come to rest overhead, quite a sight to behold.

## WILD ARCTIC

The fascinating animals of the Arctic have come to sunny Florida. Your adventure begins either by air with a "jetcopter" adventure film in a motion simulator setting or "on foot" for a viewing in stationary seats minus the stomach churning. After the film, proceed to chilly Base Station Wild Arctic, where beluga whales, polar bears, and walruses in ice-cold pools can be viewed both from above and, after winding your way down ramps, from under the water. **The by-air simulator ride has a 42-inch (3-foot, 6-inch) minimum height. Not recommended for expectant mothers; anyone with heart, neck, or back problems; or those prone to motion sickness.**

*CARA'S TIP:* The simulator ride is pretty gut-wrenching; those with even a bit of motion sickness should beware.

## The Very Best Dining at SeaWorld

Specialty dining at SeaWorld includes Dine with Shamu, a dinner buffet at Shamu Stadium including an up-close-and-personal poolside view of a training session between the killer whales and their trainers; and the Makahiki Luau, a Polynesian show with tropical cuisine. For reservations call (888) 800-5447 or book online at www.seaworld.com

**Sharks Underwater Grill.** Dine in front of the fascinating shark tank at SeaWorld's only full-service restaurant, featuring a "Floribbean" menu with an accent on seafood; grottolike setting with an amazing dining room of floor-to-ceiling windows peering into the 660,000-gallon Shark Encounter tank; pan-seared merluza, shrimp pasta Alfredo, mixed grill, steak en croute, moho pork; *children's meals:* pasta marinara, hot dog, chicken tenders, grilled chicken breast with orange glaze, fried shrimp. Open for lunch and dinner; call (888) 800-5447 for priority seating or arrange on day of visit at the information desk.

## Special Entertainment

**Mystify.** Summer show with marine creatures shown on 60-foot mist screens, 100-foot fountains, and fireworks. View it from the Waterfront harbor.

## Special Events

**Viva La Musica.** March Latin music festival with Saturday night concerts by award-winning Latin artists as well as Hispanic cuisine. Concerts included in park admission.

**Halloween Spooktacular.** Four-weekend event with costumed characters, Halloween-themed shows, and trick or treat for little goblins. Included in park admission.

**Christmas at SeaWorld.** The Wild Arctic attraction is transformed into the Polar Express Experience with a multisensory simulation of riding the Polar Express train. There's a special Shamu show, "Shamu Christmas Miracles," and the Orlando Philharmonic entertains between Christmas and New Year's with music from the *The Polar Express.*

# Discovery Cove

Swim with the dolphins at the one-of-a-kind Discovery Cove. Much controversy surrounds this type of park as animal rights activists protest the exploitation of dolphins, making the decision to participate one not to be taken lightly. However, if there is one place to do a dolphin swim, Discovery Cove is it, where extreme caution is taken to ensure the animals' safety.

That said, here is one of the best places to spend your vacation dollars. And dollars you will spend, with a full day costing as much as $289. But it is a chance to get in the water with a dolphin, snorkel in tropical coves loaded with fish and rays (sharks and barracudas are safely behind Plexiglas), and sit on relatively uncrowded white-sand beaches. Only 1,000 guests per day are allowed to enter this thirty-acre park, built at a cost of $100 million.

Discover a tropical paradise overflowing with palms and flowering plants, dripping bougainvilleas, crystal-clear blue lagoons, waterfalls, aviaries, and marine life galore. Interact with tropical fish, stingrays, colorful birds, and of course, dolphins, or just lie under an umbrella on a white-sand beach fronting the boulder-strewn, sparkling blue dolphin lagoon while sipping tropical drinks to your heart's content. It has all the makings for a great day in the Florida sun.

## Discovery Cove Basics

### GETTING THERE

From Disney take I-4 east toward Orlando to exit 71 (the same exit as SeaWorld). Turn right on Central Florida Parkway. Discovery Cove is on the right just past the entrance to SeaWorld. From Universal take I-4 west to exit 72 (Beeline Expressway/FL-528/Airport). Once on the Beeline, take the first exit (International Drive). At the traffic light turn left (you will be driving on International Drive), and at the second light turn right onto Central Florida Parkway. The entrance to Discovery Cove is on the left-hand side of Central Florida Parkway.

### OPERATING HOURS

Open from 9 a.m. to 5:30 p.m. Doors open at 8:00 a.m. for those who would like an early jump on the park. This is definitely one place where the early bird gets the worm—being one of the first in the lagoon with the dolphins. Arriving early assures a dolphin swim first thing in the morning, allowing time to explore the other areas of the park at your leisure.

### PARKING

Complimentary parking is just a short stroll away from the lobby.

## ADMISSION

The cost, depending on the season, is an all-inclusive price of $199 to $289, including a dolphin swim, or $99 to $199 minus the swim. Only those ages six and older may participate in the dolphin swim. I personally do not think the park is worth the money if there is no interest in the dolphins, and at least one person in your party must participate in the dolphin swim. Although it's certainly a beautiful spot, there really isn't enough activity for a full day unless you love the idea of suntanning on a white-sand beach. Your money would be better spent at one of the many spectacular water parks in the area.

If the price seems unreasonably high, consider what is included: all attractions, continental breakfast, lunch, snacks and beverages including beer throughout the day, a 5-by-7-inch photo of your party, parking, lockers, snorkeling equipment, wet suit, towels, fish and bird food, and a bonus admission of fourteen consecutive days at either SeaWorld Orlando, Aquatica, or Busch Gardens Tampa. Admission to all three parks for fourteen consecutive days is available for an additional charge of $70.

## RESERVATIONS

Reservations are mandatory. In busy season try to plan your visit several months in advance (reservations are taken up to one year prior). Off-season allows for a bit more flexibility. If the day you wish to visit is sold out, keep checking for cancellations. Call (877) 557-7404 or go online at www.discoverycove.com.

## CANCELLATION POLICY

Full refund up to thirty days prior, no refund if canceled within thirty days of your visit.

Discovery Cove only closes in case of lightning; once your payment is made, rain or shine, you'll not receive a refund unless a hurricane or tropical storm is approaching, in which case a full refund or reschedule is available with no penalties. Date changes are allowed up to 5 p.m. the day before if space is available. So if stormy weather threatens, try for an alternate day. There is no charge for the first date change; after that a $50 fee is assessed.

## WHEN TO COME

Discovery Cove is open year-round; however, warmer weather makes it easier to dip into the chilly seventy-seven-degree saltwater pools. Although winter days in Florida can be warm and sunny, some are downright cold, not exactly conducive to relaxing on the beach or swimming in the bracing water. If you want to avoid rain, stay away during the peak hurricane season from August through the end of October. Spring and late fall are the best times to visit.

## GENERAL INFORMATION

**Dining.** Your admission price includes an unappetizing continental breakfast, bag snacks, ice cream, and beverages (slushies, iced tea, sodas, hot chocolate, and beer) throughout the day, and a passable lunch at the Laguna Grill (pasta primavera, grilled salmon, burger, Caesar chicken salad, grilled chicken breast, hot dog, with sides of stir-fried vegetables and a variety of desserts).

**Guests with disabilities.** Those who can maneuver up to the wading areas may participate in the dolphin swim as long as they need only limited help or have personal assistance. Specially equipped outdoor wheelchairs with oversize tires for beach maneuvering are available and can be reserved in advance.

**Lockers and changing rooms.** Complimentary lockers are located near the lagoons. Leave your regular sunscreen at home—special dolphin-safe sunscreen is provided. Near the lockers are showers and changing rooms with complimentary towels, toiletries, and hair dryers.

**Private cabanas.** Available for rent are private cabanas tucked within the foliage overlooking the Dolphin Lagoon. Included are a table and chairs, chaise lounges, refrigerator, fresh flowers, and towels. A host will service your cabana for the day.

**"Trainer For a Day" Program.** This behind-the-scenes program allows as many as twelve guests per day to work with the trainers in the feeding, training, and caring of the park animals. The price of $398 to $488 (depending on the season) also covers everything included in the cost of regular admission, with the addition of an enhanced dolphin encounter and training session including a ride on the front of two dolphins in what is known as a double-foot push. Participants must be in good physical condition and at least six years old. Those age twelve or younger must be accompanied by a paying adult.

**Special occasions.** Celebrate a special occasion with the assistance of the Discovery Cove dolphins who deliver a personalized message on your keepsake buoy along with special touches perfect for a wedding proposal or birthday celebration. Combine this with a private cabana, red roses, champagne, birthday cakes, and more in a variety of packages available by contacting reservations.

## The Very Best Attractions at Discovery Cove

### AVIARY

A free-flight aviary, where more than 250 tropical birds literally eat right out your hand, is one of my favorite places to visit here. A Discovery Cove employee is on hand to distribute bird feed (some of it pretty gross-looking) and offer advice on exactly how to attract these colorful creatures. If you're holding a handful of food, be prepared; the birds seem to come at you from out of nowhere. The large bird area has wonderful and unusual varieties of toucans, pigeons, and doves, but my favorite section is the small bird sanctuary where visitors can hand-feed tiny birds including finches and hummingbirds. Oh, and enter from the Tropical River instead of walking in; it's a kick.

### DOLPHIN ENCOUNTER

The superstar of adventures here is the thirty-minute dolphin swim. After a short orientation, visitors are divided into groups of no more than eight people with two trainers to meet their Atlantic bottle-nosed dolphin. Now the fun begins! What gentle yet unbelievably strong creatures! Your introduction begins with a dolphin rubdown; you'll be amazed at how clean and rubbery their bodies are. Those timid about being in the water with dolphins (as I was) will find that their worries soon evaporate. The trainers do not allow any sudden movements, kicking, or hand slapping that might scare the animal. Continue with hand signals that get an instant reaction, such as chattering, spinning, or flips, and receive a big dolphin hug for a great photo that can be purchased later. A videographer also films the session.

Then comes the part you've been waiting for as two people at a time along with a trainer swim out to deeper water to interact one-on-one with the dolphin followed by a dolphin tow back to shore. What a ride! Your session ends with a big smooch on your new friend's nose.

## RAY LAGOON

Swim among hundreds of southern and cow-nose rays in this small, shallow water cove. Go ahead and touch them; they're gentle and, most important, have had their barbs removed.

# 11

# DISNEY CRUISE LINE

Combining a land package with a Disney cruise gives you the best of both worlds. Departing from nearby Port Canaveral are three- and four-night cruises to the Bahamas as well as seven-night cruises to both the western and eastern Caribbean, perfect for extending your vacation on a trip to sea. Other sailings include repositioning cruises through the Panama Canal, Los Angeles to the Mexican Riviera, even the Mediterranean, the Baltic, and Alaska.

While mainly geared toward adults traveling with children, the ships do offer many adults-only experiences, including special programs, their own beach at Castaway Cay, and an adults-only dining room and spa. But I do have to say that adults without children would probably be better off finding a different kind of cruise. That is, unless they are Disney fanatics and this cruise line would fit them perfectly. Regardless, do come prepared to vacation with hordes of little ones; it can't be avoided. Those traveling with children can look forward to many shared as well as adults-only activities, and kids will love the supervised children's programs and the myriad character greeting opportunities found at every turn.

Two of the ships, the *Disney Wonder* and *Disney Magic*—are lovingly designed in an art deco style, basically identical, varying only in itinerary. Each holds 2,400 passengers in 877 staterooms, many with verandas. Staterooms are spacious by cruise standards, with 73 percent of them outside cabins and 44 percent with private verandas. The much anticipated *Disney Dream* comes aboard the fleet in January 2011, a fabulous addition built on the same classic style but with more contemporary amenities and cabins. She will sail the Bahamas and hold 4,000 passengers, have virtual portholes for inside cabins, and even boast the first water coaster at sea.

New European shore excursions enhance the experience and add to the allure. There are treasure hunts in Tunisia, even a tour of Catherine's Palace in Pushkin complete with a Prince and Princess Ball with Disney princess characters. A "Port Adventure" is offered at each stop with families dividing into their own special groups: children enjoy their own mini adventure ashore with youth counselors; parents continue on with a more in-depth tour. At the Hermitage kids can visit the amazing art then create their very own masterpieces. Family Adventures are immersive, interactive tours allowing families to experience quality time together.

Those seeking deluxe experiences should book a shore excursion from the Signature Collection, utilizing intimate, upscale settings such as Tuscan cuisine cooking classes and wine tastings.

Call (800) 951-3532 or go online to http://disneycruise.disney.go.com/ for more information and reservations.

## Cabins

On the *Magic* and the *Wonder,* choose among accommodations ranging from a simple inside cabin to a two-bedroom suite with oversize veranda, media library, walk-in closet, and whirlpool tub. Twelve categories make it easy to choose what's best for you and your family. Of course, the larger the staterooms, the higher the price. You'll also pay a premium for outside versus inside rooms, the addition of a balcony, and a higher deck versus a lower one. Always ask about promotions when you call for reservations, or book far in advance and receive an early-booking discount.

Even the least expensive of Disney's staterooms are larger than those on most cruise ships. All are nautically decorated with natural woods and brass fixtures. Bedding is either a queen-size or two twin beds, and all rooms have, at the very least, a sitting area with a sofa and curtained divider. Each room comes with satellite flat panel TV, telephone, safe, a minifridge for drinks, and hair dryer. No smoking is permitted except on verandas and the starboard-side decks. Concierge service is included in the top three categories. It includes full room-service breakfast, snacks throughout the day, DVD rental, special gifts, and the services of a concierge staff to help with dining, spa, and shore excursion reservations.

Category 10 and up have a split bath configuration and offer connecting cabins. Handicapped accessible rooms are quite a bit larger than their category counterparts and are found on the back (aft) with a huge wraparound veranda. You'll need to call the special needs desk to obtain one.

### Royal Suite with Veranda—Category 1

Two luxurious suites fit this category, featuring two bedrooms and two-and-a-half baths, loads of glossy wood, a living area, eight-person dining table, media library, walk-in closets, Jacuzzi tub, wet bar, and even a baby grand piano. The very spacious veranda runs the length of the cabin. Sleeps seven; 1,029 square feet. Includes concierge service.

### Two-Bedroom Suite with Veranda—Category 2

These two-bedroom, two-and-a-half-bath spacious suites have an extended balcony. The living area has a queen-size sofa bed, six-person dining table, and wet bar. The master bath offers a whirlpool tub, double sink, commode, and walk-in closet. Sleeps five; 945 square feet. Includes concierge service.

### One-Bedroom Suite with Veranda—Category 3

One-bedroom, two-bath suites offer a separate parlor with double sofa bed as well as a pull-down bed, wet bar, four-person dining table, and extra-large veranda. There are two closets, one a walk-in. Sleeps four or five; 614 square feet. Includes concierge service.

### Deluxe Family Stateroom with Veranda—Category 4

A large stateroom with a split-configuration bath. The sitting area, separated from the bed by a curtained divider, contains a sofa bed and a pull-down bed. All Category 4 staterooms come with a veranda. Sleeps four or five; 304 square feet.

## Deluxe Stateroom with Veranda—Categories 5 and 6

Category 5 cabins are located one deck higher than Category 6. Both have a veranda and a curtain-divided sitting area with a vanity, small sofa bed, and pull-down bed. Sleeps three or four; 268 square feet.

## Deluxe Stateroom with Navigators Veranda—Category 7

The same as Category 5 and 6 except for a different type of veranda that's enclosed with a large open porthole. Sleeps three; 268 square feet.

## Deluxe Oceanview Stateroom—Categories 8 and 9

Category 8 staterooms are outside cabins on higher decks, with Category 9 cabins outside but on the two lowest decks; neither has a veranda. Sleeps three or four; 214 square feet.

## Deluxe Inside Stateroom—Category 10

Category 10 is an inside cabin without a veranda located on the two lower decks. All have a curtain-divided sitting area with small sofa bed, pull-down bed, and vanity. Sleeps three or four; 214 square feet.

## Standard Inside Stateroom—Categories 11 and 12

Category 11 accommodations are inside cabins located on the upper decks; Category 12 staterooms are inside on a lower deck. The sitting area has a curtain divider with a small sofa bed, pull-down bed, and vanity. Sleeps three or four; 184 square feet.

# Cruise Itineraries

Once the *Disney Dream* begins operation in January 2011, she will take over the three- and four-day Bahamas itineraries with the *Wonder* heading to Alaska in the summer and the Mexican Riviera the rest of the year. The *Magic* will offer seven-day Caribbean itineraries in the winter months and Mediterranean and Baltic cruises in the summer.

For now the *Disney Wonder* offers three- and four-day Bahamas cruises, and the *Wonder* seven-day Caribbean cruises, all from Port Canaveral with each itinerary including a stop at Disney's own private island, where an entire day is dedicated to fun in the sun. Here guests can swim, cruise around on paddleboats, sail, sea kayak, snorkel in special Disney-created "shipwrecks," snooze in a hammock, shop a Bahamian marketplace, and dine at a barbecue buffet on the beach. Trails and bike paths are laid out for the exercise-minded, and those who really want to relax can book a massage in one of the private beach cabanas. Da Shade Game Pavilion is the place for tennis, billiards, foosball, and basketball. Several bars scattered throughout the island sell alcoholic tropical drinks.

Four separate beaches cater to the needs of children, families, teens, and adults. Kids have their own special area called Scuttle's Cove, where a program of activities is sure to please including a new water play area for the little ones. Serenity Bay is the adults-only beach for those age eighteen and older, where private cabana massages can be prearranged. The Family Beach is perfect for those who want to spend the day with their children, and the Teen Beach offers snorkeling, kayaking, and supervised activities. The *Flying Dutchman,* from the hit movie *Pirates of the Caribbean: Dead Man's Chest,* is moored near the Family Beach. Spring-a-Leak is a new water play area with a washed-away beach dwelling theme of broken plumbing and dripping pipes, all concocted to help guests cool off in the hot sun. Pelican's Plunge Slides are on a floating platform in the lagoon with a water spray area and a dumping water bucket. And new cabana rentals on the Family Beach are a nice addition. At each stop a variety of shore excursions is available, and the good news is that they may be pre-reserved online (concierge guests 105 days prior, Castaway Club repeat guests 90 days prior, all other guests 75 days prior).

## Recreation on the *Magic* and *Wonder*

**Arcade.** Quarter Masters, the ship's arcade, features the latest in video games; located by Goofy's Pool.

**Deck fun.** All ages enjoy the shuffleboard and Ping-Pong tables, and the exercise-minded will love the outdoor jogging track on Deck 4.

**Pools.** Three heated pools are found on Deck 9, all with fresh water. The adults-only Quiet Cove pool with two adjacent whirlpools and a spa-like atmosphere really is the sedate place it is touted to be with soft musical entertainment and the adjoining Cove Café. Goofy's Pool is perfect for families with two adjacent whirlpools (one hot and one cold), and aft is the always noisy, shallow Mickey Pool with a fun waterslide for young children. The Goofy Pool area is transformed some evenings to accommodate a 24-by-14-foot LED screen where guests can enjoy feature films and sporting events.

**ESPN Wide World of Sports.** Recreation area on Deck 10 featuring basketball and volleyball courts, ping pong, shuffleboard, and running track.

## Entertainment

**Beat Street/Route 66.** On the *Disney Magic* you'll find Beat Street, an entertainment area offering three nightclubs for adults (age eighteen and older) only. At the Rockin' Bar D are DJs and live bands with music from the '70s through today and a lively dance floor. There's also Diversions, a sports pub with ESPN satellite feeds on big-screen plasma TVs with appetizers such as hot dogs, chicken wings, and such; and Sessions for a mellow atmosphere with live piano music and guest vocalists.

On the *Disney Wonder* it's Route 66. Clubs include WaveBands, where dancing to a live band or DJ-driven music playing the hits of a span of generations is the agenda along with karaoke and dance parties; the art-deco-style Cadillac Lounge (my personal favorite) for a sophisticated atmosphere, fine wines, complimentary hors d'oeuvres—including caviar—live piano music, car bucket-seats for barstools, and a '50s feel; and the sports bar Diversions, similar to the same-named club on the *Disney Magic*.

**Buena Vista Theater.** Watch Disney classic movies as well as first-run feature films in this 268-seat theater. A giant LED screen at the Goofy Pool area shows movies under the stars.

**Cove Cafe.** Wine, coffees, and pastries located just off the adult pool. For those ages eighteen and older.

**Internet Café.** Surf the Web, e-mail a friend, or find out more about your cruise activities. A fee is charged for Internet services. Open 24/7.

**Pirates in the Caribbean Party.** This after-dinner dessert buffet and pirates show at Goofy's Pool is a much-anticipated event on each cruise. Go buccaneer crazy along with Mickey followed by a fireworks show at sea.

**Promenade Lounge.** Lobby lounge featuring live easy-listening music each evening along with dance parties, trivia, and bingo; complimentary hors d'oeuvres and snacks are served in the afternoon and evening hours; skip this and head down to the adult's-only nightclubs if you are traveling sans children.

**Walt Disney Theater.** Three-level, 1,022-seat theater with original live productions each evening.

## Dining on the *Magic* and *Wonder*

Disney's dining system, which rotates through each of three restaurants, is unique. Seating is assigned, and although you'll be moving to a different place each evening, your servers as well as table guests travel with you.

At Parrot Cay there's island-style cuisine along with Caribbean music and tropical decor, and at Animator's Palette the room changes as the night progresses from black-and-white to a barrage of color with animated scenes from classic Disney movies. On the *Disney Magic* the third dining room is Lumiere's, offering fine dining and a *Beauty and the Beast* twist on the evening; on the *Disney Wonder* it's Triton's, featuring seafood and a *Little Mermaid* underwater-style setting.

Dinner is served with staggered dining. Early seating is between 5:30 and 6 p.m. Cruisers with late seating will be dining between 8 and 8:30 p.m. Preference can be requested but is not guaranteed. Disney tries to put childless adults with other childless adults, and families with children with other families. Evening attire changes nightly but most if not all evenings are resort casual (no shorts or tank tops). Aboard the seven-night cruises, one dinner is semiformal, and one requires more formal or black-tie-optional attire.

Breakfast and lunch with open seating are served at Parrot Cay and either Lumiere's on the *Disney Magic* or Triton's on the *Disney Wonder*. A casual breakfast, lunch, and dinner buffet is offered at Topsider's on the *Disney Magic* and breakfast and lunch at Beach Blanket Buffet on the *Disney Wonder* (not my favorite place to eat—too crowded and sub-par food). Beverages such as coffee, tea, soda, juice, and milk are complimentary with meals, and a self-serve soda and juice station is found just outside the buffet area. Anywhere else, beverages, both alcoholic and non, may be charged to your room.

If you want to get away from the hustle and bustle make reservations for Palo, the adults-only (age eighteen and over) dining room. Featured is Northern Italian cuisine, fine wines, and an air of romance accompanied by sweeping ocean views. Good appetizers include the tender, fried calamari with a dusting of fried cherry peppers or the buffalo mozzarella with tasty tomatoes topped with a touch of basil. I prefer the pasta (nice, fresh lobster ravioli) here over the meat dishes. Because reservations fill up quickly, make them as soon as possible (concierge guests 105 days prior, Castaway Club repeat guests 90 days prior, all other guests 75 days prior). Suggested dress at Palo is a jacket or a dress shirt for men and a dress or pantsuit for ladies. Dining is from 6 to 11 p.m. Palo also features a reservations-only champagne brunch on four- and seven-night cruises, and high tea is served on seven-night cruises. There is a $15 additional fee for dinner and brunch, $5 for tea.

Anytime the stomach starts to rumble, head to Pluto's Doghouse for hot dogs, hamburgers, chicken sandwiches, bratwurst, veggie burgers, chili tacos, and chicken tenders; Goofy's Galley has interesting and healthy choices with an assortment of fresh salads, fruit, ice cream, and wrap and panini sandwiches; or Pinocchio's Pizzeria for a slice of pizza.

In-Room Dining is offered twenty-four hours a day, with continental breakfast served from 7 to 10 a.m. and sandwiches, salads, soup, pizza, pasta, and dessert the remainder of the day and into the wee hours of the morning. Those staying in a suite may order a full breakfast.

## Services

### Vista Pool and Spa

This adults-only spa, salon, and fitness center has a long list of luxurious services perfect for a great day at sea, including many types of massage, body treatments, facials, and hydrotherapy. The Exotic Rain Forest Thermal Suite offers two types of steam rooms (mild and aromatic), dry sauna, heated mosaic tile chairs, and ice drench showers for a $15 per day charge. Spa Villas offer an indoor treatment suite that is connected to a private outdoor veranda with personal hot tub, open-air shower, and Roman-style canopied bed—a perfect romantic getaway. A salon offers manicures, pedicures, haircuts, and hair coloring. What I don't like is that you must walk through the spa to get to the fitness room, a disturbance for those who are paying top dollar to enjoy the services. Reservations can be made online at http://disneycruise.disney.go.com (concierge guests 105 days prior, Castaway Club repeat guests 90 to 120 days prior depending on your level, all other guests 75 days prior).

At the complimentary fitness center you'll find Life Fitness treadmills, stair-climbers, exercise bicycles, rowing machines, exercise machines, and free weights in a facility that comes with a fantastic ocean view. For an additional fee, personal training, Pilates, and yoga are available. Cardio and Sculpt-and-Tone classes are complimentary. Avoid the "secrets of a flatter stomach" and other such seminars, which are come-ons to sell overpriced products.

## For Adults Only

A third of all guests aboard Disney's ships are adults traveling without children, and there are many areas where no children are to be found: Palo for dining, adults-only pool and nightclubs, a separate beach at Castaway Cay with private massage cabanas, live music at Cove Café while enjoying coffee and drinks, and the soothing Vista Spa. There is also a variety of seminars on wine tasting, art, and health, as well as walking tours of the ship.

## Children's and Teens' Programs

With nearly an entire deck dedicated to children, there is a wide range of age-specific programs for kids. We all know what Disney does best, and that is cater to the needs of children. And when children are happy, so are their parents. It's a perfect combination of family time as well as playtime with others their own age. The programs run from around 9 a.m. to about midnight and are complimentary (with the exception of Flounder's Reef Nursery). Pagers are provided to parents.

### FLOUNDER'S REEF NURSERY

This is the place for children ages three months to three years; those three- and four-year-olds who are not potty trained, and therefore not eligible for the Oceaneer Club, also may be accommodated here. The fee is $6 per hour per child ($5 per additional child per hour) with a two-hour minimum. It's best to make advance reservations because only a limited number of infants and toddlers are accepted at one time. Although hours vary, the service is generally provided from 9 a.m. to 11 p.m.

## OCEANEER CLUB

In a setting reminiscent of Never Never Land, potty-trained children ages three through seven have plenty to keep them occupied and happy. For three- and four-year-olds there are such activities as Toy Story Boot Camp, Aladdin's Adventures, Do Si Do with Snow White, water games, a search for Tinker Bell, and Rescue Rangers. Ages five through seven enjoy treasure hunts and whale digs on Castaway Cay, animation classes, Ratatouille Cooking School, flubber play, and So You Want to Be a Pirate?. All this plus much, much more. Open from 9 a.m. to midnight.

## OCEANEER LAB

At Disney's ultramodern Oceaneer Lab, older children enjoy Nintendo played on a giant screen, a science lab, reading and lounge area, and computer games. Children ages eight through ten on the *Magic* and eight through twelve on the *Wonder* participate in cooking school, Kim Possible: Cruise Control, detective school, and lab workshops, and learn the secrets of Disney animation. Open from 9 a.m. to midnight.

## OCEAN QUEST

On the *Disney Magic* only is this perfect location for children ages eleven to thirteen to play video games, participate in arts and crafts, or watch a movie on one of the multiple plasma-screen televisions. A big hit is the super-cool simulation game, Ocean Quest, where they can steer a cruise ship in and out of various ports around the world from a replica of the ship's bridge. LCD screen "windows" allow them a look out over the bridge via live video feed from the actual bridge. Open from 9 a.m. to midnight.

## TEEN HANGOUTS

Teens ages thirteen through seventeen hang out at the Stack on the *Disney Magic* and Aloft on the *Disney Wonder,* where they'll find games, Internet, music listening stations, and a big-screen TV. Other activities include dance and pool parties, animation drawing, weight lifting classes, arcade nights, PJ parties, filmmaking, karaoke, and trivia games. Open from 10 a.m. to 2 a.m.

# APPENDIX:
# SUGGESTED ITINERARIES

## Suggested One-day Itinerary at the Magic Kingdom for Adults with Young Children

Although this is a suggested one-day itinerary, those with young children may want to plan for two days at the Magic Kingdom. With so many attractions for the little ones, a couple of days spent at a relaxing pace are certainly preferable over a one-day mad dash through the park, allowing time to head back to your resort for a midday nap or a post-lunch dip in the pool.

Make Advance Dining Reservations (call exactly 180 days prior at 7 a.m. Orlando time) for a meal at Cinderella's Royal Table.

Upon arrival check your daily schedule and decide when to work in the Dream-Along with Mickey show and any character greetings of interest. Then head straight to Fantasyland, pick up a FASTPASS for Peter Pan's Flight, and then ride Winnie the Pooh and Dumbo and see *Mickey's PhilharMagic* before your FASTPASS time. Afterward take in Cinderella's Golden Carousel, It's a Small World, and Snow White's Scary Adventure.

Move on to Tomorrowland, pick up a FASTPASS if necessary for Buzz Lightyear, and take in the race cars at Tomorrowland Speedway and the show at Monsters, Inc. Comedy Club.

Have lunch at Cinderella's Royal Table or eat at one of the many quick-service spots—my favorite is Pecos Bill Café for good burgers. See the Haunted Mansion attraction before finding a place for the Celebrate a Dream Come True Parade. Pick up a FASTPASS at the Jungle Cruise in Adventureland before getting in line for Pirates of the Caribbean and the Magic Carpets of Aladdin. If you're making good time, see the Swiss Family Treehouse, The Enchanted Tiki Room, or Country Bear Jamboree.

If your kids (or you) are not totally exhausted by now and want to stay for the evening SpectroMagic parade and Wishes fireworks, make Advance Dining Reservations for dinner at the Crystal Palace, a character meal with Winnie the Pooh and friends before the evening's festivities.

## Suggested One-day Itinerary at the Magic Kingdom for Adults and Older Children

If your kids are older or you're traveling with adults only, try this itinerary.

Have breakfast at your hotel or pick up a quick treat at the Main Street Bakery. Either way, try to be finished with your meal and in line for the rope drop at park opening time.

Head straight to Splash Mountain in Frontierland, and then take in Big Thunder Mountain next door.

Cut back through the hub to Tomorrowland and ride Space Mountain.

If anyone in your party is interested in the attractions in Fantasyland (as I usually am), go there now. It will probably be necessary to pick up a FASTPASS for either Peter Pan's Flight or Winnie the Pooh, so check that out first before your tour of this land begins. Ride Peter Pan's Flight, Snow White's Scary Adventure, and the Many Adventures of Winnie the Pooh. See *Mickey's PhilharMagic* and, if you really like torture, It's a Small World.

Have a relaxing lunch at either Liberty Tree Tavern or Tony's Town Square. If fast food is your choice, head to Pecos Bill's for great burgers.

See the Haunted Mansion attraction in Liberty Square before settling down for the afternoon Celebrate a Dream Come True Parade at 3 p.m.

After the parade see Pirates of the Caribbean in Adventureland.

Pick up anything of interest to you that you missed during the day. Good choices would be Buzz Lightyear, Stitch's Great Escape!, or the Jungle Cruise.

Before leaving, take a stroll down Main Street for shopping and a late afternoon snack.

If you decide to stay for the evening's festivities, make Advance Dining Reservations at Tony's Town Square for dinner (a noncharacter meal) and enjoy the park until the fun begins, or head back to your resort (easy to do if you're staying at a monorail-serviced property), freshen up, and have an early dinner before returning for the parade and fireworks.

## Suggested One-day Itinerary for Touring Epcot

For optimum enjoyment, Epcot really needs to be seen in one and a half to two days; however, the following itinerary does hit all the highlights. It may be difficult if not impossible to accomplish in busy season but entirely possible in the slower times of the year. Come prepared with plenty of energy and a good pair of walking shoes.

Have breakfast and be at the park at opening time.

Ride Soarin' at the Land, then move over to the east side of Future World to first Test Track and then Mission: SPACE.

See the attraction at the Universe of Energy and then ride Spaceship Earth.

See *Captain EO* at the Imagination pavilion.

Hop next door to the Land pavilion, where you'll want to ride the Living with the Land attraction, then head next-door to take in the Seas with Nemo & Friends.

Move to World Showcase and pick up a late lunch at one of the many quick-service spots.

Work your way around World Showcase for the remainder of the afternoon, making time between stops for shopping as you attempt to take in some of the highlights, including Maelstrom in Norway, the *Reflections of China* film, *The American Adventure* show, and *Impressions de France*. Make advance reservations at one of the World Showcase restaurants for 7 p.m., have dinner, and then roam or pick up anything you missed until about a half hour prior to the Illuminations fireworks, when it's time to search for a nice viewing spot for the show.

Go back to your hotel room and collapse.

# Suggested Two-day Itinerary for Touring Epcot

Now this is more like it, a much more relaxing two days at this massive park.

### First Day

Your first day of touring will take in all of Future World. Begin by riding Soarin' at the Land, and then see the Living with the Land attraction and the Circle of Life.

Move over to the east side of Future World, pick up a FASTPASS for Test Track, and while you wait ride Mission: SPACE and the Universe of Energy attractions.

Have lunch at the Coral Reef Restaurant; make your advance reservations for around 12:30 p.m. After lunch visit the Seas with Nemo & Friends.

Head to the Imagination pavilion to see *Captain EO* and Journey into the Imagination.

Tour Innovations and ride Spaceship Earth. Hang out, enjoying Epcot's fun atmosphere before making your way to dinner (remember to make Advance Dining Reservations weeks ahead of time) at one of the World Showcase restaurants or the Flying Fish Café at the Boardwalk.

Tomorrow night you'll be staying for the fireworks, so tonight head home for a good night's sleep.

## Second Day

Your second day will be a complete tour of World Showcase. Sleep in today because this area of Epcot doesn't open until 11 a.m. Begin your tour in Canada, where shopping and the *O Canada* film are in order.

Next tour the United Kingdom's cutesy shops and perhaps have a pint at the pub.

Break for lunch at either Chefs de France or Restaurant Marrakesh in Morocco; make your Advance Dining Reservations for around 1 p.m. Then see the *Impressions de France* show and do a bit of perfume shopping.

Visit Morocco to walk the interesting bazaars and alleyways.

Japan is next with its serene gardens and the Mitsukoshi Department Store brimming with all kinds of goodies.

Then *The American Adventure* show, a must on every patriotic citizen's list.

After America head to Italy for soft Italian leather and enjoy a glass of Chianti while you're at it.

Take in Germany and its jolly village and then move on to the *Reflections of China* film.

Next Norway and the Maelstrom attraction before your advance reservation time of 7 p.m. at one of the World Showcase restaurants. Ride the Gran Fiesta Tour either before or after dinner and stake out a place for the Illuminations fireworks at least a half hour before the show.

See Illuminations and then head for home or an evening at the Boardwalk, just a five-minute walk outside the International Gateway.

## Suggested One-day Itinerary for Touring Disney's Hollywood Studios

Plan to tour the Studios on a day when FANTASMIC! is scheduled, usually Sunday and Thursday. Arrive thirty minutes before park opening. Hopefully you've already made your Advance Dining Reservation for the FANTASMIC! Dinner or Lunch Package (see Special Entertainment at the end of the Disney's Hollywood Studios section for full details).

Since this park offers scheduled live shows, you'll need to work in the *Indiana Jones Epic Stunt Spectacular,* Beauty and the Beast Live on Stage, and the *Lights, Motors, Action! Extreme Stunt Show* when your schedule allows during the course of the day. And if you're traveling with toddlers, you'll certainly need to find time to see Playhouse Disney—Live on Stage!.

Everyone should immediately head to Toy Story Mania!, the park's most popular attraction. Then thrill junkies need to head to the Tower of Terror and Rock 'n' Roller Coaster.

Those touring with young children should plan a late breakfast at Hollywood & Vine's Playhouse Disney Play N' Dine with June and Leo from the *Little Einsteins* and JoJo and Golaith from *JoJo's Circus,* then see *Voyage of the Little Mermaid.* Or if thrill rides aren't your cup of tea, skip the scary attractions and go to the Magic of Disney Animation and the Great Movie Ride.

You'll want to plan for only a snack or light lunch. Advance reservations for the FANTASMIC! Dinner Package can be startlingly early (sometimes as early as 4 p.m.), so don't stuff yourself.

Take the Backlot Tour and then head over to MuppetVision 3-D.

Stake out a place for the Block Party Bash afternoon parade.

By now it is time for your advance reservation for the FANTASMIC! Dinner Package; if you're smart, you've made your reservation for the Hollywood Brown Derby.

After dinner pick up what you've missed before heading over to FANTASMIC! thirty minutes before showtime (even earlier if you haven't made priority seating for the FANTASMIC! Dinner or Lunch Package).

# Suggested One-day Itinerary for Touring Disney's Animal Kingdom

Be at the park gates a half hour before opening, using the time before the rope drop to walk the paths of the Oasis. Those with children may want to take in the character breakfast at Donald's Safari Breakfast before park opening.

Check the schedule for *Finding Nemo—The Musical* and decide when to fit it in (the first show is usually the least crowded). At the rope drop head straight to Expedition Everest then over to Africa for Kilimanjaro Safaris and the Pangani Forest Exploration Trail.

Explore Africa before backtracking to Discovery Island to take in the *It's Tough to Be a Bug* show. Then head to Camp Minnie-Mickey.

Work in the *Festival of the Lion King* sometime in the morning and stop for a visit at the Character Greeting Trails.

Head to your 1 p.m. advance reservation at the Rainforest Café or, better yet, the buffet at Tusker House.

After lunch it's time for Dinoland. Ride Dinosaur and take in the rides at Chester and Hester's Dino-Rama. If you have children in tow, make a stop at the Boneyard for playtime.

See the afternoon Mickey's Jammin' Jungle Parade (in slower seasons, the parade is sometimes the last event of the day, in which case it would be necessary to take in Kali River Rapids and the Maharaja Jungle Trek before it begins).

Move on to Asia to ride Kali River Rapids, and while you're waiting, walk the Maharaja Jungle Trek and see Flights of Wonder.

After Kali River Rapids you'll be soaked. Either head out to Rafiki's Planet Watch to see the exhibits or head home for a hot shower and dinner at your resort.

## Suggested One-day Itinerary at Universal Studios for Adults with Young Children

This park has enough to keep kids busy for part of a day, but remember that many of the attractions with major scare factors are not suitable for little ones.

Those with children who are not too young will want to see *Shrek* 4-D first, then Jimmy Neutron's Nicktoon Blast (younger children can sit in stationary seats).

Next head to Woody Woodpecker's Kidzone and ride the E.T. Adventure followed by Woody Woodpecker's Nuthouse Coaster. Work in the Animal Actors on Location show and A Day in the Park with Barney when you can during the day.

Break for lunch at the Classic Monster Café.

Return to Woody Woodpecker's Kidzone for wet playtime at Fievel's Playland and Curious George Goes to Town.

If your children are not too young and have a high tolerance for scary attractions, you may want to try *Twister:* Ride It Out.

Parents should utilize Universal's Child-Switch Program for rides with a high scare factor, whereby one parent stays behind with the children while the other rides an attraction, then the other parent hops aboard, leaving the first rider with the children.

## Suggested One-day Itinerary at Universal Studios for Adults and Older Children

Be at the park before opening time, allowing thirty minutes to park and another thirty to buy tickets (hopefully you've prepurchased them). Head straight to Hollywood Rip Ride Rockit, then *Shrek* 4-D and the *Revenge of the Mummy*. Move on to the World Expo area to take in *Men in Black: Alien Attack*.

In Hollywood see *Terminator 2*: 3-D, the Horror Make-Up Show, and then walk through Lucy–A Tribute.

Sometime during your day pick up lunch at a quick-service spot. My favorites are the Classic Monster Café and Richter's Burger Co. Or head outside the park's gates to one of the better CityWalk restaurants.

Move to the New York area and see *Twister*: Ride It Out and then head for Disaster! and *Jaws* (if it is open) in the nearby San Francisco/Amity area.

If you like attractions geared to the younger set, swing over to Woody Woodpecker's Kidzone (this might be the time to pick up the *Animal Actors on Location* show) and ride the E.T. Adventure. Walk back to the Curious George Goes to Town area and get wet if it's a hot and steamy day.

Head back to your hotel or plan for an evening at CityWalk.

## Suggested One-day Itinerary at Islands of Adventure for Adults with Young Children

Begin your day at Seuss Landing and make *One Fish, Two Fish, Red Fish, Blue Fish* your first stop. Proceed to the *Cat in the Hat,* then Caro-Seuss-el, and stop to play at If I Ran the Zoo. Then catch the High in the Sky Seuss Trolley Train Ride.

Head to the Wizarding World of Harry Potter to wander and lunch at the Three Broomsticks. Ride the Hippogriff, a child-friendly coaster, and if your children are not too young for loud noises, work in the Eighth Voyage of Sinbad.

Next comes Jurassic Park, where the Jurassic Park Discovery Center is a must for dinosaur-loving kids, followed by a romp in super Camp Jurassic, one of the best play areas for children in the Orlando area. If lines are short, ride the Pteranodon Flyers.

Work your way over to Toon Lagoon and let the kids have fun at Me Ship, The *Olive.*

Parents may want to utilize Universal's Child-Switch Program for attractions with a high scare factor whereby one parent can watch the children while the other rides, and then the other parent hops aboard, leaving the children with the first rider.

## Suggested One-day Itinerary at Islands of Adventure for Adults and Older Children

Be at the park before opening time, allowing thirty minutes to park and another thirty to buy tickets (which I hope you've purchased ahead). Head straight to the Wizarding World of Harry Potter to ride Harry Potter & The Forbidden Journey, Island of Adventure's newest signature attraction. Then to Dragon Challenge if you're a daredevil.

Backtrack to Marvel Super Hero Island to ride the Amazing Adventures of Spider-Man, then the Incredible Hulk, and finally Doctor Doom's Fear-fall before heading over to Jurassic Park.

Ride the Jurassic Park River Adventure then take a spin around Camp Jurassic, one of the neatest kid play areas in Orlando (don't miss the cave that leads to the amber mine) and the Jurassic Park Discovery Center.

Have lunch at Mythos before seeing *Poseidon's Fury*. If there's time, see the Eighth Voyage of Sinbad (a scheduled show).

Walk through quirky Seuss Landing and, if you are still a child at heart, ride the Cat in the Hat and Caro-Seuss-el.

Now that you are hot and sweaty, go back to Toon Lagoon to ride Popeye and Bluto's Bilge-Rat Barges and Dudley Do-Right's Ripsaw Falls before heading home.

# INDEX